Religion and Human Security

RELIGION AND HUMAN SECURITY

A Global Perspective

Edited by

JAMES K. WELLMAN, JR.

CLARK B. LOMBARDI

OXFORD
UNIVERSITY PRESS

OXFORD
UNIVERSITY PRESS

Oxford University Press is a department of the University of Oxford.
It furthers the University's objective of excellence in research, scholarship,
and education by publishing worldwide.

Oxford   New York
Auckland   Cape Town   Dar es Salaam   Hong Kong   Karachi
Kuala Lumpur   Madrid   Melbourne   Mexico City   Nairobi
New Delhi   Shanghai   Taipei   Toronto

With offices in
Argentina   Austria   Brazil   Chile   Czech Republic   France   Greece
Guatemala   Hungary   Italy   Japan   Poland   Portugal   Singapore
South Korea   Switzerland   Thailand   Turkey   Ukraine   Vietnam

Oxford is a registered trademark of Oxford University Press
in the UK and certain other countries.

Published in the United States of America by
Oxford University Press
198 Madison Avenue, New York, NY 10016

Library of Congress Cataloging-in-Publication Data
Religion and human security : a global perspective / edited by
James K. Wellman, Jr. and Clark B. Lombardi.
p. cm.
ISBN 978-0-19-982773-2 (hardcover : alk. paper) — ISBN 978-0-19-982775-6
(pbk. : alk. paper) — ISBN 978-0-19-982774-9 (ebook)   1. Security,
International—Religious aspects.   2. Religion and international relations.
I. Wellman, James K.   II. Lombardi, Clark B.
BL65.S375R44 2012
201′.727—dc23
2011044293

ISBN 978-0-19-982773-2
ISBN 978-0-19-982775-6

1 3 5 7 9 8 6 4 2
Printed in the United States of America
on acid-free paper

For Annette, Constance, and Georgia: you bring grace and peace.
—James K. Wellman, Jr.

For Greta, Chiara, and Cecilia: with gratitude and love.
—Clark B. Lombardi

Contents

Acknowledgments ix

1. Introduction: Religion and Human Security: An Understudied
   Relationship—CLARK B. LOMBARDI AND JAMES K. WELLMAN, JR.   1

2. The Dance of Desire in Religion and Human Security
   —JAMES K. WELLMAN, JR.   18

3. The Janus-Faced Relation of Religious Actors and Human Security:
   Islamic and Secular Values in Turkey—MURAT SOMER   30

4. The Role of Human Security in the Contest between the Egyptian
   Government and the Muslim Brotherhood, 1980–2010
   —CHARLES MCDANIEL   48

5. Popular Muslim Attitudes towards Violent Islamic Groups: The Case
   of Pakistan—C. CHRISTINE FAIR AND CLARK B. LOMBARDI   67

6. Networking through Religion: The Case of Malerkotla
   —KARENJOT BHANGOO RANDHAWA   94

7. Indian Muslim Leadership: Predicaments and Possibilities
   for Human Security—ROWENA ROBINSON   113

8. "A Little with God Is a Lot": Popular Religion and Human Security
   in the Land of the Brazilian Colonels—JONATHAN WARREN   130

9. Interrogating Human Security and Religion in Guatemala
   —C. MATHEWS SAMSON   150

10. Striking a Balance: Christianity and the Challenges of
    Long-Term Human Security in Zimbabwe—GLADYS GANIEL   172

11. Beyond Basic Human Security: The Role of Religious Institutions
    in Angola—JAMES TIBURCIO   189

12. In Violence and in Peace: The Role of Religion and Human Security
    in Northern Ireland—EMILY MORRISON GRIFFIN   209

13. Eastern Christianity and Human Security in Postwar Europe
    —LUCIAN N. LEUSTEAN   228

14. Washed by a Deluge: The Religious Struggle for Human Security
    in Algeria and Poland—SAYRES S. RUDY   243

15. The Soka Gakkai and Human Security—DANIEL A. MÉTRAUX   265

16. Postscript: Lessons for Policymakers about Religion and
    Human Security—JAMES K. WELLMAN, JR., AND
    CLARK B. LOMBARDI   285

Bibliography   291
Index   323

Acknowledgments

THIS BOOK COULD not have come into being without the vision and generosity of the Henry Luce Foundation. From 2007 to 2010, the Luce Foundation generously sponsored an interdisciplinary research project on "Religion and Human Security" that was based at the University of Washington's Jackson School of International Studies. The project asked whether religion had a greater effect on the human security of individuals than the scholars of human security and the architects of programs to promote human security had realized and, if so, what the policy ramifications of this were. Over the course of two international conferences and subsequent discussions a significant amount of new research was produced. This book presents some important findings from this project.

Besides the Luce Foundation, many people helped this project advance and this book come to fruition. Among them, a few deserve particular mention. Not only did the Luce Foundation provide generous support, but several scholars at the Foundation provided advice and support along the way. Among them, Toby Volkman deserves special thanks for her confidence in the project and her insightful advice along the way. In the Jackson School of International Studies, we want to thank in particular the former and current directors of the School, Anand Yang, who was deeply involved in the grant's success, and Reşat Kasaba, whose support and advice has been equally critical. Thanks are due as well to Dean Kellye Y. Testy and the University of Washington School of Law, which supported the project in a number of important ways. Other Jackson School and University of Washington colleagues have also been instrumental in the success of the project. These include: Sara Curran, Dan Chirot, Gary Hamilton, Cabieri Robinson, Gad Barzilai, Christian Novetzke, Steve Pfaff, and Steve Smith. We also wish to thank Loryn Paxton, who ably administered the Luce Grant for the comparative religion program. We are grateful too for the work of Brad King, a University of Washington graduate student in comparative religion, and Kennedy Sanderson, a University of Washington law student, who were ever able copyeditors and bibliographers throughout the long process of finishing the volume. Connie Canon, a PhD student in the Interdisciplinary Program in Middle East Studies, provided important research and editing assistance on a number of articles. As always, we could not thank enough our spouses and children: Annette Moser-Wellman, Constance, and Georgia; Greta Austin, Chiara Lombardi, and Cecilia Lombardi. Without their unflagging support and great kindness over the past few years, we would never have completed this project.

Religion and Human Security

I

Introduction

RELIGION AND HUMAN SECURITY:
AN UNDERSTUDIED RELATIONSHIP

Clark B. Lombardi and James K. Wellman, Jr.

OVER THE LAST twenty years, the study of international relations has begun to move away from its myopic focus on "state security." Rather, it has begun to turn its attention also to the study of "human security," the degree to which humans enjoy "basic" welfare and rights. Since the 1990s, some influential scholars and diplomats have argued that state security will be fragile so long as nations' citizens are suffering.[1] They have insisted that the international community should consider the promotion of human welfare as one of its core priorities.

As a result of such policy reorientations, the international community has begun to prioritize the promotion of "human security" as a shared goal. Indeed, the international community, acting through the United Nations (UN), has formally recognized that, under some extremely limited circumstances, states possess an international legal right (and indeed an obligation) to interfere in the internal affairs of other sovereign states that are failing to provide some aspects of human security for their citizens (UN Secretary General 2010: 20–22). At the same time, scholars and policymakers have struggled both to define human security in a precise manner and to develop effective strategies for promoting it.

Scholars and policymakers have come to agree that the protection of human security requires the protection not just of material welfare but also of human rights and, some say, mental and emotional security. When human security is defined so broadly, however, it is difficult to understand the mechanics by which the diverse elements of human security come to exist in or pass away from a given society. Also difficult is the process of determining how states and multilateral institutions can most effectively try to promote the multiple elements of human security. To approach these issues, policy scholars have been working with a wide range of historians and social scientists. Surprisingly, though, scholars of religion have generally been ignored with regard to the study of this material.

As a historical matter, religious organizations have always affected the material welfare of people (often through charity or the construction of norms), the ability of people to enjoy fundamental human rights (through the construction of ethical norms and legal systems), and, of course, humans' sense of mental and emotional welfare. This continues to be true. The last fifty years have seen an extraordinary period of religious revival around the world. A great deal of evidence suggests that the power of religion as a motivating force and the power of religious organizations as social actors has grown during this period (Berger 1999). Religions and religious organizations undoubtedly shape contemporary human security in many pervasive ways (Norton 2009; Nasr 2007; Fox 2008). Those who seek to promote human security should, therefore, study the impact of religion in the societies in which they are working—to understand better the dynamics of the human security situation in that country and to identify possible enemies and allies in the fight to improve human security (Appleby 2000). This book seeks to demonstrate the importance of religion to the human security situation around the world, to explore the dynamics of the relationship between religion and human security, and to provide lessons for policymakers as they think about how to develop security-promotion policies that take religion into account.

The book grows out of a series of international workshops on religion and human security that were funded by the Luce Foundation and organized by the Comparative Religion Program based in the University of Washington's Jackson School of International Studies. At these workshops specialists in these fields met, settled on a working definition of "human security," and produced case studies that explored the way in which a specific religion affected the human security of people in a particular part of the world. A selection of these studies was collected in this volume.

Taken together, these case studies make clear that religious actors all over the globe affect in major ways the human security of people. Religion's impact on human security is, however, multifaceted and defies easy characterization as either positive or negative. In some cases, religions or religious actors work cooperatively with the state; in other cases, religions work at cross-purposes with the state; and in others, they are used by states to serve in areas the state has decided it wants nothing to do. In any one of these modes, religions and religious actors can have a huge impact on human security. Religious actors are among the biggest threats to human security, and they are also among the most important safeguards (Huntington 1996; Juergensmeyer 2000; Appleby 2000). In sum, religious actors play an ambivalent role—threatening some aspects of human security while promoting others. We argue that religion has an important impact on human security in every region of the world. A religion's impact on human security in a particular region will, however, be shaped by multiple contextual factors. Those interested in understanding how human security is advanced or undercut must study the conditions under which religion can be expected *in a particular country* to help human security and the conditions under which religions *in that country* threaten human security.

The study of human security's relationship to religion is just beginning (Seiple and Hoover 2004). Even now, however, it is clear that a program for enhancing human security in a given region or country must take into account the ways in which religious groups both help and hurt the human security of people. Because of the highly contextualized nature of the relationship between human security and religion, scholars and policymakers should avoid the temptation to propose simple, "cookie cutter" techniques for dealing with religious actors in areas where human security is threatened. Those who work to promote human security in particular countries, if they wish to be effective, will need to think about the dynamics of religion and society in each of the countries where they operate, and they will need to develop policies that will diminish the negative effects of religion on human security while preserving its positive impacts (Seiple and Hoover 2004).

The introduction begins with a section on the history of the human security movement and describes some of the competing definitions of human security. The following section describes the definition of human security the participants in the workshop decided to use. We then explore the term "religion" and propose a definition we think useful in studying the relationship between human security and religion. Finally, we summarize the book's chapters, and consider some of the broader policy lessons we can draw from them.

Human Security: The Emergence of a New Paradigm in Security Studies

The roots of the modern human security movement can be traced to President Franklin Roosevelt's famous "Four Freedoms Speech" (Roosevelt 1941). In that speech, on the eve of America's entry into World War II, Roosevelt articulated a liberal vision sharply at odds with the totalitarian ideologies of fascist and communist countries then ascendant in many parts of the world. Roosevelt insisted that people "everywhere in the world" had a right to enjoy freedom of speech, freedom of religion, freedom from fear, and freedom from want. The founding of the United Nations was envisioned, at least by some, as creating an institution devoted not only to preserving peace but to guaranteeing these four freedoms (Alkire 2003: 13). During the Cold War, however, states and international security organizations, including the new United Nations, found themselves unable to develop a shared ideology that elaborated on what it would mean to enjoy these four freedoms and unable to commit to a joint program of guaranteeing them.

Thus, it was primarily in the context of the international development movement that scholars and policymakers articulated concepts and goals that reflected the spirit of the Four Freedoms speech and developed institutions that could try to achieve these goals (MacFarlane and Khong 2006: 143–163).

After the end of the Cold War, a new movement appeared, trying to refocus the attention of international security organizations on the importance of promoting human welfare. Drawing explicitly on the ideals of the Four Freedoms speech and benefiting from the practical lessons of the development movement, proponents argued that no state could enjoy national security if its people did not experience "human security." The human security movement formally emerged when, shortly after the fall of the Berlin Wall, important figures associated with the UN began to argue that, with a declining threat of catastrophic world war, the international community should begin to conceptualize and develop a world order that was to guarantee the well-being of humans and would eliminate some of the causes of international instability and conflict (Alkire 2003: 13).

In 1994, the United Nations Development Programme (UNDP) published a revolutionary document, the *Human Development Report*, subtitled *New Dimensions of Human Security*. It asked the international community to revisit Roosevelt's ideal of a world in which people were free from fear and want and to think about what it would take to achieve that goal. It argued that such an approach would be necessary to realize the promise of peace in the post–Cold War period. Importantly, while the report accepted that freedom from fear and want could be understood narrowly to mean freedom from violence and poverty, it also suggested that states embrace a broader reading. According to the report, human security, properly understood, was a "people centered concept" that required people to recognize that the essential human freedoms are interdependent. Thus, it required protection not only of people's lives but of their dignity and their market and social freedoms (UNDP 1994: 22–23).

Events that occurred during the 1990s reinforced the report's basic premise— that a failure to provide for material welfare and human rights tends to promote instability and conflict. This decade proved to be an unexpectedly challenging one for international institutions. With the fall of the Soviet Union, peace did not break out all over. Rather, regional conflicts spread in a number of regions of the world, including the Balkans. Later in the decade, a financial crisis devastated many of Asia's economies and threatened to destabilize a number of countries. In short, human misery in certain countries led to national instability and, thereafter, to international instability. Against this backdrop, the UNDP in 1999 issued the *Human Development Report 1999*, advocating a new role for the UN, so that it "could respond to broader needs of human security" UNDP 1999: 111; Alkire 2003: 14). The following year, Secretary General Kofi Anan presented a report to the United Nations that endorsed this vision. He discussed the UN's duty to protect "human security," which he defined as a concept that "embraces far more than the absence of violent conflict." Rather, it included access to interdependent goods such as "human rights, good governance, access to education and health care and ensuring that each individual has opportunities and choices to fulfill his or her own potential" (Anan 2000). From this point onward, the idea of human security began to capture the imagination of a number of important international actors.

In the 2000s, a number of highly influential figures associated with the UN and other international organizations, such as the Japanese diplomat Sadako Ogata and a Nobel laureate in economics, Amartya Sen, relentlessly advocated for the reframing of international obligations through the lens of human security. Independently and through special commissions such as the Commission on Human Security, these figures publicized the concept of human security. They have suggested that the world should adopt "human security" as a new paradigm for thinking about the rights and duties of states (see, e.g., Commission on Human Security 2003).

The success of the human security movement is demonstrated by the behavior of multilateral organizations around the world. The most dramatic development is the evolution in recent years of a controversial doctrine called Responsibility to Protect—or, among those who favor acronyms, R2P. The doctrine provides that, under certain circumstances, states will be understood to have a legal obligation not to violate the human security of their citizens and that, if they fail to meet this obligation, other states have the legal right to take whatever steps are necessary to protect those citizens. The doctrine was implicit in a report from the UN secretary general entitled "In Larger Freedom: Towards Development, Security and Human Rights for All" (UN Secretary General 2005). Strikingly, a high-profile meeting of the UN General Assembly ended with the production of an outcome document that specifically recognized that states had a responsibility to protect citizens from violations of international humanitarian law and, if they failed, that the international community had a responsibility to do so (UN General Assembly 2005). This document recognized that states had an enforceable international obligation to protect human security in only certain types of circumstances, and some think it marked a first step toward the recognition of a broader obligation to protect human security. As Carsten Stahn writes,

> The articulation of the concept of responsibility to protect is a remarkable achievement. The inclusion of the concept in the Outcome Document not only marks one of the most important results of the 2005 World Summit,

but is testimony to a broader systemic shift in international law, namely, a growing tendency to recognize that the principle of state sovereignty finds its limits in the protection of "human security" (2007: 100–101).

Stahn may have overstated the extent of the shift; the "tendency" that he identifies has not been welcomed by all. There has been strong resistance to the idea that state sovereignty can be limited by the concept of human security outside of those exceptional cases where genocide, war crimes, ethnic cleansing, and crimes against humanity threaten people. In 2010, the secretary general made clear that, under international law as the UN understands it, the legal "Responsibility to Protect" applies only to these extreme and unusual cases (UN Secretary General 2010: 23–24).

Nevertheless, even if the UN does not, at this point, support calls to coerce states to protect the human security of their citizens, the secretary general in 2010 did accept that guaranteeing human security tended to promote stability within nation-states and peace within them (UN Secretary General 2010: 20–22). Thus, after discussing the work of nongovernmental organizations and multilateral organizations aimed at promoting human security, he declared that one of the UN's central missions going forward would be to promote human security around the world. "Human security" has thus become, in a short time, a crucial concept in international relations, and promotion of human security has become a stated goal of the international community. The rapid adoption of the human security ideal, however, has highlighted some lingering ambiguities in the concept. For instance, there are still questions on how best to define human security. Even more questions remain about how the international community should try to promote it.

What Is Human Security?

A growing literature on human security already exists, and this book does not attempt to survey it. (For surveys, see, e.g., Dedring 2004; Alkire 2003; MacFarlane and Khoong 2006.) Some abbreviated discussion is necessary here only in order to explain that there are some questions about how to define "human security" and to help explain why, in this book, the contributors will define human security as they do.

As noted already, the term human security has only recently entered the vernacular of international studies. A milestone in the evolution of the concept occurred, as we observed, when the UNDP published its *Human Development Report* in 1994. In calling for the protection of human security, and "freedom from fear and want," the report specifically suggested that people could not enjoy human security unless they enjoyed seven types of protection: economic safety nets, food security, access to health care, environmental protection, personal security, community security, and political security.

As broad as this list sounds, some suggested that it was actually too narrow. In 1999, a multilateral organization called the Human Security Network was created (Dedring 2004: 67–68). It insisted that people who enjoyed the seven types of material security identified in the 1994 UNDP report might still not enjoy human security if they did not possess at the same time an equal opportunity to fully develop their human potential and human rights (Human Security Network, 1999). Sadako Ogata and Amartya Sen embraced a broader definition of human security when they led a highly publicized "Commission on Human Security." In 2003, the commission issued a report that said protecting human security

> means protecting fundamental freedoms that are the essence of life. It means protecting people from critical (severe) and pervasive (widespread) threats and situations. It means using processes that build on people's strengths and aspirations. It means creating political, social, environmental, economic, military and cultural systems that together give people the building blocks of survival, livelihood and dignity (4).

The move to adopt a broader definition of human security proved influential among multilateral organizations. Thus similar definitions were adopted by the Organization of American States in its 2003 Declaration on Security in the Americas (OAS 2003) and by the African Union in its 2005 Non-Aggression and Common Defence Pact (AU 2005).

Ultimately, the UNDP itself came to accept that it should define "human security" more broadly than it had done in its 1994 report. In its *Arab Human Development Report 2009*, the UNDP distinguished between narrow definitions of human security, which referred to protection from physical violence, and broader definitions. These broader definitions defined "human security as the liberation of human beings from those intense, extensive, prolonged, and comprehensive threats to which their lives and freedom are vulnerable." In explaining why the agency preferred a broader definition, the report noted that common sense tells us people can feel insecure even if their physical persons are protected from physical threats. Denying people physical safety or minimal material comforts is immoral and will lead to instability. But denying people human rights or psychological security is also immoral and will also lead to insecurity (UNDP 2009: 23–24). In accepting this definition, the *Arab Human Development Report 2009* seemed to imply that there is a highly subjective nature of "human security." When some feel secure, others may not. By implication, human security may be different in different cultures, in different communities, or for different individuals.

In the academic literature on human security to date, scholars have generally supported the broadening of the definition of human security—although they disagree about how broad it should be. There is awareness that by broadening it too far one creates both conceptual and practical problems (Dedring 2004: 47–52; Alkire 2006: 14–19). The addition of culturally and individually contingent components of welfare to the definition of human security exacerbated the difficulty of prioritizing and measuring the components of human security. With a few exceptions, including an important article by Leaning and Arie (Leaning and Arie 2001), few works grapple seriously with this problem.[2]

In shaping this book, it was important to establish a common definition of human security for all of the contributors. During the first of the workshops the contributors discussed the issue and concluded that it made sense to adopt the type of broad definition that the UNDP adopted. Since the research interests of many contributors centered on religious revival, there was strong support for a definition emphasizing that humans cannot meaningfully be said to be secure— and thus national and international stability cannot be ensured—if people are denied goods that have cultural value or that lend them psychological security. The strong feelings on this point are probably due to the fact that scholars of religion tend to become sensitized to the power of cultural values and mental and emotional needs. After all, religions have maintained, and arguably increased, their power in the modern world in large part because they offer access to culturally specific enjoyments, subjective goods, and, in some cases, the promise of a form of salvation (Riesebrodt 2010; Collins 2010).

In forming a definition, a number of workshop participants struggled to articulate a definition of human security that captured both the objective and subjective elements of security. Murat Somer's chapter in this book elaborates his understanding of a "Janus faced" human security—one that was much discussed at the conference. Ultimately, the workshop decided to adopt a slightly different definition, proposed by Sayres Rudy, which grows out of the definition elaborated in the *Arab Development Report 2009*.

The workshop conceptualized human security as containing three parts: (1) a physical aspect, involving protection from threats to basic human welfare; (2) a juridical piece, relating to protection from violations of human rights; and (3) a more elusive, culturally conditioned factor, relating to a sense of personal autonomy and freedom. People are thus "insecure" if they are in danger of physical harm or material want; if they are suffering grave violations of human rights; or if they feel alienated, psychologically distressed, or sociologically oppressed—for example during a period of dislocation as refugees. Working from this understanding of human security, participants were asked to produce case studies in which a religion has affected human security in a particular nation or community. Through this mechanism, we hoped to get a sense of the *degree* to which religions and religious actors affect human security in various societies and also the *nature* of the effects: Do religious actors affect material welfare, rights, or mental and emotional comfort? Do they affect these elements in a positive way, a negative way, or both? We also hoped to gain some insight into the mechanisms by which religions in different societies affect the human security environment.

What Is "Religion" and How Might It Affect Human Security?

"Religion" has long been a highly contested concept in the academy, partly because it is exceptionally difficult to define (Taves 2009). On the other hand, the term "religion" is regularly used in academic life, political life, and everyday life, and people seem to have general agreement on the types of thing they are talking about when they refer to religion. For this volume, we define religion as *a socially enacted desire for the ultimate, embodied in practices that have ultimate significance,* with the understanding that these practices include both rituals directed to gods or spirits and also obedience to moral laws with ultimate consequences. Like any definition, this has its shortcomings.[3] It avoids, however, the common pitfall of overvaluing belief and downplaying practice.

Religions are forms of cultural practice and group process, which relate human communities to what they value as ultimate (Durkheim 1915; Collins 2004, 2010). While some scholars might suggest that religion is no more than a form of culture, the majority of the world's people self-identify themselves as practicing forms of "religion" that they would argue are not merely cultural. This is because religious practices shape distinctive beliefs about the nature and ultimate purpose of the world, and in this way, religious practices are different from other forms of culture.

Furthermore, we argue that the symbolic elements of religions—the faith systems that evolve from ritual practice—reinforce the mental and emotional security that is essential to the third element of human security. In this way, these forms of religious security have unique motivating force and tend to affect human behavior in powerful ways. We submit, then, that it is primarily believers' religiously motivated practices that directly affect the welfare and rights of humans.

Security scholars and policymakers therefore need to bear in mind that in studying the impact of religion on human security, the focus should be twofold: (1) the relationship between religion as *a belief system* and human security and (2) the relationship between *religiously motivated actions* and human security. By "religiously motivated action," we mean action undertaken by a person who self-identifies her- or himself as acting in accordance with a view of the ultimate that has been learned from others and is shared with others. Barring strong evidence to the contrary, we think it is generally reasonable to accept at face value a claim that a person was acting in accordance with her "religious" beliefs, and we think that there is no alternative to doing so. Exactly how a religion affects human security in a particular setting usually—though not always—boils down to a question of how practitioners of that religion affect human security in that setting.

Framing the discussion in this way, we think it is arguable that the second half of the twentieth century and the first decade of the twenty-first century have been periods of extraordinary religious revival. As a result, religious groups all over the world are having huge effects on society—effects that would seem to have implications for the material aspects of human security (Berger 1999; Fox 2008).

In the United States, for example, evangelical Christianity has come to influence beliefs in a way that influences both political and private behavior. It has affected US foreign and domestic policy in ways that would seem to affect the human security of both believers and nonbelievers (Thompson and Wellman 2011; Green, Rozell, and Wilcox 2003). Similarly, the Islamic world in the second half of the twentieth century famously saw a spiritual revival that allowed "Islamic" political and social organizations to grow in power vis-à-vis their secular competitors (Fetzer and Soper 2005). This has had a great impact on numerous Muslim societies, including through religious violence and official policies of legal reform that aim to harmonize state laws with Islamic values. Islamic revival has also empowered private Islamic groups in numerous countries where the government has historically failed to provide basic education, health, or other basic services, and these groups have become crucial providers of material welfare (Norton 2009; Nasr 2007; Cole 2010). In many other countries as well, religious groups have exercised growing influence on government policy or have played growing roles as nonstate actors carrying out essential educational or welfare services.

The impact of these developments on human security is undeniable. One of the most publicly discussed aspects of the recent global religious revival is the fact that it has supposedly led to a rise in religious violence. In the 1990s, Samuel Huntington famously argued that religious revival may lead to a breakdown of the peaceful order by which states have agreed to deal with each other and may lead to a clash of civilizations (Huntington 1993, 1996; Lewis 2003).[4] At the same time, the role of religious actors in mediating peace agreements around the world seems to suggest that religion and religious actors also have an unusual ability to establish peace after conflicts have already started—not just religious conflicts, but other types of conflict as well (Appleby 2000). Whether religion is promoting violence or helping to end it, there is a clear connection between religion and the material aspects of human security.

Religion also has a major impact on less material components of human security, such as "basic" human rights. Religions construct ethical systems that shape the behavior of governments and communities and can, thus, help determine whether people in that state or community enjoy the privileges that are recognized by the international community as fundamental human rights. Within the confines of this discussion, religion has a complex and often controversial place. This is because religions often work to increase the fundamental rights of one group while simultaneously diminishing those of another. In cases such as this, the scholars in this volume will generally avoid any sort of cost-benefit analysis of the good and bad. Rather, we accept that religions might simultaneously have significant positive and negative effects.

Finally, if mental and emotional well-being is a component of human security, the importance of religion in promoting human security is paramount. Scholars of religion have generally tried to explain the return to religion in ideological or psychological terms. These religious movements, by their account, represent a reaction to anxieties unleashed by modernization and by the failure of secular ideologies to give people a sense of identity and control in a rapidly changing, globalizing world (Casanova 1994; Norris and Inglehart 2004).

Thus, the field of religion is ripe for use by scholars who are interested in human security. One might expect the human security community to be mining the work of scholars of religion and seeking to understand how much religions actually affect human security. Religious scholars and scholarship will be vital in determining a variety of important questions, such as whether religion tends to promote or retard human security and, if both are true, whether there are ways to leverage a religion's security-enhancing aspects while suppressing its security-harming aspects. Surprisingly, human security scholarship has, so far, shown little interest in studying religion for the purpose of answering these questions or, indeed, any others. This book demonstrates how shortsighted this is.

By bringing together a series of microstudies, each demonstrating the significant impact that religious actors have on human security, the book demonstrates first that religions and religious actors often play a decisive role in shaping the human security conditions in a society. The book shows as well that productive alliances between religious organizations and the international community are indeed possible in the area of human security. However, the book makes clear that the nature of those alliances will be different in different societies. The role of religion in shaping human security is very different in different regions. Thus, those who wish to leverage religions' productive capacities in a particular region and to minimize their destructive capacities will have to gain a nuanced understanding of the role that each religion plays and the mechanisms by which it exercises influence and will have to tailor strategies on a case-by-case basis.

The Plan of the Book

This book brings together leading experts on regions of the world in which religious actors play major roles. As noted already, these experts agreed upon a working definition of "human security." They each then provided a case study in which religiously motivated actors were affecting human welfare in the areas that they study. Seeking to understand the full range of types of impact that religion has on human security today, we gave the contributors free rein to examine whatever most interested them regarding the relationship between religious actors and human security in the regions that they study.

A theoretical chapter by James Wellman precedes the case studies; it explores the way in which contemporary scholars define "religion" and proposes some explanations for why modern "religious" movements regularly, and sometimes deliberately, try to affect what scholars are coming to call "human security."

The case studies demonstrate some of the complex and occasionally counterintuitive ways in which religious actors in the contemporary world have affected human security in particular nations or communities. Some contributors have focused on the ways in which religions harm society. Analyzing the dynamics that drive religious groups to create cultures that harm human security and the mechanisms by which religious actors bring about such harm, these studies provide insight into the challenges that promoters of human security will face in different societies. Other contributors consciously problematize what they see as a reductive equation of religion with violence and gender inequality. They focus provocatively on the ways in which religion plays an ambivalent or even a positive role in shaping the human security environment of a particular country or community. All make clear, however, that the activities of religious actors affect the human security situation in particular ways.

The first five case studies focus on Muslim religious actors in various parts of the world. They describe the threats to human security that exist in various parts of the Muslim world and the role that Muslim actors play in exacerbating or alleviating these threats. Murat Somer's contribution explores some of the theoretical issues that plague discourse about human security. He argues that if we understand the importance of both the subjective and objective elements of human security, then we can better understand the dynamics of recent Turkish politics. Somer shows that religious, nonstate actors can and do undercut human security in Turkey by acting as substitutes for state support to certain Turkish populations. His discussion introduces another theme that we will see throughout the volume: that religious nonstate actors can be used by states to shore up and take over the provision of human security allowing states to retain resources and avoid their public duties.

In the second chapter in this group, Charles McDaniel describes the evolution of the competition between the secular Egyptian government and the Muslim Brotherhood. He discusses the ways in which repression inspired the Muslim Brotherhood to provide social services the state has proven unable to provide. Initially welcoming the Brotherhood's retreat from violence and politics, the government came to fear the organization's growing political power. McDaniel stresses that the war between the Brotherhood and the Egyptian state evolved during the Mubarak era so that the two groups, who were once locked in violent conflict, increasingly came to compete as *visible* providers of human security.

Christine Fair and Clark Lombardi's chapter on Pakistan examines the phenomenon of public support for militant Islamic groups that promote violence in Pakistan's neighbors as well as in Pakistan itself. Since Pakistanis tend to self-identify as Muslims, the fact that Pakistanis support such groups might seem to support the hypothesis that religiosity coincides with an increase in violence as well as the toleration of violence. Parsing two large sets of polling data, Fair and Lombardi question such hypotheses. They find considerable data to suggest that Pakistanis do not fully understand radical Islamic groups, nor do they understand the activities in which they engage. Fair and Lombardi, thus, suggest that current data does *not* support the claim that increased personal commitment to Islam has led the Pakistani public to support Islamic groups that engage in violence either within or outside of Pakistan.

In the next two chapters, Karenjot Bhangoo and Rowena Robinson explore the behavior of religious actors in regions of India severely affected by communal violence between Hindus and Muslims. Bhangoo and Robinson each accept that increased religious violence has facilitated communal violence in India. Each focuses, however, on what she considers an unappreciated aspect of this terrible violence: that religious actors who are committed to peace and human rights have been able to harness religious vocabulary and organizational structures in order to create a "religious" argument against religiously motivated violence. Bhanghoo contends that patterns of religious conflict can be overcome if members of the competing faiths appreciate each other's differences and are sensitive to their respective religions' shared concern with human security. Robinson describes the challenges facing the Muslim minority in India as it grapples both with the physical insecurity that has accompanied Hindu resurgence and with the myriad harmful results of Islam's history of repressing women. Her chapter explores approaches that certain members of the Muslim community have employed to minimize the aspects of religious organizations that harm human security while maximizing the growth of those aspects by which human security is promoted.

The next six chapters of the volume examine Christian groups that have a significant effect on human security. The first two chapters come from Latin America. Jonathan Warren challenges a popular belief in Brazil that contemporary culture and popular religion do nothing but sustain the status quo. Through Warren's close case study of the municipality of Araçuaí, in the Jequitinhonha Valley of northeastern Minas Gerais, we find that there is something much more complex taking place on the ground. Indeed, Warren finds that the people are activated to resist oppression, even while participating in popular religious traditions—a finding that stands in contrast to popular opinion in much of urban Brazil. Consequently, as Warren argues, popular religion is the engine of advancement for human rights, health, social equality, democratization, and economic development. All of which is very much in line with the definition of human security developed in this volume.

The second Latin American chapter, by Matthew Samson, is a study of Pentecostal Protestants in Guatemala. At times, Samson's chapter seems to paint an apocalyptic view of the Guatemalan nation. This is not entirely surprising, since many have suggested that the consequences of the last thirty years of internal strife and genocide are evidence of a failed state. Others debate this judgment; Samson adjudicates the perspectives. He shows that, despite the rise of evangelical religious leaders to become leaders of the state, the culture of despair and violence continues. In Samson's close study of Pentecostal congregations he finds little to argue that these church leaders or congregations have done much to change or to corrupt the social structures of the society. At the same time, these pastors are not merely conducting health and wealth ministries, and they do make a difference in offering the people a sense of hope and self-improvement.

In the next two chapters, Gladys Ganiel and James Tiburcio give us moving portraits of Christian organizations operating in African nations and responding to situations that are precarious, to say the least, in terms of human security. Each paints an ambivalent picture of these organizations from a human security perspective. They examine the means by which religious organizations and their leaders find themselves compelled to work with—or at least not to work aggressively against—the corrupt state officials and local warlords who are responsible for the people's pain and suffering. In this regard, these chapters recall Fair's and Lombardi's chapter dealing with Pakistan, insofar as they suggest that religious actors may feel religiously compelled to promote human security as far as practicable. Not to say that such actors universally avoid harmful behaviors. They simply prefer not to given alternate opportunities.

Emily Morrison Griffin's chapter about Northern Ireland addresses communal violence in that region. Griffin questions whether the presence of strong religious communities in Northern Ireland helps or hinders resolutions across distinct religious cultures. Some have argued that religion has had nothing to do with either the conflict or its resolution, but Griffin makes a strong case that religion was essential to both. Griffin demonstrates that while religion *can* cause violence, religious groups may also be uniquely suited to ending religious and nonreligious violence. She, thus, suggests that the answer to communal religious violence may not be a policy of empowering secular institutions, but rather a policy of offering incentives to the peaceful elements within warring religious communities.

Lucien Leustean's chapter concentrates on Eastern Europe and the activities of the Romanian Orthodox Church. He underscores the resilience of religion under communism and reviews the ways that religious leaders in Romania accommodated the totalitarian government in a way that allowed for their survival. Leustean argues that a concerted program of religious and political compromises made it possible for religious groups to meet security needs, to provide services, and to act as a source of autonomy.

Sayres Rudy's chapter provides an intriguing comparative case study by bridging the Muslim and Christian worlds. Focusing on Algeria and Poland, Rudy compares the impact of religious movements that resisted autocratic state governments. This chapter addresses the puzzle of why religious protests against the state remained peaceful in Poland, where religious groups are widely considered to have benefited human security, but turned violent in Algeria, where they are widely considered to have been harmful. Rudy suggests that the explanation may rest in the fact that in Poland the government grudgingly allowed religious groups to provide for human security and to be a forum for the open expression of social desires. Algeria never permitted this. In other words the Polish government promoted the type of "compromise" that Ganiel, Tiburcio, and Leustean have noted in their own chapters.

The last case study focuses on the impact of the Soka Gakkai Buddhist denomination in Japan. Daniel Metraux illuminates the case of this Japanese minority religious sect, which self-consciously embraces a goal of human welfare. Metraux describes the methods by which the sect works for human welfare and security both in Japan and throughout the world.

As a unit, this volume provides a number of important insights about the relationship between religion(s) and human security. Perhaps most importantly, these studies confirm that there *is* an important relationship. All over the world, people rely on religious groups to provide mental, emotional, and social welfare. Because of this reliance, religions exercise considerable influence over the behavior of believers. Because secular organizations are rarely able to provide the mental and emotional comfort that religions do, religions will always be a powerful social actor. Secular organizations that wish to promote human security would benefit immensely by the creation of productive alliances between themselves and religious organizations.

The contributions to this book also make clear that, in aggregate, religion's impact on human security cannot be neatly characterized as positive or negative. Religious actors can and do play important roles both in building and in undermining human security around the world, and in some countries, they do both at the same time. Sometimes rival religious groups operate against one another. Sometimes a single group will have an ambivalent effect on human security, acting in ways that promote one aspect of human security while at the same time threatening a different aspect of human security. In demonstrating the many different facets of the relationship between religion and human security and in highlighting the myriad of contextual factors that may shape the relationship in a particular country, the book also illustrates the danger of generalizing about the impact that religious actors are having (or could have) on the human security of a given population.

By demonstrating the importance of religion in shaping the human security environment around the globe, and the degree to which religion's impact will depend on context, these chapters provide useful points of reference for policymakers. Those who wish to effectively promote human security in a particular country would be wise to carefully map the relationship between religion and human security *in that society*. Moreover, they should attempt to comprehend the reasons for that religion's success at the same level. Armed with an understanding of these groups, it should be possible to develop policies that simultaneously leverage the security-enhancing elements of local religious cultures while dampening those that threaten security.

In some societies, policymakers who have mapped the religion–human security nexus will be able to identify religious groups that aid human security as well as those that harm it. This book provides several examples of societies riven by religious violence, but where religious voices also provide the only effective voices for a durable peace. In situations like these, champions of human security can and should learn to differentiate between the two in order to act as effective advocates.

More provocatively, the book suggests that if policymakers understand the religious organizations that harm human security, they may be able to develop policies that aim to improve relations with those specific religious groups. One intriguing finding in several of these studies is that some of the religious actors who harm human security or who support actions that harm human security seem, in the abstract, to value human welfare. Some religious actors apparently cling to harmful practices either because they are ignorant of the effects or because they know no viable alternative. Thus, providing better education about the effects of violence and about alternative means of approaching the same problems may ameliorate the negative behaviors of some violent religious groups.

The ultimate lesson is that religion's impact on human security is pervasive, varied, and potentially changeable. It is likely to remain so for the immediate future. In this environment, we can only hope that this book begets many more and that scholars continue to build knowledge that will permit policymakers to engage more productively with religious actors in the service of a world in which everyone is able to enjoy all elements of human security.

Notes

1. The argument goes as follows: States that fail to protect "human security" create dissent and disorder. In so doing, states do more than weaken themselves and harm their own national security. They also create conditions such as civil war or refugee flows that can spread across borders and destabilize neighboring states. Thus, states have not only an ethical obligation but a practical interest in promoting human security.

2. Leaning and Arie's work "raises in particular the need to address cultural and psychological dimensions (which are not easy to measure), without diluting or derailing the focus and compactness of human security as a 'minimal set'" (Alkire 2006: 16).

3. In an early chapter, James Wellman discusses the advantages and disadvantages of this definition of religion and, more importantly, the vital relationship of religion, thus defined, to human security.

4. Several scholars have argued, controversially, that the Islamic revival will lead to increased violence between Muslims and non-Muslims, both state violence and non-state violence (Lewis 2003; cf. Juergensmeyer 2000; Lincoln 2003; Avalos 2005). This position has become influential among policymakers who have relied on it as they have planned the global "War on Terror" (Elshtain 2003; Walzer 2004).

2

The Dance of Desire in Religion and Human Security

James K. Wellman, Jr.

Introduction

The interplay between religion and human security is at once a sociopolitcal enigma and an often ignored aspect of the increasingly interconnected world of modernity. The constant give and take of both entities provokes consistent and continual shifts in the sociopolitical climate of every culture on earth. So, then, why hasn't this relationship been explored previously, and why is it so important that it is now and in the future? Religion and human security intersect, precisely, at the center of human social desires. These desires for safety and stability drive human security at its core. And in this complex web of desires, religion is a consistent and seemingly univeral cultural instrument that creates equilibrium and facilitates change in a wide array of potentially positive and negative ways.

Over the course of my collaboration with the various scholars involved in this research, I reexamined how religious studies, my own discipline, fits into the landscape of this work. As a result, I discovered that the dance between religion and human security is even more necessary to understand than I had realized at the project's inception. This chapter then is a theoretical reflection on the conceptual junction between religion and human security that is aimed at scholars of religion, policymakers in human security, and the growing cadre of social scientists in global religions and international affairs. I begin with a review of the concept of human security and its interaction with religion, followed by an examination of the way in which the religious and secular aspects of the state become competitors in the conveyance of human security in the modern era—a competition that continues despite the predictions and expectations of many that religion would either die or be reduced to the private sphere in the face of Western modernity. I then examine the field of religious studies and how it can be rethought in light of human security. Finally, I arrive at a new way to define religion in relationship to the delicate dance between the demands of religion and human security.

Human Security and Religion

As we mentioned in the introduction, there are no generally accepted definitions of human security, and while it is a relatively new term in the field of international studies, it is not a new idea. Rather, it is a different way of thinking about human welfare that lies in contrast to the more conventional focus on national security. That is, the focus of this volume is *not* state security and how nation-states defend their borders and powers; it is, instead, about the safety, welfare, rights, and social and subjective desires of populations within such states. This movement away from national security and toward human security is also a shift away from the "hard" power of state politics to the "soft" power of civil societies, community organizations, and yes, in our case, religious institutions and groups of all kinds (Lukes 2005; Buzan and Hansen 2009). As will be clear in the following case studies, this "soft" power is not immune to political influence, conflict, and even violence (Nye 2005; Wellman 2007). Human security entails, then, a unit of analysis that is more amorphous and difficult to grasp; nevertheless, we argue in this volume that it is a critical factor for the well-being of citizens of all states. These case studies exhibit that national security does *not* necessarily ensure human security. Indeed, some states maintain strong national security precisely to the extent that they ignore the basic needs of their populations. Thus, the focus on human security is often a matter of life and death for many populations.

As we outlined in the introduction, we define human security broadly as having three parts: (1) a concern for basic human welfare, (2) a set of inalienable human rights, and finally, (3) a more subjective factor, characterized by social desires for freedom and self-expression. Each of these parts can, of course, be described more specifically, depending on context. What is needed in human welfare in Zimbabwe, by way of food and shelter, is much different from what is expected in Northern Ireland; what is thought of as legally acceptable and normative in terms of women's rights in Egypt or Algeria is different than in Poland, Japan, or even India. All are cases in this volume.

What is socially desired by way of freedom and the human expression of power is highly dependent on context as well, but these three factors—welfare, rights, and the ability and freedom to express one's social desires—are critical to human security the world over. Further, I would argue that human security, when broadly conceived, hovers close to a basic aspect of what humans have always sought, developed, and constructed for themselves in human communities across all time and all cultures.

What acts as a prerequisite for one or the other of the three aspects of human security is again relative to time and context. There is little doubt, however, that when one of these factors is missing, human security is undercut, and if given the chance and opportunity, people seek ways to redress their grievances. The opportunity to remedy these deficits of human security is not always there, and several of the case studies in this volume, especially that of Sayres Rudy on Algeria and Poland, explore the consequences of such situations. States sometimes undercut and destroy channels of expression for these complaints, but this does not mean that the *desire* for these basic aspects of human security is not present.

For this volume, religion acts as a carrier of values and an instrument of social desire that is deeply interwoven in the warp and woof of human security. Religion is not the carrier of human security, but it is one of the core cultural systems that seeks to provide basic human welfare, organizes and shapes human rights, and bundles social desires through symbolic and ritual life that have been a part of human history from its beginnings. Roy Rappaport, in his volume *Ritual and Religion in the Making of Humanity* (1999), lays out a theory that ritual functions as a process by which humans learn to trust one another in groups and sustain themselves against internal and external threats. Ritual facilitates the social desire to create a trust that ensures a modicum of human security. From these rituals, social forms of welfare and law develop that elaborate human security and extend it across and beyond familial and tribal relations.

One can see from this volume that religions of every kind comfort people in insecure settings. They facilitate rituals that lend support in transitional moments of life and death. They offer basic human welfare to the vulnerable and create norms and legal constructs to adjudicate conflicts. They mobilize groups to resist oppression in both peaceful and in violent forms, and in many cases, they directly challenge states and governments that seek to oppress peoples with their power—justly or unjustly. Religion is the key carrier of the social desire for human security, but it is not alone in this interest. Secular cultures are competitive providers of human security as well.

Religion and the Secular

Even as I lay out the ways that religion has been one of the key cultural carriers of human security, cultural sources of secularism and the modern state have become one of the crucial challengers to religion in providing human security since the Enlightenment. Throughout this volume the competition is traced out as a kind of omnipresent shadow boxing match. We find it everywhere: in the secular state of Turkey, in the religious nongovernmental organizations of African states, and in the faith-based charities in the United States. Often, the secular world partners with religion; at other times, religion and secularism are in direct opposition. This competition is often decided by which group, religious or secular, can more efficiently and effectively protect and increase human security in any given circumstance.

This volume's case study of Egypt exemplifies this contest between the state and religious providers. In the 1992 earthquake, religious charities offered care and human security at a time of terrible tragedy—a good thing to be sure, and yet, the secular state had to negotiate the growing power of religious charities in Egypt. These charitable organizations produced their own systems of social service in order to compete for the loyalty of their citizens and the legitimacy of their own political power. Thus, these arguments are far from "merely" academic; they are deeply enmeshed in issues of power and human social desires.

Not surprisingly, this competition between a religious and secular perspective lingers and is contested in the very ways that religion is conceptualized in the modern academy. The academic study of religion is deeply enmeshed in the project of modernity. Indeed, the critical study of religion has paralleled the rise of modernity since its inception during and immediately after the Enlightenment. David Hume's posthumously published (1779) *Dialogues Concerning Natural Religion* (1981) was one of the first critiques of religious belief and perhaps the most articulate, preceding the French attacks on religion that led some Enlightenment philosophers to declare religion a form of superstition. In the nineteenth century, Ludwig Feuerbach's writings on religion provided an anthropological interpretation of religion, and Marx extended this critique to judge religion as a kind of anesthesia for the oppressed. Later, Freud called religion a neurosis—an expression of infantile desire. Each critic of this sort detailed how he or she believed religion channeled human social and subjective desires—some as an intellectual mistake, some as a social projection, some as compensation for economic scarcity, and others as a psychological comfort—each attempting to differentiate religion as a symptom of a deeper and more empirical source of human desire.

The contestation over religion and secularism in the English, German, French, Jewish, and broader European traditions were very much about politics and the negotiation of interpreting and explaining human social desires. For the English, the question was how to maintain an independent and free state, established by natural law and related to religion, though not dependent on religion for its security. For the French, the question was how to overcome the stranglehold of the Catholic hierarchy and the entrenched interests of the political elite to establish a republic free of the pressure of authorities. For Marx and Engels it was about how to overcome the terrible costs of industrialization, a modernizing force that destroyed any sense of human security for the poor and middle class. For the liberal Jews, it was to create an egalitarian culture and politics that would ensure their survival and liberate them from what many interpreted as the intellectual straitjacket of their own religion. For Europeans in general, the issue remained the continuing struggle and memory of the political and religious strife of the seventeenth century, whereby Christian states annihilated one another. In each case, religion and the secular clashed over issues of power, human security, and the sustainability of their very cultures. For many European thinkers, religion had become a barrier to human security.

Religion and the Secular State

The marginalization of religion as *the* source of governance and policy has become an axiom in the modern West. This is true at least in Western states that have sought, depending on context and time, to co-opt, curtail, and contain the power of religion. And indeed, in some minds, it appears that the secularists have won the day. But the shadow boxing continues, and there are important variations on how religion and states intermingle, collaborate, and contest with one another.

There is no doubt that fatigue over religious conflict and violence fueled many in the European and Anglo-American Enlightenments to create the era of secular nation-states. The French Revolution did its best to instill an ideology of secularism, founding a public order that sought to be free from religion. The laical order is one of the potent varieties of church-state relations that resonate in multiple nations today. The Anglo-American variety of church-state relations was much less critical toward religion, allowing that religion must be separated from the public square but arguing that religion was important for social order and personal morality (Martin 2005). The American Founders instituted the equation that the state should neither "establish a religion nor prohibit its free exercise." This created a neutral ground that has been fought over for the last two centuries. Nonetheless, for many it has acted as a guard against certain forms of political religion, on the one hand, and the emasculation of religion, on the other.

The putative victory of secularism, however, remains in question. In the shadows, religion again rises to frame and sustain human security as one of the core mechanisms of the social desires of human populations. Even in the French example, the purest template of secularism, nineteenth-century thinkers were trying to replace Christianity with what Auguste Comte called a religion of humanity; Emile Durkheim made the argument that religion provided a social glue that was necessary for a stable political life and true in its social function even though it was a metaphysical illusion.

Religion, like the moon in the night sky, continues to wax and wane on the various stages of the modern era. Just as it seems to disappear on one stage, it shines ever more brightly on another—a sign, I would argue, that religion is and will continue to be one of the most important carriers and organizers of human social desires, at least for the foreseeable future. Of course, religion is always adapted to time and circumstance, filtered by events and culture—willing and clearly able to change form when necessary, sometimes expressed in a religiously shaded secularity and at other times as a secularly tinted religion. To be sure, in many of our modern nation-states that exercise forms of modern secularity, religions persist—whether as a Hindu secular state in India, a Christian secular state in the United States, or a Jewish Israeli state in the Middle East. Indeed in Turkey, a state that has an Islamic majority, the rising question is whether or not a secularist and laic-like state can continue to persist. The purity of Turkey's secular identity seems to be at risk.

The waxing and waning of political religion is also nicely illustrated by its activity in the last century. Secularism appeared to triumph in the twentieth century, but a revival of religious politics has marked the early twenty-first century. Religion refuses to be confined to private concerns; it harnesses the social desire of communities to express grievances and the hopes of these communities as they move into the public square, making an impact on the ethos, values, and norms of the state. In this way, we see the images, intimations, symbols, and signs of various forms of civil religion—borrowing Robert Bellah's term (1975).

A civil religion is a group of working ideals—inchoate to be sure but, nonetheless, manufactured and based on deeply embedded social desires and ideas that tribes, groups, and nations have for themselves. And again, this form of civil religion can be expressed in multiple forms, whether as a pale soteriology in Chinese Maoism, in the communism of the Soviet Union or even in the more religiously robust forms of the nineteenth-century British Empire and the turn-of-the-twentieth-century American manifest destiny. In either secular or religious terms, populations and social desires are harnessed in ways that offer hope, a sense of destiny, and a feeling of purpose toward which a group or nation proceeds.

It is questionable, then, for secularists to claim purity from the soteriological language of religionists. I would argue that they often do so without realizing that they have become what they have rejected. The Soviet Union is perhaps the best example of this dilemma. The chapter in this volume on the history of the Eastern Orthodox Church under the Soviet regime makes it quite clear that the Soviets knew that, in order to survive as a political culture, they had to create a secular civil religion that could translate social desires into an ideological framework that would inspire its peoples' loyalty. And, of course, this secular religion was a colossal failure. It is one of the ironies of the twentieth century that "atheistic" and "secular" regimes, such as China, have encountered their greatest challenges in the religions of the homeland, whether indigenous, such as the Falun Gang, or transplanted, such as in the blossoming Chinese Christian community. Religions often carry peoples' social desires, at times occurring as private and local rituals and, at other times, spreading into political structures and challenging state authorities—for example, as occurred in China.

In such cases, we again encounter a conflict, not only between religion and the secular but also between religious groups and secular states: negotiating with each other; competing over how to construct, legitimize, and embody the social desires of populations; securing power; and mobilizing individuals and groups toward larger goals and programs of the state. Thus, a religiously inflected form of political power hovers around the edges of both religious and secular states, using the social desires of groups to engage in power plays of all kinds. Religious structures and symbols galvanize and organize desires for human security, but they go beyond the private affairs of the individual, passing into the public byways in forms that can and often do mobilize the identity and destiny of groups that lead not only to periods of power and peace but also, at times, to conflict and violence.

Public Religion and Religious Violence

Even as the public voice of religion was displaced in the twentieth century, many of the key theorists of religion during this era became less critical of religion than their predecessors. Scholars of religion during this period sought to retrieve religion as a central human phenomenon. Some of the most notable of these described religion as the instrument of the sacred (Eliade 1996:xvii); as a mechanism for meaning (Geertz 1973:90); as a subdimension of human experience (Smart 1999); as a relationship of social and economic exchange (Stark and Finke:278); and finally, as a carrier of moral orientation (Smith 2003:98). Religion, for these theorists, is no longer a purveyor of political power; instead, it is that which brings internal meaning and purpose. Talal Asad's well-known critique of Geertz's definition of religion noted this tendency of modern religious theorists to make religion a lucky charm of the heart, a personal and private mechanism that reflected a liberal Protestant bourgeois ethic, tucked away from the public square and domesticated for private use (Asad 1993). Anticipating the resurgence of public religions at the turn of the twenty-first century, Asad has made it clear that religion is not only for private use. It cannot be—now or ever—because religion is a reflection of social desires as much or more than it is of private ones. As such, its political implications and intersections must be taken seriously.

Undoubedly, Asad was prescient (Asad 2007). Over the last ten years, explaining religion as a source of political grievance and social mobilization has become the order of the day (Buruma 2010; Toft, Philpott, and Shah 2011). The events of 9/11 proved to the United States and the rest of the world that religion was not interested "only" in the private concerns of the individual but that it also sought a key role in public discussions about power, politics and human security. As if on cue, recent theorists of religion have been quick to arrest this resurgence and contest its power, judging it as a threat to secularity and, more pointedly, as *the* source of human violence. Some sociobiologists now interpret religion as an epistemological error and delusion, and several recent theorists of religion have judged it as a mechanism that creates scarce resources that instigate human violence. Religion is "ignorant," "immoral," and "violent" (Harris 2005; Avalos 2005). Other critics want to kill religion because it "poisons everything" (Hitchens 2009), though it would seem to be prudent to be as suspicious of their secular substitutes—something respondents to these critics have made clear (Hart 2009; Eagleton 2010).

As we have noted, religion continues to thrive in the modern world, responding to the social desires of populations and, at times, partnering, collaborating, and even creating conflict or violence. We know from much empirical research that religion often creates moral binaries that are less than conducive to modern pluralism and peace between diverse groups. To some extent, the unique claims that religions make are the source of their genius and their staying power. People share an identity in these claims that bring them social solidarity, again a powerful sense of human solidarity. But these exclusive claims create moral and cultural antinomies that have become the basis of social conflict as well as occasionally provoking the sorts of violence that are a part of all religions.

In my recent edited volume, titled *Belief and Bloodshed: Religion and Violence across Time and Tradition* (2007), I argued, similarly, that even as religions have sought human security for their own contituents, they have, at times, created violence or an atmosphere conducive to violence. In all the major religious traditions of the world, religion creates moral exemplars that promote love and forgiveness as well as moral disasters that seek to annihilate any in their path. Religion seems to be a knife with which deep social desires are cut, for both good and ill. But again, secular cultures and governments cannot claim to be free of violence and human devastation. The twentieth century showed us that secular regimes could be engines of wars and genocide that appear even more devastating than the religious wars of the past (Burleigh 2005, 2007). As Michael Burleigh asserts, secularist regimes took on "sacred causes" that were every bit "totalitarian political religions," making ultimate claims in militant language and taking genocidal actions.

A New Definition of Religion

One of the chief lessons from my own work and from reading the scholarship in this volume is the relatively consistent way that religion, as a political force in the world, is underestimated, whether by critics of religion, who imagine that it can be argued out of existence, or by more friendly interpreters, who think religion can be tamed and domesticated. The consistent theme in the modern critical study of religion is that explaining religion can reduce its power, undercut its impact on public life, and in the end, control it. Remarkably, even the *Arab Human Development Report 2009*, which addresses human security directly, sidelines religion as a critical factor in the analysis of the Arab world, which, by any criteria of analysis, is one of the most religious places on earth (Cole 2010). Indeed in the report, religion is compartmentalized as something that does but, perhaps, should not have real public impact. This privatization thesis is very much a part of the modern sociological account of religion, assuming, as many have, that religion in modernity would persist only in the privacy of the human heart (Berger 1967; Luckman 1967).

Of course, religion is no doubt a powerful personal and subjective desire in modern people, but its public expression has become equally pronounced—as Peter Berger and others have rediscovered. José Casanova created his own theory of the "deprivatization" of religion to explain its political resurgence (Berger 1999; Casanova 1994). Indeed, it is one of the great reversals of fortunes that religion, rather than being tamed by its modern cultured despisers, has come to define the modern world, taking full advantage of its accoutrements—whether by using modern technology or the structures of the state.

The assumption, for many scholars of religion, is that secularity (the separation of religion from the social and political fields of influence) is the social condition of modern life. The idea of secularity becomes a prototype of what *should be* the state-church arrangement. In this way, secularity, as a descriptor of modernity, often becomes a prescription for modernity. Secularism, as a modern ideology, not only identifies the separation of religion from the public sphere but also promotes it. Thus, the bias of secularism may not only miss the power of religion to carry human social desires but also fail to comprehend the empirical data that shows that religion continues to have a major impact on public life. Religion may be more powerful today than in any time of modern history (Berger 1999; Demerath 2003).

Thus, we turn back again to the question, "What is the source of religion's perseverance in the modern 'secular' world?" What moves people, embodied in every form of world religion, to continue not only to believe and act in the name of their religion but also to translate it into the public square? From my work, its seems clear that global religions are not simply what people believe but are also how they live and orient themselves in the world, whether relating to their family life, social life, or political life.

For many, to separate religion from daily life is like separating music from the sound that it produces. The one without the other is still notes on the page, but it lacks the dynamism that moves people to feel, think, and act in the world. In this sense, religion is more than a belief system; it is a dynamic and changing cultural mechanism that moves in time and context, expressing deep social desires, related to and overlapping many of the concerns that we have described in human security, including issues of human welfare—such as food and shelter or the guarantee of rights and laws for human communities of all types and, yes, that ever present set of social and subjective desires for freedom and self-expression.

In this way, social scientific studies of religion offer explanations of religion that can be helpful, but they tend to "freeze" systems in places that are, in reality, constantly changing, adapting, and partnering with the various elements with which they congress. One definition of religion that I developed and used in other works is that *religion is a system of symbolic and social boundaries related to a power or force experienced within and beyond the self and group—most often related to spirits or gods* (Wellman 2007, 2008). As I have edited the chapters in this volume, however, my own thinking has shifted. Theories and definitions offered by social scientists can and do guide and shape inquiry, but for many, perhaps most, people on the globe, religion acts in both history and in time. It acts to save, to comfort, to challenge, and to express and guide their desires in the world.

All of this is to say that religion is a whole lot more than simply "belief"; it involves a way of life and an intersection and investment both *with* and *in* history (Eagleton 2009). In this sense, it cannot be distinguished from the political machinations of the world. Religion, some have argued, should disappear in the modern world, but there is little doubt that it has persevered. At the turn of the twenty-first century, religion is one of the key components of international affairs, and building on the research in this volume, we have argued that religion is one of the major carriers of the social desires in human security. How might this change the way we have defined religion?

As the introduction suggests, an aspect of human security is a subjective social desire that lies not just in the mind of individuals but also in their bodies and in their wishes. By this, we mean an affective longing for something that is not simply a rational choice conceived as a correct decision but is, instead, a deeply felt sense and passion for something—a sustained preference, often developed and nurtured over years. It is social because language itself is developed in a group setting that embodies a moral order, often involving a religion that shapes preference, values, and behavior (Bourdieu 1977; Smith 2003). This affective social desire is often constructed as a core sense of freedom—a deep and sustained desire for self-determination and liberty from want and oppression. I have proposed that religion is not *the* instrument of this desire, but it is one of the facilitators of these aspirations. In this sense, I define *religion as a socially enacted desire for the ultimate.* Like any definition, there are problems; one could argue that it is too vague, that it could include many kinds of human activities, whether having to do with sexuality, family, sports, or nationalism, and of course, this is true. But it also makes the point that religion is a subjective and slippery intention that has, for many humans, been one of the avenues by which they seek contact with what they describe as ultimate, sometimes, though not always, referred to as god(s) or spirit(s). The ambiguity of the definition also underscores both how this social desire perseveres and how it is adaptable in many circumstances, even as it changes in form and expression.

Thus, a cognitive critique of religion, like the recent spate of books decrying religion (Harris 2005; Hitchens 2008), predictably has a marginal impact on the religious. Religion is not simply a belief or a cognitive claim, but it is like water dripping through cracks or light through the forest. Religion lives in the crevices of people's lives, in places of ultimacy, and it acts as a generator of energy, both personally and socially (Long 1986). In this way, religion tends, I argue, to be in the passions and affections of the body before it is even expressed. People come to religion through social networks (Stark and Finke 2000), through rituals of everyday life, through a sense of what William James called the "more" in life—expressed as ultimate experiences that take on an unconditional valence, often described as ineffable, though being illustrated using the full range of aesthetic forms (1982).

This, I would argue, is why religion is so sustaining and enduring; it touches and expresses desires that rational argumentation can neither overturn nor touch. Religion is a social desire that provides a deep sense of hope, resilience, and security to individuals and groups. The empirical basis of this is extraordinary. Against all odds, in the modern world, religion survives in places where many thought it not possible; think of China, Myanmar, and even Europe, where many have predicted the death of Christianity for a very long time (Yang 2011; Jenkins 2007; Martin 2005). In one sense, this volume shows that religion has been and continues to be a resilient source of human security.

This is not to say that when religion is expressed in public life it always comes from some pure desire of the heart. Indeed, nation-states, in the modern era, are learning or have learned that religious motivations are powerful carriers of human social desires and can be used by politicians of all stripes to legitimize power and push their agenda. Here again, we think of the case studies in this volume—on Egypt, Algeria, Pakistan, India, Poland, Northern Ireland, Latin America, and Japan—and realize that politicians throughout history have used religion to sponsor themselves and their power. But this makes the point even more profoundly; religion as a socially enacted desire for the ultimate offers to the political life of nation-states an enormous resource to galvanize and mobilize energy in the body politic toward goals they seek. One can then understand why global religions of every type are so dangerous to political regimes: they have the power to resist governments and to even topple them. Needless to say, to underestimate the power of religion in the modern world as one of the prime conveyors of human security is not only a major mistake politically but also empirically, and in terms of policy. Religion is not going away because human social desires for human security will not disappear, and religions have shown a sort of genius as carriers of these desires.

Conclusion

Despite the predictions of its demise, religion perseveres in the modern era as a potent cultural instrument of social desire and one of the important ways by which people negotiate their desire for human security. For these reasons, I claim that there is, in the human, a deep need and passion for the ultimate that at times is expressed in the core attributes of human security. The relationship of religion and human security, far from being abstract or incidental, is a critical way to go forward in thinking about the issues of human security, both now and in the future.

Thus, I argue first that religious studies must get beyond its fascination with religion as a "mere" event of sacred and private meanings. As Asad has made clear, religion has always been and will always be a matter of power and politics. Secondly, policymakers must realize that religion does not move humans with cognitive claims alone; it produces and enacts deeply felt social desires, centered on welfare, rights, and subjective aspirations for self-expression and self-determination; policymakers ignore religion at their peril. And finally, religion, as an expression of human social desire, by no means ensures peace in the pursuit of human security. This volume and its contents clearly demonstrate that religion, as an instrument of human security, has a checkered history. Like all human cultural frameworks, religion must be negotiated and, at times, restrained. The partnership of state and religion has a horrific past. At the same time, religion is a chief carrier of the human dream of human security and so it must be taken seriously. As in all things human, there are no guarantees, but the importance of keeping one's eyes wide open to religion ensures that we will not overlook such a critical element in the conditions and the potential of a secure human future.

Note

James K. Wellman, Jr., is associate professor and chair of comparative religion in the Jackson School of International Studies, at the University of Washington.

3

The Janus-Faced Relation of Religious Actors and Human Security: Islamic and Secular Values in Turkey

Murat Somer

Introduction

The main goal of this essay is to underline the Janus-faced nature of religious nonstate actors' involvement in the provision and protection of human welfare, rights, and freedoms. In doing so, it will draw on a critical examination of the case of Turkey, supported by a content analysis of three religious and two secular newspapers and interviews with Islamic nonstate actors.[1] This exercise helps us to better understand both the multifaceted impact of religious and nonreligious actors on human security and the complex concept of human security itself.

A simple conceptualization of human security may be "the welfare and quality of life of a state's inhabitants." However, closer examination reveals that human security has both an objective component (on which there may be widespread agreement across societies and individuals) and a subjective component. More specifically, it has three interrelated yet analytically distinct components: (1) a material component involving physical health, well-being, and security; (2) an idealistic and legal-political component relating to protection of basic human rights and civic, economic, and political freedoms, insofar as such fundamental and universal human rights and freedoms can be defined; and (3) a more elusive, culturally conditioned factor, marked by different communities' subjective understandings of human autonomy and values of collective freedom, self-expression, and self-preservation. It can be assumed that religious nonstate actors at times enhance human security by complementing states and secular nonstate actors. Religious charity, for example, may help to alleviate poverty by attracting more contributions from the pious. Religious human-rights watchdogs may address problems that secular watchdogs tend to overlook because of ideological prejudices, selective attention to different issues, or insufficient ability to reach out to the pious segments of society. In pursuit of religious liberties, "moderate" religious actors that embrace democratic pluralism may join forces with other pro-democratic actors and be a catalyst for the enhancement of democratic liberties in general. More directly, however, religious nonstate actors contribute to human security by virtue of the fact that their activities are not only means to achieve social, economic, or ideological ends; they are also "expressive activities." The ability to participate in these activities is an essential component of human security, insofar as freedom is an end of human development itself (Sen 1999). By participating in religious nonstate actors' activities, people enhance their own well-being by expressing and promoting their religious values and identity, fulfilling religious duties, exercising religious freedoms, and building social networks. Often, these activities also increase their participants' well-being by reducing moral dissonance, that is, by enabling them to do things and pursue lifestyles that satisfy their religious values.[2]

In Turkey, religious nonstate actors such as religious foundations, brotherhoods, communities, and associations are active in a vast array of areas ranging from manufacturing and trade to publishing, broadcasting, labor unionism, human rights advocacy, religious education, and charity, as well as building and running schools, dormitories, and mosques.[3] While these actors tend to support Islamist and conservative political parties and benefit from the successes of these parties, they are at least partially autonomous. Many view themselves as part of an Islamic "movement" that is driving rather than being driven by Islamist politics. They have survived even in periods when pro-Islamic parties were in decline (White 2002). Similarly, as we will see, while these actors are undoubtedly influenced by the complex mixture of inclusive-supportive and exclusive-controlling Turkish state policies in regard to religion in public life, they drive state polices at least as much as they are driven by them. Many of them have no organic relations with the state. They view themselves as part of a loosely defined and vastly diverse social-cultural and political movement that has anti(secular) state and antisystem characteristics in addition to a mission to transform society in accordance with Islamic guidelines.[4] To varying degrees, they have distinct organizational styles that draw on Muslim and traditional identities and practices (White 2002; Yavuz 2003). Undoubtedly, many people join these religious nonstate actors largely for instrumental reasons such as economic gain and social recognition and communitarian support. Others, however, join primarily to express their religious identity and beliefs, and to advance and exercise religious freedoms.

At the same time, I argue that religious nonstate actors can have a negative impact on human security under two conditions. First, they can do so insofar as they compete with the state agencies and secular nonstate actors that provide human security. For example, social security in a society suffers if, faced with the alternative of contributing to religious organizations, many reduce their contributions to secular organizations by more than what they give to religious organizations. Alternatively, human security suffers if states cut down on social security spending by shifting responsibility to religious nonstate actors. In Turkey, for example, the promulgation of religious charity and aid organizations has gone hand-in-hand with government policies since the 1980s that have increasingly outsourced social security provision to voluntary organizations or to formal and informal partnerships between the government and such organizations (Buğra 2008).

Second, religious nonstate actors can undermine human security if they promote values and beliefs that undercut freedoms and protections that are granted by modern, pluralistic democracies (Dahl 1998; Schmitter and Karl 1991). More indirectly, religious actors adversely affect human security insofar as they bring about social and political polarization. This happens when they promote values and beliefs that conflict with those held by the secular segments of society and when social and legal-political institutions fail to successfully mediate these conflicts.

Such conflicts arise in two areas. The first area concerns political pluralism and democracy. For example, scholars have long argued that Islamic actors have a built-in conflict with democracy for various reasons, such as Islam's comprehensive belief system that includes the realm of state.[5] Such arguments had been advanced earlier with respect to Catholicism. However, available evidence suggests that Islamist political actors have shown considerable flexibility in embracing political democracy (Nasr 2005; Bayat 2007; Browers 2009). Public opinion in Muslim societies is generally supportive of democratic government, even in the Middle East (Norris and Inglehart 2005: 146–147; Kurzman and Naqvi 2010).[6] As I will show ahead, the contents of Turkish Islamic newspapers also demonstrate Islamic actors' adaptation to pluralistic democracy. Thus, we can expect that under favorable conditions Islamic political actors would adjust to democratic government, as Christian political parties did in Europe (Kalyvas 1996, 2003). The determining factors are whether or not social and political institutions provide sufficient incentives for secular actors to adopt an inclusive attitude toward religious actors, and for "radical" religious actors to moderate, that is, choose democratic competition over religious-authoritarian hegemony, and the presence of some freedom and pluralism in the public sphere so that pluralist ideas can develop.[7]

The second area of social pluralism is more problematic. Clashes between secular and religious actors over issues such as free expression, abortion, teaching evolution theory, stem cell research, and women's and gay rights constitute social and political tensions and threaten social pluralism in many parts of the world, including advanced democracies. Moreover, available evidence shows that, while desiring political democracy like other societies, Muslim societies tend to hold more religious and conservative values than the rest of the world with respect to social issues such as gender equality, sexual liberalization, and the role of religious authorities in social affairs (Fish 2002; Norris and Inglehart 2005: 146–147). In Turkey, Muslim-conservative intelligentsia are more skeptical of social pluralism than secular intelligentsia, even though they are not less supportive of political pluralism (Somer 2011).

Thus, while advancing some religious and other freedoms, Islamic actors often promote values that undermine some freedoms that are granted in advanced democracies. Alternatively, even when religious actors do not oppose certain rights, they promote different understandings of such rights that conflict with the understandings of them by secular actors. Many Islamic actors believe, for example, that the separation of men and women in public life promotes women's freedom. This contrasts with secular conceptions of women's advancement in society, which aim to achieve the opposite. The resulting loss of consensus over the goals of democratization, and conflicts between religious and secular understandings of it, affects human security in society.

These multifaceted linkages demand that a comprehensive analysis of human security with respect to religious actors requires one to address complex questions such as potential conflicts between secular and religious understandings of democracy, human wants, rights, and freedoms. They also indicate that the relationship between religious nonstate actors and human security will be affected by a country's social structure and political system. Particularly important is the nature of the relationship between the state and religion, on one hand, and the religious and secular segments of society on the other.

The Turkish case is an ideal illustration of these complex mechanisms through which religious nonstate actors affect human security because they are vividly manifest in its current politics and social relations. As I show in the next section, the reasons lie in the country's peculiar background of secular modernization and democratization in a Muslim social-cultural context. The Turkish experience entails the social and political effects of both the exclusion and support and proliferation of religious nonstate actors. The exclusion resulted from state-led and comprehensive secularization that affected both the political and social-cultural realms. The proliferation resulted from various factors including the country's relatively advanced democratization, economic development, and integration with the world, the failures of the secular state and nonstate actors to provide sufficient social welfare, and, paradoxically, state support of religion to promote national unity and its own legitimacy. A main goal of Turkish secularization policies in early years was to make sure that the government controlled and regulated religious activities and religious actors because the latter were thought to hold at least some values that were incompatible with modernization and development. State policies thus tried to suppress and exclude autonomous religious nonstate actors from mainstream politics and society. This generated a conflict-prone and distrusting relationship between the state agencies and religious nonstate actors, fed the politicization of Islamic actors, and generated a deficit of religious freedoms.

Through relative economic development, integration with the world, and the limited yet "conditional but promising" inclusion of Islamic political parties in a competitive political system, however, the Turkish experience also created opportunities for Islamic actors to participate in political and socioeconomic lives, build symbiotic relationships with state agencies, and adapt to pluralistic democracy and market economics (Yavuz 2003; Somer and Tol 2009).[8] As I show below, a content analysis of Islamic and secular newspapers demonstrates Islamic actors' discursive adaptation to democracy. Islamic, nonstate actors thus became major players in Turkey's political and economic life. One consequence of this process was the emergence of the Justice and Development Party (AKP) as a mass party rooted in Islamism. Religious actors have gained new opportunities to influence government policies and to shape social life since the party came to power in 2002. This period boosted Turkey's political and economic development in many ways. But it also polarized society and politics in various ways. Major political conflicts occurred between the AKP and the prosecular military-bureaucratic and political actors.[9] Relations between the religious and prosecular nonstate actors became tense and polarized. As the findings of the content analysis will indicate, one source of these tensions seems to be that major differences exist between secular and Islamic understandings of secularism and social pluralism.

Turkish Secularism and the Exclusion of Religious Nonstate Actors

Turkish secularism (laicism) was originally designed to control religion in order to modernize society and to secure the autonomy of the legal-political order from religious actors (Berkes 1998; Mardin 2005, 2006; Tunaya 2007).[10] It is a product of radical reforms that took place in the formative period of republican Turkey between 1924 (the abolition of the caliphate) and 1937 (the institution of the secularism principle in the constitution), under the charismatic leadership of Kemal Atatürk. These reforms both continued and broke away from the modernization-secularization model of the Ottoman ancien régime that republican Turkey replaced. The late Ottomans attempted to reform and co-opt traditional religious institutions and official authorities (*ulama*) in the name of modernization.

Convinced of this model's inadequacy, Kemalist reformers replaced these institutions and authorities with new institutions and agencies that were either secular or under state supervision. A main target of the secular reforms was a vast array of Islamic nonstate actors such as Sufi orders. "Official Islam" was easier to manage because it was already under state control in the Ottoman system (Mardin 2006). But Sunni Islam lacks a hierarchical church system and its decentralized organizational structure harbors a wide range of actors, autonomous or semiautonomous from the state.

In the Ottoman period, religious nonstate actors such as religious foundations (*vaqfs*), *madrasas,* and Sufi orders and brotherhoods (*tariqat*) fulfilled major functions such as regulating civil relations, providing education and social security, and lending legitimacy to the legal and political order. Kemalist reforms dissolved religious courts and schools and replaced them with secular courts and schools. All Sufi orders but a few were banned. The *vaqfs* lost their autonomy and were brought under government supervision. Having thus eliminated potential opposition to other social-cultural and legal-institutional reforms, secular reformers embarked on a series of reforms such as the westernization of the alphabet and calendar, the institution of universal suffrage for both sexes, and the adoption of civil and penal codes based on Swiss and Italian models.

A comprehensive evaluation of these radical reforms in terms of human security is outside the scope of this chapter. Suffice it to make two observations here. First, the general principle of secularism is likely to have helped Turkey's development. At the end of 2008, Turkey was one of only five countries that could be considered to be an "electoral democracy" among majority Muslim states. None of these five democracies had a state religion and all had the freedom of religion as a constitutional principle (Freedom House 2008).[11]

Second, beyond the general principle of secularism, Turkey developed a model of secularism that involves heavy state regulation of religious activities. The developmental effects of this model are more controversial. At first sight, Turkish secularism resembles the French *laïcité,* which promotes a strict separation of church and state that is symbolized by its famous motto "the Republic neither recognizes, nor salaries, nor subsidizes any religion" (Kuru 2007). The Turkish constitution prohibits any law based on religion, and it is a crime for any political actor to try to base the state's workings on religious principles.[12] Looking more closely, however, one recognizes that Turkish secularism, unlike France, involves strict regulation and subsidization of the majority religion. According to Fox (2008), Turkey has the twenty-third highest score of government involvement in religion, in a group of 175 countries.[13]

The colossal Directorate of Religious Affairs regulates Muslim religious practices, and appoints and pays the salaries of all the imams in the country. According to Article 24 of the constitution, it is the state's duty to supervise all religious and moral education. In the eyes of the prosecular state agencies, these practices are aimed at checking religious radicalism and promoting a more rational and prosecular religion. A similar rationale underlies a highly polarizing ban on the Muslim headscarf in schools and government offices. Islamic nonstate actors vehemently oppose it but it has been upheld by the Turkish Constitutional Court and the European Court of Human Rights. The courts reasoned that the Islamic headscarf may symbolize antisecular politics, and, without restrictions in a Muslim-majority society, it may create religious pressures on uncovered women (Kalaycıoğlu 2005).

Such restrictions adversely affect religious liberties, and thus, human security. A detailed US Department of State report concluded in 2007 that the government "generally" respected freedom of religion, while an international ranking put the environment of religious freedoms in Turkey as "partially free."[14] It is also debatable as to whether or not the prosecular regulations serve the developmental goals that were the main motives of Turkish secularization. For example, a major goal of Turkish secularism was the transformation of the traditional Turkish-Muslim society to facilitate equal participation of women in public life. However, the legal equalities provided by secular laws did not necessarily translate into actual equality (Kalaycıoğlu and Toprak 2004: 16). Prosecular restrictions on Islamic headscarfs exacerbate this situation by making it more difficult for covered women to be represented in professional life.[15]

Turkish Democracy and the Growth of Religious Nonstate Actors

Despite the state's built-in suspicion of religious, nonstate actors, Turkish political and economic development provided important opportunities for their participation in public life. After the transition to multiparty democracy in 1950, religious nonstate actors steadily expanded their autonomy and influence through formal and informal arrangements with center-right governments, state agencies, and religious-conservative and Islamist political parties. Although it remains a taboo for politicians to publicly denounce secularism, unlike their French counterparts, Turkish politicians freely accentuate their piety in expectation of voter support. The 1980–1983 military regime actively supported Islamic, nonstate actors in a deliberate effort to use them as an antidote against rightist and leftist extremism. The subsequent civilian governments of Prime Minister and later President Turgut Özal included prominent disciples of the Nakshibendi religious order. He allowed Islamic actors more access to state agencies and the political mainstream, creating, among other things, a need-based social assistance fund administered with the involvement of local clergy (Buğra 2008). Özal's promarket and pro-international trade policies helped the Turkish economy to grow and religious nonstate actors to gain autonomy from the state. In this process, a vast array of "legitimate and illegitimate" Islamic movements emerged and employed "state-centric and society-centric" strategies to promote more Islamic models of society, politics, and economics (Yavuz 2003: 27, 35).

In 1997, the symbolic moves of the government led by the Islamist Welfare Party (RP), such as an official dinner for heads of religious *tariqats* at the Prime Ministry caused much anger among prosecular actors. The prosecular military, judiciary, media, and civil society launched a fierce public campaign known in Turkey as the "February 28 process," which compelled the RP government to resign in June. A crackdown on actual and perceived Islamist political and social-economic actors followed, causing much resentment among religious actors.[16] Paradoxically, however, this undemocratic intervention accelerated the Islamists' adaptation to pluralistic democracy. They abandoned the Islamist political discourse, which envisioned a political and economic system based on Islamic principles, in favor of a pro–liberal democracy and pro–European Union (EU) discourse as a survival strategy in the face of prosecular opposition (Bulaç 2001; Somer 2011).[17] The AKP's foundation by former Islamists as a "conservative democratic" party and its coming to power in a single party government were products of this transformation (Öniş and Keyman 2003; Özel 2003; Çarkoğlu and Rubin 2006; Yavuz 2006).

In government, the AKP has avoided any legal-institutional changes that one may call Islamist, apart from a short-lived attempt to criminalize adultery and a constitutional amendment to legalize headscarves in universities that was later annulled by the Constitutional Court. Any Islamic changes in society occurred indirectly through religious nonstate actors that were encouraged or, according to prosecular claims, favored by the government. Prosecular social and political actors claim, for example, that government recruitment, promotions, and projects systematically favor the graduates of religious *imam-hatip* schools, members of powerful religious movements, and pro-Islamic business groups (Toprak et al. 2008). Accordingly, the membership of Muslim-conservative and progovernment civil society organizations grew significantly vis-à-vis prosecular organizations.[18]

In addition to promoting more conservative conceptions of social life and gender relations, Islamic nonstate actors promote a traditional, voluntarism-based notion of social security rather than a modern welfare state. In a similar vein, the government's policies emphasize the privatization of areas such as education. According to government statistics, the number of private schools of primary and secondary education increased by 67.2 percent between 2002 and 2007, while the number of public schools increased by only 0.95 percent.[19] In private schools run by religious nonstate actors, religious groups have more flexibility than in public schools to bypass secular restrictions and, for example, to organize prayer groups or have female students wear the Islamic headscarf.

Janus-Faced Impact of Religious Nonstate Actors on Human Security

During the AKP's administration, Turkey adopted more liberal laws and reduced military influence on politics, developed a more prosperous economy, and became an official candidate for EU membership. Between 2002 and 2006 the Turkish economy grew on average 7.3 percent a year.[20] The new "Islamic bourgeoisie," composed of export-oriented Islamic-conservative businesses, was one of the sources of economic growth (Buğra 2002; European Stability Initiative 2005; Öniş 2009). These factors coupled with political stability contributed to the human security of many among both the religious and secular segments of the population, in a country accustomed to long periods of unstable coalition governments.

However, legal-political democratization and economic development came at the price of a society, politics, and media severely divided over questions of secularism and democracy, the activities of Islamic communities, secular and religious perceptions of social exclusion, and market versus state provision of human security.[21]

Optimists applaud Islamic communities as indigenous modernizers who "vernacularize modernity" via their selective openness to it (Yavuz 2003). Skeptics raise concerns about issues such as their opaque character, the secondary role they assign women in their operations, and their discriminatory practices vis-à-vis "outsiders" (Toprak et al. 2008). While the government and the religious-conservative portions of its constituencies welcomed the growing influence of religious nonstate actors, this led to a growing sense of insecurity among major segments of society about coexistence and the future of secular freedoms and protections. Meanwhile, prosecular restrictions continue to feed a sense of insecurity and exclusion among the religious segments of society, even when an Islamic-conservative government is in power. In 2007, the AKP nominated and eventually elected one of its leading figures to the presidency. But this process led to major political fissures, including an online ultimatum by the military, prosecular mass rallies against the government, and a legal proceeding seeking to shut down the party. In 2008, the Constitutional Court ruled against shutting down the party but warned it against being "a center of anti-secular activities." The government itself began to display increasingly "illiberal" tendencies after its victory in parliamentary elections in 2007, including a public campaign against the prosecular media.[22]

For example, my interviews with female members of religious nonstate actors revealed their sense of injustice caused by secularist restrictions of the Islamic head-scarf. They view these restrictions as yet another sign of secularists' exclusionary and prejudicial practices against pious people. In addition to government restrictions in public offices, they point to the practical exclusion of covered women from white collar positions in prosecular business corporations.[23] Accordingly, recent surveys show that Turks in general sense that there is discrimination against religious people; 40 percent of the Turkish public thought in 2002 that "there was oppression of religious people in Turkey," 67.7 percent of them giving the example of "headscarf/turban pressures" as the reason.[24]

In return, secular nonstate actors fear that the legalization of Islamic dress on schools grounds would create social pressures on uncovered women, since the overwhelming majority of the society is Muslim and the headscarf is viewed by many as a sign of religiosity and "good morals." Many secular women feel, for example, that women and men show less respect to uncovered women than to covered women in places such as public transportation vehicles, especially in conservative parts of the country (Toprak et al. 2008).[25] One survey found that the percentage of women using a headscarf increased from 64.2 percent in 2003 to 69.4 percent in 2007, while those using a distinctly Islamic headscarf (which secularists call a turban in Turkey) increased from 3.5 percent to 16.3 percent (Konda 2007). The wearing of an Islamic headscarf has a Janus-faced impact on women's human security, enabling more conservative women to join public life while increasing the legitimacy of religious-traditional and patriarchal social norms and practices. Accordingly, 22.1 percent of the general public, 35.9 percent of the "nonreligious," and 43.6 percent of university graduates believed that secularism, which is often understood to capture secular freedoms and lifestyles, was under threat in 2006 (Çarkoğlu and Toprak 2006: 76). Fifty-five percent of the public disagreed in 2002 that religious people were oppressed for reasons such as headscarf restrictions, and 63.3 percent thought that people were free to practice the worship requirements of Islam (Çarkoğlu and Kalaycıoğlu 2007: 129).

Education is another area of contention. Religious actors complain about government restrictions of religious education. Secular actors complain that religious teachers tend to be assigned as directors in public schools, that schools connected with religious communities tend to exclude secular teachers, and that students are encouraged or pressured to be observant of religious practices, for example to fast during the holy month of Ramadan.

While pro-Islamic actors often charge prosecular actors with being biased against religion, prosecular actors charge the pro-Islamic actors with social conservatism and with using democracy only as a means to acquire power. In order to reach a fair assessment of the implications for human security, it is useful to take a closer look at which beliefs and values religious nonstate actors promote. The following discussion focuses on three areas: political democracy, social freedoms and pluralism, and secularism.

Social and Political Pluralism, Secularism, and Turkish Islamic Actors

During my interviews with religious nonstate actors in Turkey, I made two general observations. The first is the diversity and mental flexibility of Islamic actors. One senses their eagerness to adopt selective dimensions of modernity and democracy and to reconcile them with tradition, faith, and a rural- or urban-conservative personal background. The second observation is that this flexibility meets sharp boundaries in relation to some norms of democracy and social pluralism that are accepted in western, liberal democracies. These norms relate to questions of secularism, free speech, social regulation, and public mores.

However, impressions based on personal conversations can be misleading precisely because people often try to impress each other in personal conversations. Public debates where secular and religious social and political actors discuss and deliberate issues in writing can be a more reliable indicator of these actors' views and values. Thus, I conducted a systematic content analysis of three religious-conservative (Islamic) and two secular newspapers published between 1996 and 2004 (Somer 2010, 2011).[26] In total, researchers I trained analyzed the contents of more than forty thousand relevant articles in about fifty-four hundred newspaper issues. These large numbers minimize the likelihood that the findings are coincidental.[27] In interpreting the findings, I also benefited from interviews with media representatives, persons from four Islamic nongovernmental organizations (NGOs), and editors of two Islamic newspapers.[28]

The discussions in the newspapers are a good indicator of the views and values that religious and prosecular actors promote. All are privately owned and may, themselves, be considered nonstate actors. Turkish newspapers are similar to the French press, which is more closely tied to the political field and in which newspapers assign themselves a larger role in interpreting events and shaping public opinion than the US press, which tends to view its primary role as reporting facts and contending statements (Benson and Hallin 2007). Journalists, especially columnists, tend to view themselves as public intellectuals with a mission of informing as well as interpreting events for the public in pursuit of self-appointed goals such as democratization, (secular or religious) "justice," and "modernization."[29] Most newspapers are owned by major business groups with major political and social-ideological alliances and are connected ideologically with different constituencies and social movements. *Zaman* is closely tied with the powerful Fethullah

Gülen faith–based movement, *Yeni Şafak* has close organic ties with the AKP, for which many of its writers act as formal or informal advisors, and *Milliyet* is owned by the powerful and prosecular Doğan media and business group.

Democracy

Notwithstanding secular fears, Islamic actors are supportive of democracy in general: in the three religious newspapers analyzed, only 10.4 percent of the content on democracy expressed skeptical views, that is, negative views referring to the flaws or failures of democracy.[30] More importantly, their dominant understanding of democracy changed from electoral to liberal democracy. In other words, it shifted from one that allows Islamic actors to come to power through elections to one that secures pluralism and the rule of law. This is important because one fear of secular actors is that the strengthening of religious actors will produce an "illiberal democracy," if not an outright authoritarian regime.

In religious newspapers, the ratio of the times democracy was praised primarily as liberal democracy to the times it was praised primarily as electoral democracy was roughly one (1.1:1) in 1996 and 1997. In 1998, the ratio rose to roughly two (1.8:1), and after that year the positive codings for liberal democracy were at least double the positive codings for electoral democracy.

The findings indicated a relatively higher support for democracy in general and for liberal democracy in particular in secular newspapers. The ratio of positive codings for liberal democracy to the positive codings for electoral democracy was greater than 2:1 throughout the period and was 4:1 in 1999. However, in those years when an Islamic party was elected to power (1996, 1997, 2003, and 2004), and in years that led to the elections that brought an Islamic party to power (2001 and 2002), the ratio for negative codings of liberal to electoral democracy was less than 1:1. In other words, more of the *negative* codings for democracy in secular newspapers came from electoral democracy in those years. Arguably, its allowing Islamists to come to power is a negative aspect of electoral democracy from an exclusionist prosecular point of view. Similarly, although the secular newspapers were very critical of military interventions in general, they became less critical whenever military interventions were thought to "protect secularism."

Social Pluralism

Even though religious nonstate actors embrace liberal democracy in terms of political rights, they may hold socially conservative or illiberal values. If these values promote intolerance of different life styles and identities, the growth of religious actors may undermine social pluralism, freedoms, and thus human security.

Available survey studies in Turkey suggest that social conservatism, in the sense of avoiding people with different ethnic and religious identities and lifestyles as neighbors, colleagues, or marriage partners, tends to be higher among people who consider themselves religious than among people who consider themselves not religious (Çarkoğlu and Toprak (2006: 49). The contents of the newspapers support this view. In general, religious nonstate actors are more skeptical of social pluralism than secular actors are. In the religious press, 36 percent of the content (compared to 11 percent in the secular press) related to issues of social, ideological ethnic, and religious diversity reflected negative opinions regarding the desirability of pluralism; 38 percent (as opposed to 59 percent in the secular press) reflected positive opinions, the rest comprising neutral opinions. For example, whenever the subject of pluralism stemming from different sexual preferences was discussed in the religious press, homosexuality was viewed as wrong or sick (91 percent of the times compared to 11 percent in the secular press).

The contradictions between political and social liberalism also came out during interviews. For example, two otherwise zealous and coherent advocates of EU standards of human rights asserted that gay rights were unacceptable because "homosexuality should not be supported." An otherwise daring female activist fighting for gender equality took pains to avoid shaking a male interviewer's hand at the end of a lively and candid conversation, visibly sensitive to the reactions of her male colleagues present.

Secularism

If religious and secular actors hold widely different views on secularism, it follows that the growth of religious actors can cause conflicts with prosecular nonstate actors and state agencies, undermining human security in society. In the religious newspapers, people tended to express critical views of secularism and their main demand with respect to secularism was that it should allow religion to play a bigger role in social affairs. The findings do not indicate that there was any improvement in religious actors' evaluation of secularism during the period. As expected, secular actors' evaluation of secularism was overwhelmingly positive.

In the religious press, 34 and 24 percent of the content on secularism reflected critical and supportive views regarding the desirability and consequences of secularism, in respective order. The corresponding figures were 2 and 73 percent in the secular press.

Whenever secularism was an issue, religious actors tended to refer to it as a problem, and most of the time as a criticism of Turkish secularism. Similar observations were garnered by the interviews. For example, the head of an NGO close to the AKP criticized the Constitutional Court for its 2008 warning that the party supported antisecularism, labeling the decision "politicized and biased." Later in the conversation, however, he argued, "ideally, of course, we would not have secularism" (Somer 2011: 535).[31]

But if they had the ability to modify Turkish secularism, how would religious actors change it to better fit their ideals? The findings from the content analysis show that religious actors would allow religion to play a bigger role in social affairs. The results also indicate that the primary source of value conflict between religious and secular actors vis-à-vis the secularism question does not concern the separation of religion and state. Religious actors wanted to reduce the state's exclusionary practices but did not express views in favor of reducing the Turkish state's supportive involvement in religious affairs discussed above. Although there is considerable support (30 percent) among religious actors for religion to play a bigger role in state affairs, half of the religious (48 percent) and the overwhelming majority of the secular actors oppose this idea. However, the majority of religious media actors (68 percent) wants religion to play a bigger role in social affairs, while the overwhelming majority of secular media actors do not. This divergence of preferences can cause conflicts that can undermine human security.

Conclusions

The concept of human security has objective components such as wealth, life expectancy, and rights and freedoms on which there is widespread agreement across societies, and subjective components such as happiness, safety, and different understandings of human autonomy and freedom. As for the objective components, most humans feel more secure in having access to more and better health services when they are sick and access to more effective human rights organizations when they have trouble with the law. While having access to more lifestyles and cultural diversity may please many people in Seattle as long as they peacefully coexist, such diversity may make some people feel less secure by generating frustrating choices and by threatening the continuity of beliefs, values, and communities. This indicates an effect on the subjective component of human security.

Thus, any definition of human security and, for that matter, development reflects some degree of bias. The ingredients of human security may change across societies, states, and religious and secular communities. What may increase human security for an Orthodox Jew or Muslim may differ from what may increase human security for a secular Jew or Muslim. In the same way, Buddhists and Christians and, for that matter, socialists and liberals may perceive human security differently.

A close look at the Turkish case shows that, while contributing to the objective component of human security for many and to the subjective component of human security for some, the growth of religious nonstate actors can have a negative impact on the subjective component of some people's human security through two mechanisms. The first one concerns the tensions between secular and religious understandings of human security. For example, religious actors may not accept a Millian liberal conception of individual autonomy based on the ability of adult individuals to pursue different notions of a "good life" and the associated rights to privacy and freedom from social controls (Mill 1985 [1859]). To give a more specific example, many liberal-secular Turkish intellectuals support the freedom of adults in universities to choose to wear the Islamic headscarf or veil but believe that such a freedom would subject children in elementary and high schools to parental and societal oppression (Kadıoğlu 2007). Many Islamic actors believe, however, that children need to be immersed in Islamic practices and symbols and some secular choices should be made unavailable to them in order to develop the habits that would make them good Muslims in the future (see, e.g., Karaman 2009: 162).

The second type of tension concerns issues of social exclusion and polarization and occurs even if one accepts the liberal notion that pluralism and the availability of different choices is an intrinsically valued asset for human security. There are now more human rights organizations with either secular or unsecular understandings of human rights, more charity organizations with different understandings of justice and welfare, and more newspapers and television channels with different takes on the news in Turkey primarily due to religious nonstate actors. Take the example of religious-conservative television channels. On one hand, their presence clearly increases the information available to Turkish citizens and their ability to choose between different sources of information. This potential choice increases neither subjective nor objective human security, however, whenever the norms and values promoted by these channels discourage the use of different sources. Alternatively, social polarization between the secular and unsecular gives rise to social pressures among both groups, even within families, that may limit exposure to different channels.

Policies aimed at improving human security should take into account these complex mechanisms. They should include legal and political measures to prevent social discrimination and polarization and platforms of public exchange and deliberation where religious and secular actors can try to reconcile their different values. This is a major challenge for Turkish democracy. While addressing Turkey's Grand National Assembly in 2009, President Barack Obama maintained that Turkey's secular democracy is "at the center of things [in the world]." "This is not where East and West divide," he argued optimistically, "this is where they come together." Indeed, the challenges facing Turkish democracy reach well beyond the country's borders.

Notes

Murat Somer is associate professor of international relations at Koç University, Rumeli Feneri Yolu, Sarıyer 34450, Istanbul, Turkey. E-mail: musomer@ku.edu.tr. Website: http://portal.ku.edu.tr/~musomer/. The author wishes to thank the International Development Research Centre in Ottawa, Canada, and Tübitak in Ankara, Turkey, for funding; Gad Barzilai, Dan Chirot, and Reşat Kasaba for comments and encouragement; Jonathan Fox for data; Faik Kurtulmuş for an insightful remark; and an excellent group of undergraduate and graduate students in Istanbul and Ankara for research assistance. The usual disclaimer applies.

1. The content analysis covers the period 1996–2004, and the analysis and narrative are based on events and developments in Turkey through the end of 2008. However, I was able to include some post-2008 bibliographical references while editing the final version of the essay in 2011. In my view, the social and political developments between 2008 and 2011 mainly confirmed and reinforced the observations and predictions made here.

2. For a formal analysis, see Kuran (1998).

3. By Turkish law, religious education should be provided either by state agencies or under state supervision and regulation. In practice, religious nonstate actors are involved in religious education either illegally, under government regulation, or through informal arrangements with state agencies.

4. While all Islamic political actors criticize the Turkish state's secular or secularist characteristics to differing degrees, many simultaneously defend a strong and patriarchal state as long as it supports public religion.

5. For such arguments, see, e.g., Huntington (1996); Lewis (2002); Tibbi (2008).

6. However, Muslims also tend to favor the clergy having more influence in government.

7. For moderation of Islamist political parties and movements, see, e.g., Brumberg (1997); Wickham (2004); Schwedler (2006 and 2011); and Tezcür (2010).

8. Also see Yavuz (2006) and Güney and Başkan (2008) for sanctions against Islamic political parties.

9. As of 2011, the AKP had prevailed in most of these conflicts and had consolidated its power in government.

10. The discussion here focuses on Muslim religious actors. Note that 99.8 percent of Turkey's population is *nominally* Muslim. Christian and Jewish minorities recognized by the Lausanne Treaty have their autonomous religious and educational institutions but they are restricted by government regulations and exclusive practices that have been relaxed in recent years alongside EU-led legal reforms. Other religions need first to be recognized by the state in order to have legal protection. See Fox (2008); US Department of State (2007); Aktar (2000).

11. By comparison, twenty of the remaining thirty-two nondemocracies have a state religion. Three of the democracies, Mali, Senegal, and Turkey had the principle of secularism enshrined in the constitution.

12. The Constitution of the Republic of Turkey, Article 24.

13. The Religion and State Project, available at http://www.religionandstate.org.

14. Data of Religious Freedom obtained from Hudson Institute website (http://crf. hudson.org/index.cfm?fuseaction=survey_files); before being moved to Hudson Institute, the data was reportedly collected by Freedom House.

15. Turkish women, however, are highly represented in some professions such as law.

16. Accompanying prosecular policies were aimed at undermining religious nonstate actors. For example, new legislation made religious *imam-hatip* high schools, which are state administered but largely built through local initiative and charity, less attractive, leading to a 65 percent fall in enrollment. See Bozan (2007: 21).

17. Also see, e.g., Ali Bulaç, "Modernliğin Merkezine Göç" (Migrating to the Center of Modernization), *Zaman*, April 28, 2001.

18. The membership of the Muslim-conservative labor union Memur-Sen, for example, swelled from 42,000 in 2002 to 315,000 in 2008, while the membership of the competing unions either decreased or remained the same. See Toprak et al. (2008: 113).

19. In the same period, the numbers of mosques also increased at a slightly higher rate. From 2003 and 2007, the number of mosques increased by 3.47 percent, while the corresponding rate was 2.94 percent between 1998 and 2002.

20. However, Turkey's ranking in the Human Development Index remained more or less the same between 2002 and 2005 (see http://hdr.undp.org/en/statistics/). Similarly, the country's gender gap score remained the same, and its ranking actually deteriorated from 105th to 123rd, between 2006 and 2008. See Global Gender Gap Index, World Economic Forum (available at http://www.weforum.org/).

21. For implications for democratic consolidation, see Somer (2007).

22. See, e.g., Tülin Daloğlu, "The Decline of Freedom of Expression in Turkey," *Washington Times*, March 4, 2009.

23. See the explanation on the interviews conducted in the "Social and Political Pluralism" section.

24. However, less than 1 percent indicated "turban, religion and religious pressures" as the most important problem of the country. See Çarkoğlu and Kalaycıoğlu (2007: 129, 152).

25. See interviews with religious actors in Toprak et al (2008: 116).

26. For a more comprehensive discussion of the methodology and findings, see Somer (2010, 2011). The newspapers were *Milli Gazete, Zaman, Yeni Şafak, Milliyet*, and *Cumhuriyet*. The first three are religious-conservative newspapers. Note that the terms "religious" and "secular" are used to denote these newspapers for brevity, for lack of better terms, and to abide by the popular usage in Turkey.

27. In general, I also minimized validity and reliability problems by distributing the issues among twenty analysts with no consecutive day examined by the same person

and each coder's employing the same rules and answering the same set of questions while coding the articles. The coders were also instructed *not* to try to infer the overall opinion of an article. For example, if an article on nationalism contained arguments and examples both favoring and critical of nationalism, they were instructed to code both positive and negative judgments for the article on nationalism. This reduced the role of their subjective judgments and made it possible to code the composition and changing balance of different views in the texts.

28. The NGOs are the Istanbul branches of Mazlum-Der Human Rights Foundation, the Ensar Educational Foundation, the AK-Der women's rights organization, and the Deniz Feneri Charity Foundation. The newspapers are: *Today's Zaman* and *Vakit*. In order to protect the privacy of these parties, however, I will not link comments to specific actors.

29. The Turkish word is "çağdaşlaşma," which can be translated as "adopting the contemporary level of civilization." See also Heper and Demirel (1996).

30. This skepticism is still almost double the skepticism in the secular newspapers, which had 258 negative codings, or 5.8 percent, within a total of 4,478 codings on democracy.

31. Intellectual ambivalence vis-a-vis secularism is common among Islamist actors in the Middle East. See Tamimi and Esposito (2000).

4

The Role of Human Security in the Contest between the Egyptian Government and the Muslim Brotherhood, 1980–2010

Charles McDaniel

Introduction

Over the past fifty years, Egyptian human security has continued to decline for a variety of reasons, contributing greatly to the present disorder. Among these, three specific issues are at the forefront of the crisis. First, Egyptians are increasingly challenged by poverty.[1] Second, until the recent uprising that ousted Hosni Mubarak in early 2011, Egyptians suffered profound social and political alienation. Finally, many Egyptians are continually threatened by violence, both from state and nonstate actors. During the 1970s, '80s, and '90s, a number of radical Islamic organizations engaged in violence with the apparent intent of "purifying" Egypt by eradicating insufficiently pious Muslims as well as non-Muslims, such as Copts. In response, the government of Hosni Mubarak, following the lead of the previous administrations under Gamal Abd al-Nasser and Anwar Sadat, acted to suppress dissent, particularly from Islamist organizations. This suppression extended to groups that are neither violent nor overtly political. In Egypt's deeply insecure environment, the popularity of any institution (state or nonstate) is influenced by public perceptions about its impact on human welfare. This chapter describes how ever-increasing public concern about human security in Egypt is leading to a cultural transformation of the country by reshaping the decades-long contest between the state and the most popular Islamist organization in the country, the Muslim Brotherhood.

The Muslim Brotherhood is a faith-based movement, founded in 1928, that has unwaveringly criticized the Egyptian government for being too secular as well as being profoundly unjust: qualities that it asserts are linked. The Muslim Brotherhood officially abandoned violence in the 1970s, but nonetheless, it has not been permitted to challenge the government politically—at least through open political participation. Being more or less unable to challenge the government in the political sphere, the Brotherhood has gained ground by contesting the Egyptian state in less high-profile elections and has gained popularity as a capable provider of services critical to the human security of the threatened Egyptian middle classes.

During recent decades, the Brotherhood has established itself as a religiously inspired, nonstate rival capable of outperforming the state in the provision of basic services—with the not-too-subtle subtext that if it was given control of the state, its leaders would create a stronger social services arm than the current regime elites. The Brotherhood's ability to provide services helped increase its popularity, both socially and at the ballot box.

Threatened by the increasing strength of the Brotherhood, the state responded by trying to improve the *image* of its performance in the area of social and economic welfare, even as its neoliberal agenda limited political freedoms (in particular, disenfranchising the rural population), subsidized speculative financial arrangements and upscale real estate development, and discouraged domestic agricultural production on which most Egyptians were dependent (Mitchell 1999: 461–465). At the same time, the state sought to convince the public that the Brotherhood was not, in fact, a provider of "net" human security. By publicly claiming that the Brotherhood was still linked to extremism and violence, the government portrayed the organization as one that perpetuated physical insecurity and, by impeding the tourism-based economy, increased poverty. This forced the Brotherhood to distance itself even more publicly from violence.

In short, beginning in the 1990s, both the Egyptian government and the Muslim Brotherhood understood the necessity of being perceived as a more effective provider of human security than their rival. The Brotherhood demonstrated its commitment and effectiveness in providing human security by using its captive syndicates and grassroots organizations to provide essential services the government was unable to provide. The government responded by trying to link the Brotherhood with violence and, therefore, with much of the physical and economic suffering in Egypt. As a result, the Brotherhood tried even harder to demonstrate that it was not violent. It made efforts to demonstrate a desire to engage in politics and a commitment to cooperating with a wide range of secular civil organizations.

In essence, issues of human security have become central in the decades-long political struggle between the state and the Muslim Brotherhood. On the one hand, the Muslim Brotherhood has gained popularity and credibility through its perceived ability to remedy problems of human security, such as poverty and underemployment. On the other, the state has sought to portray the Brotherhood as destructive of human security. This chapter argues that the relative popularity of the government and of its main rival, the Brotherhood, depends a great deal on each party's perceived impact on human security. By the 2000s, both groups recognized this fact. They have adapted their policies to meet this reality, and the Egyptian people have benefited from these developments.

The Muslim Brotherhood and Its Ideology

Egyptian schoolteacher Hassan al-Banna founded the Muslim Brotherhood in 1928. Initially, the group was just one of the anti-imperialist groups operating in Egypt at the time, along with secular nationalists, liberals, communists, and fascists.[2] Each of these groups was devoted to eliminating vestiges of European colonialism and had their own view of what the "new Egypt" should look like. The Brotherhood envisioned a nation whose leaders would share the Brothers' commitment to living life according to an early and uncorrupted version of Muhammad's message (Hopwood 1985: 85–89, 38–42).

From the time of publication of Sayyid Qutb's *Social Justice in Islam* in 1949, the Brotherhood demonstrated a commitment to "social justice," although the exact meaning of the term was never adequately articulated.[3] In some ways, the appeal to social justice seemed to be part of a tautological formula by which Islam was presented as a complete social and moral code that, if followed, would lead to a just social order. In Christian vernacular, al-Banna adopted an "evangelical" approach to social and religious restoration, insisting that "an Islamic nation was to be built upon the reform of individual hearts and souls" (Abed-Kotob 1995: 323). Once people committed themselves to Islam, they would implement Sharia (Islamic law) and because Sharia represents true justice, a just and equitable society would result. Drawing on modernist Islamic thinkers, the Brothers implied that literate people reading and interpreting the Qu'ran could understand much, if not all, of God's justice. Among other things, God's justice would involve protection of private property but would also require the wealthy to donate some portion of their wealth to the underprivileged.

Although their commitment to justice has been steadfast, the Brotherhood's policies and statements have been ambiguous regarding the institutional structures through which justice can be achieved and by which divine sovereignty could be implemented in a modern state. In different countries, different branches of the Brotherhood seem to have come up with different answers. The organization's adaptability has extended its physical presence but lessened ideological cohesiveness as national chapters adjust their message and strategies to local conditions.

In fact, the Brotherhood's international organization has been described as "a loose and feeble coalition scarcely able to convene its own members" (Leiken and Brooke 2007: 107).[4]

Umar al-Tilmisani, the Egyptian leader of the Brotherhood in the 1970s, illustrated the ambiguous role of politics in Brotherhood ideology. After noting that the "first level of power is the power of creed and belief," al-Tilmisani muddies the waters by asserting: "As for rule, the Brethren do not request [political power] for themselves. If they find among the nation one who can handle this burdensome responsibility ... who can rule following Islamic and Quranic mores ... [the Brethren will be] his soldiers, his supporters, and his assistants" (al-Tilmisani 1987, qtd. in Abed-Kotob 1995: 324). Even less clear is what the leaders of the Brotherhood believed would be the appropriate action the Brotherhood should take when political leaders do not live up to this Islamic standard.

Many Egyptians, particularly the emerging lower-middle and middle urban classes, were attracted to the idea that literate people could understand texts themselves, without seeking guidance from professional clerics. With the support of these groups, the Brotherhood quickly established itself as one of the most important nongovernmental organizations in Egypt.

Despite the Brotherhood's initial position as anticolonialist and antiimperialist allies in the struggle for a free Egypt, the relationship between the government and the Brotherhood has been tenuous at best and violent at worst. Throughout the 1950s and 1960s, the government dealt with opposition from the Brotherhood by imprisoning, torturing, and executing members of the group under the tenet that the Brotherhood was continually conspiring against the regime. Assassination attempts against Nasser and the more militant positions held by some members of the Brotherhood did not help change this perception (Kepel 1985). The Brotherhood officially renounced violence in the 1970s, and since then, it has been committed to evoking change through participation in the democratic political process.

Since its renunciation of violence, the Brotherhood has gradually gained prominence as a moderate Islamic movement. It has also benefited from a set of policies that effectively delegitimized many of the other Islamic voices in Egypt. Early after the Free Officers coup of 1952, Nasser and his government recognized the need for religious legitimization in accomplishing its aggressive social program. This was particularly true in light of opposition from Islamist groups such as the Muslim Brotherhood. Nasser attempted to gain control over religious institutions through steps such as taking over religious endowments and the 1961 reorganization of al-Azhar, the bastion of Sunni orthodoxy in Cairo (Moustafa 2000: 5). By taking control of al-Azhar's finances and faculty appointments, the government co-opted a venerable religious institution and conscripted its scholars for its own purposes (5). Once in control, the Egyptian government began to exploit ideological differences that had existed among Azhar scholars for years (6).

Instead of legitimizing the government, subsidization and effective nationalization of Egyptian mosques brought accusations of corruption against traditional Islamic leaders as well as intense criticism from radical Islamist groups such as Takfir wa al-Hijra and al-Jam'a al-Islamiyya (Moustafa 2000: 9–11). This conflict over religious legitimacy and authority further empowered the Brotherhood, which was viewed as a moderate voice that was not complicit with the government. Moustafa relates a specific instance when members of the Brotherhood were solicited by the government to replace the shaykhs from al-Azhar in a "prison dialogue" with recently arrested Islamist radicals. When the Brotherhood accepted the role of mediator, it demonstrated its credibility to militant Islamists as well as the Egyptian public (11).

In addition to officially renouncing violence, the Brotherhood demonstrated its willingness to cooperate pragmatically with secular and coalitional organizations. For example, Brotherhood members have been active participants in the Egyptian umbrella opposition group Kifaya. Such stances have made it unpopular with jihadists.

Nasser's Policies and the Growth of the Brotherhood

Beginning immediately after the Free Officers coup in 1952, the revolutionary policies of Egyptian president Gamal Abdel Nasser increasingly began to affect the human security of Egyptian citizens through policies of redistribution and increasing employment. From the beginning of his regime until his death, Nasser continued to pursue a socialist campaign to transform Egypt. At the same time and, ironically, as a result of these same policies, the Brotherhood's growth as a potent institutional force accelerated.

Education was particularly affected by Nasser's policies. Despite the lack of economic resources to support his program, thousands of primary and secondary schools were constructed in the attempt to provide universal education (Danielson 2007; Wickham 2002: 25). Nasser's elimination of school fees at all levels in the attempt to attenuate class differences opened the possibility for "nonelites" to receive university degrees.[5] During Nasser's presidency, enrollment at Egyptian institutions of higher education grew 325 percent, and enrollment in primary education grew 235 percent (Wickham 2002: 25).

At the same time that education levels were skyrocketing, a program of "education-vocation exchange," in which the government guaranteed employment for those who took advantage of the state's generous education subsidies, was established. These programs targeted "educated, lower-middle-class youth for extra entitlements—as well as for extra indoctrination—in order to defuse their capacity to threaten the regime's survival" (Wickham 2002: 23). The government established targets for the production of engineers, doctors, agricultural specialists, and other professionals in Egypt's system of higher education, without the benefit of market demand measures. Actual employment did not meet these targets.

For example, Geneive Abdo (2000: 85; qtng. Moore 1994: 215) describes the situation that Egyptian engineers found themselves in as follows:

> By the early 1980s, most engineers had been forced into the swollen ranks of the *muwazzafun*, state workers sitting idle in rows of desks in the labyrinth of "socialist Gothic" ministry buildings in Cairo. In the centralized economic tradition of full employment, the workers pretended to work and the state pretended to pay them. Few engineers were actually working in their chosen field. In 1993, the state still had not found jobs for those who graduated in 1984. In the words of the authoritative Western scholar Clement Henry Moore, they were "engineers in search of industry."

This emphasis on higher education contributed to a disproportionate number of educated professionals and technicians whose experience with failed state programs and lack of opportunity made them susceptible to the Brotherhood's recruitment efforts. Carrie Wickham has observed "a special irony in the fact that the largest opposition movement in Egypt derives the bulk of its support from educated youth" (Wickham 2002: 2). The Brotherhood benefited from this new disenfranchised and educated class.

The Brotherhood's Attempts to Enter Legislative Politics in the 1970s and 1980s

During the 1970s, there was a period of minor political liberalization in Egypt. While some offshoots of the Brotherhood continued to wage violence against the state, the main wing of the Brotherhood began attempting to participate in the political process by running in national elections. It was Umar al-Tilmisani, the leader of the Muslim Brotherhood, who led the organization into the field of electoral politics in the 1970s. The organization prepared for political participation by securing positions of leadership in professional syndicates. Later, the Brotherhood struck alliances with "legitimate" political parties to field candidates for Parliament, and it achieved significant gains, particularly in the 1987 parliamentary elections (Skovgaard-Petersen 1997: 210–211). Eventually, the Brotherhood became a significant political player by running candidates as independents. As a result, the organization continued to secure seats in Parliament, with a record eighty-eight members associated with the Brotherhood being elected in 2005 (Shehata and Stacher 2006: 33). Ultimately, this emergence of the Brotherhood as a major political rival threatened the government and led to renewed suppression of the Brotherhood's political arm.

The Egyptian government was unwilling to let the Brotherhood become a political presence that could compete on level ground for seats in the legislature. Government harassment of candidates and voters, in addition to government-sponsored fraud in elections, limited the number of seats the Brothers were allowed to win. Furthermore, the Egyptian Parliament ignored the demands of legislators who were members of the Brotherhood in all but a few circumscribed areas. The government was willing to let Islamists win legislative victories with respect to certain social issues, but it prevented them from influencing policies important to the regime (Lombardi 2006: 136–139; Kepel 1985: 247–248).

By the mid-1980s, it was clear that the Brotherhood would not gain significant power through national electoral politics. A lack of political power left it with no way to displace the current elites at the top of the government and no power to influence those elites to implement Brotherhood policies with respect to core political or economic issues.

Importantly, during the 1980s and '90s, the main wing of the Muslim Brotherhood did not react to its general restriction from political power by returning to arms. Those Brothers who wanted to resort to violence left the organization and joined more militant factions. Instead, the main wings of the Brotherhood attempted to engage in politics through two different modes. The first was election to nonnational offices, and the second was the provision of essential services in a way that highlighted the failure of the government to provide these services.

During the 1980s and '90s members of the Brotherhood ran, with limited success, as political candidates under the banner of various opposition parties. They also began to run for leadership positions in numerous professional syndicates, with much better results. In taking these steps, they were publicly signaling their commitment to nonviolent political contestation. At the same time, they leveraged these new positions in syndicates and took steps to demonstrate their ability to provide human security, particularly to the middle class, by providing services that the government was unwilling or unable to provide. In so doing, the implicit message was that if it controlled the government, the Brotherhood could and would provide better services than the current regime.

With the oil-inspired recession of the 1980s, the economic plight of these over-educated and underemployed Egyptians became worse. The disenfranchised professional class became a fertile ground for the Muslim Brotherhood to transform itself, and to raise its profile and influence in Egyptian society. To the consternation of the government, Islamists associated with the Muslim Brotherhood began to run for office in the national syndicates. Having won, they used the syndicates as a forum in which to organize discontented Egyptians to criticize government policies and to provide services that the government had been unwilling or unable to provide, thus embarrassing the government further.

Several scholars have noted the rather seamless transition of the Brothers from involvement in student organizations in the 1970s to professional syndicates in the 1980s that offered significant incentives for membership, such as pensions, health insurance, and assistance in procuring visas for travel abroad ('Awaḍī 2004: 95). The members of syndicates often were, in fact, the same students that the Brotherhood had targeted ideologically in the past—though now underemployed and amenable to the messages of the Brothers.

Most concerning to the government was the Brotherhood's takeover of the traditionally secular Lawyers Syndicate, winning fourteen of twenty-four seats on the Executive Council and effectively gaining control over Egypt's Bar Association.[6] Asked about the victory, lead candidate Ahmed Seif El-Islam Hassan El-Banna said, "it is proof of our popularity"; moreover, regarding the organization's goals, he added: "We want it to be an Islamic association whose members abide by Sharia (Islamic law) and fear God in all their actions."[7]

After Brotherhood candidates won syndicate elections, the administrative expertise they had gained through participation in the student unions was extended to the Brotherhood's management of the syndicates, with a commitment to address corruption in these organizations ('Awaḍī 2004: 96).[8] Ninette Fahmy sees the Brotherhood's turn to the syndicates as part of a broad-based pattern of political participation that complemented its parliamentary ambitions rather than substituted for them. However, she points to the longevity of Islamist office-holders in professional syndicates as well as continuation of ethically questionable practices as evidence that Brotherhood control of these organizations has not rid them of corruption. She notes that syndicates remain "intolerant of internal criticism and reluctant to abide by syndicate rules"; they are also subject to charges of corruption, waste, and embezzlement (Fahmy 1998: 557). Moreover, she sees the continuation of corruption under Brotherhood leadership as making the syndicates even more vulnerable to government control, since the state can highlight supposedly corrupt practices as an excuse to "tighten even further its grip on the institutions of civil society" (557–558). The Brotherhood, working through professional organizations, was able to gain an inroad into the country's social welfare system by administering member services in these organizations. It does not appear, however, that its involvement reduced the corruption that has contributed to problems of human security in Egypt.

Beginning in 1990, the Brotherhood began to leverage its successes in the syndicates to reach out to secular groups and to agitate for political reforms that would allow the organization to reenter politics. It organized meetings on "political reform" with both secular and religious opposition groups ('Awaḍī 2004: 151). The government responded by passing Law Number 100 in 1993, which required "democratic" principles to be enforced in syndicate elections. Among the new stipulations, a 50 percent turnout was required for an election to be valid, and the judiciary would undertake the supervision of all syndicate elections (153). Aggressive government crackdowns on union activities followed this legislation, and even some Egyptian officials conceded that it was not violence that precipitated such a harsh reaction by government; the apparent motivation was the Brotherhood's emergence as a rival to the government and the potentially destabilizing effects of its rising autonomy.

By this time, however, the Brotherhood had found an even broader forum in which to demonstrate both the failings of the government in the area of human security and the ability of the Muslim Brotherhood to supplement it.

Providing Services to the Broader Public

The Egyptian government's decision to deny any political voice to Islamists had unforeseen effects. It forced the Brotherhood to concentrate its efforts on human security and civil society through education, health care, law, and other sectors. Just as it had attempted to provide human security to members of the syndicates, the Brotherhood made a point to deliver human security to the public at large. Its activities allowed it to advertise its professed commitment to social service and to demonstrate the ways in which the Brotherhood could deliver it. The Brothers' effectiveness was particularly attractive at a time when the state was unable to address the people's basic security needs.

As one example, the force of the Brotherhood's implied claim that it could provide better security for the Egyptian people than the current Egyptian government became apparent in 1992. On October 13, 1992, an earthquake with a Richter magnitude of 5.9 struck the Dahshour region of Egypt, southwest of Cairo. It lasted between thirty to sixty seconds and killed over five hundred people as well as injuring approximately six thousand.[9] More than one hundred schoolchildren were trampled to death as they fled collapsing school buildings.

In an instant, the disparity of destruction in the city became a visible symbol of a corrupt and ineffective government that had enabled a glaring (and the Brothers insisted, un-Islamic) distribution of power and income, forcing its lower classes to exist in destitution and substandard housing while simultaneously catering to Western tourism and commercial interests.[10] Destruction was concentrated in the city's poorest districts and blamed on poor construction. Cairo's luxury hotels, upscale residential areas, and commercial districts escaped with minor damage.[11]

A government program to eradicate militant movements was underway at the time of the earthquake, but the disaster forced the Mubarak regime to redirect state resources to victims of the earthquake and to the security emergency that developed in the districts that were hit the hardest. Government response to the catastrophe was sluggish and inept. People in Cairo's slums collected in the streets, unable to reenter their damaged homes, and eventually, many made their way to government offices to demand action.[12]

The Muslim Brotherhood's response to the disaster in Cairo contrasted starkly with the government's ineffectual actions (Campagna 1996: 292–293). The Brotherhood established medical centers and shelters for thousands of injured and homeless Egyptians. A network of "Islamic" clinics and medical institutions, many of which were begun by the Brotherhood in the 1970s, supported the effort. Western journalists noted that the earthquake caused the Mubarak government to fear that the Brotherhood's domination of professional associations "had succeeded in forming a state within a state" (Kurtz 2007). Egyptian political pundit Mohammed Sid Ahmed asserted that the "earthquake was a godsend for the fundamentalists," noting that members of Islamist movements "portrayed the event as God's vengeance on a corrupt society. But, more important, they [used] it to show that they [could] provide services while the Government [was] ineffective."[13]

This was not the response of an impoverished class of religious zealots but rather the results of a series of government policies that created a class of academically trained and religiously motivated workers. The response of the Muslim Brotherhood to the Cairo earthquake revealed an unintended consequence of the Egyptian government's social reform policies. Kurtz (2007) observes that "[i]nstead of taking a nation of pious traditional villagers and turning them into secular modern technocrats, college students fresh from Egypt's villages were turning the nation's secular professions into Islamist bastions."[14]

Harrigan and El-Said show that the rise in faith-based services coincided with shrinking state services caused by Egyptian government policy (Harrigan and El-Said 2009: 101). The services offered by these faith-based organizations varied, extending to "day care centers, schooling, adult literacy classes, secondhand clothing shops, classes to upgrade skills, wedding and funeral services, and medical clinics" (Clark 2004b: 50).

Adding insult to injury, the Brotherhood repeatedly insisted that it did not *mean* to embarrass the government but felt compelled to step in where it was failing. For example, during the Brotherhood's response to another disaster, the Dronka fire of 1994, spokesman Mohammad Habib said: "We don't want to embarrass the government and give it the impression that we are the most active. … Our objective is purely humanitarian and has no political dimension."[15]

In reality, however, it may be difficult to assess the full scope of the Brotherhood's social and civil activities. This is due to the diffuse nature of Islamist social movements, which Asef Bayat has called "a complex web of dispersed and heterogeneous organizations, activities, and sympathies around a distinct core embodied in the reformist Muslim Brotherhood, which aimed to Islamize society at the grassroots" (Bayat 2007: 137). Most Islamic social institutions are independent, with independent financial resources, and even those linked with nationally recognized organizations often operate autonomously (Clark 2004b: 51). In addition, while the government has enacted laws requiring all nongovernmental organizations in Egypt to register with the Ministry of Social Affairs (allowing the government to supervise all social services activities), the Brotherhood registers organizations under different names. Nonetheless, in 2006, one Brotherhood member claimed that at least 20 percent of five thousand legally registered nongovernmental organizations (NGOs) are linked to the Brotherhood.[16] The provision of these social services has been suggested as a main reason for Brotherhood members winning eighty-eight seats in the People's Assembly by running as independents during the 2005 elections, and the failure of the government in similar areas as a main cause for discontent with the ruling party.[17]

At the same time, while the services provided by the Muslim Brotherhood have arguably benefited the educated, but frustrated middle class that forms the basis of the Brotherhood's membership, it is less clear whether these services have really benefited the urban and rural poor to the extent that would garner the Brotherhood political support among those classes (Clark 2004a).[18] Nevertheless, these institutions have had a large degree of success, proving an integral part of understanding the struggle between a secular government and Islamist groups (Clark 2004a).

Response of the Government

The Egyptian government was clearly embarrassed by the Brotherhood's superior response to the earthquake and frightened by the public's recognition that the Brotherhood had outperformed the state in the provision of basic services. The government responded with a major crackdown on all Islamist organizations. In 1995, the government attempted to cripple the Brotherhood's international organization by arresting many of its leaders. Estimates suggest that as many as one thousand "opposition activists," including more than three hundred Brotherhood members, were arrested during the 1995 election period in which Mubarak's National Democratic Party (NDP) attained more than 400 of the 444 seats up for election.[19] Candidates known to be members of the Brotherhood "cut deals" with police that enabled them to campaign, although with extreme restrictions.

Campagna (1996: 302) has observed that a critical component of the government's strategy was "decapitating the organization's dynamic, younger leadership and demobilizing its best organizers, while leaving most of its membership intact."

The response of the Egyptian government and that of the NDP suggests that both organizations realized that the public's support of the Brotherhood was rooted in the belief that the Brothers were providing human security to Egypt's frustrated citizens. The NDP realized the need to compete with the Muslim Brotherhood in the area of social services, even as its neoliberal policies shrank the state's role as a social service provider. As a result, the party's efforts have included programs such as passing out food packets during Ramadan and sending doctors to provide health care to the party's constituencies (Harrigan and El-Said 2009: 105).

In addition, the state cracked down on the Brotherhood, a crackdown justified by claiming that the Brothers were not in any way as beneficial to Egyptian social welfare as the government (Campagna 1996: 293–298). In fact, notwithstanding the Brothers' good work during the earthquake, the government insisted that they were linked to terrorist actions that had been carried out by radical Islamist groups and that, in addition to contributing to general unrest, these actions had harmed many sectors in the Egyptian economy (Kepel 1995: 115–118). But there was little evidence linking the Brotherhood to terrorist violence, and the director of state security for Central Egypt, Mansour Esawi, admitted the lack of any such evidence. Nevertheless, he insisted that there *was* some connection and implied that the services the Brotherhood provided were offset by the damage it caused to the civilian victims of terror and to the Egyptian economy.[20]

The government used its control over the media to emphasize that the Brothers did more harm than good, despite the image they presented to the public. *The Independent* (London) reported that "all six national daily newspapers, whether government-controlled, opposition mouthpieces, or independent as well as the main weekly magazines have, in the past week or so, broken with their practice of not criticizing the Islamists" and have "begun taking on the ideologues of the mainstream Islamist movement, including shaykhs preaching militant Islam."[21] In February 1995, the weekly magazine *Al-Musawwar* attempted to tie the Brotherhood to Islamist violence. It published an expose entitled "Secrets of the Muslim Brotherhood's World Organization," which alleged that the organization's "Capability and Hegemony" program, which focused on the goal of establishing a Muslim Brotherhood government, was meant as preparation for a new caliphate, with the desired seat of this Islamist government located in Cairo (Tal 2005: 69).

The Brotherhood's response demonstrated that it believed that the battle for public support would be won or lost based on how the public perceived each party's ability to affect human security. In an interview, a leader of the Muslim Brotherhood, Ma'mun al-Hudaybi countered that those arrested were artists, scientists, and academics who had no interest in violence:

> We regret that [the arrests] have taken place and we do not know what the reason for them is. We fear that there are some elements who want to create political crises in Egypt. This is not in Egypt's interest. This also harms Egyptian media, tourism in Egypt and its economy. It is not at all in the interest of the Egyptian people.[22]

Hudaybi's statement appears to turn the tables on the Egyptian government regarding human security; rather than the Brotherhood harming Egypt, it was the state that was fomenting "political crises," employing violence and harming the economy, while his organization promoted the peaceful progress of Egypt by supplying artists, scientists, and other professionals who support the nation's civil institutions.

Some elements of the Muslim Brotherhood were radicalized by the mass arrests and joined militant organizations. Most of the Brotherhood, however, seems to have opted for staying the course through involvement in professional organizations and participation in social service via civil institutions, believing that competing with the government in these areas was a more winnable course than the turn to militancy. The organization made extraordinary efforts to demonstrate that its beneficial activities were not tainted by any connection to violence.

The Brotherhood also took highly public steps to demonstrate its desire to use peaceful rather than violent means to protest state actions and that its members were not, as the government claimed, xenophobic radicals. The organization enabled the development of the Al-Wasat ("The Center") Party in 1997, which maintained the "Islamic civilization project," even though the group allowed Coptic Christians to be members and women to be officers.[23] The Brotherhood increasingly reached out to secular human rights groups and proposed joint responses to the government repression. Secular Egyptian human rights organizations responded to the overtures made by the Brothers, mobilizing the organizations to take action against the media blitz opposing the Brotherhood-dominated syndicates. The Egyptian Organization for Human Rights sponsored a workshop in May 1998 that brought together syndicate leaders and human rights activists to speak out against syndicate-targeted legislation, particularly Law 5 of 1995 that restricted syndicate activities and enabled syndicates to be placed under sequestration.[24]

The result of the battle for public support that occurred during the 1990s is still not clear; both the Islamists and the state continue to present themselves as the best provider of democratic and social services while portraying their opponent as less beneficial, or even harmful, to human security. The 2011 overthrow of the Mubarak regime was brought about by a mass uprising in which Islamists participated but did not lead. Although there is much to be determined as events in Egypt unfold, it is likely that Egypt will create a new constitutional system. The Islamists' ability to succeed in a new and, presumably, more "liberal" political environment remains to be seen. In the post-Mubarak age, memories of previous eras may fade or, perhaps, become distorted.

We do know that in the years prior to Mubarak's fall, there was growing doubt within the Egyptian government about its ability to win this battle of perceptions, and we know that this doubt pushed different factions to recommend very different policies toward the Brothers. Some of the more optimistic policymakers, like Hassan Abu Basha, have advocated an inclusive approach that involves moderate Islamist groups in "political measures and social-economic reforms," along with continued antiterrorist programs against militant organizations (Tal 2005: 61). Others like Fu'ad Allam, a former head of the Directorate of State Security Investigations, believe that government tolerance of Islamist groups in political society would inspire more dissidence and favor those who desire an Islamic state. Thus, they argue for strong restrictions on the Brothers' political and social activities (Tal 2005: 61).[25]

In the final years of the Mubarak regime, the hard-liners seem to have won the upper hand. In April 2008, when a handful of Brotherhood members received ten-year prison sentences for "money-laundering and terrorism," one Egyptian journalist described the sentences as some of the harshest penalties since the Nasser era and asserted that they represented the "highest degree of political exclusion to hit the [Muslim Brotherhood] over the past three years."[26] The government's increasingly aggressive stance against the Brotherhood is a continuation of policies begun in the aftermath of the 2005 parliamentary elections. In that year, 150 candidates affiliated with the Brotherhood were allowed to run for Parliament and achieved a surprisingly strong showing, attaining seventy-six seats in the legislative body.[27] Police responded immediately to the success of Islamist candidates in the initial round of voting by arresting over one thousand Brotherhood members before subsequent rounds. The police also blocked access to polling districts known to be sympathetic to the Brotherhood.[28] Despite the government crackdown, the Brotherhood continued to resist the turn to violence. That decision will probably serve its members well when they enter the political environment that emerges post-Mubarak.

Conclusion

The history of the struggle between the Muslim Brotherhood and the Egyptian government suggests that the Egyptian government's oppression of the Muslim Brotherhood, rather than eliminating its ability to challenge the government, shifted that challenge away from electoral platforms and toward the ability of each respective institution to provide security, employment, financial stability, and emergency services. From the 1970s through the 1990s, the Egyptian government's policies pushed the Brotherhood away from electoral politics. Instead of trying to debate large policy issues, the Brotherhood chose to emphasize, at a grassroots level, its abilities to provide human security. This strengthened the image of the Brotherhood as a group that was more willing and able to provide for the human security of Egyptians than the government itself.

Given the systematic political oppression that the Brothers have been forced to undergo, Sana Abed-Kotob logically asks, "why has the Brotherhood chosen to work within the system, as opposed to battling it through extralegal mechanisms?" Abed-Kotob locates the answer in the organization's foundational mission, articulated by al-Banna in the 1920s: the goal to call people to a proper Muslim life (da'wa). In his view, "the contemporary Brotherhood views the election campaign as an ideal apparatus for promulgating its message of Islam as the solution" (Abed-Kotob 1995: 331). Dissemination of the message is all important, enabling the public expression of Islam in a way that the secular Egyptian government cannot. By remaining connected to politics and integral to civil society, the Brotherhood contributes to culturally expressive activities that, in their own way, play a part in the security of many Muslims in Egypt who desire more religious involvement in the social order. Ironically, succeeding in the Egyptian electoral process could be damaging to the extent that Islamists would come to be identified with a system that they oppose and that is perceived as ineffectual and corrupt. Government restrictions do not eliminate participation, but they do provide a channel "that promotes awareness at the societal level, thus aiding in the creation of the Islamic society that is at the core of the Brotherhood's long-term ambitions" (331).[29]

However, it is important to note that the Brothers profited from their ability to provide social services. Largely forced out of politics, the Brothers targeted social service in ways consistent with their founding principles, gaining the moral high ground even as they were able to expose government corruption and preoccupation with its own security at the expense of the people. This orientation toward service enhanced the Brotherhood's prestige and its political potential in the event it was ever allowed to participate in the electoral process. Recognizing the power that came with the Brotherhood's reputation as a superior provider of services, the government tried to associate the Brotherhood with the violence of more militant groups—notwithstanding the fact that the organization sought to demonstrate its commitment to nonviolent action and willingness to cooperate with secular groups to improve human welfare in Egypt.

The Egyptian government's attempts to suppress the Muslim Brotherhood seem to have led, unwittingly, to a cycle that forced both the Muslim Brotherhood and Egyptian government to take the human security of Egyptians into account, however ostensible the account may be. Numerous chapters in this volume demonstrate that in countries where the focus is national security and not human security, the people often turn to religiously affiliated, nonstate entities with their grievances. Such is the case in Egypt, where the people, in order to procure basic services, have been forced to seek alternatives to an incompetent and corrupt government whose neoliberal policies have put the welfare of poor and even middle-class Egyptians increasingly at risk. Prompted by organizations such as the World Bank and International Monetary Fund, the government did achieve a remarkable reduction in the national deficit to a degree that amazed even the international financial institutions, but in the process it reallocated state support from the needy to bankers, entrepreneurs, building contractors, and real estate investors, consistent with the neoliberal policies that have contributed to the global financial crisis (Mitchell 1999, 457–462). According to Lehman Fletcher, these policies resulted in "growing unemployment, falling real wages, higher prices for basic goods and services, and widespread loss of economic security" (Fletcher 1996: 4; qtd. in Mitchell 1999: 4).

Religious groups such as the Muslim Brotherhood explicitly equate religiosity with a commitment to social justice. Even when they are shut out from politics—and perhaps it is especially when they are shut out from electoral politics—such groups are able to deliver real assistance to the beleaguered and to build their reputations as the types of organizations that *should* be running the government. Popular movements often threaten the survival of regimes that are failing to provide for national security. But they also call attention to the failure of the state to provide for human well-being and the long-term political costs that may be associated with that failure. Competition between these groups can move from violent or electoral contestation to a competition to be perceived as better providers of human security. In the process, religious groups may come to recognize that their credibility rests, above all, on their ability to realize the charitable goals that, they argue, define the truly religious person. As a result, governments may be inspired to try and outdo the religious opposition in the provision of human services.

In the case of Egypt, the competition between the government and Muslim Brotherhood *may* benefit the people in the long run, but this is yet to be seen. Egypt's present human security problem is the result of a continuation of the government's neoliberal policies and the Muslim Brotherhood's apparent unwillingness to develop a unified platform. The government's policies have subjected many Egyptians to an increasingly unpredictable global marketplace with little public support, and the Muslim Brotherhood has failed to develop a platform that would protect the rights of *all* Egyptians. From the standpoint of human security, if the next regime to take power in Egypt is to enjoy long-term success, it will have to promote balance among legal, political, religious, and economic institutions, as well as support both secular and faith-based NGOs, whose work advances the well-being of the Egyptian people.

Notes

Charles McDaniel, PhD, is an assistant professor in Baylor University's Interdisciplinary Core Program and serves as associate director of the J. M. Dawson Institute of Church-State Studies at Baylor. He teaches courses in church history, Christian social thought, and Islamic politics. McDaniel is the book review editor for the *Journal of Church and State*. In 2007, Rowman and Littlefield published his book *God and Money: The Moral Challenge of Capitalism*. McDaniel has numerous publications in books and scholarly journals on subjects ranging from sixteenth-century Anabaptist movements to religiously based prison ministries in the United States.

The author would like to express appreciation to Stephanie Wheatley, a graduate student in the J. M. Dawson Institute of Church-State Studies at Baylor University, for her research assistance in this project.

1. See Organization for Economic Co-operation and Development, "Egypt," http://www.oecd.org/dataoecd/13/36/40577424.pdf, accessed April 13, 2011.
2. For an early history of the Muslim Brotherhood, see Mitchell (1993).
3. For an English translation, see Qutb (1996).
4. Leiken and Brooke also comment, "Even as Western commentators condemn the Muslim Brotherhood for its Islamism, radicals in the Middle East condemn it for rejecting jihad and embracing democracy. Such relative moderation offers Washington a notable opportunity for engagement—as long as policymakers recognize the considerable variation between the group's different branches and tendencies" (107).
5. The Arabic term transliterated as *shahada* is better known as one of the five pillars of Islam: the profession of faith, "There is no God but Allah and Muhammad is His messenger." However, the word itself is translated as "witnessing" and in the context in which Wickham uses it, the word means "witnessing" the achievement of a university degree or the degree itself (Wickham 2002: 2).
6. "Islamists Take Control of Liberal Syndicate in Egypt," *Al Ahram Weekly*, September 17, 1992, available on Moneyclips; accessed via LexisNexis on May 5, 2011.
7. Qtd. in "Islamists Take Control."
8. 'Awaḍī uses the example of Abu al-Futuh as a prominent figure in the Medical Syndicate who was groomed for leadership through participation in the student movement of the 1970s. There is some controversy concerning both the political strategy of the Brotherhood and whether or not it was able to eliminate corruption within the professional syndicates.

9. Poor response of the Egyptian government combined with the fact that most of the damage occurred in poorer districts of Cairo make casualty and damage accounts suspect even to this day. See Chris Hedges, "Oct. 11–17: Cairo Earthquake; Buildings Fall Easily, Bureaucracy's Barriers Don't as Families Seek Shelter," *New York Times*, October 18, 1992, p. 3, nytimes.com, accessed April 18, 2008; Hedges, "Mubarak Asks Calms after Quake Victims Riot," *New York Times*, October 19, 1992, nytimes.com, accessed April 18, 2008; Hedges, "Egypt Tightens the Net around Its Militant Opposition: A Crackdown in Cairo Startles the Capital, and a Backlash Is Feared," *New York Times*, December 10, 1992, p. 3; Hedges, "As Islamic Militants Thunder, Egypt Grows More Nervous," *New York Times*, November 12, 1992; Hedges, "After the Earthquake, a Rumbling of Discontent," *New York Times*, October 19, 1992, p. 4.

10. Chris Hedges, "Old Cairo: Ricketiness Killed Poor," *New York Times*, October 14, 1992, nytimes.com, accessed April 18, 2008.

11. Caryle Murphy, "Earthquake Kills 370 in Egypt," *Washington Post*, October 13, 1992, p. 1.

12. Hedges, "After the Earthquake"; Hedges, "Old Cairo."

13. Hedges, "After the Earthquake."

14. The participation of educated members of society in Islamist organizations, even those that are more extreme, occurs in other groups as well. One study of the al-Qaeda organization determined that over two-thirds of a sample of 172 members had at some point attended college (Kurtz 2007).

15. Hassan Mekki, "Moslem Fundamentalists Stay Quiet about Aid to Keep Government Happy," *Agence France Press*, November 7, 1994 (retrieved February 3, 1999, from Lexis/Nexis).

16. "Egypt: Social Programmes Bolster Appeal of Muslim Brotherhood," IRIN News, February 22, 2006, http://www.irinnews.org/Report.aspx?ReportID=26150, accessed April 20, 2011.

17. "Egypt: Social Programmes."

18. Clark argues that the horizontal, intra-middle-class social ties that are strengthened through Islamic social institutions have failed to create ties between the middle and lower classes. This absence of ties between the classes has led to social institutions in poorer neighborhoods that lack the resources necessary to provide adequate services to the lower classes (952–954).

19. Peter Waldman, "Mubarak Lashes Out at Islamic Opposition Egyptian Election/ Muslim Brotherhood Was a Target of Repression during Recent Vote, and Many Feel the Government Is Only Driving It Underground," Toronto *Globe and Mail*, December 9, 1995.

20. Waldman, "Mubarak Lashes Out."

21. Adel Darwish, "Islamists under Fire in Egypt," *Independent (London)*, December 31, 1992.

22. Qtd. in "Muslim Brotherhood Spokesman Comments on Recent Arrests of Members," BBC, *Summary of World Broadcasts*, January 26, 1995.

23. Khaled Dawoud, "Islamism in Crisis." *Al-Ahram Weekly On-line*, December 31–January 6, 1998–1999, http://weekly.ahram.org.eg/1998/410/eg6.htm.

24. Egyptian Organization for Human Rights, "In Defense of the Professional Syndicates" (news release), May 26, 1998, http://www.derechos.org/human-rights/mena/eohr/synd.html.

25. Tal describes Allam as believing "that all the Islamic organizations, including the Muslim Brotherhood and terrorist groups, were of one ilk, so that even the most extensive economic, political, or social reforms would have no effect in dissuading the Islamic groups to abandon their dream of replacing government. Faced with this reality the state had no choice but to deal decisively with them" (61).

26. Khalil al-Anani, "In Focus: Risks of Excluding the Brotherhood," *Daily News Egypt,* April 22, 2008, http://www.thedailynewsegypt.com/in-focus-risks-of-excluding-the-brotherhood.html.

27. Sharon Otterman, "Muslim Brotherhood and Egypt's Parliamentary Elections," Council on Foreign Relations, December 1, 2005, http://www.cfr.org/egypt/muslim-brotherhood-egypts-parliamentary-elections/p9319.

28. Otterman, "Muslim Brotherhood."

29. Munson (2001: 487) notes that the Brotherhood "was an explicitly apolitical religious reform and mutual aid society" during its formative period in the early 1930s. It took a political turn in the late '30s in order to support the Arab general strike in Palestine and to combat "the quasi-British control" of Egypt.

5

Popular Muslim Attitudes towards Violent Islamic Groups: The Case of Pakistan

C. Christine Fair and Clark B. Lombardi

Introduction

This volume examines the contemporary relationship between religious actors and "human security," which the editors of this volume, following the United Nations Development Programme, have defined broadly as "the liberation of human beings from those intense, extensive, prolonged, and comprehensive threats to which their lives and freedom are vulnerable." Human security, as the editors of this volume see it in the introduction, contains at least three parts: (1) a physical aspect, involving protection from threats to basic human welfare; (2) a juridical piece, relating to protection from violations of human rights; and (3) a more elusive, culturally conditioned factor.

The book takes it as axiomatic that people lack human security, "if they are in danger of physical harm or material want; if they are suffering grave violations of human rights; or if they feel alienated, psychologically distressed, or sociologically oppressed—for example, during a period of dislocation as refugees." From the standpoint of human security, one of the most disturbing facets of the contemporary religious revival is the rise in many parts of the world of militant, ideologically religious political organizations. These groups are willing and able to use violence to undermine governments, which they perceive to be nonreligious or insufficiently religious. They generally try to replace these governments with ones that are explicitly religious. Although militant religious political groups are found in many parts of the world and are associated with different religions, the most visible and notorious are the shadowy families of Islamist militant groups that sometimes operate on their own and at other times operate in concert with like-minded groups around the world. As popular religiosity has increased in the Muslim world, a number of militant religious political groups have emerged.

The threat that militant Islamist groups pose to human security is potentially twofold. First, the violence they employ to achieve their goals threatens the physical welfare of people and, thus, makes them insecure. Second, the states that militant religious groups seek to impose often turn out to be affirmatively repressive or, alternatively, can be ineffective at protecting their safety, health, or human rights. Notwithstanding the harm that seems to be caused by militant Islamist groups, militant Islamist groups seem to enjoy public support in some nations. This raises important questions. Does deep religiosity in certain countries lead the public blindly to support these groups on ideological grounds notwithstanding their impact on the physical or juridical aspects of human security? Or does popular support exist in part because significant portions of the public are simply unaware of the true impact that these groups have on the physical aspects of human security? Or do elements of populations support militant groups because they support their goals, means, or both?

In this chapter, we look at Pakistan to see what polling data tells us about the sources of support for Islamist militant groups in that country. We should be clear that Pakistan is home to numerous Islamist and even militant ("jihadi") organizations, all of which are active in various ways in Pakistani society. In this chapter, we focus on a subset of Islamist groups, known within Pakistan as *askari tanzeems*. Pakistan has long been home to numerous militant groups, which have enjoyed, and indeed continue to enjoy, various degrees of state support. Since 1947, militant groups have engaged in violence in India and Afghanistan, as well as Pakistan. In recent years, these groups have also had an impact well beyond the South Asian theater. We will describe in the first part of this chapter the universe of groups that fit within the definition of "militant Islamist groups" and whose sources of support we are exploring. We make no claims about the nature of other groups, about the roles that they play in society, or about their sources of support within Pakistan.

The violence perpetrated by Pakistan-based militant Islamist groups has had grave consequences for the welfare of civilians in Afghanistan, Pakistan, India, and beyond.[1] Furthermore, in areas where violent Islamist groups have been able to establish control in Afghanistan and Pakistan, human security has suffered.[2] In the summer of 2007, one of the authors of this chapter, C. Christine Fair, commissioned a study of Pakistani attitudes toward militant groups under the auspices of the United States Institute of Peace (USIP), in collaboration with the Program on International Policy Attitudes (PIPA).[3] This chapter draws on that study and depends as well on some largely urban data collected by the Pew Global Attitudes Project,[4] and on data collected by the International Republican Institute (IRI), which was a more nationally representative sample.[5]

These studies confirm that important minority segments of the Pakistani public evince some level of support for Islamist militant groups operating from Pakistan, despite the damage that militant Islamist groups have done to human security within and outside Pakistan. The data that indicates popular support for militant Islamist groups must be read alongside other data that suggests that there is surprisingly widespread public ignorance about the activities in which these groups do and do not engage. Furthermore, in looking at the trends in Pakistani popular support for militant groups, there is also some evidence suggesting that the support may wax or wane depending on the degree to which these groups are perceived as indiscriminately violent. Other reasons for supporting these groups may have to do with the perceived efficacy of achieving their goals. In the following pages, we will discuss this data in detail and then consider its implications.

In order to approach this study, we organize the chapter as follows. First, we provide an overview of Islamist militant groups operating in and from Pakistan and catalogue the activities in which they engage.[6] These activities include limited welfare activities along with shocking acts of violence against civilians and security forces. Second, we discuss polling data that suggests important, if limited, public support for these groups and attempt to examine the roots of this support. In our analysis, we look at data addressing the degree to which Pakistanis are aware of any welfare activities carried out by Pakistani militant groups. Third, we turn to two crucial questions: (1) whether the Pakistani public supports, in the abstract, certain types of violence and (2) whether members of the Pakistani public are aware of the nature of the violence that Pakistani militant groups actually perpetrate.

Looking at the studies described above, it seems that Pakistanis are ambivalent about violence against civilians anywhere in the world and are hostile to violence against Pakistanis in particular. The data, however, also suggests a surprising lack of awareness, among Pakistanis, about the nature of the violence that is perpetrated by particular Pakistani militant groups.

We conclude that based on the data available, it is impossible to say whether Pakistanis would stop supporting militant groups if they were better informed about the nature of the militants' activities. Nevertheless, the polling data before us gives us no reason to believe that this is not true. Policymakers could explore this proposition by commissioning studies using larger sample sizes of Pakistani respondents and experimental surveying techniques (information cues) to discourage inaccurate responses to sensitive questions. And they should. For both theoretical and policy reasons, this hypothesis deserves further study. As a theoretical matter, this hypothesis, if proved, would challenge the assumption, prevalent among some theorists, that the religious revival threatens human security by creating people who are more concerned with psychic comfort than with physical security and, as a result, are prone to accept violence. As a policy matter, it would indicate that education could be an effective, nonmilitary tool to limit the sources of support that militants enjoy.

Pakistan's Militant Landscape

Pakistanis often refer to the myriad militant groups operating in their country as *askari tanzeems* (which literally means "militant organizations").[7] Prior to General Pervez Musharraf's acceptance of the US-given ultimatum to join the US-led global war on terrorism in September 2001, Pakistan's militant landscape could be differentiated by the group's sectarian orientation, its theater of operation, and its ethnic constitution. For example, there were askari tanzeems that traditionally focused on Kashmir, including the Deobandi groups of Jaish-e-Mohammad and Harkat-ul-Ansar/Harkat-ul-Mujahideen in addition to Ahl-e-Hadith organizations such as Punjab-based Lashkar-e-Taiba (LeT).[8]

Other askari tanzeems have been traditionally sectarian in nature and include the anti-Shia Lashkar-e-Jhangvi and Sipah-e-Sahaba Pakistan.[9] Both these antisectarian groups are under the sway of the Deobandi organization Jamiat-e-Ulema Islami (JUI) and are funded by wealthy Arab individuals and organizations. Notably, many of these Deobandi tanzeems have overlapping memberships, and they also have strong connections to the JUI (Zahab and Roy 2004; Fair 2004). Though they have largely disappeared, Shia sectarian groups were lethally active in the past, often obtaining funding from Iran and targeting Sunni Muslims.[10]

Since 2004, when the Pakistani military went into South Waziristan, Pakistan has experienced the emergence of a distinctive cluster of militant groups whose activists all describe themselves as "Pakistani Taliban."[11] Some "Pakistani Taliban" commanders, including Baitullah Mehsood, Maulvi Nazir, Mullah Fazlulla, and Maulvi Faqir, have operated in specific agencies. In late 2007, many of these commanders coalesced under the banner of the "Pakistani Taliban" (Tehreek-e-Taliban-e-Pakistan) under the leadership of (now deceased) Baitullah Mehsood and based in South Waziristan in Pakistan's federally administered tribal areas (FATA). Since then, they have successfully established an archipelago of micro-emirates of Sharia within large swaths of the Pashtun belt (in FATA and the Northwest Frontier Province [NWFP]).[12] (Note that the name of NWFP has changed since this survey was fielded. The territory is now known as Khyber Pakhtunkhwa. However, we have retained NWFP throughout this essay as this was the name used during the survey.) After the August 2009 slaying of Baitullah Mehsood, the coherence of the "Pakistani Taliban" was in doubt. However, after some delay and confusion, Hakimullah Mehsood emerged as the leader. Under him, the "Pakistani Taliban" demonstrated growing competence and stronger ties to other organizations, especially anti-Shia groups such as Sipah-e-Sahaba-e-Pakistan.

While the so-called Talibanization of the tribal areas was initially limited to North and South Waziristan, the phenomenon quickly spread throughout the tribal areas and into settled areas of Pakistan.[13] At the same time, supporters of the Pakistani Taliban established themselves in pockets in Pakistan's cities.[14] In April 2009, the problem of militant groups ensconced in Southern Punjab (with important ties to the Pakistani Taliban) has become apparent.[15] For example, Punjab-based groups such as the Deobandi Lashkar-e-Jhangvi (LeJ) and Jaish-e-Mohammad are allies of the Pakistani Taliban and both have conducted suicide attacks in Pakistan on behalf of the Pakistani Taliban.[16]

Finally, in addition to the above noted Pakistani groups, one finds in Pakistan several Islamist militant groups whose members are not, primarily, from Pakistan itself. Pakistan hosts groups of the Afghan Taliban, with leadership committees (shuras) in Quetta, Peshawar, and Karachi.[17] As is well known, Pakistani territory is also used by al-Qaeda. Al-Qaeda operatives are known to reside in North and South Waziristan and Bajaur among other areas in the Pashtun belt. Moreover, many al-Qaeda operatives (such as Abu Zubaidah and Khalid Sheikh Mohammad among numerous others) have been arrested in Pakistani cities.[18]

Together, these different militant groups have long been involved in fomenting violence in Afghanistan and India, particularly Kashmir. Since late 2001 and 2002, they have increasingly been involved in violent activities within Pakistan itself. Many of Pakistan's militant groups, particularly those of Deobandi background, have splintered or reoriented in terms of their targets and tactics. Many of the Deobandi groups are tightly allied to the Afghan and Pakistan Taliban and are increasingly aiming their resources at the Pakistani state even though some elements within these same groups continue to enjoy various levels of formal and informal state support.[19] Since 2006, militants have launched bloody suicide attacks against Pakistan's national security establishment, including the Frontier Corps, intelligence services, and the army. The actual numbers of suicide attacks dramatically increased in 2007.[20] The Pakistani state has not relinquished its uncritical support for many of these groups even while it has suffered significant losses battling elements of militant groups that specifically target the Pakistani state.[21] Pakistani support for groups like Lashkar-e-Taiba remains intact, even for Jaish-e-Mohammad, even though parts of that group have joined ranks with the Pakistani Taliban.

Most Pakistani militant groups were established by the Pakistani intelligence agency to prosecute the state's foreign policy goals, and thus to increase its national security, rather than to advance the cause of human security. These groups primarily recruit individuals who are interested in addressing key Muslim grievances. They are linked only indirectly to the provision of human security, and in limited ways. For example, the Afghan and Pakistani Taliban both provide a modicum of public goods, such as physical security, conflict resolution, and diminished corruption, but they have done so at a very steep price. Other groups, such as anti-Shia militant groups and those that target India, do not purport to provide public service as a part of their violent campaign.

Some of these groups, however, do have a separate organizational branch for the provision of human services. Lashkar-e-Taiba's Jamaat ul Dawa is an example. Other militant groups, such as Hizbul Mujahideen, are tied to religious parties, and benefit from the social services provided by those religious parties.

Pakistani Beliefs about Welfare Activities of Islamist Extremist Groups

As noted already, most Pakistani militant groups were organized by the Pakistani state to serve national security objectives, and they appear to be engaged in only limited and indirect attempts to provide human security. Nevertheless, it is commonplace to assume that some Pakistani militant groups enjoy popular support because they provide some benefit to Pakistani society, or at least to their supporters. For example, some posit that Pakistanis will support a specific militant group, or will at least decline to view that group as a threat, only if they perceive that group or its actions as beneficial to the Pakistani nation or to Pakistani citizens. Conversely, Pakistanis will be less likely to support groups if they perceive them to be harmful.

To explore a variety of Pakistani attitudes about militant groups, the USIP-PIPA team asked respondents several questions about specific groups as well as the actions of these groups and their impact. While this survey's main objectives were not human-security related, some of the data elements can and do inform the project of this volume. For example, the survey seeks to understand why Pakistanis support "Kashmiri" groups that engage in violence to "liberate" Kashmir from Indian rule. The USIP-PIPA team asked respondents to consider "Pakistani militant groups [askari tanzeem] that operate in Occupied Kashmir" and to indicate whether they "think that, on balance, they help Pakistan's security, hurt Pakistan's security, or have no effect either way on Pakistan's security." While the largest group declined to provide an answer (39 percent), nearly one in five believed that they "help Pakistan's security," which was somewhat higher than the percentage who believed that they "hurt Pakistan's security" (17 percent). Somewhat more than one in four believed that they "have no effect either way." We also asked respondents whether "these groups help the security of people in Occupied Kashmir, hurt it, or have no effect either way." Again, a high percentage (37 percent) declined to provide an answer. However, the largest group (39 percent) believed that they "help Kashmiris' security." Only 9 percent believed they "hurt Kashmiris' security."

Turning attention away from "Kashmiri" groups and toward groups that are focused on affecting the social and political environment of Pakistan itself, the team asked respondents to think about "groups like Lashkar-e-Taiba, Jamaat-ul Dawa, Hizbul Mujahideen, and Jaish-e-Mohammad among other tanzeems"; they were to say whether they thought these groups "provide social and community services, or are these not part of their activities?" While more than one in three refused to answer, the largest group (42 percent) did not believe that they offered such services. Nonetheless, nearly one in four *did* believe they offered social and community services. For the 23 percent of the sample who did think these militant groups offered such services, the team asked them to "mention a few services you are aware of." Open responses were permitted, and as the data in table 5.1 suggests, respondents identified madrasas and other schools along with medical care, humanitarian assistance, and financial help with marriages and burials as forms of assistance.

Despite frequent claims that militant groups are popular because they engage in widespread provision of human services, our urban survey results do not support this claim. However, it is possible that a sample that is more representative of Pakistan's population distribution, including rural respondents, would elicit different results. This does not mean, however, that militant groups are not *perceived*

Table 5.1 Services Believed to Be Provided by Pakistani Militant Groups

Service	Percentage
Deeni madrasas	22
Schools that are not deeni madrasas	15
Medical care or services	16
Humanitarian assistance during floods, earthquakes, famine	19
Financial help with marriage and burials	11
Refused/don't know	29

Source: WorldPublicOpinion.org, "Pakistani Public Opinion on Democracy, Islamic Militancy, and Relations with the US: Questionnaire," January 2008. http://www.worldpublicopinion.org/pipa/pdf/jan08/Pakistan_Jan08_quaire.pdf

by some elements of the public as groups that provide essential human services or other human security benefits even if they have no direct experience with such service provision themselves. For example, during the 2005 earthquake, militant groups were widely hailed as providing emergency assistance. The Lashkar-e-Taiba, under a new appellation, provided well-publicized relief to persons displaced by the 2009 military offensives in Swat to roust militants from their strongholds. The media coverage of these limited, but high-profile, activities no doubt fostered a sense that these groups are stepping in to fill a void where the state had failed to do so.

Pakistani Perceptions of Violence by Militant Groups and Support for Islamist Militancy

To see whether Pakistani support for militant groups is related in any way to a belief that they are benign from a human security standpoint, one might also approach the issue from the other side of the coin. Instead of asking respondents whether or not they believe that these groups provide benefits, one might ask what respondents believe about the harm they cause and the kinds of victims they target. For example, the operations of groups that target militaries may enjoy more support than those that target civilians.

Pew data casts some light on Pakistanis' support of violence in the service of Islam. The Pew Foundation has been surveying Pakistan since early 2002 as a part of the Global Attitudes Survey. For several years, Pew has asked the question given below in Pakistan and several other countries to measure support for suicide terrorism and other attacks against civilians to defend Islam:

> Some people think that suicide bombing and other forms of violence against civilian targets are justified in order to defend Islam from its enemies. Other people believe that, no matter what the reason, this kind of violence is never justified. Do you personally feel that this kind of violence is often justified to defend Islam, sometimes justified, rarely justified, or never justified?

When Pew first fielded this question to a largely urban sample in 2002, one-third of the sample (33 percent) believed that such attacks were often or sometimes justified. In March 2004, this number increased to 41 percent. In 2005, the figure declined to 25 percent, and in 2006, it declined further to 14 percent. By 2007, only 9 percent believed that such attacks were always or sometimes justified, and by 2008, support had dropped even further. At the same time, the percentage that believed it was rarely or never justified climbed from 43 percent in 2002 to 91 percent in 2008 (see fig. 5.1). This sharp decline in support for suicide attacks is likely due to the fact that, particularly since 2006, Pakistan has been the target of numerous suicide attacks, as shown in figure 5.1.

The USIP-PIPA team asked a question similar to that used by Pew and obtained similar results. When the USIP-PIPA team posed the below question, 15 percent indicated that such attacks are often or sometimes justified. Two-thirds (66 percent) said they were rarely or never justified. Twenty percent did not answer.

> Some people think that bombing and other types of attacks intentionally aimed at civilians are sometimes justified while others think that this kind of violence is never justified. Do you personally feel that such attacks are often justified, sometimes justified, rarely justified, or never justified?

While the question is similar, the USIP-PIPA question does not specifically mention suicide bombings. This, along with different sample structures and temporal effects, may explain the difference between the USIP-PIPA and Pew results.

While Pakistani views about suicide attacks and other forms of terrorism have shifted in recent years, even when such attacks were in the service of Islam, most Pakistanis sampled by Pew in urban areas are concerned about the rise of Islamist extremism. The Pew Global Attitudes project, in two years, queried a largely urban

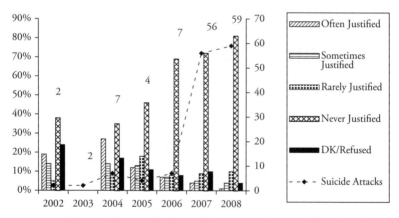

FIGURE 5.1 Pakistani Support for Suicide Bombings and Annual Numbers of Suicide Attacks in Pakistan.

Source: Survey results for all years are available in Pew Research Center, Pew Global Attitudes Survey Project, "Unfavorable Views of Jews and Muslims on the Increase in Europe," September 17, 2008, p.64.

Data on annual suicide attacks taken from South Asia Terrorism Portal, "Fidayeen (Suicide Squad) Attacks in Pakistan," updated March 2, 2009. Available at http://www.satp.org/satporgtp/countries/Pakistan/database/Fidayeenattack.htm. Readers should be aware that different sources of counts vary.

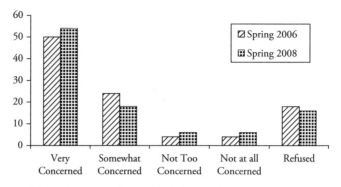

FIGURE 5.2 Pakistani Concern about Islamist Extremism.

Source: Survey results for all years are available in Pew Research Center, Pew Global Attitudes Survey Project, "Unfavorable Views of Jews and Muslims on the Increase in Europe," September 17, 2008, p.56

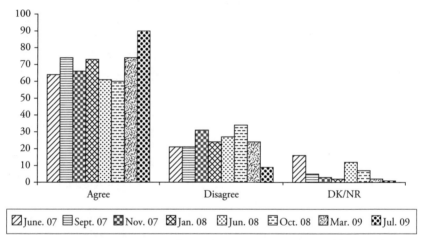

FIGURE 5.3 Agree or Disagree: Religious Extremism is a Serious Problem in Pakistan?

Source: Data for June–November 2007 is taken from IRI, "IRI Index: Pakistan Public Opinion Survey," November 19–28, 2007; data for January and June 2008 is taken from IRI, "IRI Index: Pakistan Public Opinion Survey," June 1–15, 2008; data for October 2008 is from "IRI Index: Pakistan Public Opinion Survey," October 15–30, 2008. Data for 2009 is from IRI, "IRI Index: Pakistan Public Opinion Survey," July 15–August 7, 2009.

sample of Pakistani respondents, "How concerned, if at all, are you about the rise of Islamic [*sic*] extremism in our country these days? Are you very concerned, somewhat concerned, not too concerned or not at all concerned?" As shown in figure 5.2, there were modest changes between 2006 and 2008, with more people indicating that they were "very concerned." At the same time, a slight increase was registered in those who said they were "not at all concerned." We have too little information to see if these are statistically significant differences.

A somewhat different picture emerges looking at data collected at regular intervals by IRI between June 2007 and July 2009 (fig. 5.3). In IRI's nationally representative sample, which includes rural residents as a majority of respondents, a fluctuating majority agreed that religious extremism is a serious problem. Support slightly flagged, however, between June 2007 and October 2008. After March 2009, Pakistanis increasingly came to view religious extremism as a problem. This likely had much to do with the militant takeover of Swat in the wake of yet another failed peace deal and a continued suicide bombing campaign by the Pakistani Taliban. By July 2009, an unprecedented 90 percent of those polled held this view. Given the different samples, time periods, and questions, these two surveys cannot be directly compared. Nevertheless, both polls support the conclusion that solid majorities are concerned about religious extremism in their country in a general sense.

While such questions have a general usefulness, previous survey work by C. Christine Fair and PIPA in Iran found that it is most useful to query respondents about *particular* groups of actors and targets rather than general and broad statements about violence.[22] This is likely because the general questions used by Pew (among others) are devoid of the political contexts of the group in question or of the attacks they perpetrate. Therefore, the USIP-PIPA team asked respondents about a series of militant groups operating in and from Pakistan and whether these groups posed a threat to Pakistan. The survey team provided respondents with a list of groups in Pakistan that conduct various activities. For each one, the respondent indicated whether she or he sees "these activities as a threat OR NOT to the vital interests of Pakistan in the next ten years." Respondents were asked about the following: "Activities of Sindhi nationalists in Pakistan"; "Activities of Mohajir nationalists in Pakistan"; "Activities of Baluch nationalists in Pakistan"; "Activities of Islamist militants and local Taliban in FATA and settled areas"; "Activities of al-Qaeda"; and "Activities of 'Askari tanzeems' in Pakistan."

As the data in table 5.2 demonstrates, Pakistanis distinguish between different groups. Ethnic nationalists (Sindhi, Mohajir, and Baluch) register far less concern than Islamist militants (e.g., local Taliban, al-Qaeda, and the "askari tanzeems"). In fact, a plurality finds the Islamist militants to pose critical threats to the state's vital interests and solid majorities believe that they are either a critical or important threat. This certainly suggests that many urban Pakistanis are not insouciant about these groups or even supportive, as is sometimes suggested in the media. While this is certainly encouraging, there are important minorities (14–18 percent) who do not find these groups to be a threat at all.

Table 5.2 Pakistani Threat Perceptions of a Range of Militant Groups
(Percentages)

Group	Yes, Critical Threat	Yes, an Important, but Not a Critical Threat	Not a Threat	Refused/ Don't Know
Activities of Sindhi nationalists in Pakistan	18	28	41	13
Activities of Mohajir nationalists in Pakistan	22	33	32	13
Activities of Baluch nationalists in Pakistan	17	26	41	17
Activities of Islamist militants and local Taliban in FATA and settled areas	34	26	18	22
Activities of al-Qaeda	41	21	14	24
Activities of "Askari tanzeems" in Pakistan	38	23	17	22

Source: WorldPublicOpinion.org, "Pakistani Public Opinion on Democracy, Islamic Militancy, and Relations with the US: Questionnaire," January 2008. http://www.worldpublicopinion.org/pipa/pdf/jan08/Pakistan_Jan08_quaire.pdf

IRI also asked whether respondents agree or disagree that "the Taliban and al-Qaeda operating in Pakistan is a serious threat." In 2008, fewer persons believed that these groups are a threat than in 2007. Recall that this is a nationally representative sample and includes rural respondents as a majority in contrast to the urban sample of PIPA-USIP and Pew. While the overall trends in figure 5.4 may be less than encouraging through 2008, by early 2009 Pakistani respondents increasingly viewed these groups operating in Pakistan as a clear threat, likely for the same reasons noted above.

With respect to al-Qaeda, recent fieldwork by Fair has found that many Pakistanis may not really understand what al-Qaeda is and, in fact, respond more accurately if they are told that al-Qaeda is the group under Osama bin Laden (Osama bin Laden ki tanzeem). Similarly, the author found that many did not really know what the Taliban (either Afghan or Pakistan) are, either.[23] Pew asked respondents in numerous countries how much confidence they have in Osama bin Laden specifically "to do the right thing regarding world affairs—a lot of

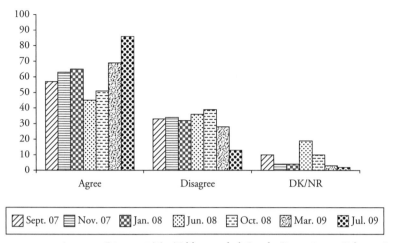

FIGURE 5.4 Agree or Disagree? The Taliban and al-Qaeda Operating in Pakistan Is a Serious Threat.

Source: Data for June–November 2007 is taken from IRI, "IRI Index: Pakistan Public Opinion Survey," November 19–28, 2007; data for January and June 2008 is taken from IRI, "IRI Index: Pakistan Public Opinion Survey," June 1–15, 2008; data for October 2008 is from "IRI Index: Pakistan Public Opinion Survey," October 15–30, 2008.

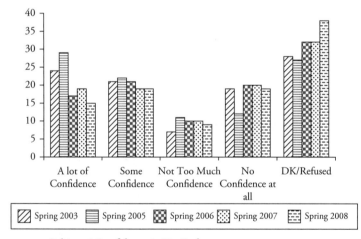

FIGURE 5.5 Pakistani Confidence in Bin Laden.

Source: Survey results for all years are available in Pew Research Center, Pew Global Attitudes Survey Project, "Unfavorable Views of Jews and Muslims on the Increase in Europe," September 17, 2008, p.58.

confidence, some confidence, not too much confidence, or no confidence at all." As figure 5.4 shows, while the percentage of respondents who expressed either "a lot" or "some" confidence in Bin Laden declined from 45 percent to 34 percent since 2003, those who have "not too much" or "no" confidence at all increased only modestly. Most notably, the percentage of respondents who indicated that they did not know or who refused to answer increased substantially indicating genuine ambivalence, increased fear in answering the question, or both. This raises a number of questions about measurement error on such issues in Pakistan.

As noted above, many Pakistanis believe that askari tanzeems present critical threats to Pakistan's vital interests. However, other data collected by the USIP-PIPA team indicates that many Pakistanis also believe that they advance the security of Kashmiris in Indian-administered Kashmir. Thus, while Islamist militant groups may threaten Pakistan, clearly they are seen to have some value when operating outside Pakistan. To probe further the kind of legitimacy that these groups' *actions* enjoy among Pakistanis in the context of Kashmir, we put forth the following question to respondents:

> In the context of the conflict in occupied Kashmir, for each of the following types of people, please tell me if you think that attacks against them are often justified, sometimes justified, rarely justified, or never justified?

The USIP-PIPA survey list included Indian policemen, Indian intelligence agents, Indian military and paramilitary troops, Indian government officials, women and children of the military, and women and children more generally. As the data in table 5.3 indicates, nearly one in five respondents believed that attacks against Indian policemen, intelligence agents, and police and paramilitary troops are "often justified." When the "sometimes justified" categories are included, support for such targets is as high as 40 percent. Support for attacks against Indian government officials was somewhat lower, with only one in four believing they were often or sometimes justified. It is interesting that even when it came to attacks in India, Pakistanis overwhelmingly rejected wives and children as legitimate targets, even those associated with the military.

While the set of questions given above focuses on the context of Kashmir, the USIP-PIPA team also asked more general questions about the legitimacy of targets, including "government institutions (like the national Parliament in Delhi and state assemblies)"; "attacks conducted against Indian targets like subways, stock exchanges, and tourist sites"; "attacks in India on families of Indian military personnel"; "attacks in Pakistan on Shia"; and "attacks in Pakistan on Ahmediya."

Among the Indian targets, levels of support are somewhat consistent, albeit lower, than the Kashmir-specific targets (table 5.4). Support for attacks against government institutions, civilian infrastructure, and Indian military personnel within India are deemed "sometimes justified" by 15 percent, 12 percent,

Table 5.3 Pakistani Support for Militant Targets (in the Context of Kashmir) (Percentages)

Target	Often Justified	Sometimes Justified	Rarely Justified	Never Justified	Refused/ Don't Know
Indian policemen	18	20	14	35	13
Indian intelligence agents	19	17	16	34	14
Indian military and paramilitary troops	19	20	15	33	13
Indian government officials	11	14	19	41	16
Wives and children of the military	1	2	8	75	15
Women and children	1	1	7	76	15

Source: WorldPublicOpinion.org, "Pakistani Public Opinion on Democracy, Islamic Militancy, and Relations with the US: Questionnaire," January 2008. http://www.worldpublicopinion.org/pipa/pdf/jan08/Pakistan_Jan08_quaire.pdf

Table 5.4 Pakistani Support for Militant Targets (Percentages)

Target	Sometimes Justified	Never Justified	Refused/Don't Know
Attacks conducted against government institutions (like the national Parliament in Delhi and state assemblies)	15	64	21
Attacks conducted against Indian targets like subways, stock exchanges, and tourist sites	12	68	20
Attacks in India on families of Indian military personnel	13	67	19
Attacks in Pakistan on Shia	5	78	17
Attacks in Pakistan on Ahmadiyya	6	75	19

Source: WorldPublicOpinion.org, "Pakistani Public Opinion on Democracy, Islamic Militancy, and Relations with the US: Questionnaire," January 2008. http://www.worldpublicopinion.org/pipa/pdf/jan08/Pakistan_Jan08_quaire.pdf

and 13 percent of respondents, respectively. Support for harming Pakistani targets (Shia and Ahmadiyya, which have been subject to decades of vilification in Pakistan) is much lower at 5 and 6 percent. Pakistani respondents appear to differentiate among these targets with substantially more support when groups target persons and institutions in India. This support also seems to increase when the violence is in the context of the Kashmir dispute.

It is widely believed outside Pakistan that some of the askari tanzeems do target civilians, even if their preferred target is military, police, or intelligence personnel. We asked Pakistani respondents to consider whether Jaish-e-Mohammad, Hizbul Mujahideen, and Lashkar-e-Taiba deliberately target civilians. Majorities simply refused to answer the question or claimed to have no opinion. However, across the three tanzeems, only 6 percent said that the group in question "has intentionally targeted citizens." Given the number of media accounts about such attacks on civilians, this low number is rather surprising. Indeed, the notorious attack on Indian Army wives and children at Kaluchak in May 2002 was widely attributed to Lashkar-e-Taiba.

The team also asked a number of questions about the Taliban. The responses suggest that Pakistanis are far more likely to condone Taliban activities when they target Western forces and much more apprehensive to do so when the victims are Afghan forces.[24]

Pakistani Support for the Government's Handling of Militancy

With respect to Pakistan's domestic security, the data in table 5.2 and elsewhere demonstrate that many Pakistanis *do* perceive these groups to imperil Pakistan. However, there is considerable discord among Pakistanis about the way in which the government has handled issues germane to these groups. To probe support for the government's various public policies, the survey team asked respondents to indicate whether they "approve strongly, approve somewhat, disapprove somewhat, or disapprove strongly of the way Pakistan's government is handling the following issues." The team probed beliefs about the situations in Indian-administered Kashmir, FATA, and the Lal Masjid.

As the data in table 5.5 demonstrates, with respect to the government's handling of Indian-administered Kashmir, solid majorities approve of the government's approach and nearly one in three approve strongly. With respect to FATA, there is considerable ambivalence with 48 percent either approving strongly or somewhat and 34 percent disapproving somewhat or strongly. Support for the government's handling of the Lal Masjid is even lower, with 31 percent lending some degree of support while a majority disapproves.

Table 5.5 Pakistani Support for Government Policies (Percentages)

Policy	Approve Strongly	Approve Somewhat	Disapprove Some	Disapprove Strongly	Refused/ Don't Know
The situation in Indian-administered Kashmir	32	36	13	9	9
The situation in the FATA	14	34	22	12	18
Religious extremism such as the Lal Masjid	12	19	27	29	13

Source: WorldPublicOpinion.org, "Pakistani Public Opinion on Democracy, Islamic Militancy, and Relations with the US: Questionnaire," January 2008. http://www. worldpublicopinion.org/pipa/pdf/jan08/Pakistan_Jan08_quaire.pdf

The international community has become acutely concerned about developments in FATA both because of the import for the international efforts to rehabilitate Afghanistan and because major terror conspiracies in Europe and the United States have important linkages to militant groups ensconced in FATA. As noted above, the data suggests considerable ambivalence about Pakistan's approach in FATA. To obtain a more granular understanding of public preferences for FATA, the USIP-PIPA team offered respondents three statements about FATA and asked which "comes closer to your view?" The statements are given below:

Statement A: Pakistan's government should exert control over FATA, even if it means using military force to do so.

Statement B: The government should not try to exert control over FATA but should try to keep the peace through negotiating deals with local Taliban.

Statement C: The government should withdraw its forces from FATA and leave the people alone.

The plurality (46 percent) believed that B, "keep peace through negotiating," best represented their view. Nearly one in four believed that A, "military force if needed to control FATA," best accorded with their preference, and a small minority (12 percent) identified C, "withdraw forces and leave the people alone." Only 18 percent declined to provide an answer. This seems to suggest that the least objectionable aspect of Pakistan's approach to FATA has been negotiating deals brokered with the militants. The USIP-PIPA team found that Pakistanis are somewhat more accepting of Pakistani military action when the target is al-Qaeda. Respondents were asked whether or not they favor or oppose the Pakistani Army entering FATA to pursue and capture al-Qaeda fighters. While 44 percent said they favored the policy, 36 percent said they oppose it.

Similar results were obtained when the USIP-PIPA team asked about hot pursuit of Taliban insurgents who have crossed over from Afghanistan. Nearly half (48 percent) favored allowing the Pakistani Army to pursue and capture Taliban insurgents who have crossed into Pakistan. However, more than one in three (34 percent) opposed it.

IRI, using a different series of questions and a nationally representative sample, uncovered similar ambivalence about the best course of action to deal with a variety of threats based in and from Pakistan, even if respondents generally agreed that they posed a threat. IRI asked respondents whether or not they agree with the statements

- "I support the army fighting terrorists in NWFP and FATA."
- "I support the army fighting al-Qaeda."
- "I support the army fighting the Taliban."
- "I support the army peace deal with the militants."

The results of these queries are detailed in figure 5.6. Most Pakistanis do not support the army fighting in NWFP and FATA; however, this opposition has declined since September 2007 and a fluctuating minority supports such fightingA similar majority opposes fighting al-Qaeda, while a minority supports it. Results were similar for the Pakistani Army fighting the Taliban. In July 2009, IRI asked a slightly different question than in past surveys. Rather than asking about support for the army fighting extremists in the NWFP and FATA, it asked whether respondents support such action in the "Malakand Division," which focused the attention of Pakistanis upon Swat. When this particular area is the focus of operations, a full 60 percent supported such action compared to 28 percent who opposed the army's fight. Three percent declined to answer.

At the same time, IRI found that a declining majority supported the army's peace deal with the militants, and this support declined precipitously, particularly in 2009, in the wake of the Swat debacle.[25] The nationally representative IRI data reveals considerably more opposition to fighting an array of militant groups and substantially less support for doing so than does the largely urban USIP-PIPA sample. At the same time, it finds more but declining support for peace deals.

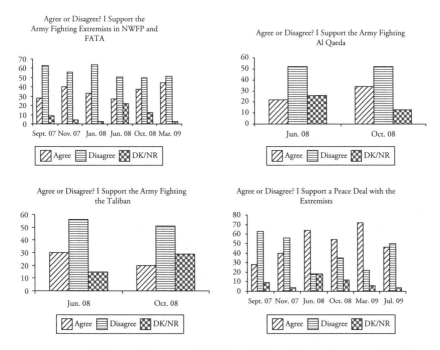

FIGURE 5.6 Pakistani Views toward Various Military Approaches toward Different Militant Groups.

Source: International Republican Institute. "IRI Index: Pakistan Public Opinion Survey," July 15–August 7, 2009," "IRI Index: Pakistan Public Opinion Survey," March 7–30, 2009; "IRI Index: Pakistan Public Opinion Survey," October 15–30, 2008. Available at http://www.iri.org/news-events-press-center/news-iri/show_for_country/1113

While the military component of Pakistan's policy may be unpopular, another USIP-PIPA survey item found that Pakistanis do support *political reform* for FATA. When asked whether they supported leaving the colonial-era and draconian Frontier Crimes Regulation (FCR) unchanged, modifying it "slowly over time such that the people there should have the same rights and responsibilities as all other Pakistanis," or "abolishing it such that the people there should have the same rights and responsibilities as all other Pakistanis," only a slim minority (8 percent) favored leaving the FCR intact. The largest percentage (46 percent) favored modification and more than one in four favored abolishing it altogether.

Thus, while there may be ambivalence about the government's policy of military action, appeasement of the militants and political reform seems quite palatable. Unfortunately, while Pakistan's political leaders have episodically made public proclamations about political reform, they have not actually initiated any such reforms of the FCR in FATA.

Conclusions and Implications

There have been a large number of polls conducted in Pakistan designed to shed light on Pakistani attitudes toward Islamist militant groups. None have been specifically designed to illuminate the relationship, if any, between support for such groups and perceptions about their impact on human security. Perhaps the time has come to do such a study. Lurking in the polling data that has been gathered to date are intriguing suggestions that such a link may exist. If that is true, scholars of the global religious revival should reflect upon this. Policymakers should also be aware of the link and should exploit it.

Two recent, large-scale studies of Pakistani support toward militant groups have confirmed that there is indeed support for such groups. However, what drives this support is not entirely clear. Most important, it is not clear whether the current level of support is rooted in religiosity and whether or not it is insensitive to concerns about the human security consequences of militant activity.

There are indications that Pakistanis *are* sensitive to human security issues. For example, they distinguish between different types of violence and, thus, are more likely to accept as legitimate attacks that do not target women and children. They are also more likely to support attacks in Kashmir and India and attacks in Afghanistan targeting Western forces than they are to support attacks in Pakistan itself. To understand how this data can be squared with Pakistani support for militant groups that have targeted civilians, including women and children, both abroad and in Pakistan, it is important to note that there is evidence that many Pakistanis do not appreciate the extent to which these militant groups are implicated in this type of violence.[26] Furthermore, as noted above, there is some evidence that a small but significant minority of Pakistanis believe that "Kashmiri" militant groups provide essential welfare-enhancing services in Kashmir, and that Pakistan-focused militant groups provide some essential services in Pakistan.

The notion that Pakistani views about militant groups are shaped by their (mis)perceptions about the human security consequences seems to be consistent with data concerning Pakistani views about government responses to militancy. The Pakistani people are ambivalent about forceful governmental action against the Taliban and toward such violent events as the 2007 Lal Masjid operation, possibly because Pakistanis believe that these actions harm the human security of civilians. Policies of negotiating with the militants in the FATA and political reform remained popular until 2009, while policies of military confrontation received less support. Even in March 2009, only a slim majority supported the military engagement. Forceful action appears to be more popular when it is directed against groups that have been identified in the public mind with violence against Pakistani civilians. Thus, when restricted to the Malakand Division, a solid majority supports such military action. Military confrontation with foreign elements, such as al-Qaeda and Taliban fugitives in Pakistan who come across from Afghanistan, is also more popular, although important and sizeable minorities still oppose military operations against these foreign, infiltrating targets.[27]

All of this data suggests that when Pakistanis take sides in the contest between Pakistani militant groups and the various governments against whom these groups violently struggle, they do not do so solely on the basis of piety. Rather, Pakistanis' allegiances may be driven, at least in part, by the way in which respondents understand the nature of the struggle and the role of these groups in those struggles. Pakistanis presumably believe that the residents of Indian-controlled Kashmir are deeply oppressed, and they themselves live in a state that has failed to provide essential services in an effective manner. As we have shown, Pakistani support for militant groups exists alongside ignorance about the nature of the activities that militant groups engage in. Some Pakistanis mistakenly believe that certain militant groups advance the human security of Kashmiris in Indian-administered Kashmir. A minority of Pakistanis believe that militant groups provide some services that the Pakistani government does not. Conversely, the Pakistani public seems to underestimate the harm caused by militant groups. Significant numbers of Pakistanis seem generally disinclined to express support for violence of any sort, either by militant groups *or* by the Pakistani or US military forces opposed to those groups. They also seem to have a remarkably poor appreciation of the violence with which militant groups are associated.

All of this suggests that religious revival in Muslim countries like Pakistan may not have changed the political calculus in such countries as much as some theorists have suggested. In Pakistan, the polling data does not support the claim that religious sentiment and piety are sufficient to drive support for militant groups that target civilians. In fact, it contains data that seems inconsistent with such a claim. The international community and its allies among the antimilitant/antiextremist elements within the Pakistani government and civil society may not be grappling, as some have feared, with a populace that is coming overwhelmingly to believe that religious ends will justify actions that cause widespread harm (particularly within Pakistan). Further study is needed to confirm whether this hypothesis is correct.

If Pakistani support for militant groups today rests, even in part, upon a lack of public knowledge about the net costs of these groups' activities in human security terms, then policymakers should take note. One policy question is whether the international community and antimilitant elements within the Pakistani government can change people's perceptions about the relative value of militant groups in human security terms with regard to their foes in the state and civil society. If so, the loss of public support for militant groups should either weaken militant groups or cause them to change their tactics. Some benefit could presumably be gained by well-planned operations to educate the Pakistani public about the actual harm that militant groups cause as well as the benefits that the state provides. This is a job for Pakistani institutions and leaders, and it will require legitimate voices and media outlets lest such efforts be understood as Washington-inspired conspiracy.

Obviously, to maximize the effectiveness of such a message, the international community and nonextremist elements within the Pakistani state civil society would also be well advised to improve their performance in providing human security to the Pakistani people. This would include providing services that militants gain support from providing and learning to battle militant groups in a manner that minimizes the suffering of the Pakistani people. It will likely mean in some measure addressing the politics of militancy and resolving those political concerns and objectives that resonate with their supporters.

Notes

C. Christine Fair is assistant professor at Georgetown University. Clark Lombardi is associate professor of law at the University of Washington School of Law and adjunct associate professor of international relations at the Jackson School of International Studies. The views expressed herein are attributable solely to the authors and not to their employers or the funders of their research.

This chapter draws on data presented in a paper by C. Christine Fair presented at the Institute for Defence Studies and Analyses in Delhi in February 2008 and published as "Pakistani Attitudes towards Militancy in and Beyond Pakistan," in V. Krishnappa, Shanthie Mariet D'Souza, and Priyanka Singh, eds., *Saving Afghanistan* (New Delhi: Academic Foundation, 2009), pp. 93–112.

1. As many of the European terror plots have had connections to Pakistan, the insecurity generated by these groups extends well beyond the Southern Asian region. See Agence France-Presse, "Number of Militant Recruits on the Rise: Report," October 19, 2009, http://www.google.com/hostednews/afp/article/ALeqM5hk4vEsPivpw-ckQBWx39wuGvuDeKg; Craig Whitlock, "Washington Post: Europe Not Alone in Seeing Citizens Lured to Warzone for Paramilitary Training; Americans Head There Too," *Washington Post*, October 19, 2009, Archive copy available at http://www.sltrib.com/nationworld/ci_13594235.

2. Even if it were true that the Afghan and Pakistani Taliban provide security in the areas under their control, undercut government corruption, provide basic dispute resolution of family and land-related issues, and address some popular grievances, a claim regularly made by their supporters, they do so at a high price. They have imposed rules that severely infringe on citizens' rights under domestic law and

under international humanitarian law. Women have been especially victimized. These groups fail to provide essential state services such as education, clinics, and sanitation among other public goods typically provided by the government.

3. One of the authors, C. Christine Fair, working under the auspices of USIP, in collaboration with research staff from PIPA, developed a comprehensive questionnaire to probe Pakistani public opinion on a wide array of domestic and foreign policy concerns. These questions pertain to public attitudes to numerous militant groups operating in Pakistan, including al-Qaeda, the Taliban, various *"askari tanzeems"* engaged in Kashmir, sectarian militant groups, and ethnic militant movements such as the insurgency in Baluchistan and previous conflicts in Sindh. Questions to ascertain views about policy issues covered the government's handling of the crisis in the Federally Administered Tribal Areas and at the Red Mosque, among other public policies. The instrument also queried respondents' opinions about several kinds of militant targets, e.g., Indian police, women and children of armed forces personnel, civilian targets such as parliaments and national assemblies. The survey was conducted from September 12 to 18, 2007, just before President Pervez Musharraf declared a six-week state of emergency and before the assassination of Benazir Bhutto. The sample included 907 Pakistani urban adults, selected using multistage probability sampling, who were interviewed at home in nineteen cities across all of Pakistan's provinces. The margin of error is +/− 3.3 percent. The bulk of this chapter derives from analyses of these data. See Fair, Kull, and Ramsay (2008).

4. See the website for the Pew Global Attitudes Project available at http://pewglobal. org/.

5. See the home page for the work done by IRI on Pakistani public opinions, available at http://www.iri.org/countries-and-programs/middle-east-and-north-africa/Pakistan.

6. This study does not include militant groups that are organized along ethnic lines such as the Baloch or Mohajjir militant groups.

7. This section draws from Fair (2008, 2004).

8. While these groups are often referred to as "Kashmiri groups," this is a misnomer as they have few ethnic Kashmiris among their ranks, and most of these groups do not operate exclusively in Kashmir. Indeed, Lashkar-e-Taiba and Jaish-e-Mohammad have long operated throughout India, and Deobandi groups have, in recent years, begun operating in Pakistan. Both LeT and Deobandi so-called Kashmiri groups have also been operating in Afghanistan against US, NATO, and Afghan forces. See Fair (2009a). There are, one should note, other "Kashmiri groups" operating under the influence of the Islamist political party Jamaat-e-Islami such as al-Badr and Hizbul Mujahideen, which tend to comprise ethnic Kashmiris and have retained their operational focus on Kashmir.

9. Many of these groups have been proscribed numerous times, only to reemerge. Many now operate under new names. This chapter uses the names most likely to be familiar to readers.

10. Since the onset of sanguinary sectarian violence in Iraq and Iran's 2006 victory in Lebanon, some have suspected that Iran may once again be involved in inciting anti-Sunni violence in Pakistan. However, allegations of Iran's involvement are not, at this point, supported empirically.

11. The rise of this movement seems to have coincided with or was precipitated by the Pakistani military operations in FATA as well as US strikes in FATA by unmanned aerial vehicles. See "Many Killed in 'US Drone Attack,'" *BBC News*, April 1, 2009. The 2006 US drone strikes at Damadola (Bajaur) in an effort to eliminate Ayman al-Zawahiri and the October 2006 drone strike against an al-Qaeda affiliated madrasa in Chingai village (Bajaur) are widely seen as the catalyst for the suicide attacks against security forces in FATA and NWFP. For more facts about this attack and its consequences, see Fair (2009b).

12. Baitullah Mehsood claimed many allies, all of whom seek to establish in various degrees Sharia (Islamic governance) across the Pashtun belt in Pakistan including the FATA and settled areas such as Swat, where the Tehreek-e-Nafaz-e-Shariat-e-Mohammadi or Movement for the Enforcement of Islamic Law (TNSM) has been active and successful in coercing the state to accede to granting sovereignty. In late February 2008, two dissident commanders, Mullah Nazir of South Waziristan and Gul Bahadur of North Waziristan, set aside their differences with Baitullah Mehsood and forged the Shura Ittehad-ul-Mujahiden. See Abbas (2007a, 2008) and Syed Shoaib Hasan, "Profile: Baitullah Mehsud," *BBC News*, December 28, 2007, http://news.bbc.co.uk/2/hi/south_asia/7163626.stm. Pakistan has considered Maulvi Nazir an ally because he helped oust or kill numerous Uzbeks in South Waziristan. He is considered to be a dedicated foe of US and NATO forces as he dispatches fighters to Afghanistan. Gul Bahadar has had a number of differences with Baitullah Mehsood.

13. Talibanization next spread to Bajour after Waziristan. Most recently, the Pakistan Taliban has emerged in areas that had previously been peaceful, such as Mohmand Agency, Orakzai, and Kurram. It has also emerged in the frontier areas of Bannu, Tank, Kohat, Lakki Marwar, Dera Ismil Khan, and Swat. Throughout the summer of 2007, Pakistan's Frontier Corps along with the Frontier Constabulary battled the Pakistani militants associated with the TNSM, which seized the Swat Valley in late October. See Fair (2007).

The valley was wrestled from the militants when elements from the Eleventh Corps entered the fray, and Pakistan's armed forces remained engaged in Swat until the early 2009 peace deal was forged. This deal ceded sovereignty to the TNSM in the guise of government-sanctioned imposition of Sharia (Nijam-e-Adil) in Swat and Malakand. There is very little scholarly literature on this phenomenon, with most coverage taking place in the popular press or security publications. See, *inter alia*, Yusufzai (2007). See also Fair (2007: n. 8); Abbas (2007a, b); Idrees Bakhtiar, "Between the Lines," *The Herald*, July 2007; Ghafar Ali Khan, "The Lost Frontier," *The Herald*, July 2007; Owais Tohid, "The New Frontier," *Newsline*, April 2004,

http://www.newslinemagazine.com/2004/04/the-new-frontier; Tohid, "The Warrior Tribes," *Newsline*, April 2004, http://www.newslinemagazine.com/2004/04/
the-warrior-tribes; Zahid Hussain, "Al-Qaeda's New Face," *Newsline*, August 2004,
http://www.newslinemagazine.com/2004/08/al-qaedas-new-face. For a recent
article, see Anand Gopal, "Pakistani Taliban in Swat Refuse to Give Up Arms:
The Militants Had Struck a Deal to Relinquish Their Weapons in Return for
Islamic Law in the Region," *Christian Science Monitor*, April 16, 2009, http://www.
csmonitor.com/World/terrorism-security/2009/0416/p99s01-duts.html, accessed
January 15, 2012.

14. Pakistani Taliban supporters were ensconced in the Lal Masjid until the Pakistani
security forces launched Operation Silence in July 2007 to oust them. See Zahid
Hussain, "The Battle for the Soul of Pakistan," *Newsline*, July 2007, www.newsline.
com.pk/NewsJul2007/cover1july2007.ht . See also Fair (2009b).

15. See Sabrina Tavernise, Richard A. Oppel Jr., and Eric Schmitt, "United Militants
Threaten Pakistan's Populous Heart," *New York Times,* April 13, 2009, http://www.
nytimes.com/2009/04/14/world/asia/14punjab.html.

16. The Jaish-e-Mohammad leader, Masood Azhar, was close to the Taliban. In fact,
Jaish-e-Mohammad, which shares considerable membership and infrastructure with
LeJ, was the first South Asian Islamist group to use suicide attacks in the region. In
that 2000 attack, Mohammad Bilal, a British Pakistani, attacked the Indian Army
headquarters in Srinagar. Information from author interviews with Pakistani journalists and a terrorism analyst in February 2009. Also see Emma Brockes, "British Man Named as Bomber Who Killed 10," *The Guardian,* December 28, 2000,
http://www.guardian.co.uk/uk/2000/dec/28/india.kashmir.

  While it is tempting to view this as a "new theater" or even as a future site of a
redux of the Talibanization of Swat in the heartland of Punjab, these sites of militancy are interrelated.

17. The Afghan Taliban remains focused on ousting foreign forces in Afghanistan,
overthrowing the Karzai regime, and restoring a role in governing Afghanistan.
See, *inter alia*, Senator Carl Levin, "Opening Statement of Senator Carl Levin,
Senate Armed Services Committee Hearing on Afghanistan and Pakistan," February 26, 2009, http://levin.senate.gov/newsroom/release.cfm?id=308740; Barnett
R. Rubin, "Saving Afghanistan," *Foreign Affairs*, January–February 2007, http://
www.foreignaffairs.com/articles/62270/barnett-r-rubin/saving-afghanistan.

18. See comments made by National Intelligence Director John Negroponte cited in
"Al-Qaeda 'Rebuilding' in Pakistan," *BBC News Online*, January 12, 2007, http://
news.bbc.co.uk/2/hi/south_asia/6254375.stm; Kronstadt (2008).

19. While their targets have included President Musharraf, they have also included
other high-value military and civilian leaders. Al-Qaeda leaders continue to operate
and plan attacks from the tribal areas, including, until his death, Osama bin Laden,
as well as Ayman al-Zawahiri, Abu Ubaidah al-Masri, and Abu al-Yazid. Recent
attacks and plots—such as the successful July 2005 attack in London, a transatlan-

tic plot foiled in 2006, and a plot to attack US and German targets in 2007—have connections back to Pakistan's Pashtun belt.

20. That said, the afore-noted innovation in targeting seems to have occurred in 2006 in response to US attacks on sites in Bajour. For example, on November 5, 2007, a suicide attacker assaulted army recruits doing exercises in northwest Pakistan, killing at least forty-one soldiers and wounding dozens. This attack was reportedly in retaliation for the US strike on a purported madrasa on October 30, 2007, which killed eighty-two persons. See Pamela Constable and Kamran Khan, "Suicide Bombing Kills 41 Troops at Pakistani Army Base: Attack Called Reprisal for Strike on School," *Washington Post*, November 9, 2006, http://www.washingtonpost.com/wp-dyn/content/article/2006/11/08/AR2006110800397.html.

21. While Pakistan considers some of the militant groups to be allies, e.g., the Afghan Taliban and the so-called Kashmir groups, it has acted against some other groups, such as the TNSM and elements of the Pakistani Taliban, suffering serious losses in the process. For details of the actions and the consequences, including the possible creation of a broad Pashtun insurgency framed in Islamist terms and what seems to be the "Pakistanization of al-Qaeda," see generally Fair (2009b).

22. See USIP, "USIP and PIPA Give Advance Briefing on Unprecedented In-Depth Poll of Iranians," January 16, 2007, http://www.usip.org/programs/projects/iran-working-groupl.

23. During recent enumerator training in April 2009, the author and her collaborator, Jacob Shapiro, found that few enumerators really knew what al-Qaeda was. Given low familiarity among enumerators, it seemed doubtful that they could adequately explain it to a respondent. This may explain why the nonresponse rate for al-Qaeda-related questions is higher in Pakistan than it is elsewhere.

24. As is well known, one of Washington's concerns about Pakistan is the sanctuary that the Taliban forces enjoy in Pakistan. As the Taliban were the clients of the Pakistani state for several years and given that the reversal of the official policy of support encountered some resistance, the team wanted to explore Pakistani beliefs about the Taliban and its activities. The team first queried respondent beliefs about Taliban activities by asking respondents to think about "attacks by the Taliban against NATO [Western] troops in Afghanistan" and indicate whether they "approve of them, disapprove of them, or have mixed feelings about them? Do you feel that way somewhat or strongly?" Thirty percent strongly or somewhat approved. Only 15 percent disapproved and another 18 percent had "mixed feelings." The remaining 37 percent were refusals or "do not know" responses. Next they were asked about "attacks by the Taliban against Afghan troops and police in Afghanistan." Only 5 percent strongly approved and another 13 percent approved somewhat. In contrast, 29 percent disapproved somewhat or strongly while 14 percent had "mixed feelings." The remaining 38 percent did not provide a response.

25. IRI found stronger support for this option than did USIP-PIPA, although the two results cannot strictly speaking be compared, due to different samples, time frames, and questions.

26. Pakistanis also fail to recognize the role of Pakistani state institutions in supporting these groups and their violent operations.

27. US and other foreign military operations are deeply opposed even when the targets are foreign and seeking refuge in Pakistan from Afghanistan.

6

Networking through Religion:
The Case of Malerkotla

Karenjot Bhangoo Randhawa

Introduction

Religious intolerance in its various forms as well as the violence and extremism that it has produced now plagues many parts of India, threatening human security. It is appropriate and timely for policymakers and researchers alike to look at a town that has witnessed many outbreaks of violence in the past but still holds peace as the norm in order to understand how the welfare of different groups is sustained through interreligious understanding of religion.

The *Times of India*, in 2002, declared Malerkotla an "Island of Peace" and more recently a segment was produced by the National Film Network titled *The Legend of Malerkotla: A Tale from the Punjab*. The former princely state of Malerkotla, located in Northern Punjab, is a place where riots did not occur during Partition. In this unique, Muslim majority town, there are four distinct religious groups that live in close proximity to each other, and yet, the overall pattern of peaceful plurality in the town has resulted in the avoidance of violence even when the threat has loomed close by.

The focus of this research project was to look at how religion is negotiated and understood between two groups, Muslims and Sikhs, often understudied or studied solely in isolation from each other. The narratives, practices, and teachings between and among these religious groups are a part of the peaceful civic engagement to which this community in Northern Punjab is dedicated. Religious associations, expressions, and activities have helped to build social capital and stabilize peace, thereby strengthening human security.

This study argues that when religious groups are well connected through a strong civil society network such as that which exists in Malerkotla, there is a greater opportunity for peaceful coexistence to prevail. Based on ethnographic research conducted in the Punjab, this study demonstrates that religious historical narratives, rituals, and daily practices are necessary to help maintain peace but are not sufficient on their own. Religious groups in this town are interconnected through civil society networks in which religious expression and social capital help to actively engage members of the society in relationships that create a dialogue for peace. This research examines how religious nonstate actors have been able to institutionalize religious influence within structures of civil society, helping build social capital and stabilize peace in addition to practicing peaceful sharing of sacred spaces and rituals.

Background

Malerkotla is located in the Indian state of Punjab in the district of Sangrur, just south of Ludhiana and to the west of Patiala. After the Partition of India, Malerkotla become the only Muslim majority town on India's side of Punjab. According to the 2001 census, the total population of Malerkotla is estimated to be 106,802, of which about 75 percent is Muslim and the other 25 percent are Sikh and Hindu. The minority Sikh population in Malerkotla mostly comprises Jat Sikhs, commonly agriculturists. Of the Muslim population in Malerkotla, over 90 percent are Sunnis and a small percentage are Shias. Although the population of Malerkotla is relatively small in comparison to larger Indian cities, such as Delhi and Mumbai, it serves as an important case study for several reasons. First, it is located in a state that has witnessed a great deal of religiously motivated violence not only during Partition but also as a result of terrorism in the 1980s and 1990s. Studying a place of this size and nature helps to isolate linkages and key factors that aid the maintenance of peace. More particularly, when studying religious expression as a function of civil society, one can better isolate possible causes of peace and conflict such as historical conflict incidences, political economy, and social exchange. The reasons for peace or the structure of these networks can then apply in a larger setting where there is religiously based hostility. Malerkota's residents participate in a shared consciousness, helping to construct peace. In the case of these individual agents working to strengthen and promote peace and a peaceful reputation, it is important to explore how the dynamics of interpersonal exchange can transform rigid belief structures and suspicion in the face of larger collective violence.

Today, Malerkotla is a significant industrial center in the Punjab; it is seen as a leader in agriculture and hardware production. Many of the industries here are devoted to the production of refined oil, vegetable oil, desi butter, zinc sulfate, spray pumps, carrier stands (put on the back of bicycles), washing soap, rippers (an instrument used for cutting wheat), combines (a machine that cuts wheat and jeeri), and harumba hardware (used to cut wheat and rice). Out of the 42,399 hectares of land that are part of Malerkotla, approximately 37,300 are devoted to agriculture (Khan and Ghai 2000). Several major crops reap the highest return in the agriculture industry: wheat, chickpeas, mustard seed, lentils, peas, cauliflower, and potatoes. Several major factories in Malerkotla contribute to the economic success of the town. The main industries operating factories include those producing hardware, spinning mills, and athletic equipment. Major factories in Malerkotla include Arihant Spinning Mills, Sohrab Textiles, Rashid Brothers (racket manufacturers), Chaudary Hardware Factory, Chand Factory, and Star Impact Factory (makers of sporting equipment and shoes).[1] Nearly 75 percent of the employees in factories like Arihant Spinning Mills are from Bihar. Although these employees live locally in residences, the language they speak is different from that spoken by Malerkotla's citizens and their involvement in the community is limited. Furthermore, most of the materials produced in these factories are transported outside the Punjab.

Generally, the government of Malerkotla has been backed and controlled by Muslims; it has a long history of rule by the nawabs, followed by state rule that was first imposed in 1953. From 1458 to 1954, there were twenty-two Muslim rulers in total. The city was almost taken over by the Sikhs during the time of Maharaja Ranjit Singh (r. 1801–1839) but was ransomed by Utala Khan, who was the nawab at the time, for the price of 1 lakh, 50 rupees. After this time, Malerkotla came under British rule (Zubairy 2000: 26–30). In postcolonial times political power resided with the nawab's family and the family of Haider Sheikh, the Sufi saint who founded the town of Malerkotla more than five hundred years ago. In more recent years, the town has been governed by the Congress Party or Akali Dal. Parties like the Bharatiya Janata Party (BJP) have never had much success in Malerkotla. Politicians have visited Malerkotla on many occasions, making note of the exceptional legacy of peace that has endured as well as taking the lead on initiatives designed to help the residents in Malerkotla, often giving speeches encouraging them to continue to work together as an example of peaceful coexistence.

Research Methodology

This ethnographic research is based on 120 interviews collected in Malerkotla, 60 with Sikhs and 60 with Muslims. The interviewees were selected from individuals who lived in both the "outer" and "inner" pockets of Malerkotla, including but not limited to academics, religious leaders, and politicians who adhere to values and beliefs derived from Sikhism or Islam. Informal, in-depth interviews furthered my enquiry, and participant observation also took place at various sites where devotees gather for religious ritual and prayer, including Haider Shaikh dargah, dargah of Shah Fazl, and Gurdwara Hadanara. The most important question asked in this study was what is the present structure that allows people to utilize traditional religious value systems in supporting peace or conflict?

Relations in Malerkotla: Historical Narratives

It should be noted that before Partition, the history of the former princely state of Malerkotla is colored with violence and conflict. Reflecting on these historical and traumatic events and the fact that diverse religious groups live in close proximity, one expects that violence might penetrate this community easily, but since Partition, the legacy of peace has remained strong. I outline several key historical markers that help one identify why peace is a proven success and not just an anomaly. There are many events that make up the local bloody history of Malerkotla prior to Partition, including brutal incidents involving the attack on the Kukas by the British as well as the attacks by the Namdharis and Sahib Singh Bedi.[2]

It is also important to outline the broader historical relationship between the Sikhs and Muslims on a larger scale in the Punjab. Much of the tension between Sikhs and Muslims dates from the conflict of Sikh Gurus and the Mughal emperors over the power to rule. From the time Guru Arjan Dev Ji was tortured at the hands of the Mughal ruler Jahangir in 1606, the two sides engaged in intense warfare for more than 150 years.

Another significant part of Malerkotla's violent history is the attacks involving Sahib Singh Bedi in 1796. Bedi, a direct descendent of Guru Nanak Dev Ji, attacked Malerkotla in retaliation for cow killing and the killing of a close relative of Guru Gobind Singh Ji by the nawab of Malerkotla. Another incentive for attack by Bedi is said to have been the the Vaada Ghallughara (the great massacre) of Sikhs that took place at Kot Rihra in 1762, in which the nawab of Malerkotla is said to have had a role. An estimated twenty-five thousand to thirty thousand Sikhs were killed in this massacre (Shani 2007).

In 1872, another disturbing and violent local episode involved the British when Namdharis attacked Malerkotla because of the killing of cows by Muslims and the British.[3] Although the Kukas caused only minor damage, the British retaliated by killing sixty-nine Namdharis by cannon and without proper trials. Today there is a large sword-shaped statue with holes in it representing each death; the smaller holes represent the children who were killed. The statue serves as a symbolic reminder of the atrocities witnessed in Malerkotla and of the perennial possibility of violence.

As a result of Partition, Punjab was essentially divided between India and Pakistan, and the displacement of populations was traumatic. Sikhs in Western Pakistani Punjab migrated east to the Indian capital of New Delhi, and Muslims in Indian Punjab migrated to Pakistani Punjab. The massacre that occurred during partition created wounds that may seem to have healed but continue to ripple through generations. Scars remain, and residents of Malerkotla who had family and friends living outside the town during the Partition and the massacre in Punjab remember these events with great pain today. They also feel tremendous pride at Malerkotla's ability to become a safe haven for those who stood threatened by violence. In 2006, the Namdhari Shaheed Girls College dedicated an arts performance to those who suffered during the atrocious events, evoking great sadness and remorse for the violence surrounding Partition and attesting to the fact that the memories of Partition are far from forgotten.

In many cases, past injustices fueled episodes of violence by reinforcing Muslims' negative stereotypes of non-Muslim Asians and vice versa (Muzaffar 2005).[4] Therefore, one of the ways to understand how cooperation and peace have been sustained in Malerkotla is to look at its religious communities and how they have dealt with these injustices and perceptions. When asked to explain why peace has prevailed despite events that threaten to disrupt it, most residents of Malerkotla refer to popular narratives of the *haa da naara*, which include the events that occurred during Partition, as an explanation. The dominant narrative of the *haa da naara* involves an event that took place during the time of Guru Gobind Singh. When the sons of the last guru were bricked alive by the governor of Sirhind, Wazir Khan, a close relative of Khan's, Sher Mohammad Khan, the nawab of Malerkotla, protested against the killings of these children as a way of converting the Sikhs in the region to Islam. Walking out of the court in protest, the nawab did not see his request fulfilled but gained the respect of Sikhs in the region. His humanitarian act would be remembered by many in later decades, and the lessons gleaned from his gesture would resonate among the people of Malerkotla during the violent period of Partition. Religion and the connection through historical memory was a central feature of conflict in the region, but it was also central in resisting it.

When probed about peace and conflict in Malerkotla, many respondents spontaneously expressed pride in their town's ability to withstand the violence that engulfed the rest of the Punjab during Partition. Participants discussed why their town was unique and peaceful despite the history of violence in Malerkotla as well as between the two religious groups. Table 6.1 lists the three main reasons given for the prevalence of peace in Malerkotla.

The most common reason given for peace in Malerkotla was the story of how Sher Muhammad Khan protested the killing of the Guru Ji's two sons.

Table 6.1 Reasons for Maintenence of Peace

	Muslim Respondents	Sikh Respondents
Haa daa Naara (Sher Mohammad Khan and Guru Gobind Singh Ji)	36	47
Haider Shaikh	13	0
Bhaichaara (Brotherhood)	1	3

This was stated by eighty-three of the one hundred respondents in the town. This story continued to resonate through and after the time of Partition and continues to be told today. In her work, Bigelow (2010: 123) recognizes that "harmonious interreligious relations continue in Malerkotla, even during times of strife in other regions, and so the town enjoys a reputation as a communal utopia." Two narratives, the haa da naara (which is the protest of the killing of the two *sahibjadis*) and Partition, dominate the narrative landscape, but "it is a mistake to assume that one of these reasons for peace is the 'right one'" (Bigelow 2010: 124).

While these two narratives both contributed to later peace, they are linked by the perception that peace at Partition depended on *haa da naara*, making the latter the causal as well as the chronological predecessor of the latter. Bigelow (2004: 228) goes on to say that a reinterpretation of *haa da naara* as a factor in peace occurred after Partition, since there was not a complete state of peace between the two events. How have these incidences prevented violence in Malerkotla after later potentially disruptive events, such as the killing of Malerkotla Sikhs in Operation Blue Star of 1984? The main point here is that, despite past violence in Malerkotla, there was less after *haa da naara*, and the town's capacity for maintaining peace increased. Partition was a dramatic test of the sentiment for peace, but the town had already confronted the threat of violence on several occasions between the time of *haa da naara* and Partition.

The territory or "place" of historical memory is precious for Muslims as well as Sikhs. My research examined why residents have stayed in Malerkotla. I was fortunate to speak not only with residents of Malerkotla but also with Muslims who left the town and now live in Lahore, Pakistan. One businessman, who owns an extensive dental-supply business in Lahore, spoke candidly about his decision to escape Malerkotla for Pakistan when the riots were most violent. He has not visited or seen any of his family since Partition, and while he is happy that his decision resulted in economic prosperity, he expressed a strong sense of attachment to Malerkotla. Muslims who left Malerkotla and have lived in Pakistan for years still consider the town to be their first home. Muslims have always been a majority in this town, and it remains a precious place to those who left it for Pakistan. Other Muslims in India see the town as a central community, since they are still a minority elsewhere, constituting only about 13 percent of the population nationwide and 2 percent statewide.

The shared sacred site of Haider Shaikh is the largest tomb shrine in the region and an example of both respect and the nonoccurrence of syncretism in shared spaces. Observing the religious practices at this tomb and speaking with some of the devotees, I saw that this site allowed for all to come and display different styles of prayer. Sikhs usually *matataak* (bow to the tomb and touch their foreheads), whereas Muslims do not, praying instead to Allah through the saint. But the power of the saint to fulfill prayers at his shrine is contested by neither faith.

In her research, Bigelow asserts that the sharing that takes place at a sacred site, particularly the tomb of Haider Shaikh, is a reason why peace has been maintained in Malerkotla. The fundamental difficulty in claiming that a sacred space is able to regulate peace is noted by Bigelow herself (2004: 6): "this study is a challenging project for I am attempting to describe a non-event, a state of peaceful exchange at a shrine that is sacred to Muslims, Sikhs and Hindus in a town populated by all three groups." In light of trying to "prove" this, it is essential to consider the obvious and opposing perspective that sacred sites have provided an impetus for conflict numerous times in India's communal violence history, one such incident being Ayodhya.[5]

Understanding precisely the type of religious sharing that takes place becomes vital for one to make the assumption that peace occurs because of it. The issue of sacred space sharing is broken down according to power dimensions between diverse religious groups, and the key is to understand how power imbalances manifest in this sharing. When groups coexist peacefully, we cannot assume that it is because tolerance and understanding are practiced. Hayden asserts that this can also be categorized as a passive form of intolerance—almost a type of noninterference. It cannot be misunderstood as embracing of the other. Hayden, thus, argues that there is a primary difference in the type of tolerance that one practices (2002: 205): "There is a difference, though, reflected in dictionary definitions of 'tolerate,' between the negative definition of noninterference ('to allow, permit, not interfere with') and a positive one of 'to recognize and respect' while disagreeing with others' beliefs and practices." An example of the kind of negative tolerance that Hayden describes is that of Palestinians who share physical space with Israelis but are still segregated. This situation demonstrates that space sharing is not always a prerequisite for peace. Although the situation in Israel is distinctly different than the case of Malerkotla, the actual layout of Malerkotla reflects a similar dynamic in that sacred space, such as the tomb of Haider Shaikh, is shared, but Muslims, Hindus, and Sikhs live in separate areas of the city. The Muslims inhabit inner Maler, and the Hindus and Sikhs live in the surrounding Kotla area.[6] Furthermore, the space that is shared is managed predominantly by Muslims who are descendants of Haider Shaikh.

According to Hayden (2002: 210), an individual's control over a certain space is dependent on the "configurations of power in the polity in which he lived and those that have succeeded it." His example of a shrine at the village of Madhi, Pathardi Taluka in Ahmadnagar District, Maharashtra, is a good example of this. In years past, the Muslims recognized this site as the *darga* of Shah Ramzan Mahi Savar and the Hindus recognized it as the *samadhi* of Sri Kanobah. It is decorated as a dargah and is home to a yearly festival attended by twenty thousand Hindu and Muslim pilgrims. However in the 1990s, its meaning shifted because many symbolically Hindu icons were introduced into its surrounding area. According to Hayden, the shift in the shrine's meaning was linked to the Babri Masjid-Ram Janmabhumi incident but also represented a new kind of "communalism" based more on politics than on tolerance.

One might assume that if there is a general level of consensus about the history and origins of a shine or a saint, conflict is less likely. One can say that the nature of Haider Shaikh's tomb is not conflictual and has, therefore, not resulted in any type of conflict, but this does not necessarily mean that there is an active type of tolerance going on. Another issue that arises when looking at the practice of space sharing has to do with site management and who has the power to control the activities and practices (such as making offerings) that take place at the shrine. In Hayden's example, the British rulers were invested in maintaining the peace between Muslims and the Hindus because conflicts could threaten the stability of the empire. This led the British courts to recognize that Hindus had some right to the proceeds of the Madhi shrine, a ruling that guaranteed them a certain degree of control over it. Hayden (2002: 215) does not see this result as the product of natural tolerance but rather as the product of those syncretic processes that are accompanied by contestation for the rights to control the space. When such a contest occurs on the larger scale of a village, the idea of religion as a political ideology becomes stronger than religion practiced as faith.

As mentioned in the case of Haider Shaikh, the control of the tomb is largely in the hands of the Muslims, and the outside of the tomb is very visibly representative of a Muslim identity. Its architecture resembles the Islamic style with the Muslim crescent displayed at the front entrance of the tomb. This confirms my argument that the symbol of Haider Shaikh is not a fair representation of all religious groups in Malerkotla. I believe it is the understanding of religious traditions and respect that helps to form the basis of cooperation that takes place here. If cooperation is the result of religion, here must be evidence that religious ideas have been exchanged and that a deeper understanding has occurred because of this exchange; it needs to be clear that what is seen is the product of religious sharing and respect and is not the product of something else, such as passive intolerance or syncretic practices. Sikhs, Hindus, and Muslims worship at the tomb for different reasons and in different ways. Sikhs and Hindus bow their foreheads, while Muslims do not. Sikhs and Hindus also pray directly to the saint, whereas Muslims pray to God with the saint as the messenger. Although the tomb of Haider Shaikh was not the central part of this research, it must be highlighted as an important example of the way residents interact, demonstrating the peaceful plurality of the town.

Systems of Conflict Resolution

Many of the residents of Malerkotla expressed great pride in being a part of a peaceful town in which religious communities exercise tolerance, acceptance, and mutual understanding. This religious tolerance contributes to the building of a strong civil-society structure that resists violence. The few incidents with the potential to instigate violence that do occur are dealt with in ways that illustrate the strong civil-society network and its embedded system for resolving conflict. In the interviews, some respondents mentioned three major incidents (table 6.2).

In response to the question, "Have you ever been involved in any peace-building type of activity with members outside your religious group?" many respondents talked about the killing of a cow in the mid-1980s. Although this Hindu-Muslim dispute did not involve Sikhs directly, a few Sikhs were members of the peace committee that settled it, and many others remembered it vividly as a conflict their community had endured and overcome. Cows are a sacred symbol of livelihood for Hindus and Sikhs, who have condemned their slaughter for centuries, while Muslims see them as a legitimate source of meat. The parties that gathered to address this particular killing included Hindu and Muslim leaders as well as a deputy commissioner and the superintendent of police. One difficulty was the lack of proof as to who had committed the crime. Initial blame fell on some Muslim youths, who eventually begged for forgiveness. One of the Muslim

Table 6.2 Conflict Incidents Most Frequently Mentioned

	Muslim Respondents	Sikh Respondents
Arati/Namaz conflict	20	5
Cow killing	15	33
Burning of Holy Qu'ran	35	0

respondents noted that "there was a rumor that Muslims had done this by *halal*. Peaceful committees were established and an intervention was conducted.There was conflict prevention and *thukrow nee hoya* [no physical violence occurred]." A leader of the Muslim community noted that "an innocent Hindu man was killed and a curfew was placed for 10–15 days, after which a meeting was set up to discuss the incident, at which Hindu representatives were quite upset." At that meeting, the Muslims present declared a moment of silence to show respect for the murdered Hindu. The formation of a peace committee, which included members of all three religious communities and reflected the different testimonies that had been gathered, helped to calm animosity and to prevent an eruption of revenge or counterattack by those who felt justice had not been adequately served. From that point, the conflict did not become enlarged and peace-building efforts were successful.

Another incident mentioned by many residents involved the proximity of the houses of worship of the three faiths, the *mandir*, *masjid*, and *gurdwara*. In the 1930s a Hindu group started singing a *katha* in a building that was close to the Lohar's Masjid (mosque), interfering with the *maghrib namaz* reading by Muslims.[7] The ensuing rioting took the life of one Hindu, and some months later there was a similar conflict over prayer times. J. C. Donaldson of the Indian Civil Service dealt with the dispute, declaring that past practices should be resumed with the *arati* at Chaudrian Mandir taking place after the evening namaz at Masjid Bafindagan (Bigelow 2010: 112). It was only the leadership among the community and citizens' willingness to take active responsibility for the situation that prevented it from escalating. One retired Sikh schoolteacher spoke of the results for the community at large:

> The fact that this dispute was handled in a good way was very significant for our community. It means that everyone could save face and we can still visit each other's *mandirs*, *gurdwaras*, and *masjids* even when they are nearby. We respect each other's way of religious life and we can understand why things are important to them.[8]

Many felt that if this incident had not been resolved, animosities and tensions would have persisted, impeding the ease with which local residents of Malerkotla could attend each other's functions, such as weddings and funerals, and share in each others' times of happiness and mourning.

Another, more recent conflict occurred during the 2002 elections, when a Holy Qu'ran was found burned in the bathroom at the Sorod Road masjid. The incident could have erupted into violence, but the community surrounding the masjid quickly convened to discuss the issue and decided that it was an unfortunate political act that should not give rise to animosity. The community then discussed possible repercussions and considered what steps could be taken to reestablish order and to ensure peace. Residents take pride in the peace that characterizes their town and in helping to maintain that peace, which is a vital part of their history. One young resident claimed that "one of the differences in our city is that there are about 7–8 *nasalaan* [generations] of people living here in the same houses for generations. You can't find that in larger cities like Ludhiana. The strength of our *poorvaj* [forefathers] comes through in the generations of people that have lived here."[9] Residents are acutely aware of this reality and reputation and the lengths to which their forefathers have gone to protect it. This historical legacy is what motivates residents to continue the tradition of peace and uphold their town's reputation.

Until recently, there have been very few formal systems of conflict resolution in Malerkotla and its surrounding areas in Ludhiana. The recently implemented complaint-redressal mechanism, known as *suvidha,* is a system of conciliatory intervention in which police and citizens review pending complaints in a one-day camp format (where grievances are heard, in an outside location).[10] When my research began, three such camps had been held in the Ludhiana District, disposing of 302 complaints, but I discovered that, even if they had heard of the committee, most residents did not know of their purpose or function. However, a year later (2006), information about the process had been distributed through contact with the Sub District Magistrate's (SDM) Office, and an office representative explained that there had been four camps held by that time with a fifth scheduled for February 18, 2006. At the camp itself, twenty-two departments are represented, and the hearing of grievances is scheduled once a month at the local government college.

The SDM's office also operates a grievance subcommittee, established in 1993–1994, in which nominees from various departments gather once a month to hear ten to fifteen cases. Police exercise vigilance when a larger community conflict is anticipated. Recently, the controversial cartoon images of the Prophet Mohammed brought together Muslims of Malerkotla in a protest to express their outrage, but the protest was peaceful and provoked no violence or destruction.[11] Within the Muslim community of Malerkotla, a *Panchayat* was formed in 1981–1982 to help settle matrimonial disputes in accordance with principles of Islam.[12]

Civil Society

The concept of civil society is important in this research for several reasons. Understanding the strength of religious ideas in Malerkotla's public sphere as well as how peace is maintained provides insight into how public institutions serve as links in which religious exchange flourishes. In addition to the more traditional

Western liberal paradigm, the influence of religious value systems are seen as having an increasing role in civil society, a term that usually refers to the governing level between the state and the people. For the purpose of this study, "civil society" refers to "clubs, religious organizations, business groups, labor unions, human rights groups, and other associations located between the household and the state organized on the basis of voluntarism and mutuality" (Hefner 2003: 349). Civil institutions can serve as powerful representations of spirituality and religion and can, thus, be critically important in enhancing human well-being and security. Civil organizations encourage important exchanges that can reinforce relationships across religious divides.[13] In Malerkotla, civil society is a platform of public exchange and deliberation, where nonstate actors reconcile different values and enhance their own well-being by expressing and promoting values and ideals through social networks. The close relationship between civil society and religion is at the very heart of the community, precisely where human security can be measured and strengthened. All such micro components, including those pertaining to the role of civil society and civil religion, were considered in assessing the strength of Malerkotla's public sphere and examining how public institutions provided linkages and spaces in which religious exchanges flourished.

One example of a strong civic organization in Malerkotla is the Jama'at-i Islami, founded by Abul 'ala Maududi (1903–1979). According to statistics gathered from the Malerkotla office in February 2006, this group has 18 or 19 working members, 50 workers, and 250 associates; a spokesperson said that the organization claims a total Malerkotla membership of 1,500. One member said that the largest challenge for the organization is a misunderstanding of what it stands for, particularly its classification by the government as a terrorist group. Currently the organization issues approximately thirty publications, but its members noted difficulty in getting approval for a publication called *Chanan Monara*, published in Punjab but currently available only in Urdu. The Jama'at-i Islami leans less toward involvement in politics and more toward strengthening social welfare and providing services to the community.

The behavior of Jama'at-i Islami in Malerkotla in comparison to branches elsewhere in India must be emphasized. Though organizations like the Jama'at-i Islami often have a reputation of adhering to strong fundamentalist beliefs and practices that might fall outside the organization's platform, Jama'at-i Islami focuses on social obligations as opposed to political aims and has achieved an immediate outcome of bringing people together to discuss issues of faith. In Malerkotla, this group has extended interreligious dialogue and reached out to help broaden conversations across religious divides.

In fact, there did not seem to be any extremist groups operating in Malerkotla; groups like the Rashtriya Swayamsevak Singh and BJP have not achieved any successes in the electorate. This lack of extremist dogma reflects the great amount of interfaith dialogue. For example, Jama'at-i-Islami hosts events in Malerkotla's neighboring rural communities around the holiday of Id Milan, inviting members of different religions to share in the celebrations. The organization also holds weekly meetings, open to the general public and often conducted in outdoor venues such as stadiums, in order to reinforce the message of the Qu'ran. This shows its capacity for a type of "bridging" social capital among religious groups, extending to generate a broader identity for the group outside its immediate circle, while at the same time displaying "bonding" tendencies by focusing on its internal strength. These types of organizations help to strengthen ways in which religious groups negotiate peace with each other, showing that dialogue and positive interaction can create foundational strength.

Inclusive Political Processes

Historical religious memory is very significant in Malerkotla and proves to be connected with the idea of shared memories in the sense that most politicians often include the town's unique history in their speeches and mention the bravery of the Nawab Sher Muhammad Khan and the haa da naara. According to some of the residents interviewed, this is also a common part of speeches at college events and local functions.[14] State-level politicians visit often, making a point of mentioning Malerkotla's exceptional status within the Punjab. Captain Amarinder Singh, formally chief minister of Punjab, visits often and was there in 2006 to announce the setup of a medical college and funding for daughters of economically poor Muslims. Simranjit Singh Mann is also in the hearts of many Muslims who were touched by Mann's protest against the Babri Mosque demolition. It is, in fact, a newsworthy occurrence when a politician such as Captain Amarinder Singh does not visit Malerkotla for the holiday of Eid and comment on the peaceful history of the town.[15]

The religious integration of Malerkotla politics can also be seen in the fact that Muslim candidates sometimes run for office while representing non-Muslim parties. For example, in 1977 Hajji Anwar Ahmad Khan won office while representing the Shiromani Akali Dal (SAD) party, which is a Sikh-dominated political party in the Punjab. Sajida Begum, who is one of the wives of Nawab Iftikhar Ali Khan, was reelected as a SAD candidate in 1980 (previously elected in 1972), and Nusrat Ali Khan (representing the Akalis) held this office next. Nusrat Ikhram Khan was elected in 1997, bringing the Khan family back into power.

The trend appears to be the same in Malerkotla's local politics, which are under the purview of the Municipal Committee. Although most of the committee's members are Muslim, with some elected Sikhs and Hindus, its president was a non-Muslim from 1951 to 1979 (Bigelow 2004: 500). Local political battles never seem attributable to religious divisions. During the 2002 elections, Kewal Kishan Jindal (Hindu) was physically assaulted before a council vote for Municipal Committee president, and Faqir Muhammad (Muslim) was then elected to the post. In March 2003, the people in Malerkotla demanded another election in which M. S. Bholi (Hindu) was elected president. Bigelow argues (: 510–512) that while this seems like an "interreligious dispute" on the surface, the fact that the backing for each of the candidates involved mixed religions does not support this view. Rather, the demand for a new election was held in reaction to the assault on Jindal, a highly respected figure, who expressed concern for the breakdown of law and order.

Several conclusions can be drawn from looking at politics as a factor in the maintenance of peaceful relations. At the political level, actors can influence the greater whole, helping create sustained cooperation among residents. Interviews and historical documentation indicate that Malerkotla politicians often use their support for a religiously integrated society to promote their platforms, which may in turn reinforce the town's harmonious state of relations. They do not try to create cleavages within the electorate. Politicians often affiliate with parties whose members are generally of a different religious background from their own, making it impossible to say that Malerkotla politics are characterized by religious divides. It is clear that political leaders have helped to maintain peaceful relations by using religious narratives as a main part of their election platforms.

Economic Life

The effect of economic factors on the town's overall relations can be seen in the community role of commercial organizations. Rashid Brothers, a large racket-manufacturing business, has supported the construction of a masjid for Malerkotla as a community and more specifically for its employees so that they can leave work to read namaz. Another noteworthy example of organizational involvement with the community is that of Sohrab Textiles, a spinning-mill company, which has created Sohrab Public School, an English-language boarding school whose mission statement consists of Malerkotla's blessing from many religions. Both the principal and the chairman of the school are Muslim, but the students come from various religious backgrounds. The connection of a business with this educational initiative indicates the potential of the economic sector for building strong networks and ties within the community.

Interview respondents involved in businesses with a migratory labor pool expressed different opinions about the effects of business on civic life. Nearly 75 percent of the employees in factories such as Arihant Spinning Mills are immigrants from Bihar. As noted earlier, their language is different from that spoken by Malerkotla's citizens, and their involvement in the community is limited. Other workers come from Orissa, Rajasthan, and Madhya Pradesh. One business owner explained:

> People don't stay in the city, and when they do they stay in quarters that are separate from the main city core. Also, because people are from surrounding states, there is a different style of language and dress that is often not so easily assimilated into the rest of the city, partly because the workers are not there to stay in the city. Therefore they might be less invested in maintaining and creating relations within the city.[16]

It is apparent that business organizations can help to maintain peaceful relations when they are directly linked to community networks and functions, but the city's use of outside investment and outside labor does not have a strong impact within Malerkotla's multireligious society.

Social Relations

Religious activities and the exchanges that take place during celebrations, festivals, and other events often provide an opportunity for people of different religions to connect as a community, to interact, and to learn about the other's faith. The religious activities that most prominently serve these functions include the Hindu and Sikh holiday of Diwali and the Muslim holidays of Baqr 'Id and Id al-Fitr. Some of the Malerkotla Muslims and Sikhs interviewed during these events talked about the days of observance and what it meant to celebrate them with neighbors of different faiths. One respondent said, "We celebrate every year with our neighbors: they give us sweets for Diwali and in turn we give them sweets for Id. It doesn't make any difference to us and we have lived like this for years. This does not happen in many places in the Punjab and we are fortunate to have such shared celebrations in our town."[17]

Id Milan is a cross-religious celebratory gathering hosted in honor of Id Milan by many organizations and attended by politicians of various faiths, including the late Sajida Begum—the last nawab's youngest wife and former member of the Legislative Assembly. Other religious festivals that involve sharing include Guru Nanak Dev Ji's *janampurb* (birthday celebration) and Holla Mohalla.[18] Sikhs in Malerkotla gather annually at the Kuka Walla Kalar, a memorial to the sixty-nine Namdaris who were executed by the British in 1872. Thousands of people, including many non-Sikhs, attend the anniversary of the execution on January 17, 18, and 19 every year. Such historical observances demonstrate the important role of cultural memory and the power of sharing through religion. Ideas of peace are derived from Islam as well as Sikhism and from various sacred texts and teachings across the Punjab. Malerkotla is exceptional, however, for the frequency with which residents talk about religious sharing and the knowledge that they have gained of the other's traditions despite differences that may exist. Further, they stress the common elements of the different religions. One Muslim factory owner expressed the following ideas about communal harmony in Malerkotla:

> We all have a responsibility towards our neighbor here in Malerkotla, and it is only the concept of equality that helps us to maintain a state of no conflict. In 1992, during the Babri masjid incident, we did not celebrate Eid, and instead, we donated money to the restoration of the temple. Everyone's religions pray for peace; the Sikhs for example say *kirt karo, vand ke shako*.[19]

Even when respondents noted differences between Sikhs and Muslims with respect to religious practice, they talked at great length about the acceptance people have of both religions and each other's traditions, highlighting the active engagement in interfaith dialogue and practice:

> When Muslims come to the gurdwara, they do not participate fully in all of the traditions, such as taking *karahprasad* and bowing the head down to the Granth Sahib, but they do show respect with their presence and that is enough. When there are differences amongst the people, one must remember that we are all from the same god, and communicating this makes it more likely that we can all work together: *Aval Allah noor upaa-i-aa, kudarat ke sabh bande, ayk noor tesabh jag upaji-aa, kaon bhale ko mande.* (First, Allah created the Light; then, by His Creative Power, He made all mortal beingsFrom the One Light, the entire universe welled up. So who is good, and who is bad?)[20]

This pride in Malerkotla's reputation has heightened its status as a unique example of peace at the state level in Punjab where many prominent people have come and participated in events that help mark its unique history. The daily activities and exchanges that are performed through a strong civic network have further demonstrated that it is an active commitment to engage in peace that has helped sustain this town's reputation.

Conclusion

Understanding is the most important step in transforming conflict, and in Malerkotla, it has sustained the communities through times when the potential for violence loomed close by. The will and determination of the people of

Malerkotla to build strong networks was necessary for transformation to occur and violence to be avoided. The understanding facilitated in Malerkotla through religious traditions is strengthened by religious dialogue, a microlevel element of broader collaboration. I found that understanding the basis of the "other" religion's teachings and respecting each other's traditions fostered a unique kind of dialogue that thrives in Malerkotla today. Malerkotla's exceptional status as an oasis of peace is no secret in the Punjab; residents here make it a point to mention the blessing given by Guru Gobind Singh Ji as just one reason for the enduring peace. Residents take an active role in committing to the ongoing legacy, a fact that stands out during turbulence at both the state and national levels. During the 1980s and '90s, when the Punjab was plagued with terrorism, Malerkotla remained untouched. It is this legacy that residents take pride in and which is kept alive through commemoration and celebration of all that is unique. In 2006, when the twelve published cartoons of the Prophet Mohammed in Denmark sparked worldwide controversy, Malerkotla residents immediately planned a peaceful protest. Although police were on hand, they typically serve only as an added precaution.

One key consideration in guiding nonstate religious actors in their role of helping to strengthen human security is to establish more cooperative relations between religious communities. In Malerkotla, I witnessed how religion works alongside many other elements to maintain positive relations among various groups. The religious exchanges that take place within the social fabric of society and the understanding born of close interactions all contribute to the existing peace. Communities' knowledge about each other's religions become part of the political and historical narratives shared by community members and leaders to promote peace. Peace-building activities and conflict resolution processes are also critical elements in the ongoing facilitation of positive relations, but these smaller transactions need participatory channels that are found in the civic structure. The connectivity found within civil society organizations and across groups has proved to be crucial in helping Malerkotla remain peaceful and, thus, in strengthening human security.

There are several questions derived from this case that could prove fruitful in other contexts where religion plays a role in conflict. One might ask whether the factors contributing to violence are in fact local or if they are linked to the larger system. If there are factors specific to the context, what can local leaders and institutions do to transform the conflict? What components of the civil society could possibly forge peaceful networks? What strengths are present and what categories within civil society would need to be developed? For example, is local administration or leadership a more effective peace builder than political parties and representatives? What types of neighborhood committees could partner with local authorities or government offices to tackle disputes resulting from a larger conflict? The goal is to systematically understand the linkages that exist between religion and civil society components and to truly identify the function of religious expression. In Malerkotla, it is religious expression and understanding that has helped to forge such strong civil-society networks, but it is also the reputation of peace that is reabsorbed into the daily interactions between religious groups. Local authorities and government offices commit to establishing conflict resolution mechanisms as a preventive measure in making sure residents have an option other than violence. Politicians and other officials celebrate the exceptional status of Malerkotla, a practicethat has served only to help residents further understand the depth of their pride and commitment to preserving the reality of their goals.

Notes

Karenjot Bhangoo Randhawa is currently assistant professor in the Program on Negotiation, Conflict Resolution and Peacebuilding at California State University, Dominguez Hills, and is Adjunct Faculty of Law at Straus Institute for Dispute Resolution, Pepperdine University. She conducts training and workshops in cross-cultural, conflict resolution and consensus building for public and private entities. She has completed a PhD from the School for Conflict Analysis and Resolution, George Mason University. The author wishes to thank the International Peace Research Association for funding support.

1. Arihant Spinning Mills is part of the Vardman Group owned by S. P Oswal. This factory is the largest exporter in Punjab in terms of yarn and the unit in Malerkotla is the largest in Northern India.
2. Namdharis consider themselves Sikhs and are also known as Kukas. *Kuk* in Punjabi means "scream" or "shout." Because they chanted sacred hymns, they became known as Kukas. Namdhari means devotees of *nam*, meaning those attached to God's name.
3. See "Kuka Massacre at Malerkotla," www.namdari.org.
4. This point is also supported by Jan Van Butselaar (2005) in the same volume, who argues that the main challenge then becomes "healing" these memories of historical injustices.
5. In 1992 Ayodya, a city in Uttar Pradesh, became the epicenter of communal violence in India sparked by the destruction of the Babri Mosque by Hindu nationalists.
6. This information comes from a map of Malerkotla produced by the Malerkotla City Council in 2005.
7. A namaz is the telling of a story of a religious context, sometimes chanted along with instruments.
8. Personal interview, February 15, 2006.
9. Personal interview, February 24, 2006.

10. K. S. Chawla, "'Suvidha' to Redress Grievances," *The Tribune* (Chandigarh, India), March 11, 2005.

11. AFP, "Indian Islamic Court Issues Fatwa to Cartoonists," *The Sydney Morning Herald*, February 1, 2006. The twelve published cartoons of the Prophet Mohammed in Denmark's *Jyllands-Posten* newspaper sparked worldwide controversy in Muslim and non-Muslim nations causing protesting and violence (Flemming Rose, "Muhammeds ansigt" ["The Face of Muhammad"], September 30, 2005).

12. A panchayat allows grievances and issues to be heard within a social setting or circle that can influence the party or parties. See Saberwal and Jayaram (2003); Madsen (1991, 1996).

13. Muslim organizations in Malerkotla include the Muslim Welfare Society, Maulana Abdul Kalam Azad Memorial Society, and Muslim Social Reforms Panchayat.

14. The chief minister, Captain Amarinder Singh, was in town on January 17, 2004, to pay tribute on the anniversary date of the Kuka Sikh martyrs.

15. Sushil Goyal and Vikrant Jindal, "Cabinet Expansion Next Week, Says Amarinder," *The Tribune* (Chandigarh, India), January 18, 2004.

16. Personal interview, February 12, 2006.

17. Personal interview, February 4, 2005.

18. For the Sikhs, Diwali is the celebration of the sixth Guru Hargobind Ji who traveled to Amritsar after being in the custody of Mughal rulers. Sri Harmandir Sahib (also known as the Golden Temple) was illuminated with lights and fireworks. Holla Mohalla is celebrated a day after Holi. The annual festival occurs at Anandpur Sahib and was instituted by the tenth Guru Gobind Singh Ji to gather Sikhs for preparation of defense and mock battles in a time when Sikhs were fighting against the Mughal Empire. Each year the martial tradition is carried on for three days and thousands travel for miles to take part in *langar* (community kitchens) and *sewa* (community service).

19. Personal interview, February 14, 2006. *Kirt Karo* means to work honestly and *Van ke Shako* means to share what you have with those around you, especially those who are less fortunate.

20. Personal interview February 10, 2005.

7

Indian Muslim Leadership: Predicaments and Possibilities for Human Security

Rowena Robinson

Introduction

This study examines the relationship between the Indian state, Muslim nonstate actors, and the inherent relationship between religion, secularity, and human security. The chapter focuses on Muslim activists and secular leaders in western India. I focus particularly on Mumbai and Gujarat where, in recent decades, targeted attacks on Muslims have occurred. In fact, in both these cases, the state has been indicted for its complicity in the violence (Varadarajan 2002; Barve 2003; Krishna 2003). These events and their aftermaths provide a window through which we can observe nonstate Muslim activists directly contesting with the state for the sake of increased human security. As is noted in the introduction to this volume, human security includes the provision of welfare, human rights, and a socially subjective view of human autonomy. Because of a large Muslim population, the Indian state cannot limit its jurisdiction to the protection of property. It must also include the defense of Muslim rights as well as the recognition of Muslims' social and subjective desires for self-expression and autonomy. When human security is sacrificed for national security, grievances arise from marginalized groups. The full provision of human security for the Muslim community is a critical step toward its members' ability to trust the Indian government, but my research indicates that even within these oppressed communities, there are subcultures that are marginalized within the context of their Muslim communities. These minorities sometimes choose to move outside the religious community in order to pursue their rights, as well as their political and social desires. The situation is complex, but the data indicates that if human security issues are not addressed, the resultant grievances often lead to unrest, and eventually violence.

Methodology

This research is based on interviews with Muslim religious leaders of different sects and persuasions as well as Muslim secular campaigners. It was conducted largely in Mumbai and two cities in the state of Gujarat, Ahmedabad and Baroda. The work focuses on those areas hit most by the violence of the previous years. The interviews were unstructured or semistructured in nature and were aimed at exploring the different responses to the Muslim community-state relationship. I employed qualitative research methodologies for the study. During the course of research, I had occasion to speak with several Muslim secular activists and religious leaders, and I explore further the insights of that research here.

The foci of this chapter are local religious, youth, and activist groups. These are identified primarily by their engagement with the issues of welfare and support emerging out of the impact of ethnic violence. The chapter focuses on leaders of the following religious groups: (1) Jamaat-e-Ulema-e-Hind, (2) the Jamaat-e-Islami, (3) the Islami Relief Committee (Gujarat), (4) World Islamic Network (Shia), (5) Najafi Trust (Shia organization), (6) Tablighi Jamaat, (7) Raza Academy, a well-recognized Barelvi group, and (8) the Mumbai-based Islamic Research Foundation.[1] The activities of these organizations have considerable spread; several are pan-Indian in reach, and they have been actively involved in rehabilitation and interaction with the state and community in the aftermath of ethnic violence in Mumbai and Gujarat. With respect to groups that work with Muslims but do not have a religious orientation, I focus on: (1) Awaaz-e-Niswaan, (2) Vikas Adhyayan Kendra, (3) Rahat Welfare Trust, (4) Nirbhay Bano Andolan, (5) Muslim Youth for India, (6) Modern Youth Association, (7) Sahiyar, (8) Karavaan, and (9) specific zonal divisions of the Mumbai Mohalla Committee Trust. Again, these groups have been selected because of their active and long-term engagement with the victims and survivors of ethnic conflict in the region.

The accounts of activists cited below exhibit the particularities and commonalities that shape individual trajectories of involvement in community activities and the work of ethnic amity. Each individual is defined by his or her own particular history, family context, gender, and personal experiences, but there are also many commonalities. These may emerge from the shared experience of violence, but they are shaped more often by the discourses of activism learned through engagement with nongovernmental organizations.

Militancy, Social Exclusion, and Human Security

Over the last few decades, violence against Muslims has increased in India. In Mumbai during 1993 and in Gujarat during 2002, several thousand Muslims were killed, and many more were rendered homeless and without livelihood. On the whole, the social, political, and economic indicators exhibit the exclusion and vulnerability of Muslims in India. This chapter analyzes the work of Muslim, nonstate actors in both Mumbai and Gujarat based on both secular and religious factors. Greater human security is the goal, sought by both religious and secular agents, but it is difficult to preserve a balance to which both parties will consent. Indeed, to speak of only two sides is reductive. During my research, I found that women within Muslim communities often felt that their human security was compromised because of the male Muslim leadership. Within marginalized communities, women were doubly disaffected. The plight of women in such groups provides one impetus for the occasional intervention of secular activists and the state, but these interventions are not always effective or even helpful. Nevertheless, the desire for human security is a powerful source of mobilization and motivation. Human security grievances, when ignored or denigrated, do not go away. They fester until an opportunity is presented for such grievances to be expressed.

When groups are socially or politically excluded, their human security is compromised, as their self-actualization is diminished. At times, such marginalization provokes a radical response (Hasan 2001, 2004; Hasan and Menon 2004). The Indian state's response to this radicalism is typically repressive. When one examines the social, economic, and political place of Muslims in modern India, one finds that the community is largely socially excluded (Razzack and Gumber 2002; Government of India [GOI] 2006). More recently, with the rise of Islamic militancy, the popular understanding is that Indian Muslims are prone to violence, and as a result, they become the "natural" suspects in incidents of terror. This was particularly apparent following the bomb blasts of Mumbai in 1993, which were traced to Muslim groups operating from outside the country.

In the wake of violence in Jammu and Kashmir, and in Gujarat, there have been bomb blasts and gun attacks in several parts of India. These include an attack on Parliament, recent bomb blasts in Mumbai trains, and on November 26, 2008, an attack in Mumbai by gun-wielding militants. In some cases, local Muslims were found guilty and indicted; in others, however, the evidence implicated militant sources outside of India. Violence, of course, may be perpetrated in the name of any religion, not just Islam. In the 1980s, Sikh militants used violence to further the cause for a separate homeland, and in recent times, militant Hindus have been suspected of violence against religious minorities. Thus, while a genuine fear of militancy in the name of Islam may not be dismissed, the vilification of an entire community cannot contribute to a solution. Indeed, such a view undermines human security by provoking violent responses from oppressed populations.

Over the past two decades, various events have contributed to the spread of fear among many groups, especially minorities (Wilkinson 2005; Krishna 2003).

Among these, recent political shifts are paramount. For instance, national-level political parties such as the Bharatiya Janata Party and some of its allies have publicly questioned the value of Indian secularism. This has created a sense of unease among minorities such as Sikhs, Muslims, and Christians, who have increasingly been the target of state violence (Basu and Subrahmanyam 1996; Bhargava 1998). In many incidents of violence, scholarly and investigative reports have identified the state's complicity (Dayal 2002; Concerned Citizens' Tribunal—Gujarat 2002; Human Rights Watch 2002, 2003). But perhaps no minority group has suffered greater social and political deprivation than Indian Muslims.

Indian Muslims: A Deprived Community

Muslims comprise just over 12 percent of India's population, but of the 593 districts in India, only 9 are predominantly Muslim. The main areas of Muslim concentration are in the Indo-Gangetic plain, in Jammu and Kashmir, in Kerala, in Assam, and in south-central India (GOI 2006: 30–31). This data helps to explain the lack of human security of the 9 percent of Muslims in Gujarat, who are scattered across many villages and districts and who, after 2002, were systematically removed and not allowed to return.

The average standard of living of Indian Muslims is among the lowest in the country. The literacy rate is far below the national average, and this gap is even greater in urban areas and among women. In fact, there is a significant disparity between the educational status of Muslims and that of other socioreligious categories. Both mean years of schooling and attendance levels of Muslims are low in absolute numbers and in comparison with other socioreligious groups, admitting regional variations. In higher education, the differences between Muslims and others stand out even more sharply (GOI 2006).

Worker population ratios are lower for Muslims than any other socioreligious community, and this is even truer in rural areas. Muslim women fare even worse in both rural and urban areas, and they are especially underrepresented as workers in urban areas. A high percentage of Muslim workers are self-employed, particularly in urban areas (GOI 2006). This concentration of self-employment—street vending, small trades, and small enterprises—ensures that the community as a whole is far more exposed to the disruption and damages caused by urban conflict and violence. The low level of Muslim asset accumulation further intensifies the vulnerability of this group, which exacerbates even more the threat to its core sense of human security.

The general state of Muslim employment is a concern because it is indicative of the community's sense of well-being and economic security. As employees, Muslims typically work as casual labor and are very poorly represented in regular, salaried employment. Their participation in formal sector employment is far lower than the national average. Muslim men are overrepresented in street vending (more than 12 percent as opposed to the national average of less than 8 percent), while women tend to work from home to a much larger degree than average (70 percent versus 51 percent). Muslim participation is relatively lower in professional, technical, clerical, and managerial work, particularly in urban areas. Further, Muslim working conditions (length of contract, social security benefits, and the like) are poorer than those for other socioreligious groups (GOI 2006: 108). Muslims are also poorly represented in defense and security-related activities. Diversity in the police forces has a place in producing greater impartiality and promoting the trust of citizens, but the number of Muslims in "public order and safety activities" at the central level is about 6 percent while that of Hindu upper castes is 42 percent.

With respect to other social and physical infrastructure, Muslims are poorly served. Muslim-concentration villages, as the census of 2001 shows, are not well served with *pucca* (properly built) approach roads or local bus stops. A large number of Muslim-concentration villages lack post and telegraph services. Further, there is a clear inverse relationship in small villages between the proportion of Muslim population and the availability of educational infrastructure. In most states, the proportion of Muslim-concentration villages with medical facilities is lower than the proportion of all villages with such facilities (GOI 2006: 139–149). These facts indicate possible biases in public service provisioning in Muslim-concentration areas.

Human Security and Indian Muslims

Human security for Indian Muslims should involve the protection of lives, livelihoods, and basic human rights, as well as the subjective sense of the ability to express their grievances. Today, however, they feel threatened by police bias, social alienation, and political hostility. Police raids, surveillance, and curfew mechanisms leave them uneasy. In many places, one sees the growing ghettoization of Muslims. Discrimination appears to operate in ensuring that such areas remain poorly serviced by civic bodies, and Muslims, even in urban areas, often find that their names and their religion become liabilities in the search for housing in good localities.

The *madrasa* (Muslim religious schools) and the mosque are under increasing scrutiny. There is clearly a perceived threat of the spread of different radical ideologies. Nevertheless, experience has shown that militancy is best prevented when communities have faith in the state, the law, and the police. The argument of this volume is that human security of vulnerable populations must be taken as seriously as the national security of the state. One without the other threatens both. The Indian state is a quintessential case study of that conceptual assertion. Agents of the state need to interact continuously with local-level committees and with other civic groups in society. The need for quick and impartial action in times of civic and ethnic violence is of even greater importance. The legal apparatus must be impartial in order for basic forms of civic trust to flourish; otherwise, human security is undercut and grievances increase.

Civil Activism

Altaf is a young Gujarati who started working within his community after the violence of 2002. He has retained links with nongovernmental organizations by working for communal peace and justice. He talked about how he learned that communal peace could only be a part of a complex of engagements; some of these involved dealing with a range of activities that residents found difficult to negotiate. His daily activity consisted of following up on compensation cases, helping people acquire voter identity cards, making them aware of available government grants and benefits, and assisting them in acquiring such grants. On the ground, trust constructed on the basis of these myriad actions fed the larger project of building social trust and political involvement as well as links across communities.

Altaf is among the more ordinary members of the Muslim community, who do not identify themselves as "religious" leaders, for whom work in relief and rehabilitation has woven into a wider concern with social activism and improvement within the community. Such activists see themselves as "secular" in orientation. Their stance toward some aspects of their faith can be described as ambivalent, but they are often called upon to interact with local religious leadership and these interactions can be lively if not obviously troubled by a degree of tension. As another local-level Muslim secular activist said in Mumbai: "We cannot think only of Muslims. Everything is not a community issue. Many larger and more critical issues are at stake: fundamental rights, justice, and so on."

Some of these grassroots workers systematically distance themselves from those who exclusively pursue the cause of religion. Sajjid from Mumbai's Jogeshwari (East) makes this clear, asserting:

> We do not involve ourselves with religious activities at all. Ours is the only organization in the area that is engaged in social activities within the community. Apart from religious activities, there were no organizations that were involved in social activities. Today, on our own strength, we have set up several such local-level organizations that do not run madrasas, are

engaged in the work of communal harmony, building community-based associations, and bringing out protest marches on the streets in connection with different issues.

Disdain toward *all* religious matters raises its own problems as I discuss below. Altaf did not have a great deal of education and is certainly not a fluent speaker in English. His spoken Hindi is passable, but his education has been largely in his local tongue, Gujarati. By his own admission, it was his interaction with an international nongovernmental organization (Action-Aid) and the training he received from it that helped fuse his somewhat hazy social ideas into a more highly developed worldview. He became aware of larger developmental issues and the place of peace and conflict resolution in realizing the goals of community development.

Feroz Ashraf, from Mumbai, is another such secular activist. In 1993, Ashraf was forced to move out of his home in a Hindu-dominated locality in Mumbai to another suburb in Mumbai considered safer because of its Muslim-concentration. This enforced dislocation led to a different turn—a move toward engagement with the problems of his local area. Ashraf's life-long bent towards leftist politics clearly framed his critique of Muslim local religious leadership as well as his understanding of the issues that ailed the community.

Pyar Ali Khapadia was a postal employee for most of his life; today, at seventy, he lives in the heart of Ram Rahim Nagar in Ahmedabad. Thirty-four years ago he moved to this riverside location after his house was destroyed in the communal carnage of 1969. That experience sensitized him to the dismal danger of persistent intercommunity aggression. He set up the Ram Rahim Nagar Jhopadpati Nivasi Sanstha (Ram Rahim Neighborhood Association), bringing together Hindus and Muslims of the area with a commitment to preventing aggression. It was no easy task, and there were always those who defied persuasion. Nevertheless, the central thrust of his message was clear—violence must be prevented for people's own interest. He worked continually to bring others in the neighborhood around, and in 2002, Ram Rahim Nagar remained an isle of quiet in a city torn by communal strife.

Pyar Ali's is an education sustained and augmented by an active engagement with the everyday issues and politics of his neighborhood rather than one obtained in the classroom. He does not think of communities as benignly unstructured entities; for him, the interests of the deprived within those communities are of crucial concern. Communal violence is intensely associated with class and privilege, with the underclass and the underprivileged bearing the brunt (see, for instance, Gupta 2000; Engineer 1984).

For a Muslim woman, the engagement with difference may involve a greater degree of friction. Sophia Khan, in Ahmedabad, comes from a background she self-consciously describes as orthodox. She completed her education, including an advanced degree in law, in the face of constant pressure from her family that she should abandon her studies for matrimony and the home. Her teachers fostered her tentative interest in social work. Later, she found herself steered toward a greater concern with gender issues. The awareness of being "Muslim" and, therefore, "Other" remained, reinforced by well-intentioned educators who urged her to work for "her community."

In 2002, Sophia had to assume a Hindu name and make an identity card in that name to allow her, despite her position as a social activist, to move through the city to help in the relief work. She had to carefully strategize, adopting a non-Gujarati name so that she would not encounter questions about her caste identity and would be able to explain away her frequent lapses into Hindi when she speaks. According to Sophia, she fits no "stereotype" of the Muslim woman. She does not use the veil and wears her hair short. It is more usual for a Muslim woman of her age to wear the veil and to have long, well-groomed hair, but Sophia marks out her difference by breaking with these expectations. Her struggles exhibit the difficulties of the Muslim woman activist who has to contend not only with the perceptions of the Hindus (who think of the "veiled" Muslim women as backward) but also with expectations of femininity within her own community.

Here again, the complexity of advocating for human security, for welfare, rights, and social desires, is not just a matter of nonstate groups (whether secular or religious) against the state, but also how to negotiate differences within religious communities where gender and class create inequalities that undercut human security and foment more fragmentation within these oppressed communities. And indeed, as we see below, some religious groups seek not only equality with the state but, at times, political autonomy that adds yet another layer to how these conflicts can play out in the field.

Religious Engagement

The Jamaat-e-Islami has been involved in relief work in different parts of India. While it has a radical political position, aiming ultimately at setting up of an Islamic state, on the ground it negotiates its stance far more pragmatically. It is different from the Jamaat-e-Ulema-e-Hind with regard to the posture adopted toward the state. For instance, the Jamaat-e-Ulema-e-Hind was against Partition and did not believe that Muslims needed their own political unit.

Thus, the Jamaat-e-Islami tends toward a position wherein the Indian state is considered illegitimate, but the Jamaat-e-Ulema-e-Hind accepts the state's boundaries and its legitimacy. On the ground, the Jamaat-e-Islami combines the reworking of individual lives and practices in terms of Islamic principles with the effort to mediate with nongovernmental organizations and non-Muslims for the purposes of social activities and "living together [with non-Muslims] in the *mulk* [territory]."

In the violence of Mumbai and Gujarat, destruction and loss had by no means been confined to the city slums; it visited commercial pockets and middle-class neighborhoods. Further, for some, the experience of violence was not the first. In the light of this, conversations with community leaders working with survivors of riots raised several questions. How did a community exposed more and more frequently to violence attempt rehabilitation at the very sites? Coping with violence might raise queries for gender roles and expectations, but how are these to be contended with? What was the experience of community leaders contacting the state? While ordinary Muslims negotiate their own way through such concerns, they are also exposed to the teachings of their community or *jamaat* on them. Any statement coming from the *jamaat* leader is taken seriously by Muslims and influences the way in which they act or interpret issues and events.

Increasingly, religious leaders have begun to try to influence and direct arrangements of rehabilitation and settlement in the wake of ethnic violence. They have had close involvement with riot relief operations, particularly in recent times. One Barelvi leader explained:

> After the Gujarat riots of 2002 we held a press conference by the Ulema to appeal to Muslims to come back to places where there were more Muslims. Wherever Muslims are in a minority, they are targeted the most. After 1992–93, people moved individually but now the Heads have announced it and want it to happen. Earlier, they had thought it [residential pattern] should be cosmopolitan.

For Shia groups, living in communal neighborhoods has long been a preferred custom. Nevertheless, certain members of these groups, often highly educated and wealthy, deliberately choose to live along with others in their social class in cosmopolitan, affluent neighborhoods rather than in more socially heterogeneous, and usually crowded, ethnic quarters (Engineer 1989). In Gujarat during 2002, many such families were the conscious targets of violence, and as a result, they endured ridicule by religious leaders. Further, in the wake of violence, some religious organizations worked to relocate Muslims at new sites, away from mixed neighborhoods. From the Jamaat-e-Islami, Hasan said:

> Most of the rehabilitation has been done in the same areas. We have not worked to displace people. Morally, we try and give them courage. Tell them it is their *zameen* [land], *basti* [village], they should not leave it. …
> In some cases, we bought land and rehabilitated them nearby at a new site, complete with surrounding walls, *pucca* houses, and so on.

With respect to the call for justice regarding injury, death, and even rape, religious leaders expressed reluctance to pursue these causes. While some differences emerged, on the whole there was a sense that Muslims could not expect anything from the Indian state and should, therefore, not rely on it too much. Certainly, questions of male and community honor were significant for religion-based organizations refusing to pursue cases of rape and violent crimes against women. The sense that "Muslims have to look after themselves" came through very strongly. This was particularly so for those aligned with the Jamaat-e-Islami. The Jamaat-e-Ulema-e-Hind expresses greater faith in Indian law, but both groups, together with other religion-based organizations, unified in condemning the state's recent attacks against Muslims. Here again we see where basic forms of human security are undercut, there is distrust; state mechanisms are delegitimized, which, in the end, sets up a dynamic of potential violence and civil unrest.

Gender, Modes of Struggle, and Forms of Leadership

Among Muslim secular activists, there is an acute awareness of how community and women's issues chafe one another, particularly in the wake of heightened communal consciousness and targeted violence. Secular activists often cite "Mumbai 1992–1993" and "Gujarat 2002" as moments that fundamentally altered the very ways in which gender issues could or could not be addressed. Hasina, a Muslim woman activist working both in Mumbai and Gujarat, mentioned how issues had been redefined in the wake of violence:

> The impact of Gujarat or the Mumbai riots on Muslim women is tremendous. There is a sense of oppression from two sides: from within by conservative and fundamentalist forces and from outside by Hindu communalist forces. ... Muslim women get marginalized. In an atmosphere of communalism, women's questions do not get centralized; this needs to be done. How do we look at women? In the kind of atmosphere in Gujarat, should we raise the women's question at all? Or only that of the identity of Muslims as a community, a minority?

Her statements evoke a sense of being pulled by contradictory affiliations emerges:

> In education and social advancement, Muslim women are very poor, and there is a great deal of violence and pressure on the community. As it increases, the community is further ghettoized, and minority politics

increases. Our *samaj* [society] is backward. There is so much violence—is there place for us? Where do we go?

Women's rights issues ranging from the misuse of provisions for divorce under Muslim Personal Law to questions of maintenance in the event of divorce are all pushed into the background in the face of targeted attacks against the community. Muslim religious leaders rage against the foregrounding of such issues when, as they argue, the whole community is under attack. Women activists are castigated for even bringing up such issues (Jeffery and Basu 1998; Williams 2008).

Further discomfort centers around the fact that concerns over violence against Muslim women are the ones that religious leaders would rather not see addressed. As secular activists assert, communal violence always has a negative impact on women; in its wake, the male community elders seek to regulate women's mobility, their dress, their behavior, and the like. In Gujarat, for instance, men remain reluctant to admit incidents of rape and are known to have applied pressure on women to prevent them from reporting such incidents at all. There are activists who believe that the stance of religious leaders is detrimental to what they consider to be the "wider" battle—that of the gender struggle or of human rights issues. Regardless of the climate of communalization, Muslim women's concerns within the larger concern of the rights of women in general should not be marginalized.

Thus, we see ways in which, even in marginalized groups, there are subcultures, in this case women, who experience even greater alienation; they are made to feel guilt for expressing their own social desires for equality over and against the wider Muslim community. This research indicates that the provision of human security is a powerful consideration for communal welfare. When it is denied to any given population, social and political unrest are not uncommon.

Working with Each Other

Working with overtly religious leaders or caste elders is also an issue that several activists find contentious. Sajjid, for instance, as I earlier recorded, refuses to link himself with any sectarian or religious groups. The association, funded by local contributions, initially called itself the Muslim Youth Association. However, to dissociate it from any connection with religion and to stress its "progressive" character, it soon renamed itself the Modern Youth Association.

Sajjid and the other young men associated with the group worked with nongovernmental associations in relief and rehabilitation work in the months and years after the violence of 1992–1993. This interaction exposed them to a complex of ideas concerned with social issues, secularism, justice, and globalization. From this, the idea of forming the association emerged. Among other activities, the group organized several public protests. It also runs a small book bank, lending school books to poor children in the neighborhood, and works to build communal amity through arranging collective neighborhood celebrations. These celebrations often involve Hindus and Muslims, helping to mediate local tensions and to encourage a joint approach to shared concerns such as sewage collection and road maintenance.

Ashraf keeps aloof from religious *jamaats*. While he relies on some support from individuals and nondenominational, nongovernmental organizations, he remains largely an independent worker. Concerned with issues of communal amity and education, he tutors underprivileged youths, both Hindu and Muslim, to help them through school. His attention focuses on individual youths in the slums, and he encourages students as far as their abilities will take them, even assisting them with information regarding employment opportunities. When he moved to Jogeshwari, Ashraf started going to the local mosque. However, this was not for the purpose of participation in the prayers. He aimed to know how people thought and what the *maulvis* preached in order to be able, perhaps, to contest these ideas in the course of his interaction with Muslim neighbors. He expressed considerable contempt for the kind of Muslim who focuses only on religious matters without addressing the problems of poverty and educational backwardness that confront the community.

There are others who distance themselves from the *maulanas*. Several women activists in Gujarat and Mumbai talk of tense engagements with religious leaders who insisted on men and women saying *namaz* in the relief camps in order to be entitled to assistance and were openly derisive of violence-hit Muslims who had opted to stay in ethnically mixed areas, implying that they had only got what was coming to them.

Such activists do not wish to underline their or their community's "minority" or "Muslim" identity but to align their struggles as citizens with other deprived or oppressed groups, including women, Dalits, tribal members, and the economically disadvantaged. This alignment is not always assumed or easily achieved. It is apparently much easier for the Muslim clergy to act against the state's attempts to restrict personal laws or against a proposed visit of the Israeli president than it is for clerics to stand together on issues not viewed as directly affecting the community.

Muslim activists who work primarily with the Muslim community often feel the pressure to remain silent regarding questions of women's rights or justice in the wake of targeted attacks from outside, *and* they do not always find themselves in agreement with the views of religious leaders. On the other hand, Muslim activists who work on issues of social justice and rights, regardless of the religious question, are also sometimes reluctant to push too far. One stressed:

There is just so much pressure on Muslims right now. Ever since the Shah Bano case, Mumbai violence and now Gujarat they are so much the target. … Yes, divorce [and] abandonment of women without proper maintenance—all these are issues of concern, but right now the community is hurting terribly. It would not be fair. … It would be a further violence to take up these things right now.

How far should the issue of justice be pushed? Religious leaders, on the whole, seem to minimize the importance of the pursuit for justice in individual cases. Shakeel Ahmed in Mumbai leads Nirbhay Bano Andolan (Be Fearless Movement), a group based entirely on voluntary effort that works to educate the poor and marginalized with regard to human security issues of rights and justice for empowerment. Shakeel provides the local groups he works among with careful information about legal and official procedures, modes of follow-up for cases, and the rights of common citizens. *Nyaya* (justice) forms the pivot of his social thought. His work with the victims and survivors of violence shaped an ethic of peace that centered around the notion of justice. He has been at the forefront of the campaign to ensure that the indicted be brought to book and has also been engaging with victims' families in their struggles for compensation and justice. He argues:

> *Nyaya* is not a question only about Muslims; it is an issue for the whole *samaj* (society). … Every problem is seen as being one of a community, either Muslims or Dalits or whatever. … Justice is an issue for the society as a whole. People question why we must pursue this. Why reopen old wounds? [*zhakham hare karne ki zaroorat kya hai?*] However, without *nyaya*, from where will peace come in society? If people see that the government is not giving justice, they will take the law into their own hand.

Conclusion and Implications

Throughout this chapter I have shown that the struggle for human security is not only a difficult one but one that has unexpected complexities. The obvious and sustained deprivation of the Muslim community in India has led to great unrest and terrible violence. The Indian perspective on Muslims obsesses over how to undercut Muslim militancy. In India, as in many of the other locales discussed in this volume, national security trumps human security. When this occurs, neither goal can be fully actualized. I have also discovered that the Muslim community is far from a monolith. In addition to Muslim women seeking social actualization, the various religious and secular organizations, some desiring political autonomy, further muddy the situation on the ground. In this sense, the problem is more complex than it first appeared and has more to negotiate. In any case, groups and individuals that are marginalized, whether religious or secular, seek a core set of human security goals, and it is the continued thwarting of these goals that might provoke violence and unrest.

How these groups go about expressing their desire for human security and the strategies that they take are also different. As I have shown, there is a significant dissonance between religious and "secular" Muslim populations. The attitudes of Muslim religious and secular activists toward the state and toward legal processes are notably different. While both regard the state as corrupt and biased against Muslims, the attitudes toward redress and governance differ. Muslim secular leadership critiques the state, but it does not attempt to supplant it or remove Muslims from under its protection. On the other hand, religious activists sometimes speak of the state as redundant or express views that turn community members away from engagement with it.

The unintended consequences of removing Muslims from the protection of the state can be catastrophic, particularly for women. By asking Muslims not to file or follow up cases for justice or insisting that they reside in community-specific areas makes Muslims physically, socially, and economically more vulnerable. Muslim women are further marginalized if issues concerning maintenance or gender equality are left out of the processes of legal intervention and state legislative control.

Nevertheless, there is real ambivalence toward the Muslim faith, particularly from Muslim secular activists who interpret the faith as unfriendly to women. On the other hand, many activists have not rejected the possibility of working with religious leaders to facilitate a broader understanding of Muslim faith and culture. Many of these activists would likely acknowledge that faith is integral to the daily life of most Muslims; leaving religious elders out of the loop diminishes the activists' own credibility with their community, vastly decreasing the interested audience. While some would like to work only with those leaders who are willing to contemplate the possibility of reinterpretation of religious doctrine for contemporary life, there are others who believe that even the conservatives must be accorded attention.

Organizations, such as the Jamaat-e-Islami or the Jamaat-e-Ulema-e-Hind, play a crucial role in postviolence situations. Muslim religious organizations are among the first to offer assistance to victims and survivors. For instance in Gujarat, during 2002, a large part of the relief work was in Muslim hands. Further, as Sophia argued, religious organizations are also now beginning to understand that things have got to change, particularly with respect to education for women:

"[Religious leaders] know now that things cannot go back to being just the same as before. . . . Some changes will have to come."

Another Muslim woman activist from Gujarat offered this comment:

> We should not leave the opportunity to engage with the *maulvis*. We need to involve them so that they do not stonewall all our efforts. Further, we cannot decide whom to work with on the basis of personalities; we have to address the questions that they are raising. We find it possible to talk with the Tablighi Jamaat leader [in our area]. He raises the question of values: submission to God's will, setting a good example for others. . . . Can we ignore these? Even if we disagree on some points, we have to dialogue [and] slowly build more areas of agreement.

Even Shakeel admits the practicality of strategic but selective interaction with religious ideologues:

> We think we should work only with secular people; but we realized that we need to engage with other people of different ideologies also. . . . [I]n local-level issues decisions have to be taken. In our areas, there are issues—displacement, corruption etc. [At such time] we have to work together, whatever the ideology.

Thus, there are differing approaches: one admits common ground only on nonreligious issues of public or local level interest; another sees conversation on spiritual matters as a way of encouraging religious leaders to participate more in civil concerns or to at least not oppose these. A third, even more proactive, strategy actually tries to converse with religious leaders for the reframing of human security concerns.

Sophia, Hasina, and others are engaged in this third form of interaction. They do this through discussions relating to provisions within Muslim Personal Law.[2] Further, at their own level and in their own limited regions, activists continue to raise questions about Muslim men's violence against women and about Muslim women's need for and access to education, emphasizing that these cannot be sidelined because of communal attacks. Indeed the attacks must spur *more*, not less initiative.

With regard to Muslim issues in the postcolonial period, the state has tended to act in paternalistic ways, assuming that it knows what is good for the community. Second, political compulsions have dictated that token gestures are occasionally made toward Muslims, but their real socioeconomic problems have been neglected. Third, the stress on national security issues has led the state to look at

Muslims largely from the perspective of containing militancy and to ignore the core features of human security. This has led to tragic results.

What this chapter shows is that the state must redress on a constant and consistent basis the economic deprivation and social exclusion that the Muslim community faces. The state should act impartially, not alienating the community as a whole in the fight against militancy. Militancy is a part of a national security agenda, but militancy is related to a lack of human security. If an entire community finds itself excluded, this could lead- to conditions conducive to the flourishing of activities against the state. Positive outcomes, such as in the social, economic, and juridical spheres, can do much to alter this. Even more important is the need for quick and impartial action in times of civic and ethnic violence.

Furthermore, no community is a monolith. Different kinds of leaders have differing responses to the state or community issues, but they are talking with each other at various levels. The state should allow the dialogue that has already emerged among different Muslim groups to come up with agreed-upon solutions for the community. In this regard, Muslim women's groups need to be involved in working together with other Muslim groups in the search for solutions. These solutions, if coming from below, are likely to be better accepted by the community and more effective, but it is true that Muslim leaders might resist some of the movements from below and that the state is not always ready to act on behalf of the marginalized. Nonetheless, the rising political awareness of many Muslims, particularly Muslim women, has unleashed expectations at the popular level creating forms of "soft" power that are not easily ignored. The kind of grassroots activism described in this chapter has had an impact on a broader level. Women activists have been working with Muslim national-level leaders in attempting to amend some of the provisions of Muslim Personal Law, particularly those relating to marriage and divorce. This is a visible way in which community-level activism is feeding policy formation. In the atmosphere of greater awareness that prevails today, it would be difficult for either the state or Muslim leaders to ignore such moves. The moment is opportune for state and nonstate religious actors to find ways of working together by understanding that human security is the very foundation for India's future national security.

Notes

Rowena Robinson is professor of sociology in the Department of Humanities and Social Sciences, Indian Institute of Technology Bombay, India. She is the author of *Christians of India* (Sage, 2003) and *Tremors of Violence: Muslim Survivors of Ethnic Strife in Western India* (Sage, 2005) and the editor (along with Sathianathan Clarke) of *Religious Conversion in India: Modes, Motivations and Meanings* (Oxford University Press, 2003).

1. The Jamaat-e-Ulema-e-Hind is a strongly anti-imperialist organization of Islamic clergy formed during the British period. It was against Partition. In Pakistan, it functions as the Jamaat-e-Ulema-e-Islam. The organization follows the Deobandi school of Hanafi Islam. Deobandi Islam derives its name from the small town of Deoband, where a Deobandi Dar-ul-Uloom came to be established. The movement itself precedes the setting up of the Deobandi Islamic school of learning. It was an anti-British movement, which also espoused a literal and austere interpretation of Islam. Some Indian Deobandi Muslims lean toward an admiration of the Saudi Arabian religio-polity. Deoband teachings manifest a distrust of other cultures and seek to purge Islam of Western and modernist influences and to establish the Quran and Hadith ("sayings" of the Prophet) as the sole sources of tradition. Deobandi schools have sought to purify Islam of such popular practices presumably borrowed from Hinduism as the veneration of idols and visits to the graves of saints.

   The Jamaat-e-Islami was formed in 1941 in Lahore on the initiative of Maulana Syed Abul Ala Maududi. The organization split up on Partition into the Jamaat-e-Islami, which continued to function in Pakistan, and the Jamaat-e-Islami Hind, which functioned in India. The Jamaat-e-Islami is opposed to the separation of religion and politics and claims to strive for the ultimate installation of a polity based on Islamic principles. The institutionalization of the Tablighi Jamaat took place under Mohammad Ilyas in the 1920s. The unit of preaching was the *jamaat*, which consisted of a small group of teachers who went around from place to place educating Muslims in correct Islamic practice. The *jamaats* often consisted of ordinary Muslims who could be trained to preach and participate in the work of Islamization.

   Barelvi Islam is a school of thought founded by Maulana Ahmed Raza Khan Al-Qaderi, a contemporary of Maulana Ashraf Ali Thanvi of the Deoband school. Unlike Deobandis, Barelvis believe in the powers of the Prophet and the saints and in supplication at *dargahs* (tombs of saints). Barelvis are influenced by a variety of Sufi practices, including the use of music (*Qawwalis*) and intercession by their teacher. Barelvis believe in the intercession between humans and the divine through a chain of holy *pirs* (saints) ultimately reaching the Prophet.

2. Personal laws for different religious communities in India were codified by the British. Thus, Hindu and Muslim Personal Laws existed at the time of Independence. Under Nehru, Parliament reformed Hindu Personal Law, bringing in many modern revisions that improved the status of women under the Law. However, Muslim Personal Law was not touched. In the 1980s, the issue of Muslim Personal Law became very controversial. In particular, the absence of a provision for the maintenance of a divorced woman came under scrutiny. Other areas of controversy include the provision that a man may marry four wives or divorce any one of them by the simple procedure of thrice saying the words "I divorce you."

8

"A Little with God Is a Lot": Popular Religion and Human Security in the Land of the Brazilian Colonels

Jonathan Warren

Introduction

The racially inspired elitism that saturates Brazilian society has often led to a pat dismissal of anything associated with the general public or what, in Brazil, is referred to as "*o povo*" (the people). On both the left and the right, individuals interested in civilizing, modernizing, and developing Brazil have typically defined the culture of o povo, including their religion, as an impediment to progress.

The great Brazilian filmmaker Glauber Rocha offers an example of this dismissive view of popular religion, at least as a means for advancing human security. In his film *Black God, White Devil* (1964), he depicts popular religion, especially its messianic forms, as an ineffectual mode of popular resistance in Brazil. Like so many other cosmopolitan modernizers, Rocha suggests that popular religion's putative impotence in producing substantial change stems from its narrow focus on the afterlife and the metaphysical, rather than the quotidian and mundane. Consequently it is presumed that the institutions, identities, discourses, and policies that undergird socioeconomic marginalization are left unexamined, uncontested, and therefore unchanged. In the words of the film critic Ismael Xavier (1982: 141), "messianic rebellion ... distances [the people] from the official church. It frees them from the domination of the landlord and boss, but in their place proposes only the passivity of prayer and the initiatory rituals that will define them as elect in the moment of cataclysm."

The municipality of Araçuaí, in the Jequitinhonha Valley of northeastern Minas Gerais, challenges this commonplace theory of popular religion. In these once forbidden lands of Brazil, the embrace of popular religious traditions, including messianic ones, has not reinforced the passivity of the oppressed. Indeed its embrace has provoked a transformation of the consciousness, identities, and praxis of o povo. Consequently, popular religion has been a cornerstone for the advancement of human rights, health, social equality, democratization, and economic development. All of which is very much in line with the definition of human security developed in this volume.

"Colonelism"

In the 1960s, the Jequitinhonha Valley was the third poorest region in the world. There were no telephones, running water, or sidewalks. The majority of the population lacked any formal education and were, thus, generally illiterate. Severe health problems such as chagas disease[1] were commonplace. Even basic health care was unavailable. Older residents recount that it was not unusual to see people dying on buses, while in the process of seeking medical care. This state of affairs is especially striking since the area was, and continues to be, a region extremely rich in natural resources, especially minerals such as uranium and lithium.

The reasons for this immense poverty were centuries in the making. In the eighteenth century, diamonds and gold were discovered in Diamantina, the mountainous (*serra*) region, occupying the headwaters of the Jequitinhonha River. The quantity of minerals was such that it paid for the complete rebuilding of Lisbon after an earthquake and tsunami devastated it in 1755. In order to ensure that this wealth was taxed and protected from other European powers, the Portuguese Crown created a forbidden zone between the littoral region of southern Bahia, Espírito Santo, and northern Rio de Janeiro where these areas border the mining region of central Minas Gerais. Given that it was illegal to settle or construct roads through this region, it became a refuge for indigenous people such as the Borun and Tikmãa.

With the invasion of Portugal by the French during the Napoleonic Wars, the Crown fled to Brazil in 1808, where it set up its court in Rio de Janeiro. Coveting the lands and minerals in the forbidden lands, the colonists intensified their complaints about Indian intrusions onto the plantations that bordered this region. These complaints found more sympathetic ears after the court relocated to Rio de Janeiro. The first act of King John VI upon his arrival in Brazil was to lift the ban on settlement and declare a "just war" on the Indians in this region.

The objective of the war was twofold: colonization and ethnic cleansing. Outnumbered and outgunned, indigenous people were brutally conquered. Survivors, especially the orphaned children, were enslaved as a means of destroying indigenous identities and culture (Soares 2010). The mercenaries in this genocidal war were rewarded by the Crown with land, slaves and the ersatz nobility title of "Colonel."² Many of the colonels brought with them slaves, primarily of African descent, who mixed socially, culturally, and biologically with the indigenous survivors of the war. It was this mestizo population that formed the socially marginalized labor force of the region. If they were not slaves, they worked as subsistent farmers, artisans, day laborers, or domestic servants in small villages on or near the plantations.

In 1850 Brazil's first land law was passed. It favored the further concentration of the land into the hands of a few. The law required that landholders register their land hundreds of miles away in Rio de Janeiro. The costs of such a journey prohibited small landholders from registering their land. Without title to their lands, the colonels were able to easily appropriate the lands of small, mestizo landholders and force them to live on the peripheries of the plantations as tenant farmers or share croppers in slave-like conditions. They were called "*agregados*" or aggregates.

The outcome of these processes was that the colonels became very powerful. Yehuda Cohen, in *Why Religion?*, sums up the situation well: "They possessed economic and political power over the local government and over the means of law enforcement.... They maintained monopolistic control over agricultural production and commerce and controlled the best lands. They maintained power even through unlawful means" (2003: 432).The resulting social order was a kind of racially inflected feudalism. The people were landless, extremely poor, and socially, politically, and economically at the mercy of their patrons, the colonels. Moreover the peasants were cast as racial subalterns. Physical features, histories, or cultural practices associated with indigenousness or blackness were hyperstigmatized. Indigineity and blackness, the dominant ancestries of these subalterns, became a racial stain and source of shame.

Freire's Disciples

In 1964 the Brazilian military carried out a coup d'état against João Goulart, who as vice president became president when the democratically elected Jânio Quadros resigned. US president Lyndon Johnson described it as a great day for democracy (Huggins 1998). In reality it was a major setback not only for democracy but also human security. The predominantly white, middle and upper classes had become increasingly uncomfortable with the demands by o povo for access to health care, land, social security, and education. In a society that was barely a generation removed from slavery, such challenges to the social order were alarming to people of means. Even though the suggested policies were modest (for example, calls for universal access to public schools), they were perceived as exceedingly audacious. O povo, largely viewed as racially inferior riff-raff, were behaving as if they were social equals. From an elitist vantage, they were "uppity." And so the numerically small but powerful middle-class and elite sectors were largely supportive of the military coup. Predictably, the military regime enacted a series of policies that served to only further erode Brazilian human security and animate the authority and status of the colonels in places like the Jequitinhonha Valley. It was during this darkest hour that the seeds for change were sown.

In 1969, a Dutch friar, Franciscus Henricus van der Poel (aka Frei Xico, b. 1944), arrived in the Jequitinhonha Valley. During this time, liberation theology had influenced the thinking of many in the Catholic Church, including approximately half the bishops in Brazil (Löwy 1996). Frei Xico was also touched by this theological movement. He went to Araçuaí with a vision that it was the church's responsibility to prioritize the poor and search for ways to help them advance human security in the mundane world in which they lived.

Liberation theology had political and philosophical roots in Marxism. Along with this often came a Leninist elitism in which it had been determined what the poor's true identity should be and what was best for them. They were to identify as "workers" or "peasants" and advance their own liberation and society's modernization by distancing themselves from their "feudal traditions." This led to defining popular culture, be it religious or otherwise, as a backward impediment to progress and human security. In this way, more critical views within the church dovetailed with the general elitism in Brazilian society noted above. It also echoed the conventional position within the church, which had largely looked with suspicion on popular religious practices. The second Vatican had been a challenge to this perspective but besides the laity being taught in their native language, little had changed in Araçuaí by the 1970s.

In interviews with Frei Xico,[3] he notes a pivotal moment that led him to question his attitude toward the culture of o povo. A celebration during Holy Week prompted him to confront the inadequacies of his theoretical convictions. He performed a mass on Good Friday, enjoyed a beer afterward, and went to sleep content with a day's good work completed, only to be awakened in the middle of the night. Following the sounds, he returned to the church to find it alive with people.

> Initially I thought what ugly singing. People shouting. Spitting rum. Attacking one another. I thought it was ugly. Then I thought I'll wait until they stop and encourage them to go to bed. I observed the music they were singing. It echoed the music of love one heard on the radio and I realized that they had a faith or love that I didn't have. There were prostitutes singing with such force, such conviction, that it left one speechless with emotion. And so I began to see the other side. I became very emotional. I went up front, as planned, after the music had stopped and I said the opposite

of what I was originally going to say. I said "This is very beautiful. You can sing as long as you want and next year I want to stay the whole evening with you" and I left. That for me wasn't theory. It was a moment when you see something and make a decision. The next day people told me that when I entered the church the people thought I was going to prohibit it because the priest at the time (who is now the retired Bishop) prohibited it at the time. Only after I left there, five years later, the priest prohibited it.

This experience generated a crisis in his thinking. A self-identified socialist and liberation theologian, he was confronted with his theoretical biases against popular culture: "Socialism, in my opinion, got weak because it never valued the religion, the culture, the vision of the poor. Liberation theology had the same defect. ... I was certain that what I had seen did not fit these concepts. So I decided to abandon my ideas, my baggage, to leave them behind. I perceived I needed the courage to abandon beautiful theories."

Like many of his contemporaries, who were also reaching similar conclusions about the shortcomings of socialism and liberation theology, he turned to the ideas of Paulo Freire.

> Money is not basic to helping the poor. It certainly helps but it is not the most important thing. The first step is to help the people to value that which they already have. This I learned from Paulo Freire. Value their history, culture, ideas, leaders, their faith ... give value to what they have. When this happens a person is going to have self-esteem.

Even though Paulo Freire's writings were banned in Brazil during the military dictatorship, which lasted until the mid-1980s, smuggled copies of his seminal text, *Pedagogy of the Oppressed* (1968), served as a key point of reference for intellectuals and activists concerned with advancing human security. Working with sugar cane workers in the northeast of Brazil in the early 1960s, a region similar to that of the Jequitinhonha Valley, Freire developed a methodology for enabling poor communities to turn from being objects, "those who are known and acted upon," to subjects, "those who know and act" (Freire 2000: 20). He argued that power was largely reproduced through subjectivities rather than force. And activists who took an elitist approach that was dismissive of the culture, value, perspective, and identities of the poor—the prevalent vantage of the Catholic Church, leftist activists, and conservative modernizers—changed nothing. Despite their intentions, however well meaning, they merely substituted one paternal order for another.

Freire focused his so-called pedagogy of the oppressed on literacy, in part because literacy at that time was required to be able to vote. Many of his disciples advanced his methodology through different means. Frei Xico, for one, focused on excavating, nurturing, and celebrating popular culture. Rather than using literacy campaigns as a tool for transforming subjectivities and advancing human security, Freire's approach, he emphasized the culture of the people and most especially popular religion as a tool for "helping the people to value what they already have."

One of the first concrete steps taken in this direction began in the shower. As there are no ceilings in most homes in the Jequitinhonha Valley, sound carries readily from one room to the next. While bathing, Dona Fila, the cook for the parochial house where Frei Xico lived, would sing while preparing meals. She sang the songs that the people had often sung while carrying out their daily chores. Listening to them as he bathed, he was moved by their beauty. These songs inspired him to establish Trovadores do Vale (Troubadours of the Valley), a choir that performed the songs of the people of the valley.

The members of the choir, encumbered as they were with a kind of internalized colonialism described by Frantz Fanon (1952) in North Africa, were initially reluctant to perform the songs of o povo. Peoples' feelings of inferiority and inadequacy were reflected and intertwined with how they saw their own culture. According to Frei Xico they would say, "Ah no, this is not beautiful, no, we are not going to sing this, no." Dona Fila herself considered them "*bobagem*" (foolish). Frei Xico recalled that "they wanted to perform the songs that they heard on the radio. They were embarrassed and ashamed of their own culture. And when the choir eventually appeared on TV, the director of the bank and hospital," the descendants of the colonels, or what the people refer to as "*os grandes*" (the Big Ones) "reacted badly." They interpreted these shows as yet another way of signifying the Jequitinhonha Valley's lack of modernity, its backwardness. According to Frei Xico, there was the general mentality that "this culture didn't have any value." However as this cultural movement grew and more outsiders affirmed their music, "the people," recalls Frei Xico, "began to believe and have confidence in their culture and themselves."

The Folklorists

Perhaps the most influential person to be affected by the Freireian inspired embrace of popular culture was Maria Lira Marques. Lira, a woman of African and indigenous descent, was born in Araçuaí in 1945 and was raised by her mother, a washerwoman. At the invitation of a friend, she attended one of the first rehearsals for the Trovadores do Vale.

> At the first choir rehearsal that I attended, I saw myself in everything that was happening. They sang the "cantos de roda," the "batuques," and these songs I knew from home. My mother would sing them when she was ironing

clothes, and working around the house. ... So it was something that I knew intimately. I just didn't understand that it had value. That day I came running back home. I was so happy. I said, "Mom, there at the church ... you should see ... everything that they sing are songs that you know. ..." And she said to me "You look like a wild cow!" All the times that she remembered that moment, she said, "You arrived just like a wild cow!"

Lira was so excited, she explains, because for the first time in her life her culture, the music of her mother and her neighbors, was being affirmed. Perhaps most importantly it was being validated within the church, an institution of high regard in the Jequitinhonha Valley. The fact that a friar within the Catholic Church, who was a European white man, saw the beauty in this music, helped to legitimize it in the eyes of the people like Lira, who asserted that "it changed my sensibilities."

Almost immediately, she became insatiably curious about popular culture. She would pester her mother and others to sing as many songs are they knew. As she recalls, Frei Xico perceived this awakened passion and invited her to participate in the choir as both a performer and researcher.

I went to meet the people, and ... I asked them "What is the lullaby that you know? The work songs?" They passed them along to me, and sometimes they weren't aware of the value that these songs had. Sometimes they were ashamed to teach them to me. I'd challenge them: "The priest sings this. We are singing this. This has value!" After I began challenging them and showing them the importance and value of these songs, they would give me more [songs]. I went about copying them down. When I had filled my notebook, I would go with a recorder saying "Sing this, sing that" and they would sing it all. For me this wasn't difficult, as I'm "povo" [one of the people]. For me this was very easy. I began to invite Frei Xico to come with me. ... He began to go with me to meet the people and visit them in their homes. And so the research continued growing like this and he told me, "Oh, Lira, you really know what it is that we are doing." And he began to give me books to read. ... He gave me Câmera Cascudo, Renato de Almeida, folklorists. And ... like this, the research took shape. Eventually we reviewed everything that we had done and we chose the most beautiful songs to record. This was our first disk, which is called *Ainda bem que eu cheguei* [*It's Good That I Arrived*].

Together they became a formidable research team. They shared a sense of calling with respect to popular culture and its documentation. Moreover they complemented one another exceptionally well. Frei Xico had formal training, knowledge of and access to libraries and other research materials, and an authority that came with being a friar, white, European, and male (Warren 2000). Lira, as she notes, brought an insider's perspective. This afforded an access to popular culture and its meaning that would have been difficult, if not impossible, for Frei Xico to ever develop alone. Lira also, according to Frei Xico, brought to the table a different set of sensibilities:

> Lira is very different than me. When we pass a place with homeless children, she cries. She is touched by the differences. I'm thinking of my nephews, she'd say. Or when we passed an MST (*Movimento Sem Terra* or the Movement of the Landless) encampment, she gets very emotional. I also think it's wrong but she reacts differently than me to facts. This favored our relationship immensely.

Importantly Frei Xico was able to avoid much of the elitism and paternalism that so often emerges when the power imbalance is so skewed, especially in a context such as Brazil. They had to become equals. Not equals in the sense of being equivalently situated vis-à-vis the myriad axes of power but equals in terms of respect and reciprocation. Frei Xico put it this way:

> We discovered that we were friends. To be friends you have to be equals. It wasn't simply a story of Lira helping me, but me also helping Lira. So it was a process. ... For example, I would pick out anthropology books and ask her to read them. She'd mark the whole book up. I'd think, why did she think that this part was so interesting? Lira Marques, black woman, from the Jequitinhonha Valley, seven years of schooling ... and I'd think, "Why the hell didn't I see that?!"

Thus rather than fashioning himself as the teacher, the expert who was there to help the poor whom he pitied, he understood that he too was a student who had as much, if not more, to learn. This posture was evidenced repeatedly. For example, in reflecting back on the ceremony he stumbled upon late at night during Holy Week, he told me that he learned about faith from the people there. Here were people much less fortunate than himself and yet they had a much deeper faith in God than he had. Or note his advice about collaboration with o povo:

> The plans that o povo have to improve the country ... they will be revised, rethought. I can't say what will happen; what those plans should be. It's o povo who will decide. They will choose the path forward. One has to have patience. One cannot intervene and say "Now you're going to do this!"

These are not the words of someone who sees the people as unenlightened objects who must be sheparded in a predetermined direction. As he notes, the path forward is open and not for him to decide. It was this perspective that helped him and Lira to become comrades.

And so Lira and Frei Xico documented seemingly every aspect of popular culture: culinary traditions, burial rituals, oral histories, knowledge about the fauna and wildlife, methods of child rearing, construction and agricultural techniques, iron and leather work, and so on. Their obsession with the quotidian produced copious volumes of recordings and field notes that had to be organized in some fashion. It was Lira who pushed for a deeper consideration of popular religion, which then became the analytical framework for ordering their data.

> I woke up a curiosity in Frei Xico. ... Without asking him, I began collecting ... prayers. The prayers against one's enemy, to get rid of a snake in the bush, for rain. ... This all scared him. But he didn't tell me at that time. ... He only told me this many years later. If he had told me then his fears, it could have embarrassed me. I was very timid. So he didn't tell me for fear I would stop. He read what I collected and began reflecting. He began to see their value and wanted to understand more. What protects these people are their prayers. For someone who has resources, they go immediately to the doctor. However for someone who doesn't have money ... they seek out those resources that they have in order to defend themselves, right? So it was a vast work, documenting the wisdom of the people. We even researched at the cemetery, getting those sayings that they have on the tombs. For example, "Little with God is a lot, a lot without God is nothing." Sometimes as a child we wouldn't have enough to eat. My mother would say, "My daughter, little with God is a lot, a lot without God is nothing." She was trying to give meaning to our hunger. She was saying that we should be content in the little that we have because in the future we won't be hungry. ... This speaks a lot about faith, right? ... And so we began to see how everything is linked. The homemade teas, the charms and the prayers, everything is linked together. This [insight] gave birth to the dictionary on popular religion.

Thanks to Lira's initiative, they began to see how, as Frei Xico puts it, "religious life is not separate from the life of the people, it is entwined with it." And this understanding ultimately led Frei Xico to organize the 240 cassette tapes of recordings, 2,000 slides, and 5,000 pages of ethnographic notes as an encyclopedia on popular religion in Brazil. This 2,000-page book, which took eighteen years to complete, is, according to Frei Xico, the first encyclopedia about popular religion in the world.

The Subjects of History

The power of the colonels was sustained partially through the use of patronage and *jagunços* (hired assassins). Yet the biggest barrier to change is rarely force or other material constraints but rather people's consciousness. This, of course, has been the conclusion of many of the great social analysts of the twentieth century such as Gramsci, Foucault, Bourdieu, Said, Fanon, and Freire. And so it is no coincidence that as Lira's and others' sensibilities were altered by the burgeoning cultural movement, so too was political power.

In the late 1970s the democratization movement within Brazil began gaining traction. It was advanced in part by a 1979 amnesty law, which allowed intellectuals and activists in exile to return to Brazil. A rejuvenated labor movement energized by Luiz Inácio Lula da Silva, who led a series of successful strikes in the industrial ABC district of São Paulo, also pushed it forward. These confluences led to the establishment of an anti-Leninist leftist labor party that was outside the control of the state. The Workers Party (PT—Partido dos Trabalhadores) was legally recognized in 1982, and Lula quickly emerged as its leader. Eventually, in 2002, this former shoeshine boy from northeastern Brazil, with little formal education, would become president of the republic.

It was during this transition period, when the PT was struggling to achieve legal status at the federal level, that Lira set out to establish the PT in the land of the colonels. She became the first president of the PT in Araçuaí because, according to her, "nobody else wanted to be president." Working behind the scenes, she orchestrated, managed, and carried out the labor-intensive and often tedious work of administering the requisite paperwork, networking, producing and distributing an underground newspaper (*Portador*), and "conscientizing" the people.[4]

She was, of course, ideally situated to build the Workers' Party. As a folklorist, she was already meeting regularly with hundreds of people to record their kernels of wisdom. This combined with the fact that she was one of the people allowed her to move seamlessly among o povo. Perhaps better than anyone else, she intimately knew their troubles, philosophies, art, and dialect. She was also very unassuming. She herself says that she is not a gifted public speaker. Her appearance and background as a short, black woman who sang songs with the friar, documented the culture of the "insignificant, little" people, and was not on the surface a rabble rouser easily led her to be underestimated as a serious political threat. Finally, she brought a different awareness, one less marked by patronage and a negative self-imagery and more by an understanding of one's agency. This was thanks, at least in part, to her involvement with Frei Xico and the larger cultural movement they had helped to birth.

The initial group of party members consisted exclusively of o povo. Indeed Lira was very concerned that one of os grandes would try to enter the party.

> I was afraid that maybe someone wealthy, maybe a doctor, would want to enter [the party]. I wanted to restrict the party due to my fear that they would take the party out of our hands. They have the power to do this. The people who were participating in the party were all very poor…very poor and many of them were illiterate. Os grandes with their sweet talk … with the formal education and credentials that they have … I was so afraid of them taking over the party. I didn't believe that they would enter for the good of the party. I was always worried that they would take the party from us.

During the first election in which the PT ran a candidate, they lost. After a few more years of grassroots work and deepening the cultural movement, the party was able to elect one of their candidates, Manuel Pinheiro, to the city council. Lira remembers that os grandes did everything that they could to co-opt him.

> The second time we were able to elect Manuel but he suffered the wounds of Christ. He was the only member from the PT and the others were all of opposing parties. … Every project that was brought up [by the PT] wasn't approved. Nothing was approved because he was only one person [on the city council]. And when the meeting was over, they kept Manuel there, looking for a way of getting Manuel into the mayor's office to try to convince him into changing his party affiliation. He suffered a great deal. He'd often arrive in my house so confused. That pressure that they put on him to leave the party. … . We counseled him, advised him not to leave. They tried to get him to change sides, they offered him money, but God helped us and he stayed with the party.

A pivotal moment for the party happened when Lula, the national leader of the Workers' Party and presidential candidate at the time, was going to visit Araçuaí. Permits were required and Lira, as the president of the PT, had to secure them:

> I ended up going to see the chief of police, with the vice-president. We arrived at the police station … and then he said to me, "Well, Maria, Lula's coming here, right?" and I said "Yes, sir." with a fear that I can't describe. "Maria, neither you nor Lula will change the situation in Brazil. Brazil will only get worse." And then he began to lecture us. We didn't say

anything, only he spoke. He spoke of Russia, of Japan, ... and I just kept nodding. And then he asked me, "Oh, Maria, do you read the Bible?" and I said, "Sometimes I read it." "Ah, it is a strong book; my most powerful weapon." ... And then he started to speak about the revolutionaries in the Bible and he started to insult the church [descer o pau na igreja]. He spoke badly about the church, priests, nuns, and then said again that the most powerful weapon he had was the Bible. After this he lectured us about Getúlio Vargas, Jango, Jânio Quadros. ... Mr. Sartega began to speak about these [former Brazilian presidents]. He went on and on about them. It seemed like he wanted to get us to open our mouths, but we didn't say a word. We kept our mouths shut as we were trained. ... I thought I'm not going to say anything, let him make a fool out of himself. And then he said, "Well, Maria, I am a very experienced man, and in the past the people ate beans and potatoes, but they ate them contentedly. Today they eat meat, rice and beans and are unsatisfied." I stayed quiet. We kept silent. Then he told me, "What do you do, Maria?" And I said, "I'm an artisan." He wrote this down and asked for my parents' names. "You, sir, over there, what do you do?" And Mr. Paiado said, "Me, I lived in the country, I lived as an *aggregado*, I moved to the city, and today I live as a *biscate* (handyman). As I'm old, I can't bear hard work anymore, I live more as a handyman. I clean people's backyards." He said "Well, Maria, now your names are going to the Secretary of Public Security." And I was afraid but I didn't show it, and I didn't say a word. I let him talk. And after he said, "Well, Maria, tomorrow you can come pick up the permit. You can come here to pick up the permit." This gave me such joy. I asked myself "Is this really going to happen?" And that was it. "Go with God, Maria," and I said, "Amen, go with God as well" [laughs]. And we went out, and when we got outside, I gave thanks to God as it seemed like all the weight of the world had been lifted from my shoulders.

This interaction demonstrates the role of consciousness and change. The threats of violence or sanctions were in the air and hence Lira's fear. But in all the interviews with Lira and other activists during this time, no one mentioned a killing, beating, or imprisonment. No doubt the memories of physical retaliation were fresh in peoples' minds, especially in light of the recent history of slavery and the ongoing neoslave relationships, and so even their implicit suggestion must have struck fear in the hearts of most. However what this incident helps to illustrate is that what ultimately held people in check was an intimidation anchored in their inferior status as o povo, an inferiority that was internalized. The order of the colonels rested on a culture in which individuals like Lira were made to feel small, unintelligent, unworthy, and uncomfortable. Thus, as long as Lira performed the obsequious, docile subaltern, the chief was reassured. But had it not been a performance—had Lira seen herself as the descendant of inferior races, a member of a worthless community, then she would have never set foot in that office, let alone have organized a political party to challenge the authority of "the Big Ones." His condescending, patronizing lecture would likely have awakened all her insecurities about being a little, insignificant person and led her to back down. And so it was a cultural framework, a symbolic order, on which power was anchored. And as the cultural movement, built as it was in the affirmation of popular religion, began to undermine this interpretative order, as people began to see the value of their culture and themselves, colonelism became unhinged.

Postrevolutionary Araçuaí

Remarkably, Lira helped to build a party that, in 1995, swept os grandes out of power. Maria do Carmo Ferreira da Silva or Cacá (b. 1947) who had come to Araçuaí from Belo Horizonte as a student through Project Rondon,[5] was elected mayor. In the land of the colonels, it is no exaggeration to call the election of a petite black woman, who was also a PT candidate, a revolutionary change.

Cacá's administration instituted a number of changes such as participatory budgeting and budget transparency. To this end, councils, which were made up of local experts and interested citizens, were set up to oversee various government ministries. The councils set priorities and helped to ensure that public monies were used appropriately. In the past, one individual or family dominated all the ministries of government with little or no transparency or oversight. The establishment of these councils reduced corruption dramatically, and consequently, public services, such as health care, were delivered more efficiently, cost-effectively, and widely. Moreover this kind of inclusion of o povo in the governing process helped to forge, at least according to the local scholar and activist Geralda Chaves Soares (b. 1945 to a small, white landholder in the neighboring town of Itinga), a different idea of citizenship:

> Before one just elected a group and put them there like a saint. It was like selecting a saint, put him there on the altar and then simply believe that he'll make miracles. Now it's different. We feel more responsible for life here. Things have become more collective. We see that a state by itself doesn't work. [Without sustained engagement] you end up doing the same foolishness.

The political victory of Cacá gave the cultural movement an institutional basis and support that led to an explosion of civil society. For example, incensed by the poor performance of the public schools, Cacá invited a nongovernmental organization, the Center for Popular Culture and Development (CPCD), to Araçuaí to help improve the quality of education. In a highly unusual move, CPCD took over as the local secretary of education in 2003. Significant efforts were then made to mobilize the entire community to participate via parental associations, community agents, book follies (modeled after the traditional Christmas season celebration, Folía de Reis), and a large number of circle discussions. This methodology was central to CPCD's teaching philosophy, which its founder and president, Sebastião Rocha (b. 1948), an anthropologist of African descent, developed through his fieldwork in Mozambique. CPCD has also created a successful after-school program, Ser Criança. The curriculum is play-based, anchored in the culture of o povo, and aims to foster a positive association with learning. CPCD has also set up a trade school, o Fabriqueta, for teenagers. Not only do they learn administrative skills, but they develop an expertise in local arts: furniture making, painting, iron work, clothing design, and so on.

Since coming to Araçuaí, CPCD has launched a development program called Sustainable Araçuaí. As part of this program, it introduced a permaculture farm in the region in an attempt to advance sustainable agricultural practices that are viable in an arid climate and also to counter the environmental devastation the region has suffered during the past two hundred years. This model has been picked up by the local indigenous communities, three of which, the Pankararu, Pataxó, and Aranã, expanded in the wake of Cacá's election. Two of these communities have their own reservations and have strong linkages with a myriad of other social movements. A *quilombo* community,[6] the Bau, has achieved federal recognition. It was supported in this legal process by Cacá's administration, indigenous leaders, and the urban black movement. This urban black movement, it should be added, owes a debt to Frei Xico, who played an important role in rejuvenating what is now one of the city's central cultural events: the Festival of the Rosary. This festival pays homage to the Bantu ancestors from whom many Brazilians descend. It is also a day in which the racial order is reversed; blacks can honor their royalty and assert their dignity.

The Trovadores do Vale is now one of eight choirs in the region. CPCD was involved in setting up a Children of Araçuaí choir that has been involved in major productions with premiere artists like Milton Nascimento. It has used its proceeds to build a cinema where young people can learn filmmaking and have a high-quality cinematic experience for free. Local artists have gained more recognition; their work is showcased in major museums and attracts visitors from afar. Additionally, there are now various venues such as Labyrinth, Ortelão, and Luz da Lua for individuals involved in this cultural movement to meet, share their ideas, present their art, and introduce them to artists and ideas from outside the region.

Geralda Soares described this burgeoning civil society as comparable to an unstoppable river.

> It's like a river. It doesn't work if you try to control it. The river runs alone. When there's an obstacle, an island or rock, the river goes over it or around it. If it's too big, it just goes around it. Look at this region today. With so many struggles ... I see that the people continue moving forward. Today with so many political debates and battles, with all the difficulties people face, we have the Labyrinth cultural center. It is a cultural reference point for organizations, news, music ... a place where people can meet. Luz da Lua (Moonlight) ... where you can see a good film. You can get together to watch soccer games at Ortelão. Cinema de Meninos Araçuaí ... what a beautiful thing, teams of youth producing documentaries. One also sees artists like Lira who everyday gain more recognition and achieve greater perfection. The indigenous people who have such rich art using the seeds from the region. They have taken the seeds from a common plant used to feed the cattle in the region and make beautiful bags from it. They use feathers and other things from the region. There is pottery and wood working, ... This movement is like a river. It keeps going. If a big obstacle gets in its way, it will continue.

Impressive as these changes have been, Frei Xico believes that the biggest accomplishment that the political victory ushered in has been with respect to peoples' sense of their agency as history makers. The Workers' Party in Araçuaí "allowed people to see that there were other options. It helped o povo to realize that they could be in charge. This became the greatest change during this process. Eventually they came to believe this."

In outlining the changes, one can be left with an overly positive image of the present. Despite CPCD's success in improving education, in which "marked improvements were found in children's performance" (2009), the mayor who took over after Cacá, José Antonio Martins, did not renew the agreement with CPCD. This is in part due to the fact that the culture of patronage is still very strong, if not dominate, in the region. Lira notes:

> When one compares it to how it was, when nobody had anything, one sees that there is a lot more space opened up. The children are more alive, they are attending meetings of the movements, we are learning, organizing. ... What still is a challenge is the system of "favors." A rich person doesn't owe anyone "favors." But the poor. ... There's still lots of people who need "favors." To go to the doctor, for example. If you have money you just get

in a plane and fly to the doctor in Belo Horizonte. It's different for poor people. This dynamic of favors is horrible. This system of favors and obligations leaves one imprisoned. People become dependent on those with power. It's all because of poverty. A person with money conquers everything. They don't need "favors."

Most agree that one of the largest challenges continues to be poverty and jobs. This was why CPCD launched the Sustainable Araçuaí project with the aim of creating an economy in which people were able to earn a living wage in the valley. Presently a large number of men, approximately70 percent of the young men in the region, are migratory workers. They spend nine months of the year working in near slave-like conditions as sugarcane workers in São Paulo. This puts tremendous strains on families. This is how one of the workers described the situation:

My name is Antonio. I'm thirty-nine. I had to leave to work. I left with my two brothers. We went to São Paulo to cut sugarcane. … It was necessary because there is little work here. We earn too little. As many here say, slavery ended but only if you put "slavery" in quotation marks. Many work earning only $8 a day. This doesn't pay for anything especially if one has a large family. So people go to cut sugarcane in order to earn more money. I worked fifteen years cutting sugarcane. The first time I went was in 1987 with my dad. That's where I learned to cut sugarcane. … It's hard work. One works from four in the morning until six in the evening. The more you cut, the more you earn. The more you work, the more you earn. Since I had little formal education, this was really the only option available. Here one works from seven in the morning until six at night earning $8 or less. I would cut more than one thousand meters of sugarcane each day. The places I worked only employed the best cutters. At the minimum one had to cut ten thousand kilos a day or ten tons. I would cut thirty-three tons a day between March and November including Saturdays and Sundays. That's why I was called "Champion." I would earn up to seven minimum salaries (about $2,000 per month). … It's awful to spend eight or nine months away from one's family. One's whole family is here. It's awful. But it's the only option we have.

The elitism that still saturates Brazilian society does not allow for a sustainable development model nationally or in locals like Araçuaí. Even most policymakers within the Workers' Party are attracted to the grand development projects, such as dam construction, and back monocultural agricultural production. Indeed the basis of the recent economic boom in Brazil is driven by commodity exports rather than manufacturing and increased productivity. This traditional mode of production has roots in the colonial period and has rarely left o povo any better off. Ultimately these practices are anchored in a perception that o povo and the lands that they inhabit have little or no strengths to build on. The eucalyptus plantations, which are encroaching on the Jequitinhonha Valley, are only politically feasible if the dominate perception is that the valley is largely a wasteland. How else does one explain a development strategy that only further devastates the environment and displaces o povo who reside there? Such a project for economic growth would be viewed as what it is, asset stripping. And so, one sees that there is still a great deal of cultural works that needs to take place before a viable development strategy can be realized: one that will produce jobs that will enable people to stay in the region.

Conclusions

Some of the theoretical and policy insights for those concerned with advancing human security that can be gleaned from the experiences in Araçuaí are the following:

First, a blanket dismissal of popular religion is obviously a mistake. It was the excavation and nurturing of popular religion in the Jequitinhonha Valley that helped produce change. Its affirmation did not lead to "the passivity of prayer" but rather helped to turn o povo into subjects. Indeed its embrace proved key to *conscientização*. The valorization and performance of popular religious traditions inspired a transformation in subjectivities. It contributed to the sociopolitical revolution that took place in the Jequitinhonha Valley.

Second, many leftist critics see little space within the contemporary Catholic Church for advancing human security given the purge of liberation theologians that began with the papacy of John Paul II. Frei Xico's experiences challenge this conclusion. He and his work were obviously important contributors to the changes in Jequitinhonha Valley. In interviews with him he underscored how the church consistently supported and appreciated his work. Church leaders encouraged him to write his ideas and present his research. They published two of his books as "official books." He was given several years' sabbatical to pursue his research. And he was never pressured into becoming a priest even though priests were in high demand. The biggest amount of pushback he encountered was from a few colleagues:

> There were a few colleagues that called me "Crazy Xico" (*Xico Doido*). And I didn't care if amongst themselves they called me crazy. I understood why they called me Xico Doido because I do so many things differently

than other priests. I embraced this identity. I created a clown that I take with me to any event that I attend. Even sometimes I'll take it to mass but only in those contexts where the people know me or have known me well for some time and so have stopped laughing. They don't even notice the clown anymore. It's better that they call me Xico Doido than that guy who thinks he knows better than anyone else. And so Xico Doido, the court jester, the critic standing next to those who have power, that's who I want to be. The one who thinks. That's what I want to be.

The third lesson is related to global engagement. It is noteworthy that many of the agents of change, Frei Xico, Mayor Cacá, and the anthropologist, Tião Rocha, were not from Araçuaí. What allowed them to be successful protagonists for advancing human security was their ability to take on the horizontal role of collaborators rather than that of the didactic expert who had already determined what the truth was and how it was achieved. Another factor was linked, ironically, to the hierarchies that they were trying to undermine. As outsiders who signified sophistication, erudition, and intelligence, largely because of their links to putatively more modern geographies such as São Paulo, Belo Horizonte, or the Netherlands, their attention mattered more. Their affirmation carried a great deal of weight in confirming the value of local culture and peoples. I was reminded of this during an interview I conducted with Antonio, the Bau migrant worker quoted earlier. At the end of our thirty-minute interview, Antonio observed:

> Sometimes one visit gives us strength. Your visit today is very important for us. It strengthens us. It's like giving us a plate of food. You're not just filming us. You're incentivizing us and helping us to grow, to have a deeper understanding. Now if someone asks if I've already spoken with an American, I can now say yes.

It was this kind of validation by outsiders like me, outsiders who embodied civilization, modernity, and development, that helped to spark a revolution. Hopefully, this chapter will help to sensitize fellow cosmopolitan citizens to the fact that global engagement, especially that which is guided by the Freirian tradition of collaboration, humility, and mutual respect, can be a potent means for advancing human security.

Notes

Jonathan Warren is chair of the Center for Brazilian Studies and associate professor of international studies at the University of Washington, Seattle. He has written extensively on racial identity formations and antiracism. Some of his publications include *Racing Research, Researching Race: Methodological Dilemmas in Critical Racial Studies* (New York University Press, 2000) and *Racial Revolutions: Antiracism and Indian Resurgence in Brazil* (Duke University Press, 2001). His latest project is a comparative study of culture and development in Brazil and Vietnam, titled *Cultures of Development: Vietnamese and Brazilian Modernities Compared*.

The author notes: I am indebted to far more individuals than I can thank here. However, I would like to give a special note of appreciation to Geralda Soares, Margaret Griesse, Angelica and Scott Macklin, Jim Wellman, Sanjeev Khagram, Tony Lucero, Paulette Thompson, and my family, ba ngoai Michelle, Kiên, and Nghĩa Warren.

1. Chagas is a tropical parasitic disease transmitted to humans and other mammals by hematophagic insects of the subfamily *Triatominae* (family *Reduviidae*). In the early, acute stage, symptoms are mild and usually produce no more than local swelling at the site of infection. The initial acute phase is responsive to antiparasitic treatments, with 60–90 percent cure rates. After four to eight weeks, individuals with active infections enter the chronic phase of Chagas disease, which is asymptomatic for 60–80 percent of infected individuals. Twenty to forty percent of chronically infected individuals eventually develop life-threatening heart and digestive system disorders.

2. Noble titles were largely unattainable by local elites.

3. I have been conducting ethnographic research in Araçuaí since 1995. After an initial research period of one year, I have returned at least once every two years for several weeks to a month at a time. The interviews with Frei Xico, Lira Marques, Geralda Soares, and others quoted in this chapter took place in either July 2009 or November 2010. I conducted the interviews in Portuguese, in collaboration with Angelica Macklin. The interviews are to be included as part of a documentary film project, focusing on culture, political change, and development in the Jequitinhonha Valley.

4. *Conscientização* is a term Friere borrowed from Frantz Fanon (*conscienciser*) and popularized both in Brazil and abroad. Arlene Goldbard (2006) defines "conscientization as an ongoing process by which a learner moves toward critical consciousness. This process is the heart of liberatory education. It differs from 'consciousness raising' in that the latter may involve transmission of preselected knowledge. Conscientization means breaking through prevailing mythologies to reach new levels of awareness—in particular, awareness of oppression, being an 'object' of others' will rather than a self-determining 'subject.' The process of conscientization involves identifying contradictions in experience through dialogue and becoming part of the process of changing the world."

5. Project Rondon was a program set up by the military regime in the 1970s. It focused on bringing college students, at least 90 percent of whom were white and from mid-

dle- and upper-class families, from the major urban centers to poor, rural areas like Araçuaí. The hope was that these partnerships would help these regions to modernize, develop, and advance their human security. Many also hoped that the program would build a greater sense of national unity and defuse some of the radical student movements mobilized against the military regime.

6. *Quilombos* originally referred to fugitive slave communities that were numerous in Brazil during slavery. The biggest and most famous one was Palmares (1605–1694), which was larger, territorially, than most European countries. Six Portuguese expeditions tried to conquer this republic of approximately eleven thousand inhabitants. Eventually it was defeated by an army organized by the governor of Pernambuco, Pedro Almeida. The term "quilombos," today refers to black communities that are culturally distinct in certain respects from mainstream Brazil. Quilombos are constitutionally entitled to land, schools, and cultural protection. There are presently several thousand quilombos in Brazil (Arruti 2006).

9

Interrogating Human Security and Religion in Guatemala

C. Mathews Samson

While evangelical growth might be Latin America's biggest social movement, it's wise not to exaggerate its importance. Fervent believers in miracles, it makes sense that some evangelicals guarantee no less than a radical transformation of the region. But social change requires much more than a religious transformation. If the underlying socio-economic conditions stay the same, the same social ills will remain.

JOSÉ OROZCO, "Latin America: Evangelical Christianity Moves the Masses"

ON DECEMBER 29, 2011, Guatemala marked its fifteenth year since the definitive 1996 ("Firme y Duradero") peace accord was signed. The signing of this accord brought an end to a thirty-six year civil conflict that caused some two hundred thousand deaths and the displacement of as many as 1.5 million people. By many measures, things have not gone particularly well in the intervening years. Despite four peaceful transfers of power in presidential elections, discourse of a "culture of violence" or a "culture of impunity" persists in public pronouncements regarding citizen well-being, and many people still lack access to employment, education, and health care. Guatemala has one of the highest murder rates in the Western Hemisphere (forty-eight per hundred thousand inhabitants in 2008 as compared to Mexico's rate of fourteen),[1] and the daily struggle against violence, combined with an unresponsive judicial system, creates a sense of insecurity that threatens human welfare both physically and psychologically.

Some analysts propose that Guatemala is a failed state, and in fact, the country's lack of security continues to create problems for governance and democratic consolidation. Perhaps the most vivid example of this is the "state of siege" that President Alvaro Colom imposed in late 2010 and early 2011 in response to violence committed by the Mexico-based Zeta drug cartel. The sight of a center-left government calling out the troops against its own population in a nation with Guatemala's history of military aggression raises significant human rights concerns. The nexus between violence and security is symptomatic of a host of threats to societal cohesion and bodily integrity that includes other issues such as gang violence and feminicide (*feminicidio*) that have been the subject of much controversy in recent years (Thale and Falkenburger 2006; Sanford and Lincoln 2010). Other observers note that sectors of Guatemala City have become gated communities in a place where there are said to be more private security guards than police.[2]

In the face of the apocalyptic language about the current state of affairs in Guatemala (Shifter 2011), it is significant that the term "failed state" does not remain unchallenged.[3] Some of the resistance to the "failed state" designation comes from segments of civil society (nonstate actors) in responding to the insecure political and social scenario. This chapter examines the potential contribution of religion, particularly Pentecostal Protestantism, to ameliorating human security problems in Guatemala. The definition of human security used in this volume has three components: a concern with human physical well-being, a juridical aspect that includes human rights, and a more general "culturally conditioned" component related to the need for "freedom, self-expression, and human autonomy." An ethnographic reading of the Guatemalan context demonstrates that insecurity poses threats to the populace both psychologically and physically. I argue that, in the face of such threats to well-being, the burgeoning Pentecostal presence plays an ambiguous role in contributing to human security in postconflict Guatemala. There can be little doubt that Pentecostal communities possess resources that can contribute to the betterment of human welfare, but the direct evidence for major contributions in terms of physical or juridical security is rather thin.[4] In taking such a stance, I am also arguing that the most significant contributions of Pentecostals are made at the community and individual levels rather than in the realm of national social policies and political agendas.

Pentecostal Presence in Contemporary Guatemala

In Guatemala, religion frequently makes the news; in part, this is because the country has one of the highest percentages of evangelicals in Latin America (34 percent of the population). It is not the evangelicals, however, but the Roman Catholic Guatemalan Episcopal Conference (Conferencia Episcopal de Guatemala [CEG]) that consistently acts as a promoter of human security. Evangelical voices are more diffuse and represented most prominently by the Evangelical Alliance (Alianza Evangélica), which was founded by Guatemala's "historical" Protestant churches in the 1930s, as well as by a group of neo-Pentecostal clergy who pastor megachurches in the capital.[5] These pastors, some of whom self-identify as apostles, have typically allied themselves with probusiness agendas while simultaneously promoting a prosperity gospel that links personal salvation to the progress or salvation of the nation (Cantón Delgado 1998: 211–257).[6]

In contrast to the neo-Pentecostals, classical Pentecostal denominations have filled social and religious vacuums in dispersed rural communities and in marginal urban neighborhoodswhere people face constant threats to their physical and emotional well-being. Most residents in these areas live without private security or adequate social services, and they are often forced to confront issues of human security with whatever resources happen to be at hand. Pentecostalism seems more likely to contribute to human security by responding to individual needs and the sense of community identity rather than influencing political or social policy. With regard to the potential Pentecostal contributions to human security in Guatemala, I agree with Pentecostal scholar Bernardo Campos that "it is in the realm of civil society that Pentecostalism will make a key contribution to dictating the future of the region's social system" (1996: 49).

Since the early 1960s, the popularity of Pentecostalism in Guatemala has increased dramatically. According to a survey sponsored by the Pew Forum on Religion and Public Life in 2006, some 85 percent of Guatemalan Protestants are Pentecostal. When both Pentecostal Protestants and charismatic Catholics are included, 60 percent of the population of the country adheres to some version of what the study refers to as "renewalist" religion.[7] Pentecostalism, then, is a crucial component of the growth of Protestantisms that began to receive so much attention in Latin America at the end of the twentieth century. David Stoll's *Is Latin America Turning Protestant?* and David Martin's *Tongues of Fire: The Explosion of Protestantism in Latin America* were both published in 1990. By 1991, the second of Guatemala's two Protestant presidents had entered office and drawn attention to the sea change taking place in the region.

It is crucial to note that both of these presidents had ties to neo-Pentecostal communities and that both left office under suspicion and opprobrium. One of these men, Efraín Ríos Montt (1982–1983), was a Guatemalan general who came to power through a military coup. He was famously associated with a congregation called El Verbo (the Church of the Word). During his tenure in office, the military carried out a scorched earth policy, and he has since been accused of genocide. The other, Jorge Serrano Elías (1991–1993), was associated with the El Shaddai congregation. He fled the country after an unsuccessful self-coup (*autogolpe*) in 1993 that would have dissolved Congress and left him as the sole governing authority. Ríos Montt continues to live in Guatemala and has had a long political career, including a period as the president of Guatemala's Congress and an unsuccessful run for the presidency in 2003. Serrano Elías lives in exile in Panama and has been accused of various forms of corruption but has thus far evaded prosecution. The actual and symbolic presence of these two men on Guatemala's political stage is important because it gave further impetus to the preoccupation with Protestant growth in Latin America during this period. There have also been many prominent evangelicals in the Guatemalan Congress, but they typically do not run on religious platforms. Moreover, several attempts at forming political parties based on evangelical ideals or "biblical principles" have garnered little support in elections since the end of the war (Samson 2008). The efficacy of such parties was tested again in the national elections of 2011 when the longtime pastor of the neo-Pentecostal El Shaddai congregation, Harold Caballeros, made a bid for the presidency under the banner of a party called VIVA (Vision con Valores—Vision with Values), a party he founded for the 2007 elections before he was prohibited from running for missing a registration deadline.

Although some scholars have studied the role of evangelical contributions in Latin American transitions to democracy in the late 1990s (see Gaskill 1997; Steigenga 2001; Freston 2008), no specific contributions of evangelical religion to human security have been discussed. Only a few studies have examined the impact of what might be called progressive Protestantism or Pentecostalism, demonstrating that they have been active in social movements and the protection of human rights. Other studies have considered conversion and the importance of Pentecostal social networks. In general terms, studies of Pentecostalism continue to focus more on issues of internal organization, congregational worship styles, and the impact of Pentecostalism on particular groups such as women.[8]

The ethnographic approach employed here examines Pentecostal practices both at the congregational level and within the context of Guatemalan security concerns. Donald Miller (2007: 443) has suggested that Pentecostalism can become "the engine of hope, which offers people purpose in the face of despairing prospects." There is truth in this statement, and one might even go so far as to argue that Pentecostal forms of worship and practice are responses to globalization, modernization, and concomitant threats to security. For Pentecostals, however, the experience of the Spirit is real and holds out the possibility for transformation, a term that includes both healing (*sanación*) and liberation (*liberación*). The implications of this emphasis on personal empowerment need to be delineated in order to gain a more complete understanding of Pentecostal contributions to human security.

Religious Pluralism and Human Security in Guatemala

Although the essay focuses primarily on Pentecostalism at the local level, it is important to take note of Guatemala's complex religious landscape—beyond the growth of the various Protestantisms that have put an end to the Catholic religious monopoly (Chesnut 2003). In Guatemala, there is also a third force of religious activism growing out of the Maya cosmovision, often referred to as *costumbre* (custom). Charles Reilly argues that all three streams of religion— Catholic, Protestant, and Maya—have contributed to bettering human security in postconflict Guatemala:

> The Catholic Church does play a huge role in providing social services, education, and health care that, especially in rural regions, would be otherwise lacking. Evangelical churches grew rapidly over several recent decades, especially in the cities, forging close community cohesion, increasing their social services, and, sometimes, political involvement. At the "high church" level of Catholic hierarchy, ecumenical and Evangelical confederation, collaboration is frequent. True, at the village level, deafening decibels of competing religious microphones may prevail on Sunday morning, but on balance, both at the national and local level, the churches have helped build peace. Especially among Mayans, religious practice has positively reinforced the identity of a people who had only experienced discrimination (2009: 44).

This is an expansive view that reflects the depth of religious and social pluralism in contemporary Guatemala as well as the tension between these groups.

On the Catholic side, the advocacy of the Catholic bishops for social justice during the last two decades of the war and in the postconflict period has been the most visible sign of religious engagement with Guatemalan society. This engagement is consistent with the religious dominance of the church since the colonial period, and it represents the continued cultural influence of Catholicism in the present.[9] Even so, the Catholic hierarchy has had a mixed record. Under the leadership of Archbishops Mariano Rossell y Arellano (1939–1964) and Mario Casariego (1964–1983), the official church often took conservative positions such as supporting the coup that brought an end to Guatemala's "democratic spring" in 1954 or resisting the reforms of Vatican II and other progressive social agendas. Individual Catholics, particularly those associated with either Catholic Action or other progressive catechist movements within the church, were persecuted greatly during the period from 1978 to 1983, the period referred to as "*la violencia.*" On the other hand, beginning with the period of the devastating earthquake of February 1976, segments of the church, including the CEG, spoke out against Guatemala's inequitable social structure and oppressive political environment, largely through a series of pastoral letters in the late 1970s through the early 1990s.[10] The bishops also played a crucial mediating role in the process that would result in the signing of the final peace accord.

After the signing of the accord, the Archdiocese of Guatemala's Human Rights Office established the Recovery of Historical Memory Project, one of two truth commissions formed following the end of the Guatemalan conflict (Proyecto Interdiocesano 1999). Bishop Juan Gerardi, who had promoted the commission and presided over the release of the final report in Guatemala's Metropolitan Cathedral, was bludgeoned to death in the garage of his residence two days later on April 28, 1998 (Jonas 2000: 62).[11]

In the mid-2000s, Bishop Álvaro Ramazzini received death threats for supporting indigenous communities in their struggle against the establishment of a gold mine in the western highlands. Under his leadership in 2007, the Diocese of San Marcos formed the Pastoral Commission on Peace and Ecology. In addition to mining issues, Ramazzini has also been active in various land rights issues, challenging Guatemala's skewed agrarian tenure system that keeps the most fertile lands in the hands of a relatively small proportion of the population.

The emphasis placed on the environment and social justice concerns in the highlands clearly demonstrates the Catholic Church's concern for a range of human security issues. The CEG also holds regular press conferences to comment on issues such as the situation of violence in the country or concerns relevant to the church's understanding of the role of the family in society. Some of these stances are contentious, as when the church aligned with certain evangelical leaders in the late 1990s to oppose the UN-sponsored Children and Youth Code because of its supposed intent to do away with parental authority (*patria potestad*) over their children (Samson 2008: 77–81). Nevertheless, participation in such public debate contributes to the democratic processes that are necessary for the advancement of human security.

Approximately half of the Guatemalan population belongs to one of the twenty-two Maya language communities that have been largely excluded from access to political and social power during what activists often call the "five hundred years of conquest." One analyst, writing about the role of the Maya Movement in Guatemala, notes that the recovery (*reivindicación*) of Maya spirituality is a key component of the movement, "but what is important is how the element of inclusion [in society] is conceived within this process of transformation as an elemental motivator of change, respect, and the search for equilibrium and harmony within Guatemalan society" (Morales Sic 2007: 251; my translation). This drive for respect and harmony is crucial for human security, and Maya religious traditions provide a key resource in this regard. At the same time, struggles for cultural rights and even the language of cultural autonomy used within the Maya Movement can also make Maya identity a site for contestation in the political arena.

The Protestant situation is complex, partly because of the heterodoxy within the evangelical community itself. The historiography of the peace process frequently seems to downplay the role of the international Protestant community, particularly the Lutheran World Federation, in helping to initiate the process. Marginally more attention has been given to the participation of local ecumenical organizations such as the Evangelical Alliance or the Maya-based Evangelical Conference of Churches of Guatemala (Conferencia Evangélica de Iglesias de Guatemala [CIEDEG]). Both of these have played important roles in promoting public stances on issues affecting the nation, with CIEDEG frequently focusing on issues of social justice and reconciliation. Guatemalan evangelicals from these groups, and others, participated in the processes leading to the final peace accords, including the National Reconciliation Commission. Under the leadership of Bishop Rodolfo Quezada Toruño, the National Reconciliation Commission established the Grand National Dialogue in 1989 as a way of involving civil society in the negotiations (Jeffrey 1998: 13–15).

Practical Theology and Contributions to Human Security

Any consideration of Pentecostal contributions to human security in Guatemala entails an examination of the link(s) between theological perspectives and the practice of congregational life. In an article on Guatemalan Pentecostalism, written around the time that the war ended, Everett Wilson argued that "[a]lthough popular Pentecostalism [had] become a religious alternative for many socially marginal Guatemalans, the movement [was] still too small, inexperienced, and divided to display much political importance or independence" (Wilson 1997: 154). He went on to say that the greatest strength of these groups "may lie primarily in the development of human capital, cultivating civic culture among popular groups." This argument resonates with an approach focused on the congregational level, contextualizing the contribution of Pentecostal communities to social and political security in Guatemala and elsewhere in Latin America.

In order to assess how their theological perspective relates to human security, I focus here on two congregations that are directly related to the Full Gospel Church of God (Iglesia de Dios del Evangelio Completo, IDEC). The IDEC is the oldest Pentecostal denomination in Guatemala. Dating to 1932, the IDEC was founded near Totonicapán, a departmental capital in the western highlands. Depending on the source, it is the first or second largest Protestant denomination in the country, along with the Assemblies of God. The denomination has a missionary history and represents what might be called "classical Pentecostalism," even as it demonstrates a form of Pentecostal faith and practice that draws its inspiration from and has become indigenized in Guatemalan culture.[12] In 2009, the IDEC had 204,190 members, 2,263 churches, 870 missions, and 3,179 ministers.[13] The denomination's history and its social involvement with nearly all of the diverse ethnic groups in the country make the IDEC a compelling case for developing an understanding of the potential contributions of Pentecostalism to human security.

The makeup and character of these two congregations reflect radically different social and ethnic contexts in the department of Quetzaltenango, which is about four hours' travel southwest of Guatemala City. During a recent field season, I briefly attended a regional conference of church leaders in the course of arranging a meeting with an IDEC pastor and traveling with him to his community for an interview. He is a Mam Maya pastor who lives in the municipality of San Juan Ostuncalco in an *aldea* (village) that is 95 percent Mam. I met him at the urban Lluvias de Bendición (Showers of Blessing) congregation in the regional commercial center also known as Quetzaltenango, traditionally considered Guatemala's second city in both cultural and economic terms. When I arrived at the church, a gathering was in process that included both Maya and mestizo leaders from throughout the surrounding district. I observed about an hour of the meeting as the leaders, including a small number of women, were exhorted to engage with mission and to promote the unity of their denomination—*una sola iglesia* (one single church)—because it is *la* Iglesia de Dios, *the* Church of God. When the meeting ended, participants were encouraged to take home posters with a large eye peering back at the viewer. The pupil in the eye was an image of the world with clouds above it, and the eye was placed over a statement that was simply titled "*Visión*":

> *We desire to be a Church*
> *full of the Holy Spirit, in constant growth,*
> *of thousands and thousands of Christians that congregate*
> *to worship God in spirit and in truth,*
> *that has a profound passion for the lost*
> *and a commitment with world missions,*
> *discipleship, the establishment of new churches,*
> *and that knows how to extend its hands to help those who suffer.*

For members of the IDEC, this statement is a vision of what they might call the full or complete Gospel, and it is rooted in a sense of community that indeed extends to the ends of the earth.

I had gained an appreciation for Pentecostalism's inclusive sense of geography a few days before when I attended a service led by the same Mam minister. He had preached about the events leading up to Pentecost in the book of Acts when the risen Jesus directs the gathered apostles to wait for the arrival of the Spirit. At its arrival, they would become witnesses in Jerusalem, in Judea, in Samaria, and to the ends of the earth (Acts 1.7–8). When I attended a Sunday service in Guatemala City the year before, I was handed a bulletin filled with news of congregational activities, and a praise band opened the service with song lyrics projected onto a screen so that everyone could participate. At another point in the service, a video clip was to support the pastor's sermon. In San Juan, the praise (*adoración*) music was done a cappella, and the prayers—which I was assured were just prayers and not speaking in tongues—had most of the congregation on their knees in front of their plastic chairs. Everyone prayed aloud in a particular manner so that a whistling tone pervaded the small *templo*. The front wall of the church was painted with a nature scene of the kind that is prevalent in the Maya congregations of the highlands—complete with snow-capped mountain peaks and the ever-present open Bible, this time with the words "De Jehová es la tierra y su plenitude" ("The earth is Jehovah's and its fullness"), most likely from Psalm 24.1. Seating was segregated by gender, as is the custom in Mam communities. Most of the men, on the left side as I faced the *plataforma* where the chancel area would be in more liturgical traditions, were in Western dress, often with dark jackets or sports hoodies as a buffer against the evening chill. The vast majority of the women, who occupied the second and third seating sections in the middle and right side of the congregation, wore the traditional Maya blouse and skirt (*huipil* and *corte*). Most of the children sat with their mothers, although a few did stay with the men for the duration of the service or *culto*.

Although singing and Bible reading were in Spanish, most of the preaching was in Mam with a few Spanish interpolations. When the minister addressed the situation of the apostles in Acts, he painted a cognitive geographic map for the congregation in which the Apostles' movement from Jerusalem to Judea was mirrored by the congregation's mission extending from the local community to the broader nation of Guatemala. With his words, he described a transcultural space—a place where Maya people interact with Ladinos, or mestizos, in contexts broader than those of the immediate community. It was a moving approach to a text about the presence of the Spirit being with the disciples even as they went out to the ends of the world. I, of course, cannot be certain of how the congregants heard this proclamation, but in the postconflict situation where violence and discrimination are not relegated to the past, and in a place where continuing migratory patterns lead from mountain communities in Guatemala to Mexico and the United States, it was a powerful invocation of context and experience. It was a new word, and a somewhat unexpected one, even after all these years, as I watched many of the women bring leaves for wrapping tamales and lay them on the raised chancel area as a *primicía*, or first fruit offering.

While this particular service connects with the bucolic sense of life in San Juan and most highland communities, the preaching is not always so expansive. The service also belies the shifting nature of the community, including a number of community members who have indeed migrated to the North with all the expense and vagaries that such a journey entails. Prayers are often said for those who have undertaken the journey, and another Sunday would also have the cultural influence of different musical instruments, the drum set (*batería*), keyboard, and guitar-based instrumentation that is now common in churches of almost all denominations.

The larger issue here is how the experiences in a religious service of this type articulate with life beyond the congregation itself. A couple of weeks after the service I accompanied a friend and member of the congregation on a hike to a Maya ceremonial site that was marked by three crosses high on a hilltop overlooking the village. It is a place of special significance where the community's Maya spiritual guides (shamans) sometimes gather for ceremonies involving the burning of incense and the counting of the days of the Maya ritual calendar. Frequently these ceremonies are used to request rain for the *milpa* (cornfields) at the beginning of May and to give thanks if the rains have arrived early. Adjacent to the Mayan ceremonial area was a bare space, covered with leaves, where evangelicals sometimes climb the mountain for fasting, vigils, and prayers—without the use of symbols such as the cross—but also to ask for blessing and to give thanks.

At the community level, sacred space is shared, negotiated, and contested across religious and cultural boundaries. In reviewing my fieldnotes I am reminded, however, that the purpose of the expansive vision of the place in the Pentecostal world is "to fulfill the work of the evangelization of the world" (Acts 20.21). On one hand, evangelization is a partisan activity that may support human security by affirming a particular ethnic identity even as it creates rifts by downplaying aspects of the same identity (e.g., Maya *costumbre*). On the other hand, the same chapter of Acts that exhorts the evangelization of the world includes an affirmation that repentance is for Jews and Gentiles alike. This suggests the possibility of a less contentious engagement with neighbors. And while I cannot speak for the members of this particular congregation, others have noted the possibility of practical alliances between Maya Catholics and evangelicals and those who insist on the necessity of promoting the continuity of Maya worldviews.[14]

In the urban context, returning again for a Sunday service with the Lluvias de Bendición congregation, I was again struck by my surroundings. My immediate impression was that this was not a congregation shuttered in its four walls ("los cuatro paredes de la iglesia"). I arrived a little early from wandering around the street, not knowing the start time. People were slowly gathering to music from a choir of mostly young people dressed in red on the raised platform with a dance team directly in front of the congregation (also in red with streamers and tambourines in hand). A bongo-type drum set was on the stage, and the building was crowded. I estimated when the place was full that it there might be as many as 275–375 people. To one side of the platform was a signboard with a small map of

Guatemala and the words "¡Piensa en grande ... Haz cosas grandes!—Joel 2.21 Un pequeño país, un gran país. La diferencia está en nuestras manos." That is, "Think big ... Accomplish great things!—Joel 2.21 A small country, a great country. The difference is in our hands."

That morning's sermon also provoked me to reflect on the role of social action in Pentecostal congregational life. Although the profound implications of endemic violence for human security were not addressed, other social issues were addressed that I was not accustomed to hearing about in Guatemala. I was struck by how directly the minister addressed urban social problems. The onset of the winter rains, including Tropical Storm Agatha, had caused numerous landslides and even a few deaths. A couple of zones within Quetzaltenango had been affected, and reference was made to the difficulties that a drainage system designed for 200,000 people caused when the population of the metropolitan area had risen to at least 800,000. In addition to comments on the sensitive health problems of children and young people with HIV, the sermon at times sounded like a discourse straight out of some environmental seminar one might attend in the United States. The preacher commented on the use and disposal of plastic bags and expressed concern over the growing dependence on automobiles. He urged the congregation to at least maintain their vehicles in order to prevent further contamination of the environment.[15] The tone of the sermon was both didactic and passionate in a nonjudgmental way. Language of spiritual warfare was enjoined because both Satan and pollution were implicated in causing infirmity.

These preoccupations were certainly grounded in a concern for community and a particular vision of healing. Citation of scripture was essential, and classical Pentecostals insist that they are people of the book as well as the Spirit. The textual evidence links the congregation tightly to its own tradition of practice and leads the community to a direct response to the personal and societal issues confronting people on a daily basis: "Jesús sana; mi iglesia es una comunidad sanadora" ("Jesus heals; my church is a healing community"). This statement is directly related to both the definition of human security used in this volume and Fen Osler Hampson's notion that "human security should be widely construed to include economic, environmental, social and other forms of harm to the overall livelihood and well-being of human beings" (2008: 231).

In my interview with the pastor, he was quite clear that the true gift of the congregation was its emphasis on evangelization, although some attention had to be paid to social issues broadly construed. This has the appearance of a progressive Pentecostalism, but it is not liberation theology or liberal Protestant social justice teaching of the North American type.[16] During the service, I also noticed a call-and-response refrain that was repeated several times, a refrain about the congregation's having been blessed so that it could be a blessing to others. This bit of liturgy seemed quite unusual in what is considered to be a noncreedal tradition. In asking about this, I received an answer that affirmed both the theological and the experiential perspectives from which Pentecostals approach their religious practice. The emphasis remains on healing, and this is the work of Christ (presumably through the Spirit):

> Yes, based on Galatians 3.13, where it says that Christ redeemed us from the curse of sin and the law. So ... we confess that we are redeemed and bought, [out of] the curse of sin, poverty, infirmity, and death—well, death in the sense of spiritual death, right? We're all going to die. ... But death for Christians is a gain according to the Apostle Paul in Philippians 1. ... He is in a difficult situation, but wants to be with God, and [well], what does he do in the world to continue serving the church and society? ... He says, "I don't know what to do, but for me to live is Christ, and to die is gain." So, given this, we include [the notion] that sin is the biggest curse that [confronts] humanity. Right? Poverty, because they taught me when I entered in the Gospel [*evangelio*] that being poor was a blessing, that the poorest one is the most holy. But studying the scripture, I realized that poverty is a curse. You can't bring about the Kingdom of God without wealth. Sickness ... I am just now giving a series of studies based on [the idea] that Jesus Christ is the healer [*el sandador*]. ... Galatians 3.13 is the base of this confession ... not a confession of the Church of God as a mission or denomination, but it is from the local church.[17]

This is an important statement reflecting how Pentecostal practices embody a sense of spiritual empowerment in addition to more traditional experiences of the Spirit such as speaking in tongues and divine healing. It is also language about local empowerment that links theology and social engagement as Pentecostals respond locally to social problems, responses that constitute a significant source of social capital on Guatemala's pluralistic religious landscape. Such social capital contributes to society in the voluntaristic sense of Tocqueville, and some see Pentecostal churches as fields for the development of democratic culture. In a country with one of the world's highest rates of income disparity and in which 70 percent of the economy is outside the formal sector (Briscoe and Rodríguez Pellecer 2010: 18), communities such as the IDEC straddle differences of ethnicity and class on a persistent basis. Evangelical discourse of the community of *hermanos y hermanas* (brothers and sisters) draws attention to imaginaries that do, at least on the conceptual level, transcend the quotidian divisions indexed by language of separation and dissimilarity.[18]

The relationship between theology and practice becomes clearer in the spiritual valence of the language of illness and healing. Pointing beyond the needs of the individual to the possibility of living out beliefs in a practical sense beyond the formal gatherings of the congregation, the commentary is about following in the footsteps of the healer. The key is the idea that, in being with God, people are freed from sinfulness, sickness, poverty, and death. While not precluding supernatural intervention, this discourse of liberation is decidedly "this-worldly" in the Weberian sense. Riches are not evil in and of themselves. Rather, poverty is a curse, and some resources are necessary if one wants to bring about the Kingdom of God. The discourse operates on spiritual and practical planes and is not a capitulation to a full-blown prosperity gospel where riches and social status become signs of being blessed.

The minister also indicated the futility of a teaching that places spirituality at some remove from current material difficulties. Emphasizing that the Kingdom of God is one thing and the Kingdom of the Earth is another, he said reflection on these issues requires an analysis of the situation. He questioned the kind of teaching that, loosely translated, declares, "We have a mansion in heaven, but we are screwed here in the earth" ("Tenemos una mansion en el cielo, pero estamos fregados aquí en la tierra").

The exact meaning of such a statement requires further scrutiny from the standpoint of considering Pentecostal contributions to human security. I also attended the congregation's weekly *"noche de milagros"* ("night of miracles") service, which was led, almost entirely, by the laity. Most of those leaders were young people, probably in their late secondary or postsecondary school years. There was much prayer and song in a service designed to last exactly an hour and a half. The first forty-five minutes to an hour built to an emotional crescendo with people slowly filling the *templo*. This period reached a climax with the "release" of communal prayer in which most members of the congregation simultaneously prayed aloud. This was less about speaking in tongues and more a type of catharsis; some cried, and a few people were prostrate on the steps of the platform. The message was similar in some ways to what I had heard before: "Tu eres aquí para vivir y consolar" ("You are here to live and console"). Always there seemed to be an invitation to share what people experienced in the confidence that "Jesús, tu eres el amigo que me ama; tu eres mi esperanza" ("Jesus, you are the friend who loves me; you are my hope"). The mood mellowed somewhat when a young man took his place from behind the plexiglas pulpit and gave a twenty-five to thirty minute discourse about Rick Warren's book *The Purpose Driven Life* (*Una Vida con Propósito*). The minister appeared only for a few closing announcements, a closing prayer, and informal benediction.

I still wasn't sure if the Spirit had come. Instead of a "real" sign that the Spirit had appeared, such as fainting or speaking in tongues, the rather low-key and ritualized praying and crying simply reached a crescendo and then slowly died away. The practices I had witnessed seemed mundane, but they were no less meaningful in their ordinariness. One might even argue that the "this-worldly" face of Pentecostalism tied up in empowerment, healing, and consolation is another type of liberation, one that connects the personal and the societal as people respond to the various circumstances in which they find themselves. Beyond deprivation, participation becomes a crucial source of empowerment, enabling people to act in the world from a more confident stance. Among Pentecostals, this has been referred to as an "apprenticeship" model (Petersen 2004: 297–299), but it grows from a larger sense of commitment in a congregation that sends its members out to heal in response to their experiences of healing in their own lives.

The congregation of Lluvias de Bendición stresses that people are blessed and healed in order to offer blessing and healing to others. The scope of what happens in the two contexts discussed here is limited from the standpoint of human security, especially when other studies have demonstrated how some Pentecostal organizations are involved in the delivery of social services in a variety of specific ways—for example, responding to the needs of individuals desiring to leave lives of gang activity, or standing with people who have participated in urban land invasions (Petersen 1996: 136–146; Vásquez and Marquardt 2003: 119–144).[19] At the same time, with regard to the emphasis on healing, Douglas Petersen is correct in asserting that "bydeveloping self-esteem within the impoverished, by providing them hope and by arming them with skills applicable to the larger social system, Pentecostalism enables participants to take part in the achievement of the larger social struggles for a better life and a more secure future" (2004: 305). This accurately captures the place Pentecostals occupy on Guatemala's pluralistic religious landscape.

Discussion

My argument in this chapter is that by examining the Pentecostal experience, particularly Pentecostal liturgical practice and theological perspectives, we can gain a better sense of how Pentecostalism might act within the context of human security. In a focus group with IDEC leaders taking a course at a denominational seminary in Guatemala City, a question about the relationship between the baptism of the Holy Spirit and salvation elicited a majority response that "solo Cristo salva" ("only Christ saves"). It might be argued that this seeming diminishment of the role of the Spirit is the fruit of an educational process among leaders in that particular group. One might also conclude, however, that an honest accounting for upward mobility and higher levels of education among Pentecostals will result in some of the same patterns of church attendance and relationship to personal faith that have been experienced by historical denominations that have lost considerable ground to Pentecostals since 1960.[20] Much has been written about the global resurgence of religion in recent decades, and this is one of the pieces for framing the discussion of the relationship between religion and human security in this volume. As the story continues to unfold, we should be forewarned that higher levels of education and development in the global South might lead to further processes of secularization and disenchantment.

I have argued elsewhere that the contribution of Guatemalan evangelicals to democratization and postconflict reconciliation has been ambiguous at best (Samson 2008). My view of Pentecostal contributions to human security is similar. The research does suggest that the members of the next generation are participating in a type of leadership school (or apprenticeship) that will not take long to bear fruit in civil society and, by extension, in the political arena. But this very success in providing space for leadership development may cause some to distance themselves from Pentecostal traditions and identify with other movements that provide meaning in broader contexts. As others in this volume have argued, it is at their own peril that authorities ignore the power of religion to move people. Certainly this is the case, but there is no universal pattern to how people are moved and what moves them over time.

Daniel Levine's comments regarding evangelical contributions to democratic transitions in Latin America demonstrate both the limitations and the potential location of Protestant (and Pentecostal) contributions to human security:

> Evangelicals did not play a particularly prominent role in most of the region's transitions to democracy, and I think it fair to say that with the exception of cooperation in human rights work, and (in the Central American cases) cooperation in helping broker an end to armed conflict, the weight of the evidence suggests that the potential impact of evangelicals on democracy is greater through indirect means. With the gradual consolidation of competitive civilian politics, the presence of evangelicals, self-consciously identified as such, in ordinary political activity (campaigns and elections, office-holding, associational life, lobbying) has become a well-established fact throughout the region. (Levine 2008: 216)

The issue of human security transcends the question of contributions to democracy, but in both the political arena and in particular concerns related to human security, the role of religion is conditioned by a range of other social and political factors. Careful scholarship on these issues in a variety of contexts support Timothy Steigenga's conclusions based on a combination of survey and qualitative research:

> In Guatemala, the trend is that pentecostalized religion generally contributes to civil society by encouraging volunteerism, self-help, space for public dialogue, and an ethic of equality before the law. It should come as no surprise that the ongoing political effects of pentecostalized religion in Guatemala will be less visible at the level of party organization and protest activity and more pronounced in terms of community building, self-help, and resource mobilization (2007: 271).

These localized political effects are more reflective of social movements than political parties, and they accurately describe the nature of the diffuse Pentecostal movement in the country. I also agree with Steigenga's conclusion that "the degree to which these activities translate into a stronger civil society or facilitate a political culture of clientelism depends upon the larger institutional and political context of Guatemalan democracy."

In reaching these conclusions, I have intentionally not addressed neo-Pentecostalism and its embrace of a type of "health and wealth" or "prosperity" theology that reflects "the belief that health and wealth only come to those who obey God and that individuals who suffer do so because they are sinful" (Steigenga 2001: 9). While variations of this theology can be found in a variety of venues, it is most commonly found among neo-Pentecostals whose perspectives often mirror the preoccupations of the elite sectors of the country.[21] These groups should not be left out of the discussion, and a recent study by Kevin O'Neill (2010) focuses on how members of the neo-Pentecostal community (particularly in the El Shaddai congregation) assume the "weight" of "Christian citizenship" within civil society, largely through practices of prayer and spiritual warfare. The view of citizen agents acting in support of state power and its ability to benefit the populace certainly seems to be a way in which religion can potentially contribute to human security. This is especially the case when neo-Pentecostals are described as "politically active, focusing on the moral dimensions of Guatemala's well-being—crime, divorce, and corruption" (10).

Nevertheless, O'Neill's impressive ethnographic look inside a particular neo-Pentecostal congregation largely fails to address the complicated relationship between the increasingly diverse neo-Pentecostal community and the elite power structure in Guatemala.[22] O'Neill mentions disparaging comments about Maya history and culture made by minister Harold Caballeros in one of his early books (96–101), but the conclusion that such "off-putting" perspectives demonstrate how "democracy's ideal citizen is active, responsible, and willing to participate for the greater good" (101) is less than satisfactory from the standpoint of human security. The character of such discourse in a country with Guatemala's history is important for any consideration of how one group's actions can affect another group in their struggle for self-expression and autonomy. While all Pentecostals will resort to discourses of spiritual warfare in determined circumstances, the issue of religious competition over against a vibrant religious pluralism is also raised by this example.

I mentioned earlier Caballeros's intent to run for presidency in the recent elections. The party's website puts the dual-edged sword of religious discourse in relation to human security on full display. On top of the page is a quotation by Caballeros: "I have FAITH in God, FAITH in Guatemala and in the unbreakable spirit of all Guatemalans" ("Tengo FE in Dios, FE in Guatemala y en el espíritu inquebrantable de todos los Guatemaltecos"). Still, he is an attorney by training with a reputation for honesty, and he negotiated an electoral alliance with Encuentro por Guatemala (Encounter for Guatemala). The Encounter is a center-left party, led by the respected Nineth Montenegro, who founded the Mutual Support Group (known as GAM in Spanish) in the 1980s as an organization dedicated to finding family members who had been "disappeared"—abducted by security forces during the war (and frequently their bodies never found). The coalition party received 6.24 percent of the 4,426,871 valid votes cast in the first round of the elections, a total of 276,192 votes.[23] This was a stronger showing than prior candidates running on some version of biblical or evangelical principles, and the coalition strategy might indicate a political direction for future alliances between religious groups with political aspirations and established political parties. At the same time, it points toward the necessity of such strategies in a pluralistic and multicultural nation.[24]

The eventual winner of the elections was Otto Pérez Molina, a retired army general whom human rights groups have accused of complicity with genocide during Guatemala's civil conflict.[25] Pérez Molina was the runner-up in the 2007 elections, and his win was the fourth consecutive preseidential election in which the runner-up in the prior election won in the subsequent election. He ran a campaign based on the application of the *mano dura* (iron fist) as a response to the forces creating insecurity—narcotrafficking, corruption, and poverty—within Guatemala, and his tenure will be closely scrutinized over the next four years.

Conclusion

Fifteen years after the end of Guatemala's devastating internal conflict, the study of Pentecostalism has much work ahead in the effort to understand the indigenous nature of Pentecostal practices in light of contemporary religious and ethnic pluralism. I take seriously John Burdick's concern in a recent review article on several books regarding Protestantism in the region that future research needs to take a stronger hand in addressing Pentecostal theology while moving beyond, in his words, being "bogged down in fairly mundane descriptivism" (2010: 176). He is even more direct in pointing us toward a path for future research: "it is time to get up to speed in relevant theoretical literatures, such as those in political economy, geography, communication studies, and political ecology, if we want to understand some of the deeper forces that are shaping religion on the continent today."

The order of the agenda is correct. We are hard pressed to see religion as determinative of social change in the region; rather it is one arena of human activity among others, and in ecological terms we might argue for a coevolutionary perspective that is at once systemic and multicausal, addressing the intersections of religion and larger forces such as globalization, border crossing, and network building in transnational space and through local responses to human desires for spiritual and material sustenance. Security should be added to Burdick's list as an area for sustained research.

At this juncture, the broader contribution of religion to processes of security in Guatemala can be interpreted in a number of ways. From the vantage point of Pentecostalism, one implication is that the theme of healing (*sanación*) potentially allows these particular religious communities to make a singular contribution to human security in the context of the dismal security situation described at the beginning of this chapter. Healing holds out the possibility of societal transformation and liberation. This was highlighted for me when I interviewed the director of a regional education institution associated with the Church of God. After I described my research, he responded by making a strong statement that social science research was needed for his own denomination in Guatemala. He framed his thoughts in terms of a question about how the church reacts to security issues: "The culture of violence is affecting us greatly. And what is the church doing?" After mentioning several problems such as social exclusion and corruption, he then remarked on the necessity of understanding and interpreting such phenomena. He concluded, "We greatly need social scientific study. ... The church in Guatemala is an experience-based church" (*"una iglesia empírica"*). In contrast to the neo-Pentecostal vision he ended with a statement that it is a challenge (*reto*) to govern but that it is also a challenge for *el evangelio* to touch and transform social reality.

Hope for transformation is at the heart of Pentecostal contributions to human security in Guatemala. Insecurity surely tests the ability of the Spirit to liberate individuals and communities from illnesses of all kinds even as Pentecostals themselves project the Spirit into new spaces of activity. The response to social concerns will be employed in discourses that attend to poverty, violence, and illness, but these discourses will be embodied in the Pentecostal cultural repertoire of healing, prophecy, and evangelism. These three, in the end, address and enflesh the concerns of human welfare, rights, and human autonomy that make up the pillars of human security addressed in this volume.

Notes

C. Mathews (Matt) Samson has been a visiting assistant professor of anthropology at Davidson College since 2006. He received his doctorate from the University at Albany, State University of New York in 2004, and his primary research is on religious change and ethnic identity among Maya evangelicals in postconflict Guatemala. He is the author of several articles and *Re-enchanting the World: Maya Protestantism in the Guatemalan Highlands*, published by the University of Alabama Press in 2007.

1. See International Crisis Group, "Guatemala: Squeezed between Crime and Impunity," *Latin America Report*, 33, June 22, 2010, and "Mexico Safer than Canada," *The Economist*, August 27, 2010.
2. The article where these observations are reported actually paints a far bleaker picture in saying that the ratio of private security personnel to that of the police and army is on the order of "five to one in Guatemala and four to one in Honduras." See "Central America: The Tormented Isthmus," *The Economist*, April 14, 2011, p. 28.
3. International Crisis Group, "Guatemala," p. 17. From the standpoint of governance in Guatemala, the counterdiscourse would include recognition of Colom's 2007 election in the first instance, especially given his original political affiliation with the party of the Guatemalan National Revolutionary Unity, and the establishment, also in 2007, of the International Commission against Impunity in Guatemala (CICIG) (Briscoe and Martín Rodríguez 2010: 15). The CICIG has authority to examine cases without being bound by the constraints of the Guatemalan judiciary. In 2009, its investigation of the release of a video made by the attorney Rodrigo Rosenberg predicting his own assassination and laying the blame squarely on the president played a significant role in clearing Colom's name and perhaps preserving the presidency itself (International Crisis Group, "Guatemala," pp. 20–21; Briscoe and Martín Rodríguez 2010: 15–16). The story is at once indicative of the concerns for human security that continue to pervade Guatemalan society and a sign that some of the historical patterns of elite control of the mechanisms of state and lack of transparency within the social and political structures might yet be challenged. See the details in Grann (2011).
4. Although I use the words "Protestant" and "evangelical" interchangeably in this chapter, the preferred term of self-identification among Mesoamericans is "evangelical" (*evangélico*).
5. The historical denominations in this context are the first five Protestant denominations to establish a formal presence in Guatemala, beginning with the Presbyterians

in 1882. The other denominations are the Church of the Nazarene, the Primitive Methodists, the Evangelical Quakers, and the Central America Mission. The list itself provides an indication of the diverse streams of tradition that contribute to Guatemalan evangelicals even before Pentecostal presence becomes prominent. See Garrard-Burnett (1998) for the essential history of the Protestant beginnings in the country.

6. The case of neo-Pentecostals in Latin America has some unique characteristics that are beyond the scope of this essay. I will refer to them at different points because they are an essential part of the larger Pentecostal panorama, and their historical legacy and visibility in the capital and some of the other larger urban areas in the country is remarkable on several levels. Candidates running for the presidency, for example, participate in prayer breakfasts with these leaders in similar fashion to such events in the United States. Steigenga has argued that these groups are "unique" to Guatemala (1999: 173), and it is true that even the term neo-Pentecostal has been most prominent in the consideration of Protestantism in Guatemala and Brazil. As these groups expand and cross boundaries in the context of their own missionary work, they also become more internally pluralistic while simultaneously taking on the character of denominations with congregations in diverse parts of the city or the nation as a whole. See Steigenga (1999) and Cantón Delgado (1998).

7. This figure represents 62 percent of Catholics and 85 percent of Protestants. See Pew Forum on Religion and Public Life (2006).

8. The seminal works for recent scholarship in this area are Martin (1990) and Stoll (1990). The literature is growing in addition to the scope of the research. On political engagement, see Garrard-Burnett and Stoll (1993); Freston (1993, 2001, 2008a); Steigenga (2001); and Steigenga and Cleary (2007). Representative of the work on Pentecostals and social movements, particularly in Brazil, are Burdick (1998) and Selka (2007). For progressive Protestantism, see Kamsteeg (1998); López (1998); and Samson (2003). Studies of networks and conversion would include the work of Smilde (2007) in Venezuela. Cleary (1999) provides a summary of the early work and the state of the research on Pentecostalism at the turn of the millennium.

9. The constitution upholds religious freedom, but the Roman Catholic Church is given *personalidad jurídica* (legal status).

10. On this history, see Klaiber (1998: 222–229) and Steigenga (1999: 154–159).

11. Four people were convicted of the murder, including a retired colonel in the army, a sergeant in the presidential guard (Estado Mayor Presidencial), and an auxiliary priest who lived with Gerardi. In many ways the case is an example of the role of "occult powers," frequently with ties to the military, in sowing insecurity and impunity in Guatemala. The convictions were remarkable at the time because they involved military personnel.

12. For details on the early history, see Garrard-Burnett (1998: 37–38, 2001).

13. The IDEC keeps detailed records, and membership numbers fluctuate from one month to the next.

14. Steigenga (2007: 272–274) deals with these issues, and a section of his article references Virginia Garrard-Burnett (2004) who has considered the possibility of an "inculturation theology" that implies Maya influence on evangelical practices. Molesky-Poz (2006) addresses some of these themes from the Maya standpoint.

15. The issue of plastic bags is interesting because I have heard Maya over the years either argue that Maya people don't use plastic or, in another context, that the ubiquitous bags cause cancer. The discourse is problematic on many levels, but it requires further analysis. Clearly there is an environmental concern being expressed, and despite the many conveniences wrought by plastic in the Western world, perhaps there is another message for those who engaged with issues of the environment and environmental justice. The symbolic valence of this issue is powerful, and the security concerns embedded in this kind of language seem directly related to the purposes of this volume.

16. The term "progressive Pentecostalism" comes from Miller (2007: 435). In his version, such Pentecostals are responding to community needs in a variety of ways, but they are not dealing with what liberationists might refer to as structural injustice. Of course, the hope for healing and social transformation can operate at all levels of society.

17. Galatians 3.13 in the NRSV is as follows: "Christ redeemed us from the curse of the law by becoming a curse for us—for it is written, Cursed is everyone who hangs on a tree." Themes of redemption as well as of healing are prominent in this pastor's discourse.

18. See Chesnut (1997) and Smilde (2007) for consideration of the need for healing in response to poverty and the importance of evangelical networks in Brazil and Venezuela, respectively. As indicated in this study, healing and community are recurrent themes in one form or another in most studies of evangelicalism in Latin America, and these themes play into the interrogation of religious contributions to human security. Some studies will focus more on material and political issues, while others will focus on the ineffable character of religion, both of which need to be taken into account.

19. On land invasions, see the segment on the indigenous Central American Pentecostal denomination Samaria in the video *Precarious Peace: God and Guatemala* (Worcester, PA: Gateway Films, 2003).

20. On this issue, see the statistics presented in Wilson (1997) and Gooren (2001).

21. See Sanchíz Ochoa (1998: 51–55) for the history and the establishment of some of the most prominent of these congregations.

22. For more on this particular issue, see the brief review essay by Steigenga (2010). The essay demonstrates the importance of maintaining a historical perspective in analyzing contemporary religious change in Latin America. Also addressed in this essay is the work of Garrard-Burnett (2010) dealing with period of the dictatorship of Guatemala's first evangelical president, José Efraín Ríos Montt.

23. These figures are from Acuerdo No. 1319–2011 of Guatemala's Supreme Electoral Tribunal (http://elecciones2011.tse.org.gt/resultados.oficiales.primera.vuelta.2011.php) and "TSE Convoca a Segunda Vuelta Electoral en Guatemala," *Prensa Libre*, September 27, 2011.

24. Parties running on such platforms deny being established as strictly evangelical parties. The VIVA website can be found at http://www.visionconvalores.com/ (accessed December 29, 2011). Caballeros exudes success in his persona, and it should be noted that he has moderated some of his discourse in recent years, at least partially in an effort to broaden his appeal to more secular audiences. In fact, he spent several months leading up to the elections appealing a ruling that again disqualified him from running for the presidency because of a constitutional clause prohibiting ordained ministers from occupying the office. Caballeros argued that he resigned from his ministry in 2006 when he decided to enter the 2007 elections. In a split vote (8–5) on August 16, Guatemala's Corte Suprema de Justicia (Supreme Court of Justice) issued a stay of the earlier ruling against him by the Supreme Electoral Tribunal (Magdalena Medina and Óscar Herrera, "La CSJ Ampara a Caballeros para que Participe por la Presidencia," *El Periódico*, August 17, 2011). The first round of the elections was held September 11.

25. "Otto Pérez Molina Gana la Presidencia de Guatemala con 54.27% de Votos," *La Jornada*, November 7, 2011. Other sources have pointed out that Pérez Molina also participated in the negotiations of the peace accords and was a signatory to the final document.

I O

Striking a Balance: Christianity and the Challenges of Long-Term Human Security in Zimbabwe

Gladys Ganiel

Introduction

Zimbabwe ranks last in both the Economist Intelligence Unit's "Quality of Life Index" and the New Economics Foundation's "Happy Planet Index."[1] The poor quality of life and lack of happiness that these indexes identify can be linked to the Zimbabwean state's inability to provide a secure environment for its citizens. That environment has been increasingly precarious since 2000, when groups of young men began to "invade" white-owned farms. The farm invasions were symptomatic of a wider breakdown of the economy, as well as of law and order, which has been facilitated by political oppression and state violence (Holland 2008; Hill 2005; Bhebe and Ranger 2001).

President Robert Mugabe and his Zimbabwe African National Union— Patriotic Front (ZANU-PF) party have dominated the political scene since independence in 1980 and have presided over the country's collapse (Hill 2005; Raftopoulos 2004a, b). ZANU-PF entered a power-sharing government with the Movement for Democratic Change (MDC) party in 2009, following contested 2008 elections (*BBC Online* 2009a). But socioeconomic deprivation and human rights abuses remain widespread (Amnesty International 2009).

The Zimbabwean state is still unable to ensure that its citizens can freely pursue livelihoods that would lift them out of poverty, nor can it ensure that its citizens live without the experience or threat of violence. It is in this context that Christian organizations—which constitute the largest and most pervasive segment of Zimbabwean civil society—are providing essential social services and spaces in which alternative political configurations can be imagined and discussed

(Raftopolous and Alexander 2006; Mukonyora 2008). Accordingly, this study engages two questions that are of central concern to this volume. First, it asks how are religious groups providing aid to those in need? Second, it considers the ways in which religious groups promote long-term human security by facilitating the development of politically empowering networks and ideas.

The context of this study is the obvious *lack* of human security in Zimbabwe. The Zimbabwean state is officially Marxist and secular. In practice, however, it is authoritarian, and its leaders have attempted to co-opt and control religious groups that they see as threatening state power. Comparative studies of African states demonstrate that religious actors choose a variety of options in such contexts, ranging from withdrawing from the public sphere to supporting oppressive dictators, challenging the state, and focusing on humanitarian concerns (Freston 2001; Ranger 2008). African evangelical/Pentecostal/charismatic (EPC) Christians[2]—previously dismissed by scholars as apolitical—are becoming increasingly active socially and politically. Accordingly, this chapter presents a case study of an EPC congregation in Harare. The study demonstrates how the congregation provides short-term human security by responding to the needs of the poor, while at the same time creating space where people can develop the "self-expression values" necessary for long-term human security. The case study also demonstrates that even under authoritarian states, religious actors can actively choose to balance the immediate demands of short-term human security with the sometimes competing demands of long-term human security. Policymakers can benefit from a greater understanding of how religious actors strike this balance and from a greater appreciation of the variability, flexibility, and religious resources of EPC Christians in such contexts.

Context: Human Security in Zimbabwe

Zimbabwe is plagued by what Muchena (2004: 262) has called a "culture of violence." This includes large-scale events ranging from the Gukurahundi massacres of Ndebele people by government-sanctioned Shona troops in Matabeleland following independence to Operation Murambatsvina, the government's systematic destruction of the homes of MDC voters after the 2005 elections. It also includes the commonplace violence of police against protesters and voters at election times, the violence against new recruits in Zimbabwe's security forces, and the violent rhetoric of Mugabe. It extends to the media in that foreign journalists have been banned and local independent outlets have been harassed by the state, including raids and damage to their properties (see Hill 2005: 89–104; Bratton, Chikwana, and Sithole 2005). The Zimbabwean state has nurtured this culture by using violence as a political tool to quell dissent.

While pervasive violence is a threat to citizens' human security, this has been compounded by the deteriorating economy. After the 1979 Lancaster House Agreement, which laid out the terms for the cessation of warfare and the transition from white-run Rhodesia to an independent Zimbabwe, the white-led agricultural economy was left largely intact. Zimbabwe was at one point the world's second largest tobacco exporter and its food production was such that it was known as the breadbasket of Africa (Orlet 2005). But Zimbabwe inherited a large foreign debt from the Rhodesian government (Bond and Manyanya 2002), and ZANU-PF's land redistribution program did not proceed at the intended rate (see Hill 2005: 72–73). Britain, the former colonial power, withdrew its support of land redistribution, citing a lack of transparency and accountability ("UK Policy on Zimbabwe" n.d.). In 2000, ZANU-PF proposed a constitution that would give more powers to Mugabe as president. Within days of this being defeated in a referendum, Mugabe announced a large-scale land redistribution project that amounted to gangs of youths seizing white-run farms. The "invasions" were accompanied by government-led, antiwhite rhetoric that heightened tensions. Some farmers were murdered (Hammar, Raftopolous, and Jensen 2003; Sachikonye 2004). At the time of my fieldwork in 2007, the annual inflation rate was 2,200 percent and 80 percent of Zimbabweans lived below the poverty line (*BBC Online* 2007a). The last inflation figure to be released was in July 2008, when it had reached 231,000,000 percent (*BBC Online* 2009b). Food became scarce both in the shops and in the countryside, and people struggled to provide for themselves and their families. State provision for health and education was all but abandoned. Doctors, teachers, and civil servants either went without pay or did not earn enough to cover the inflation rate, conditions the government attempted to alleviate in 2009 by paying them in foreign currency (*BBC Online* 2009c).

The Zimbabwean state is a threat to the human security of its own citizens. But international nongovernmental organizations (NGOs) and local civil-society groups have begun to step into the breach left by the state (Raftopoulos and Alexander 2006). With 75 percent of Zimbabweans practicing Christianity, churches and related organizations occupy a significant part of this public space (United States Department of State 2007; see also Mukonyora 2008). In most rural areas, the church and the school are the only public institutions (Dube 2006: 8). This means that Christian organizations and congregations are some of the most prominent, trusted, and viable institutions within the country (Raftopoulos and Alexander 2006).

The power and influence of the churches is recognized by ZANU-PF to the extent that it has attempted to co-opt some prominent religious organizations and clerics. For example, the government has pursued relatively long-established, mainstream groups such as the Zimbabwe Council of Churches (ZCC), the

Evangelical Fellowship of Zimbabwe (EFZ), and the Catholic Bishops Forum.[3] These groups annually collaborate to hold a National Day of Prayer. In 2006, it was attended for the first time by Mugabe, which resulted in an unusually small turnout since many Christians boycotted the event (United States Department of State 2006). Broadcasts on state-run television showed clerics laughing and praying with Mugabe and enjoying a meal. Prominent clerics and representatives of these groups publicly condemned religious opponents of ZANU-PF such as the Christian Alliance and the then Catholic archbishop of Bulawayo, Pius Ncube (Bird 2006). At this time, prominent church activists were increasingly targeted and arrested using the infamous Public Order and Security Act (United States Department of State 2006). In 2007 Ncube was accused of having an affair with his secretary. Ncube's supporters suspected this was a government plot to distract from his criticisms of Mugabe. Ncube resigned as archbishop and has not been as prominent since the incident (*BBC Online* 2007b, c). Mugabe also has won the support of some prominent religious figures such as Nolbert Kunonga, the former Anglican bishop of Harare. The Anglican Church removed him from his post in 2007, after which he formed his own church.

There have since been violent attacks on Anglicans attempting to worship in Harare. Anglicans claim the perpetrators are ZANU-PF youths and the police, whom they accuse of "beating up worshippers, including women taking the Holy Communion" (*BBC Online* 2008). Further, Chitando (2005) argues that ZANU-PF has appropriated Christian rhetoric to justify its actions, including the seizure of farms. This ambiguous and uneasy relationship between church and state is echoed in the relationships between church and state in other African nations. Like Tiburcio's study of Angola in this volume, the Zimbabwean case demonstrates the threat of religion to state legitimacy, the dangers for religious actors in mixing church and state, and the importance of religion to a state's moral standing in the wider world. But it seems that religious actors are mostly junior partners in the relationship between church and state. When religious groups remain outside the state apparatus, they lack power and can be marginalized, and when they venture inside the state apparatus, they can be marginalized because they are more easily co-opted.

Christianity and African Politics

The relationship between church and state in Africa is often framed in terms of the churches and their contributions (or not) to democratization (Gifford 1995, 1998; Anderson 2005; Ellis and Ter Haar 2004; Jenkins 2006, Ranger 2008; Sanneh 2008). Haynes (2004) argues that the churches' contributions to democratization have been minimal in most cases. A recent contribution to this debate is Ranger's (2008) edited volume. In the introduction, Ranger makes two important distinctions. First, he divides Africa's democratic history into three phases, examining the role of the Christian churches in each. This allows us to see how the role of the churches in politics has changed over time. Second, he distinguishes between the role of the mainline or missionary-initiated churches such as the Catholic, Anglican, and Methodist denominations and the role of EPC churches. Ranger sees the influence of the mainline denominations giving way to the EPC churches, which previously were not prominent in African politics.

Ranger says the first democratic revolution consisted of anticolonial struggles for independence in the 1950s and '60s, in which the mainline churches had prominent but ambiguous roles (Zimbabwe's anticolonial struggle came later, in the late 1970s). Some churches supported white-led minority regimes, while others spoke out against them. He contends that across the continent, EPC churches either supported repressive regimes or withdrew from politics.

After independence, the mainline churches that had allied themselves with those fighting for independence enjoyed good relations with new majority rule governments. But by the 1980s, Ranger says there was a "second democratic revolution." Drawing on Gifford's edited volume, titled *The Christian Churches and Democratization in Africa*, Ranger concludes that "[the mainline churches] offered the only alternative networks to those of the dominant party. … The churchmen still retained enough moral authority to act as arbiters and judges" (2008: 13). EPC churches were not prominent during this era.

But EPC churches have been central to what Ranger calls the "third democratic revolution," which he dates from the early 1990s to the present. He argues that African states are experienced by their people as weak, violent, bankrupt, and immoral. Some mainline churches have attempted to respond to the abuses of the state, but their efforts appear to be stagnating. On the other hand, EPC churches have been more effective in attracting people to their ranks. Rather than relying on the "speaking out" approach that has been used by the mainline churches, he asserts that EPC churches are developing a "democratic culture" that is empowering people at the grass roots (22). This culture is largely an unintended consequence of the activities of EPC Christians, who see their primary goals as converting others to Christianity and worshipping God—*not* promoting democracy. Western scholars, more so than African Christians, are responsible for linking EPC Christianity with democratization. Ranger's argument is similar to an earlier "cultural potentiality argument" about EPC Christianity (see Freston 2001). EPC Christianity was said to produce a voluntaristic culture where participation in church congregations and other Christian institutions helped people acquire skills necessary for democratic citizenship (Maxwell 2000, 2005; Martin 1990, 2002; van Dijk 2003). Freston (2001) admitted that these arguments were not grounded in much empirical evidence, but Ranger's volume begins to provide it (see also Ganiel 2010a). At the same time, Jenkins (2006) identifies continent-wide trends of Christian political engagement, arguing that some people in Africa identify with the difficult economic and political situations portrayed in the Bible. Miller and Yamamori (2007) arrive at similar conclusions in their global survey of what they term "progressive Pentecostalism," going so far as to assert that

> this movement seeks a balanced approach to evangelism and social action that is modelled after Jesus' example of not only preaching about the coming kingdom of God but also ministering to the physical needs of the people he encountered.
>
> This movement reflects the increasing maturation of Pentecostalism as it develops from being an otherworldly sect to a dominant force in reshaping global Christianity (212).

For them, progressive Pentecostalism is complementing and may be replacing Liberation Theology as a vehicle for empowering people in the world's most impoverished regions. They identify progressive Pentecostalism's strengths as using imagery that is harmonious, pure, and organic, and emphasizing Jesus's example of nonviolence (214–215). This perspective balances earlier treatments of EPC Christianity that saw it as either apolitical or preoccupied with the "get rich quick" prosperity gospel.

Scholars' more recent focus on the progressive action of EPC Christians demonstrates that there is more to the churches' role in politics than challenging state abuses by "speaking out." This more expansive understanding of the role of the churches fits better with a human security rather than a democratization framework because it emphasizes improving the lives of the poor *as well as* empowering people to express themselves in the public sphere. The case study in this chapter demonstrates tensions between supplying basic needs and political empowerment—both of which are necessary for long-term human security.

Case Study of Mount Pleasant Community Church

Most ethnographic case studies do not claim to be representative of wider trends. Rather, such studies are designed to provide detailed analyses of overlooked microlevel processes that the analyst judges to have social or political significance. This was the rationale behind my selection of Mount Pleasant Community Church (MPCC) in Harare, where I conducted fieldwork during February–April 2007. The following reasons affected my decision: first, studying a *congregation* rather than a prominent Christian organization would provide perspectives that were missing from the information that was coming out of Zimbabwe that focused on organizations and clerics; second, it would reveal how laypeople were coping with Zimbabwe's deterioration; third, given EPC Christianity's growth and prominence, it would demonstrate how people associated with that expression of Christianity were responding to the crises. The congregation was multicultural with black (mostly Shona) and white congregants. The elders were an Ndebele man and a white man. Between 100–150 people attended the main Sunday morning worship service. The ethnic makeup of the congregation was about 80–85 percent Shona, 10–15 percent white, and 5 percent Ndebele and other Africans and Europeans, as well as those from other nationalities. Harare is a predominantly Shona city so this explains the high percentage of Shona. Whites were overrepresented in the congregation given that they are well below 1 percent of Zimbabwe's overall population. MPCC was located in a relatively wealthy suburb near the University of Zimbabwe, and congregants were disproportionately well educated, young (under thirty-five), and middle class. MPCC, then, is atypical of congregations in Zimbabwe, but all of the above factors combined to make it a fruitful site for a case study.

I used an open-ended, inductive approach to identify research questions. My methods included participant observation at worship services and prayer meetings, informal conversations, and interviews. My most basic concerns were finding out what people thought was important about their congregation and their thoughts about the future. The congregation met in some form six days a week, so I interacted with people almost daily. I conducted eighteen in-depth interviews with congregants, including seven Shona, seven white Zimbabweans, two Ndebele, one white European, and one from another African nation. They were divided equally between females and males. Whites were overrepresented because of their preponderance in the over-forty age group. I wanted a perspective of the early days of the congregation, and most people who had been attending the congregation for a number of years were white. This is because MPCC began as a nearly all white congregation in 1997.

The insights from the case study come from analyzing a process of change within MPCC, what people in the congregation called "deinstitutionalization." The best way to understand deinstitutionalization and its relationship with human security is to provide a description of how the process has occurred (see also Ganiel 2008, 2009, 2010b).

The Process of Deinstitutionalization

People dated the start of deinstitutionalization to 2002, when elders and congregants together decided to start small weekly prayer meetings. By 2005, people were meeting for prayer five days a week. Congregants said they felt God speaking to them during this time, telling them that they were relying too much on the structures of the congregation, such as Bible study groups that met during the week and events like women's meetings and men's breakfasts. As time went on people began to consider even the small Bible study groups too structured. So the congregation replaced these with smaller discipleship groups that met in people's homes. These lasted till 2006, when they were discontinued in favor of meeting informally in homes and attending prayer meetings.

Deinstitutionalization also involved revamping the way MPCC's prayer meetings and main worship service were conducted. In my observation of the meetings, it was difficult to tell if someone was "in charge" of them. A prayer meeting would usually begin with someone reciting or reading a passage of the Bible, saying a prayer, or singing a song. That worked as a cue for another person to find a scripture, prayer, or song that built on the theme developed by the previous person. People said they relied on the Holy Spirit to prompt them as they shared their thoughts and feelings. The Sunday morning worship services played out in a similar way, although a worship band was present and an elder or lay leader had usually prepared a sermon. But at least the first hour of the service was given over to spontaneous prayer, worship, and testimonies. Sometimes this went on for so long that the prepared sermon was never given, and a congregant shared an impromptu sermon instead. Elders said that this way of worshiping reinforced the biblical idea of the "priesthood of all believers" and their own decisions to move away from full-time, paid employment by the congregation. MPCC also made a dramatic change to the worship space. Previously, the congregation met in a high school auditorium with chairs arranged in rows facing the band and the preaching area and elders seated near the front, but they reorganized this space, placing the band in a corner and arranging the chairs in concentric circles with an open space in the middle. People entered this space when contributing to the service, and elders sat among the people in the circles. While a free-flowing style is typical in many charismatic churches, MPCC seemed to be taking it a step further because the elders were self-consciously decreasing their prominence at these events. This goes against a trend identified in Maxwell's (2007) study of the Pentecostal Zimbabwe Assemblies of God Africa denomination, in which some leaders of congregations assume an authoritarian style.

When people spoke with me about deinstitutionalization, they invariably framed it in "spiritual" terms. They understood it as a process through which they were growing closer to God. They said that removing the "structures" of congregational life meant that they now related directly to God through prayer and Bible study. They also said their deepening relationship with God allowed them to build stronger relationships, starting with others in MPCC and then moving on to people in the wider society. Because people understood deinstitutionalization in spiritual terms, they did not make connections between the breakdown of institutions in Zimbabwe and changes within their own congregation, even when asked directly about this. Even so, some of the innovations brought about during deinstitutionalization directly address problems created by the breakdown of the Zimbabwean state. These have, in some cases, improved the human security of needy people who receive practical assistance from MPCC. MPCC also has created a safe space for its own people, where they can explore spiritually, socially, and politically empowering ideas. In the context of an authoritarian state that is ostensibly Marxist and secular but has attempted to co-opt and control religious groups, these *religious* discourses at least implicitly challenge the authoritarian, political, and religious claims of the state. There is significant tension in safely providing services for the poor beneath the radar of such a state and developing these empowering discourses.

Human Security through Addressing Human Needs

All the congregants whom I interviewed said that deinstitutionalization had led to an increase in the congregation's social activism, including new initiatives to care for orphans, widows, and the rural poor. To put it in the terms of this book, people recognized that the human security of their fellow citizens was threatened. Even if people did not publicly blame government policies for this, they were aware that the government was not responding to these human needs. They saw the churches, and their relatively wealthy congregation, as well placed to take up the provision of basic services. People I spoke with said this was a Gospel imperative, as in Luke 12.48: "For everyone to whom much is given ... much shall be required." People responded to these needs by drawing on existing networks within and outside their congregation and creating new networks. People told me that the number of volunteers for service had increased and that those who already worked or volunteered for NGOs felt more supported in their work. One woman said that, in other congregations, people saw "Christian work" as only what their particular congregation was doing and overlooked people working for NGOs. But deinstitutionalization had allowed people at MPCC to see NGO work in a new light. NGO workers were no longer under pressure to attend meetings to "prove" that they were engaged in Christian work. Liberated from the tyranny of meetings, these people said they felt energized and legitimated in their work.

I observed people from MPCC visiting orphans and widows in a high-density suburb and a rural congregation. When visiting orphans and widows, people brought food, clothing, and toys to the neediest families. Then they had conversations with them, offering tips on cultivating backyard vegetable gardens or job training. They prayed with people. The woman who organized this project saw her primary role as an evangelist—one whom God uses to save souls rather than to simply provide them with material sustenance.

MPCC's activism in the rural areas also combined practical care and evangelism. MPCC had identified two rural partner congregations, and the congregation organized two types of events for them. Since MPCC has a number of medical doctors, one type was a medical mission. People from MPCC went to the rural congregation for an evening service, stayed overnight, and the next day set up tents in which people received free medical care. There also was a tent for prayer and spiritual healing, where people from MPCC who were not doctors offered support. The other type of event combined evangelistic mission and fellowship. This involved driving to a rural congregation for an evening meal, bringing food and supplies. After the meal, people from MPCC erected a movie screen in a field, on which they projected the *Jesus Film* dubbed into Shona. After the film, people were encouraged to accept Jesus as their savior. The next morning, a Sunday, the two congregations shared a service outside under the trees. MPCC returned to its partner congregations on at least a bimonthly basis, aiming to sustain the relationship rather than providing one-off relief. These responses built on the strengths of people at MPCC and provided direct material benefits to people who—largely as a result of the policies of a corrupt state—had become unable to meet their own basic needs. People at MPCC were keen to point out that these actions were not "political." Focusing on "social" activities such as these, they were not harassed by the state. In fact, the state seems content to allow religious groups to continue supplying these and similar services. The work of these religious groups relieves the state of the responsibility to provide basic health and social services, enabling it to use state funds for more cynical purposes such as enriching ZANU-PF party members or buying the loyalty of the police and military. While further research is necessary to evaluate the effectiveness of religious networks in Zimbabwe in responding to human needs, the example of MPCC demonstrates that, at the microlevel, activist congregations can improve people's human security. Keeping a low public and political profile, at least in the short term, may be necessary for religious groups to continue providing basic services, but this approach, while effective in responding to immediate needs, may unintentionally prolong state abuses.

That said, there are numerous factors at play that keep authoritarian regimes in power. For example, the remittances sent home by Zimbabweans in the diaspora benefit their families but artificially prop up the crumbling economy and allow the government to get away with its lack of economic reform. It is perhaps unfair to blame religious and civil society groups, or Zimbabweans in the diaspora for that matter, for prolonging the rule of an authoritarian state that they do not have direct control over. Their motivation for assisting the poor or their families is an end in itself, not a step toward some greater political good. It may be unrealistic and unethical to expect people to forgo these compassionate acts for the fleeting promise of a better political future.

Human Security and Empowerment

Some degree of human security is necessary for people to exercise political power, whether that is within civil society or the voting booth. Most people are not able to become politically involved, or to speak out against corrupt and authoritarian governments, until their basic needs for survival have been met. Inglehart and Welzel (2005) have argued that socioeconomic development and stability are crucial prerequisites for the emergence of "self-expression values" such as individualism and autonomy. As a relatively wealthy congregation in a nation where there is widespread poverty, people at MPCC not only have the resources to assist the poor, they also are among the few Zimbabweans with the resources to develop self-expression values. Indeed, there is evidence that people at MPCC are doing so by constructing biblical discourses that (at least implicitly) critique the injustices perpetrated by the Zimbabwean state.

Research on "new social movements" has confirmed that discursive change is crucial for achieving social change because people require new vocabularies to justify their actions (Touraine 1978; Eyerman and Jamison 1991; McAdam, McCarthy, and Zald 1996; see also Ganiel 2007). Through analysis of my interviews and consulting my field notes, I identified four major discursive themes that occurred during MPCC's deinstitutionalization process: relationship (with God and with others), acknowledging difficulties and injustices, waiting and persevering, and serving (Ganiel 2008). These discourses were grounded in passages from the Bible. These included Old Testament prophets who condemned the rich who were oppressive of the poor and Psalms that named the injustices experienced by God's people and cried out for the Lord to do justice. When giving a testimony, people often quoted something that another person had said in another meeting, thus legitimizing and reinforcing it. They also drew on what they called the witness of the Holy Spirit, which conferred an extra gravity and authority to their words.

In March 2007 I met with the elders and presented them with a report on my research. It identified the themes above, which they agreed were accurate. But they thought that "persevering" fit better in the "acknowledging difficulties and injustices" category rather than being linked with "waiting." It is beyond the scope of this chapter to provide examples of the content of each of these discursive themes (for more see Ganiel 2008, 2009, 2010b), but I have identified some examples of the uses of these discourses at a typical Sunday morning service. For example, a man stands up and says God has given him a message for the church in Zimbabwe. He reads from 2 Kings 6, where the king of Syria wants to go to war with Israel but the prophet Elisha informs the king of Israel of the king of Syria's plans. The king of Syria sends troops to surround the city, and Elisha's servant panics. Elisha tells his servant, "Those who are with us are more than those who are with them," and opens his servant's eyes so he can see the hills full of God's horses and chariots. Elisha blinds Syria's men and the king of Israel asks if he should kill them, but Elisha says to show them mercy and to provide them with a feast. After that, the men return to Syria and there is peace. The man interprets this scripture, saying that the church in Zimbabwe has panicked, and like Elisha's servant, members have only looked at events with their physical eyes. He says he hopes that "whatever our enemies are, God would open our eyes to the thousands [on our side]," and that God wants to raise the church up as an "army" in Zimbabwe. Then a woman stands up and says that her heart started beating heavily when she heard him speaking, so she knows she should speak. She says God is asking, "what are you doing with church?" She reads James 1.27: "Religion that God our Father accepts as pure and faultless is this: to look after orphans and widows in their distress and to keep oneself from being polluted by the world." She says that she works with orphans every day and then urges others to participate in the congregation's visits to orphans and widows.

These discourses can be understood as political in the Zimbabwean context, in that the man acknowledges warlike enemies who have frightened the church in Zimbabwe. His discourses also can be understood as empowering because he tells his listeners that with God's help they can change their situation. The mercy shown to the king of Syria's troops provides a model for peace between former enemies, which could apply to Zimbabwe. When the woman identifies the church's power as the ability to change society by serving orphans and widows, her discourses also can be understood as empowering because they encourage people to act. In an interview with another woman the following week, she mentioned this woman's testimony about service and said that she thought the churches should continue serving, yet go beyond it:

> I talked to [a leader from another congregation] and he said the church should stay out of politics. I see his point, but at the same time I just think that the suffering that's happening as a direct result of what the government has done ... that surely it's time for the church to stand up and make a difference. You hear the stories: like in Germany, when all the Jews were killed, and the church sat back and did nothing. Are we doing the same thing?

For this woman, the discourses she heard in church supported the idea that she should engage in activism alongside the poor and prompted her to contemplate challenging the government. No one spoke more critically than this about the government. As I discussed earlier, doing so could jeopardize the congregation's social activism. Some congregants, like this woman, thought that people in their church should speak out, but this was a minority view. It might then seem that the words spoken at MPCC could have no real role in promoting the political changes necessary for enhancing *long-term* human security, which clearly must include significant reform of the Zimbabwean state.

Given ZANU-PF's concerted and at times desperate efforts to co-opt the political messages of religious leaders, it can be concluded that the regime feels threatened by educated Christians to whom the Gospel is a message of hope for victims of oppression. The political message of these Christians has remained largely implicit, but discourses that draw on biblical themes or stories to help people make sense of Zimbabwe's current situation have encouraged people at MPCC to become more socially active. It is not an impossible leap to imagine this congregation and others developing explicitly political discourses that challenge the state and demand reform as other Christian groups, such as the Christian Alliance, already have done, but it is difficult to balance the tension between staying below the state's radar, effectively providing essential services, and engaging in political action that might one day help create a free society in which staying below the radar is unnecessary.

Further, a major feature of MPCC's deinstitutionalization process has been a levelling of authority as the elders, and other leaders stepped back from prominent positions. Elders and congregants alike explained this as an example of "servant leadership," which they equated with biblical stories such as Jesus washing the disciples' feet. Here, power is not wielded through violence or authoritarian laws. Rather, power is linked to service by giving away time, money, or possessions. People in MPCC had the power to contribute to their congregation through their participation in worship services, prayer meetings, and social activism. Through speaking with them and observing their activities, I can conclude that they believe that their spiritual and social efforts can and will bring about change. They feel empowered by MPCC's model of servant leadership. In a context where political power is backed up by violence, such a model—though admittedly not widespread—provides an alternative example of how the exercise of power could be imagined, whether in congregations, other civil-society groups, or even at the level of state politics. MPCC has created a congregational culture of empowerment and self-expression that values active participation rather than submission to authority. The congregation has gone beyond providing for people's basic physical and material needs. It is creating a space where people can imagine alternative ways to distribute spiritual, social, and perhaps even political power. Such spaces could prove crucial in a context where the authoritarianism of ZANU-PF has been shaken by the power-sharing arrangement with the MDC. For example, the MDC prime minister, Morgan Tsvangirai, has pledged to reduce restrictions on civil society and to lift restrictions on the press, which may encourage civil-society groups to assume more overtly political roles.

Conclusions

One of the aims of this volume is to understand under what conditions religious groups may undercut or promote human security. A key condition is the nature of the state. Zimbabwe is a case where there is a supposedly Marxist and secular state, but it is actually authoritarian and has attempted to control religious groups that it perceives as threatening its power. The state's powers have not yet been significantly altered by the new power-sharing arrangements. Such states place considerable restraint on religious actors, but religious actors do not all interact with the state in the same way under these conditions. Some religious groups challenge the state in the public sphere. Such challenges can be seen as an attempt by religious actors to promote long-term human security, which in Zimbabwe depends upon the reformation of the state. But such challenges also threaten people's short-term human security because the state may attempt to oppress or co-opt these groups, often using violence. Other religious groups provide essential social services but do not publicly challenge the state. This can be seen as an attempt to promote short-term human security as, in many cases, people's very survival depends on the intervention of these religious actors. But simply providing social services may ultimately jeopardize long-term human security because this does not prevent the state from carrying on with its damaging policies. Still others, like the EPC Christians at MPCC, have provided for the needs of the poor *and* have created spaces for people to develop empowering networks and ideas. MPCC holds within it a significant tension as it both provides short-term human security and creates a space where people are developing the "self-expression values" necessary for long-term human security in the context of a reformed state. While Martin (2002) and Freston (2001) have made similar arguments about the potential for EPC Christianity to function in such an empowering way, no studies have *definitively* demonstrated a direct relationship between values acquired in EPC churches and political empowerment (Robbins 2004: 135).

Further research on a variety of religious groups in Zimbabwe would shed light on why some choose to challenge the state, work behind the scenes, or attempt to balance the tension between short- and long-term human security by strategically doing both. My case study method does not allow for this sort of comparison, but the MPCC case demonstrates that even under authoritarian states religious actors have some flexibility. They actively and strategically choose different options for interaction with the state and other groups within civil society. The MPCC case also demonstrates that EPC Christians are not always apolitical or focused on the prosperity gospel as has so often been assumed.

The emergence of EPC Christians as social and political—rather than simply religious—actors could well be one of the most significant developments in twenty-first-century Africa. A major finding of all the most recent research on African EPC Christians is that they want a place for Christianity in the public sphere. EPC Christians are having ongoing and unresolved debates about how African church-state relationships should be configured. These debates are more likely to be manifest in their various practical projects and actual interactions with the state, rather than in theological journals, but EPC Christians, for so long operating at the margins of mainline Christianity in Africa, may be especially well placed to advocate for configurations in which the churches self-consciously distance themselves from state power. This can be seen at the microlevel at MPCC in its emphasis on "servant leadership." Such churches might begin to articulate their role as prophets who shun political power, acting as watchdogs that challenge the state to act justly. As the MPCC case demonstrates, EPC Christians can be resourceful and dynamic when it comes to creating safe spaces for people to develop empowering networks and ideas.

Some general policy points flow from these conclusions. First, policymakers should be able to distinguish between short- and long-term human security and to understand the tensions between them. At various times, it may be necessary to sacrifice long-term human security for the sake of short-term human security or vice versa. Second, policymakers could benefit from a better understanding of EPC Christianity, including its diversity, flexibility, and the spiritual and cultural resources that it can draw on to provide aid to those in need and to help people develop "self-expression values." Third, policymakers should be aware that the goals and motivations of religious groups may be vastly different from other NGOs or state actors. Religious groups may not share (Western) policymakers' or (Western and African) secular NGOs' goals of regime change or democratization. EPC Christians may at times serve others, not in a bid to win power for themselves or promote democracy, but simply because that is what they understand Christ would have them to do. For this reason, secular policymakers may find religious groups baffling or frustrating partners, who may be unwilling to compromise their religious activities for the sake of political goals. This could prove important in Zimbabwe, where Western policymakers refuse to channel funding through the government, distributing it rather through NGOs and civil-society groups. For instance, in June 2009, Tsvangirai met President Barack Obama in Washington, D.C. Obama promised $73 million in assistance for Zimbabwe and said the United States would consider Tsvangirai's advice when it came to distributing the funds through various sectors (Lobe and Mattern 2009). Since Christian organizations and congregations make up one of the most viable sectors within Zimbabwean civil society, they could be poised to receive significant foreign assistance. This presents both an opportunity and a danger for religious groups, in that they may suddenly have more resources to carry out their lifesaving work, while at the same time, they run the risk of being co-opted by foreign funders. In addition, if the state comes to see religious groups as a source of foreign cash, it might intensify its attempts to co-opt them. Finally, policymakers could benefit from a thorough documenting of the present range of Christian and secular organizations. This would provide policymakers from outside Zimbabwe with better information about how to distribute funding. It also would aid the various organizations themselves, enabling them to work *together* more efficiently and effectively. This is crucial for long-term human security because it can provide Zimbabweans—religious and secular alike—with the resources and the freedom to build relationships with each other, helping to create an empowered civil society that can balance state power.

Notes

Gladys Ganiel is an assistant professor and coordinator of the Conflict Resolution and Reconciliation program in the Irish School of Ecumenics, Trinity College Dublin at Belfast. The author wishes to thank Mount Pleasant Community Church for its cooperation. The research received funding from the Association for the Sociology of Religion's Fichter Grant and the Trinity College Dublin new lecturer's start-up fund. Thanks to participants in the Luce Symposium, Karin Alexander, Isobel Mukonyora, and Terence Ranger for comments and Therese Cullen and Shae Savoy for proofreading.

1. Information on the Quality of Life Index can be found at http://www.eiu.com/ and http://www.economist.com/media/pdf/QUALITY_OF_LIFE.pdf (accessed July 18, 2009). Information about the Happy Planet Index can be found at http://www. happyplanetindex.org/ (accessed July 18, 2009).
2. There are significant literatures that define and analyze evangelical, Pentecostal, and charismatic Christianity, which are beyond the scope of this chapter. Ranger (2008), Jenkins (2006), and Freston (2001) all point out the historical develop-

mental links between these expressions of Christianity, and consider them part of a broader movement. I take that broad view, conceiving EPC Christianity as having core characteristics including an emphasis on the Bible as an infallible guide to faith, an imperative to evangelize, and an emphasis on deeply felt religious experiences (conversion, speaking in tongues, etc).

3. There is division within the ZCC, EFZ, and Catholic Bishops Forum about the degree of support for ZANU-PF, and whether or not it is appropriate to challenge the state.

11

Beyond Basic Human Security: The Role of Religious Institutions in Angola

James Tiburcio

Introduction

As defined in this volume's introduction, human security comprises the basic welfare, human rights, social desires, and subjective interests of a given population. In the past, a focus on national security has led to the oversight of vast populations on the ground. The situation in Angola is a classic example of this gap between national and human security, and as a result, churches and other welfare groups have come to the aid of Angolans ignored by their national regime. These groups, mainly led by Christian churches, work to improve basic human welfare by responding to the need for hope and the desire of neglected or abused populations to attain a voice in their future. Nevertheless, as we see in Glady Ganiel's chapter in this volume, patrimonial and authoritarian regimes have an acute interest in maintaining their hegemony, often to the detriment of populations under their control. Therefore, religious organizations must work in the delicate zone between accommodating to corrupt regimes and ministering to the needs of a destitute population. Simultaneously, many of these religious groups further complicate their political stance by working to foster a democratic transformation.

Indeed, this chapter argues that the next step for religiously affiliated, human rights organizations in Angola is direct involvement in politics. More specifically, they should act as a catalyst to accelerate long overdue democratic reforms. Increasingly, religious organizations are realizing that a more active political role could lead to more human, social, economic, and political security than any amount of direct material aid projects. Whether or not such a role is even possible in the context of Angola's centralized regime is a complex issue. Would not Christians simply be co-opted by a powerful state bureaucracy? Recent studies (Freston 2008; Ranger 2008) have shown a mixed set of results regarding Christian involvement in different national contexts, including Latin American as well as sub-Saharan countries, among them South Africa, Nigeria, Kenya, and Mozambique. How similar or different has the Angolan experience been?

Catholic, Protestant, and evangelical institutions are active in Angola today; most of them originate from the United States, Canada, Switzerland, Portugal, Italy, and Brazil. Some have been active for over a hundred years, focusing on medical care, agricultural development, and a variety of relief work. Christian institutions, including churches, schools, and aid groups, also provide a reliable link to connect foreign governments, international donors, and nongovernmental organizations (NGOs) with the poorest communities. These groups provide basic social services, such as aid distribution, health care, and education (Jayasinghe 2007). In some developing countries, including Angola, the activities of these organizations are often listed as factors that contribute to the continuation of chronic state deficiencies. This is caused by their assumption of responsibilities associated with general human security without pursuing a partnership with local government agencies (Connor et al. 2005). Many believe that the Angolan government should invest more of its revenue in social services since continued privatization of basic services further distances the Angolan state from its citizens (Ostheimer 2000).

Increasingly, nongovernmental organizations take governmental responsibilities upon themselves, allowing the government of Angola to indefinitely postpone investment in key areas. Consequently, their activities are conducive to temporary improvements in human security, but in the long run, they often create dependent behavior by state authorities, permanently siphoning funds from social service projects (Tiburcio 2008). Nonetheless, their essential services have been recognized by society in general as well as the government, and a number of religious leaders are well known and regarded by their communities and beyond (Ferris 2005).

As a result, religious institutions and their leaders have taken tentative steps toward becoming more involved in general political and governance issues, both in the capital and in provinces. Based on statements made by leaders of the two most politically active churches in Angola, the Methodist and Catholic Churches, such involvement should be directed toward countering corruption, authoritarianism, and the patrimonial presidential regime; pushing for reforms in the oil industry; advocating broad political reform; and, eventually, calling for and presiding over a truth and reconciliation commission (Gifford 1995).

For these goals to occur, there must be a general commitment to democracy and democratic values among religious groups. In other words, society as a whole, and churches specifically, must "demand democracy"; that is, churches would demand democratic forms of government and reject any form of nondemocratic government (Bratton and van de Walle 1997). This is critical step toward creating a culture of human rights, giving a voice to populations made invisible by a corrupt regime, and ensuring a full panoply of human security where welfare, rights, and voices of the people are heard as equals in the context of civil society and political power.

I took two important aspects into consideration in writing this case study; first, though evangelical Christians have been the group with the highest growth rates in the last twenty years, restricting the study to their role would be shortsighted as the nascent seeds of democracy in Angola are a collective responsibility, not restricted to a specific branch of Christianity, or even faith-oriented organizations, but rather to the whole spectrum of society. Second, following the attainment of Angolan independence from Portugal in November 1975, a continuum of religious institutional initiatives were created, aiming to influence both the Angolan military and political reality in general. Despite the fact that the Catholic Church actively supported the metropolitan regime during the colonial period, Catholics were among the first to openly confront the two most important political forces in Angola after independence. Catholic institutions lambasted the Popular Movement for the Liberation of Angola (MPLA) and the National Union for the Total Independence of Angola (UNITA), regarding their treatment of their own people in addition to the management of the war and state. Apart from criticizing the opposing sides, the Roman Catholic Church accused the MPLA government of violating the right to freedom of religion in 1977 (Oyebade 2007). There is little evidence to suggest that the Catholic Church acted out of self-interest or as part of a coordinated push in line with the liberation theology of the late 1970s.[1] Rather, period documents indicate that the criticism was a reaction to increased pressure on the Catholic Church, and all Angolan religious groups, to approve the centralized government's authoritarian rule.[2] Later, those initiatives overlapped with Protestant initiatives, and presently, the protection of religious freedom is sustained by ecumenical forums and various independent organizations.

Furthermore, recent studies by Woodberry and Shah (2005) have found persuasive evidence that there is a correlation between the current growth rates of Christianity and democracy, especially regarding evangelical Christianity in the global south. Based on that study, it is plausible to argue that continued and persistent Christian participation in Angolan politics could lead to greater democratic participation and the eventual expansion of human rights. Yet as Woodberry and Shah (2005) point out, "opposing hierarchy and liberating individual consciences in religion does not automatically make one a foe of authoritarianism and a friend of liberty in politics."

As Ganiel's chapter reveals in the case of Zimbabwe, religious actors in Angola also face marginalization and co-optation from a secular, patrimonial-authoritarian regime. Confronted by a neglectful state, religious actors are often compelled to enter their countries' political arena, often without much success. However, Angola's case suggests that a political role has the potential to be more effective than inaction. Although the present political regime exhibits no signs of change, religious actors have determined that remaining on the sidelines is not an option with the human security of the Angolan people at stake.

Background

Any discussion of Angolan politics must take into consideration the context of its recent history. In 2002, Angola emerged from a fratricidal war that left millions dead, displaced, or maimed. The nation comprises a total area of 1,246,700 square kilometers, with an estimated population of 16 million. Most Angolans are Christian, and although there is a general lack of accurate data regarding almost everything in Angola, we can estimate that around 43 percent of the population is Roman Catholic, with 25 percent belonging to African Christian denominations. Ten percent attend Protestant churches, for example, Congregationalists (United Church of Christ), Methodists, Baptists, and Assemblies of God. Five percent belong to various Brazilian evangelical churches, including Universal Church of the Kingdom of God, God Is Love, and a number of others.[3] A small percentage of the population adheres to animism or traditional religions; it is possible that the majority of Angolans still retain some sort of traditional beliefs and engage in them either alongside or in addition to an "official" religion, and there is also a Muslim community of eighty to ninety thousand, largely composed of small West African and Lebanese communities (United States Department of State 2008).

Knowledge of the nation's history also facilitates comprehension of the potential role that Protestants and Evangelicals play in contemporary Angolan politics. Their very existence was intertwined with the country's political awakening. As early as the 1930s, the Catholic Church was present in most of Angola's territory. Nonetheless, due to its close identification with the large Portuguese settler population and the central Portuguese government's restrictions on religious orders, it remained intimately linked to the colonial government, until independence in November 1975.[4] According to David Birmingham, though:

> The Catholic Church was not . . . a mission church with a mandate to proselytize, heal, and educate. It was a branch of the metropolitan church. . . . Only in the far south did a Catholic mission church of French and Alsatian parentage make a predominant impact. In the rest of the country, the

colonial regime left a partial educational, spiritual, and medical vacuum that Protestants sought to fill. (2006: 101)

Therefore, Protestant and evangelical missions are concentrated in specific regions, usually with a specific denomination dominating any given region. Historically, they have concerned themselves not only with Angolans' souls but also with their basic, human security needs. Baptist missions were the most active in the northern provinces, a region almost exclusively inhabited by the Bakongo ethnic group. The Methodists concentrated in the areas around the capital, Luanda, and the surrounding provinces of Bengo, Cuanza Sul, and Malange, home to the Mbundu people. The Congregationalists spread their mission churches through the central plateau, where the largest ethnic group, the Ovimbundu, dominated (Marcum 1978).

In a strongly Roman Catholic environment, just being a Protestant was considered oppositional to the colonial government, and "although missionaries did their utmost to avoid conflict with civil authorities and to instill concepts of law and order among their converts . . . [Protestant missionaries were] seen as a threat by Portugal" (Birmingham 2002).

All the same, Protestant and Catholic organizations provided the only educational opportunities available to the vast majority of Angolans, but even so, having the chance to be educated in one of their institutions was another feat of fortune and hard work. Concomitantly, these churches, schools, mission posts, and charities were the only available choices for Angolans to learn organizational and public speaking skills, which are essential for the development of civil society in addition to being mainstays of political aspiration. As a result of these opportunities, mission school graduates founded the three most significant liberation movements during the independence struggle. The primary founders of these movements were Agostinho Neto of the MPLA, son of an Mbundu Methodist pastor; Jonas Savimbi of UNITA, son of an Ovimbundu Congregationalist minister and railroad worker; and Holden Roberto of the National Front for the Liberation of Angola (FNLA), son of a Bakongo Baptist mission worker (Birmingham 2002).

Following the fall of the dictatorship in Portugal in 1974, the Portuguese began hasty preparations to leave the country. At this point, the multipolar, ethnically based movements that had been fighting each other in addition to the Portuguese embarked on an all-out war, aided by the Cold War rivals and their regional allies, but none of the movements attained national appeal. Unable to cooperate in a power-sharing government, they established an agreement between all movements as well as the new Portuguese government. This agreement was planned to last until national elections took place, but war continued nonstop for twenty-seven years, excepting a brief interlude in 1991–1992 (Clarence-Smith, Gervase 2003).

Protestant churches, especially the Congregationalists and Methodists, viewed the fall of the Salazar regime in Portugal as a new era. They believed that restrictions on their work would be lifted, or at least lightened, under a more liberal government. Unfortunately for them, the new Portuguese government almost immediately abandoned the colony to its own luck (Schubert 1999 [1997]).

Following independence, the support of the Protestants for the independence movement did not pay off. A considerable number of temples, mission posts, and schools were quickly attacked or destroyed; leadership and church members were persecuted. On a number of occasions, pastors, teachers, and those responsible for small communities were killed, and mission buildings were plundered and burned to the ground (Schubert 2000).

Apart from their primary ethnic divisions, Christian churches were also forced to "take sides" during the long civil war. The Congregationalist Church was regarded by the state as the church of UNITA; it was generally ostracized in government-held areas. As the war stretched on, the urban part of the Congregationalist Church was able to continue its religious and charitable activities with little hindrance. Meanwhile in rural, UNITA-controlled Angola, Congregationalists thrived in almost total isolation from their city brethren. Baptists became less significant in the national context as FNLA faded from Angola's political and military life. Nevertheless, Baptists were able to maintain a nearly national presence, despite the relatively small number of adherents and the fact that a considerable number took refuge in what is now the Democratic Republic of Congo. On the other side, the Methodist Church came to be regarded as the official state Protestant church. In aftermath of the battles around Luanda in November 1975, it became the first church to recognize the MPLA government and Agostinho Neto's regime (Freston 2004).

Dissent and Conformity

In the civil war years that followed independence, any political dissent from religious organizations was strongly frowned upon by the government, and such dissent could result in reprisals, persecution, or death. In the case of foreigners, such dissent often resulted in expulsion from the country. The May 27, 1977, coup attempt and the ensuing purge still resonated. On that occasion, the MPLA responded with extensive and violent repression to an equally violent revolt, led by one of its main cadres, Nito Alves. The traumatic experience quieted all surviving regime opponents, and the following fourteen years were characterized by fear, passive resistance, and silence. As soon as the MPLA was in control of most urban areas, it installed a single-party Marxist-Leninist dictatorship. Churches and religious organizations in general were forbidden from having any role in education; it became a monopoly of the party-state (Messiant 2008).

In the years of blood and iron, there were tentative efforts to influence the political scenario, especially by the Catholic Church's use of pastoral letters. Most of these used subtle language to attack the status quo. Among these, some of the most important were "On War and Religious Freedom," of November 1976; "On Reconciliation," of February 1984; and "On Peace," of July 1988. The boldest pastoral letter, because of its content and context, was published on November 11, 1989. In this letter, archbishops and bishops called on those in high places to consider the plight of their fellow Angolans, to put down their weapons, to embrace all as siblings, and to work for peace. Laden with symbolism, the letter denounced the violation of the recent cease-fire, the return to war, the chaos reigning in the country, the conflict of interests between those in power and the poor, and the hate speech used by both sides.[5]

The bishops not only denounced, they also possessed what seemed at the time to be a completely visionary proposal: the end of the single-party regime, a real search for peace, a long overdue cease-fire, peace talks, relaxed economic control, and free elections. It was the first time since 1977 that anyone in Angola confronted the state in such an open manner. The impact of the letter was measured by the Angolan state reaction. The MPLA used all state media—the national television and radio networks, the *Jornal de Angola*, and political rallies—to threaten and condemn what it labeled an act of state treason. Catholics were accused of siding with the Unites States and the UNITA "armed thugs," as well as engaging in illegal political activities that, in the government's view, only benefited the enemies of the Angolan republic (Heywood 2006).

On the other side, some churches seemed to deliberately choose not to see, hear, or speak against corrupt government practices.[6] Schubert (2000) argues that the Methodist Church and its related organizations watched silently for nearly twenty years after independence, supporting a government for what it symbolized, rather than what it practiced, and they, therefore, became accomplices to a perverse regime that rapidly departed from its initial promises.

The Methodists had been in Angola since 1885 and were especially active in regions where revolts had taken place against the colonial regime. In the late 1960s, a number of pastors were arrested. Some were killed, and others went missing as a result of the Portuguese colonial regime's repression.[7] The "Africanization" of the leadership of the Methodist Church, which began in 1972, did little to prevent accommodation with the Marxist regime of the MPLA.[8] This problem was not restricted to the Methodists. All religious institutions were faced with the option of collaborating with the new regime or having their activities either curtailed or banned. In such circumstances, churches were frequently unable to develop an independent or relevant role (Schubert 1999 [1997]).

The Secular and the Sacred in the Angolan State

The MPLA pronounced the new Angolan constitution of 1975, which was revised in 1976 and 1980. It endorsed a socialist political and economic system and instituted a secular state. At the time, Roberto de Almeida, the MPLA Central Committee secretary for ideology, information, and culture, "admonished church leaders not to perpetuate oppressive or elitist attitudes, and he specifically warned that the churches would not be allowed to take a neutral stance in the battle against opponents of the MPLA-PT regime" (Federal Research Division of the Library of Congress 1989).

In the first ten years following independence, the MPLA's secularist stance was balanced by an ideological rift within the ranks of the party's highest cadres. The more reactionary government members strongly opposed and resented any religious participation in postcolonial Angola. However, Agostinho Neto and his successor, Jose Eduardo dos Santos, continued to accommodate religious leaders in the name of stability (Federal Research Division of the Library of Congress 1989).

The Marxist regime was never completely secularized, nor did it officially support any religious group despite the fact that animistic beliefs and allegiances with religious leaders permanently lurked on the sidelines. Despite a few episodes of persecution and even purges, the MPLA was never perceived to be a totalitarian oppressive/repressive regime as the colonial government had been. The only things that were sacred to the independent Angolan state were the oil reserves and the diamond mines, the sole sources of revenue for the Angolan elite. Religion was generally regarded as either a nuisance or an ally, depending on the circumstances.

During the same period, UNITA established a totalitarian, Maoist concentration camp in the regions it occupied; at this camp, opposition was answered summarily, often with bonfires. Following UNITA's withdrawal into the bush, religious structures were integrated into the movement, barring any kind of criticism. For the movement's leadership, there was no space for any interference in political issues. Churches were required to restrict themselves to their spiritual and social responsibilities and to steer clear of matters outside of church "walls."

The Evangelical Congregational Church in Angola (United Church of Christ) is the largest Reformed church in the country and is favored among the Ovimbundu, the ethnic group to which Savimbi belonged. In the first decade of the war (1975–1985), it was assimilated into UNITA. Just as the Methodists were accused of omission regarding the MPLA, Congregationalists are often identified as having not only ignored UNITA's brutal activities but also of having actively taken part in the war effort.[9] Although UNITA did not hinder other churches from working within its area, Congregationalists did enjoy certain privileges, such as direct access to UNITA's leaders and more freedom of movement.

Congregationalists became the backbone of UNITA's education and health system for some time after 1975. As UNITA lost ground to MPLA, however, the influence of the Congregational Church and its participation in politics declined. The involvement of the church in politics on UNITA's side had a positive, though ephemeral, impact on human security levels for specific regions. The cost of that involvement turned out to be extremely high, and the church is still marginalized in MPLA strongholds and Angolan politics in general (Schubert 1999 [1997]).

From 1976 to 1990, only the International Committee of the Red Cross (ICRC), Médecins sans Frontières (MSF), and Caritas Internationalis (Catholic relief agency) were allowed to carry out humanitarian activities in UNITA-held territory. In the brief period of peace from May 1991 through October 1992, more than fifty humanitarian NGOs and United Nations agencies entered Angola for the first time, but as fighting once again broke out, practically all international personnel had to abscond from the interior of the country to the relative safety of the capital city of Luanda. For two years after the elections of 1992, the war was many times more destructive and brutal than in all of the previous seventeen years combined. A thousand civilians were reported killed each day. Fighting moved from rural, sparsely populated areas to populous urban centers, and in towns such as Kuito, the situation deteriorated to such extreme levels that "[t]he dogs ate the dead, and the living ate the dogs" (Richardson 2000).

At first, local international agencies' staff and religious leaders took over the management of relief efforts in rural areas as foreign workers were forced to leave because of security concerns. In later political and operational negotiations, allowing United Nations High Commission for Refugees airplanes to land in some UNITA-held areas became practically the sole responsibility of local church leaders (Richardson 2000). Nonetheless, as soon as there was peace, religious leaders in rural areas were relegated to their previous apolitical roles.

Peace without Democracy

In 2001, the Angolan government agreed to accept a mediation effort by religious organizations in partnership with the United Nations, following a string of failed peacekeeping missions. At first, it seemed to be an encouraging step toward peace. Unfortunately, in retrospect, there are indications that the initiative was a misleading sign of goodwill. By allowing a more participatory, broadly based effort in facilitating negotiations with UNITA, the government bought itself time in order to carry out its plan of cornering and killing the rebel leader, Jonas Savimbi, before anything concrete could be achieved. In so doing, the government appeased growing demands from Angola's civil society for an immediate truce and a return to negotiations. The slow and difficult negotiation process was also blamed on the United Nations and the churches, thus diffusing protests that the MPLA was no longer interested in negotiating. In February the following year, Savimbi was located and killed in the province of Moxico, bringing the war to an abrupt end (Grobbelaar 2003).

In September 2008 the second legislative elections in Angola's history took place. The MPLA, the governing party since 1975, consolidated its hold on power. Now, more than ever, government officials and the head of state have a tighter grip on the nation's destiny. Following nearly thirty years of war, peace was achieved in 2002 by the barrel of MPLA's weapons. Such a hard-earned bone will not be let go so easily; the government now feels vindicated, legitimized, and justified, as all peace missions, agreements, and international and national initiatives failed to stop the rebels. Only the MPLA was able to put an end to the war, and as a result, all opponents to the regime were either annihilated in battle or, after the September 2008 election, relegated to political insignificance through the ballot.

Angola's unicameral political system, dominated by a single party, has been continuously strengthened by a 34-year-long presidential mandate. Needless to say, the national parliament is merely a formality, or rather an employment agency for the five hundred most influential families in the country. Calls for political change fell on deaf ears, and it was only in the late 1990s, following its renunciation of Marxism, that the Angolan government began allowing some freedom of opinion and association.

Since 1985, the Angolan government had been moving away from a socialist experiment toward a market-oriented economy. By 1999, privatization of almost all state-run businesses, such as farms, factories, and services had been completed. State ministers, armed forces generals, and public servants had become the new millionaires of the Angolan economy, in line with other former socialist republics around the world.[10] The MPLA moved away from Marxism to paternalistic capitalism devoid of any genuine ideological content.[11]

Securing Human Security through Political Participation

Slowly, religious organizations became more active in the political realm. That is not to say that churches and other religious organizations did not play crucial responsibilities in localized political issues in previous years, but it was only in 1999 that the long period of distrust and partisanship was overcome enough to form the

Inter-Ecclesial Committee for Peace in Angola (COIEPA). This umbrella organization brought together the most politically oriented religious associations in Angola: on the Protestant/evangelical side, the Council of Christian Churches of Angola and the Angolan Evangelical Alliance; representing the Angolan Catholic Church, the Episcopal Conference of Angola and São Tomé (CEAST). Since its foundation, COIEPA has become the organization responsible for raising international awareness about Angolan religious entities. Nevertheless, it has failed to become a nationally recognized religious organization in Angola itself. Most of its political activities have been aimed at promoting peace building and reconciliation initiatives on municipal and provincial levels. For these efforts, COIEPA was awarded the Sakharov Human Rights Prize in 2001 by the European Union, but the organization has as of yet failed to become a focal point of faith-based political awareness programs. Though it is well known internationally, churches and other organizations under its umbrella continue to give preference to advocating their initiatives via denominational channels instead of using a united and shared vehicle (Comerford 2004).

Present Outlook

The church-led, peace-based policy of 2001 was deemed unsuccessful because it failed to secure peace fast enough (Vines et al. 2005). Had religious organizations been able to carry out their strategy, their place in shaping the postwar political and social system probably would have been assured. The end of the war was so sudden and unexpected that faith-based organizations and churches did not have a contingency plan to respond to the situation. On the other hand, there is no evidence to suggest that the government would have included religious groups if they had had a plan or even if they had presented a completely unified front.12

Formidable hurdles remain to prevent regime-changing influence from Christian factions. More specifically, economic and political realities in Angola appear insurmountable as the president's office controls the political and military life in Angola; it also has complete control of Angola's resources. The patronage system is deeply embedded in Angolan society, and most civil-society actors are enclosed in the network of patron-client circles and cycles (Shaxson, Neves, and Pacheco 2008).

Co-optation has been widely used by the government since independence, and Angola's churches have been subjected to it as much as any other organization. In 1980, the MPLA invited two priests and a bishop from the Roman Catholic Church to join the National Assembly. The invitations were refused, ostensibly on the grounds that the invitees would be unable to perform their ecclesiastical and political duties (Heywood 2006). The true reasons, though, were that such a move would configure a ratification of the dictatorial, one-party regime and in that way further limit the church's ability to confront the state. On the other hand, such an invitation could have been a unique, though improbable, opportunity to influence the system from the inside. The episode provides evidence of the fact that religion itself has never been a source of conflict in Angola, though religious groups have been the victims of violence. Rather, religion has been and is a secondary issue that has been employed as a political instrument by the government and its opposition.

Jose Eduardo dos Santos, Angola's second president since 1979, established a secular, patrimonial, and authoritarian regime and has been known to buy allegiance, not just from his cohorts but also from the opposition. In a country still recovering from a long and devastating war, few religious organizations are self-sufficient. In addition to government funding, most Angolans depend on donations from international governments and private enterprises from inside and outside Angola. Though all types of external funding are believed to have strings attached, governmental funding is a restraining factor on any civil actor in any country. In Angola, a nondemocratic society, conflicts of interest and limitations imposed by accepting public money are even higher, especially considering that it is the state's money, not the tax payers'. Governmental funding is distributed through a number of channels but mostly by the different state ministries, such as the Health Ministry, or through public companies, such as Sonangol, the state oil monopoly. The dispute over funds and the lack of transparency are particularly worrisome in the context of Angola.[13]

The end of the Marxist-Leninist, one-party rule in Angola and the introduction of a multiparty electoral system did not result in higher levels of human security in Angola. There is still a long way to go for the achievement of "participation in voting, in discussion, in self-assertion and self-help, in the establishment of a democratic culture both within church and state" (Ranger 2008). According to Freedom House (2009), Angola is not a free country, though there have been advances in what concerns popular participation: general elections in 1992 and legislative elections in September 2008. Nevertheless, the last electoral process was responsible for further concentration of power in the hands of President José Eduardo dos Santos, who has been in power since 1979.[14] Human rights violations are common, and corruption is endemic to the public and private sectors. In 2008, MPLA won more than 81.64 percent of the popular vote against the 10.39 percent of its historical rival, UNITA (table 11.1). Apart from being a highly centralized regime, most of its income comes from a single source, oil, which accounts for over 50 percent of the gross national product, 95 percent of exports, and 80 percent of government revenues (World Bank 2007).

Table 11.1 2008 Angolan Legislative Elections Results

	Total Votes	Percent of Total Valid Votes	Number of Seats
MPLA	5.266.112	81,64%	191
UNITA	670.197	10,39%	16
PRS (Partido de Renovação Social)	204.478	3,17%	8
ND (Nova Democracia)	77.405	1,20%	2
FNLA	71.600	1,11%	3
Other parties	160.615	2,49%	0
Total	6.450.407	100,00%	220

Sources: Comissão Nacional Eleitoral, in Govender and Skagestad (2009).

In a controversial move, Angola's Constitutional Court closed twenty political parties that received less than 0.5 percent of votes in the 2008 legislative elections in January 2009. As a result, only six parties were left, despite the fact that, according to the country's law, those political parties that were closed are allowed to regroup under different names and try once again to obtain the minimum number of votes in the next electoral contest. The 2008 elections merely acted to confirm the regime's power, the presidential elections, scheduled for the second semester of 2009, never materialized, and the 2012 election are set to be nothing but a formality to confirm José Eduardo dos Santos in a de facto lifelong office. In all likelihood, the six opposition parties would have their own presidential candidates, but none of them has attained a significant national recognition and, thus, would not represent a genuine challenge to the ruling party's candidate.[15]

As indicated in a European Union (EU) report (2008), the multitude of political parties combined with a lack of political skills, continuous infighting, and deep divisions have debilitated some of the most promising opposition parties. The government uses the opposition's feebleness to its own benefit as it freely manipulates the constitution and the pliable judicial system to subdue the prodemocracy movement. Simultaneously, the president simulated free and fair legislative elections, knowing his party would win, and strengthened his government's incumbent dominance to an unprecedented four-fifths majority in the Parliament, according to an EU Election Observation Mission in Angola on September 5, 2008.

Most religious institutions have adopted a cooperative stance toward the government, rather than being confrontational. Participation in the recent legislative elections, as well as in the scheduled presidential elections, was strongly encouraged by church leaders, and many churches have declared their willingness to collaborate directly with the government. During the 2008 election, religious institutions employed their staffs to mobilize the population to register and to vote in addition to encouraging congregations to participate in the electoral process in general. Some denominations invited the National Electoral Council to use their premises as registration posts. Most acknowledge that the role played by churches in the 2008 elections was positive and understand that some projects should be continued and started anew in the scheduled presidential elections.[16]

Just as is the case with the population in general, churches feared a civil war if the losing side disputed the September 2008 election results. In that context, religious leadership appealed to their congregations to register and cast their vote as a sacred and patriotic duty and in the spirit of national reconciliation. Understandably, there was little room for disputing either the voting irregularities or the use of state resources and media by the MPLA. When the opposition finally accepted the results of the ballot, there was universal relief, but now, there are renewed fears that the next years will be a reenactment of the one-party period and that, just as before, the new election will be controlled by the MPLA (Wright 2008).

International advocacy groups working directly or indirectly in Angola would prefer a more openly critical role from local religious institutions in an interdenominational bid to ensure political security. However, international faith-based organizations mostly avoid addressing political issues themselves for fear of alienating authorities and, in turn, endangering their permits to operate their human security programs inside the country. Despite such fears, religious groups have tried to decrease violence, to reconcile political opponents, and to generate a peaceful social environment. As previously stated in this chapter, international and national religious institutions are welcomed by the government as being essential service providers but only as long as their activities are focused on improving basic human welfare or promoting state-approved citizenship programs. Any independent advocacy for human rights is rejected by the regime. A full sense of human security, where all voices are heard and respected, remains a deeply embedded hope, but only a hope for now. In theory, international donors encourage recipient religious organizations to become more involved in actual governance issues, but currently, there are no religiously based parties in Angola. Further, due to operational and legal limitations, the creation of new political parties remains an insurmountable challenge in the present Angolan political environment (Kukkuk 2007). There have, however, been successful cases of localized, grassroots-level democracy-building programs in Angola that could be emulated by religious institutions.

An encouraging example is that of America's Development Foundation's (ADF) 20-month program (February 2005–September 2006), which is funded by the United States Agency for International Development (USAID) in fourteen communities of the Planalto Central district (Central Plateau). This program is called the Angolan Citizens Participation Initiative and it comprises "[a]ctivities contribut[ing] to participatory local development while building citizen participation and fostering productive engagement between communities and local government." This practice "achieved important results that paved the way to stronger democratic governance in the provinces in which it took place" (America's Development Foundation Angola Citizens 2007). The program was based on three key components: "citizens' meetings to define local priorities and elect representative Community Development Groups (CDGs), which were trained as effective interlocutors with government and project managers; promoting dialogue and partnerships between communities and local government; and implementing local development projects that responded to priorities that were identified by participating communities" (America's Development Foundation Angola Citizens 2007).

The program was a success, partly because it gave the community an opportunity to participate and share costs, but the maintenance of the program was compromised because of its finite funding period. Presently, local religious institutions offer the best option for international partnerships of this kind, especially in the continuation of the projects. Usually, churches and other related institutions have a longer life span and, often, a permanent nature that can offer prolonged support long after external assistance has left (America's Development Foundation Angola Citizens 2007).

Church-based higher education institutions are increasingly prominent and potentially influential incubators of human security. As of 2009, the largest is the Catholic University of Angola, which was officially launched by CEAST in February 1999. Portugal, South Africa, Norway, Spain, Italy, and, most importantly, the United States have contributed to the establishment of the university. Within the university, USAID and the Norwegian Embassy support the existence and continued work of the Center for Economic Studies and Scientific Research (CEIC), an independent think tank, housed in the Catholic institution. The CEIC has already produced new market-oriented analyses and publications. In 2008, another institution, the Methodist University of Angola, had its inaugural lecturers. Though these steps are promising, it is still premature to predict how deep an influence these institutions will have in Angola's civil and political landscape in the coming years (Hasdorff 2006).

In a country where nearly 60 percent of the population is illiterate and only 14 percent of domiciles have televisions, radio stations are critical to national relevance; currently, 38 percent of households in Angola own a radio set. Because of the importance of radio broadcasting, restrictions on private radio stations are a serious handicap to religious institutions' influence in Angola. Until 1974, the Emissora Oficial, Rádio Clube de Angola, Rádio Ecclesia, and several others were available to Angola's population. Shortly after independence was achieved, the MPLA's Voz da Revolução (Voice of the Revolution) and FNLA's Voz de Angola Livre (Voice of the Free Angola) also started to operate in shortwave. Soon after independence and until 1992, the MPLA prohibited all private media, but despite this prohibition, UNITA supported its own shortwave propaganda weapon, Voz Resistência do Galo Negro (VORGAN—Black Cockerel Voice of Resistance) until 1999, when it was finally shut down (Human Rights Watch 2004).

Presently, the only religious radio station, and possibly the only nonstate radio, with the technical capacity to broadcast nationally on longwave is Rádio Ecclesia, owned by CEAST, which is licensed only in the capital city of Luanda. The government has a virtual monopoly over the media in the provinces. Although there are private radio stations in Benguela, Cabinda, Luanda, and Lubango, government-friendly individuals and corporations own them, and most are strictly music stations. Other religious groups do not own radio stations in the country, and as a result, they are only able to buy airtime on commercial radio stations. As a result, they are subject to a number of restrictions and a great deal of self-censorship in order to avoid problems (Human Rights Watch 2004).

Conclusions and Recommendations

According to a 2001 United Nations survey, Angolans consider churches to be more trustworthy than governmental and international agencies. Religious organizations have earned this trust because, in most cases, their goal is to deliver basic human security needs to Angola's people. They have rallied to secure housing, food, and education for Angolans and have made tentative steps toward a program of human rights, but the voices of most Angolans remain relatively powerless. Because of these circumstances, I argue that Christian institutions are a latent civil and political force, biding their time. Postwar political contestation is becoming more and more difficult as the government attains partnerships and consent from churches. Nonetheless, faith-based institutions have the potential to become role models that can generate the necessary momentum for an increased influence of civil society on governmental decisions and, in due course, can advocate for a full expression of human security, including welfare, rights, and a voice for the people of Angola. Change is likely to come from a united, Angolan effort to influence the regime from the inside. Change will have to come from inside the regime at the same time as Angolan civil society pushes its government to be more responsive to human security needs and the demands of the Angolan people (Instituto Nacional de Estatística 2002).

I argue that, for the sake of a full expression of human security, religious institutions should continue their partnerships with governmental institutions, especially in civic activities such as registration and voting. These actions engender mutual respect and appreciation, essential ingredients in participative democracy. Simultaneously, religious institutions—churches, schools, and aid groups—must maintain their independence, especially financial, in relations with the government. Financial independence is crucial for the continued moral bearing of a society that accepts bribery as a legitimate recourse in everyday life. It is also crucial because it is the very foundation on which trust in these groups is built. Without trust, the legitimacy of religious groups as a source of human security would disappear.

Of course, the monolithic nature of the MPLA thwarts any significant opportunities for increased participation in politically relevant issues. The characteristics of most Angolans' survival struggle facilitate dialogue and not defiance. For that reason and considering the present political landscape in Angola, it is self-defeating to advocate open and direct opposition as the way toward human rights and a democratic polity. Rather, a multidirectional, multifaceted, and holistic approach is necessary.

Given the certainty of presidential election results, churches should call for provincial, municipal, and communal elections as a way to encourage further democratic processes in the country. Local elections would allow for more popular participation in local issues in addition to offering more people a chance to experience the possibility of real democratic contests and preparing local leaderships for the dynamics of democracy. In the long run, grassroots projects modeled on the ADF experience are the future basis for a democratic Angola. Religious institutions, both national and international, should engage in sustainable programs that sow the seeds of a genuinely democratic culture where human rights are acknowledged and human security empowers all citizens to take part in a true Angolan democracy.

Reconciliation initiatives are another facet to be pursued by religious organizations. A formal truth-and-reconciliation process is unlikely to be accepted by the ruling party in the foreseeable future. Even so, a general, self-imposed societal blackout of the recent past does not help bring about durable peace. General impunity as a means to promote peace is historically inadequate and is not conducive to sustainable public security and order. Religious institutions have the ability to pursue "micro" reconciliation processes within their areas of influence.

Foreign contacts and aid can play a decisive role not only by providing financial means but also in promoting actual governance practices within religious and general civil society organizations. International donors should encourage transparency and open accounting practices in order to instigate an environment of accountability from the bottom to the top of Angolan society. Democratic values and inclusive management practices must be infused into the very institutions that are to influence society at large and, ultimately, the national government. A culture of dialogue and compromise needs to be created at grassroots organizations' level and democratic governance must be seen as a viable, successful management and governing method. In a country that has always been governed by decree and coercion, practical examples of democratic interplay need to be multiplied and proliferated in all provinces and municipalities.

Religious organizations, in conjunction with international NGOs and the government, should make training courses available for local, traditional community and church leaders to promote democratic principles, civic tolerance, and participation. Simultaneously, continued pressure should be applied to the government to allow church-owned radio stations (most importantly, Radio Ecclesia of the Roman Catholic Church) to broadcast nationally in FM. An ecumenical radio station could be the answer to the high costs involved in implementing and operating such a venture.

Additionally, detailed field research is called for in order to assess Angola's religious institutions' demand for democratic government and governance. Presently, there is a lack of empirical data in all areas, including preferences and general commitment to democracy surveys. All of this is to say that religion can have an important and powerful role in bringing about the full expression of human security in Angola, not only in terms of basic welfare, but in infusing within its culture the voices of the voiceless and giving a population its first taste of human rights and democratic political power.

Notes

James Tiburcio teaches at the Faculty of Politics and International Relations of the Centro Universitario do Distrito Federal (UDF) and at the Ibmec Institute; he is also a PhD candidate at the Center for Sustainable Development, University of Brasilia (UnB), Brazil, where he also teaches in their Environmental Science undergraduate program.

1. Smith (1991: 209) asserts that "[l]iberation theology did not take these regions [by storm]. Indeed, liberation theology remained a primarily Latin American phenomenon."

2. For more details, see Cahen and Messiant (1998).

3. See Giga-Catholic Information, "Catholic Church in Republic of Angola (Angola)," http://www.gcatholic.com/dioceses/country/AO.htm, accessed January 23, 2009.

4. For an interesting summary of the period, see *Angola: Christianity*, available at http://www.country-data.com/cgi-bin/query/r-578.html.

5. CEAST, "Mensagem aos Responsáveis Políticos do MPLA-PT e da UNITA, a Todo o Povo de Deus e aos Homens de Boa Vontade," Luanda, 1989.

6. The MPLA government had recognized the following churches in the 1980s: the Assembly of God, the Baptist Convention of Angola, the Baptist Evangelical Church of Angola, the Congregational Evangelical Church of Angola, the Evangelical Church of Angola, the Evangelical Church of South-West Angola, the Our Lord Jesus Christ Church in the World (Kimbanguist), the Reformed Evangelical Church of Angola, the Seventh-Day Adventist Church, the Union of Evangelical Churches of Angola, and the United Methodist Church. See *Angola: Christianity*, available at http://www.country-data.com/cgi-bin/query/r-578.html.

7. For further discussion of this history, see Péclard (1998: 660).

8. According to reports from the United Methiodist Church, "[i]n Luanda, for instance, there were three United Methodist congregations in 1961; the number had risen to 14 by 1975. In 1975, there were between 40,000 and 45,000 members of the Angolan United Methodist Church, and more than 100 ordained and supply pastors. The number of members had reached 110,000 by 1987 and is now [1996] estimated at more than 175,000." See "The United Methodist Church of Angola," GBGM News Archive, http://gbgm-umc.org/africa/angola/angolumc. html, accessed August 4, 2009.

9. According to a 1994 Amnesty International Report, the identification with UNITA led to persecution by government troops in urban areas, following the resumption of the war in January 1993. See Amnesty International, *Amnesty International Report 1994—Angola*, January 1, 1994, http://www.unhcr.org/refworld/ docid/3ae6a9f654.html, accessed June 30, 2009.

10. For a compelling report on the subject, see Global Witness 2002.

11. Tony Hodges (2004) called the Angolan regime "Petro-Diamond Capitalism."

12. Although Vines et al. (2005) suggest otherwise, the government was determined to run the process autonomously, and the surprise advantage was part of its strategy.

13. In a recent episode, a bishop from an Evangelical Pentecostal church was accused of embezzlement by his brethren. Apparently, Sonangol bestowed the church 1 million American dollars for the construction of a school and a medical clinic. The bishop responsible for the negotiation of the grant allegedly transferred the amount to his private bank account in order to safeguard it from being used for purposes other than its original purposes. Apparently, the bishop returned the donation to Sonangol, claiming the headquarters of the church in Portugal wanted to send the money abroad instead of building the health clinic and school. See "Antigo

bispo da Igreja Maná devolve um milhão de dólares a Sonangol," May 22, 2006, and "Bispo da Igreja Maná refuta acusações," July 14, 2006, Luanda Antena Comercial Angonotícias, www.angonoticias.com/full_headlines.php?id=10045;www.angonoticias.com/full_headlines.php?id=10715, accessed January 22, 2009.

14. Voter registration did take place in the first semester of 2009, but elections have yet to happen.

15. See "Tribunal Constitucional extingue vinte partidos," *Jornal de Angola*, January 21, 2009, http://www.jornaldeangola.com/artigo.php?ID=99680&Seccao=politica, accessed January 22, 2009.

16. See "Igreja Católica está disposta a colaborar na preparação das eleições presidenciais," *Jornal de Angola*, January 3, 2009.

12

In Violence and in Peace

THE ROLE OF RELIGION AND HUMAN SECURITY IN NORTHERN IRELAND

Emily Morrison Griffin

Introduction

The essays in this volume examine the contexts and circumstances in which religion is an instrumental factor, either of peace or of conflict, in the pursuit of human security. This essay examines the relationship between religion, the desire for human security, and the circumstances that provoked the conflict of Northern Ireland. The importance of religion to the conflict has often been underestimated, being dismissed as a convenient party demarcation or merely an ethnic marker. In reality, it has played a fundamental role in identity formation and party mobilization in the rise of Irish nationalism, Irish unionism, and the conflict in Northern Ireland known as the Troubles (1968–1998). Religious, nonstate actors, in their pursuit of human security, have had a dramatic influence on the overall political environment in Northern Ireland. Religion has been central to the identity conflict, and religious leaders have used religious doctrine, religious rhetoric, and other nonstate parties to provoke the sectarian divide. Additionally, while religious, nonstate actors have fought for human security in Northern Ireland, the perceptions of human security have, in turn, shaped and recreated the face of religion in the province.

With this in mind, I examine the conflict in Northern Ireland in light of existential security theory. I suggest that during the Troubles, Northern Ireland was caught in a self-reinforcing mechanism of continuously strengthened effects of religiosity, polarization, conflict, and existential threat. The rise of modernization in Northern Ireland as the United Kingdom joined the European Community/Union introduced an external change into that self-perpetuating mechanism, which contributed to the development of the Good Friday Agreement (GFA) in 1998.

The importance of recognizing the religious nature of the conflict has significant policy implications for the continued success of the agreement. While the signing of the GFA was an invaluable step toward resolution, further steps will need to address religiously motivated fears and the mutually exclusive identities of the communities involved. More broadly speaking, the conflict in Northern Ireland presents a useful case study for policy formation in other conflict areas where states are trying to negotiate social harmony and to understand the relationship between religion and the pursuit of human security.

I begin with the theory of existential security proposed by Pippa Norris and Ronald Inglehart. By examining the tradition of religion and politics in Northern Ireland in view of this theory, I introduce the centrality of religious narratives and symbols in the conflict and later resolution. I also review the historical conditions that created a hostile situation of human insecurity in Northern Ireland, both for Catholics and Protestants. This will familiarize readers with the historical context of the Troubles and serve to illuminate the prevailing "competing histories"[1] of the religious actors. I describe the introduction of the Protestant minority into Ireland, the initial religious hostilities, and the developments of the interreligious conflict that resulted in social stratification, the rise of Irish nationalism, and Irish unionism.

After we recognize the strength of the political and religious divisions in the region, the important question for Northern Ireland must change: as Adrian Guelke remarks "what needs to be explained, it would seem, is no longer the intractability of the conflict, but rather what made the Good Friday Agreement possible?" (2003: 105). This essay addresses this question via a new perspective on the theory of existential security. I examine the influence of religion on human security in the conflict and the later peace agreement, drawing upon survey data from several sources during the era in Northern Ireland preceding the Troubles. Finally, I determine the impact of religion and religious nonstate actors in the conflict, to what extent secularization has occurred in Northern Ireland, and the influence it may or may not have had on the peace process. Thus, in order to understand human security in Northern Ireland, both during the Troubles and after the GFA, we must also understand the relationship between human security and religion.

Religion and Human Security in Northern Ireland

There has been a "disinclination among many sociologists to assign religious belief anything but a subordinate role in the lives of the people they are studying" (Hickey 1984). I argue, as do other scholars in this volume, that by *not* recognizing the role of religious nonstate actors, we may seriously hinder our capacity to understand the issue of human security. As discussed in the introduction, we define human security in three parts: "(1) a physical aspect, involving protection from threats to basic human welfare; (2) a juridical piece, relating to protection from violations of human rights; and (3) a more elusive, culturally conditioned factor, relating to a sense of personal autonomy and freedom." Thus, I argue that where populations feel insecure, religious identity conflicts come to the fore. These conflicts create situations where government institutions are no longer able to provide adequate security guarantees for the majority of their citizens (Ross 2007: xiv). Here I ask, "What role have religious nonstate actors played in the pursuit for human security in Northern Ireland?"

In *Sacred and Secular: Religion and Politics Worldwide*, scholars Pippa Norris and Ronald Inglehart emphasize the relationship between religion and human security. The authors argue in their theory of existential security that groups are more likely to emphasize the central importance of religion in situations of perceived existential threat. They suggest that natural disasters, HIV/AIDS pandemics, economic insecurity, political oppression, drug crimes, ineffective health care, and civil wars are all examples of situations that would reasonably cause a population to feel that their lives were in danger (Norris and Inglehart 2004: 64). In these situations of compromised human security, or existential threat, the authors insist, "religion . . . assures people that the universe follows a plan, which guarantees that if you follow the rules, everything will turn out well, in this world or the next. This belief reduces stress, enabling people to shut out anxiety" (64). More simply, in instances where people feel that their human security is threatened, they will adhere more closely to religious ideologies. On the other hand, if a population feels secure, the population will become less religious.

Critics have remarked that Norris and Inglehart fail to develop theoretically the social psychological and cognitive mechanisms that would cause these results (C. Smith 2006: 623). However, terror management theory (TMT) also supports the effect of heightened religiosity in circumstances of insecurity. Founded on the writings of Ernest Becker, psychologists base TMT on the assumption that knowledge of the inevitability of death causes extreme anxiety. Culture, ideologies, and worldviews create a kind of buffer from this anxiety, which psychologists call a "worldview defense" (Van den Bof 2008). When awareness of mortality is increased, a person adheres more closely to his or her previously held ideologies and worldviews, which provide this buffer.

Jeffrey Seul argues that religious worldviews have the superior ability "to serve the identity impulse" (1999). They lie nearer to the core of one's identity because other elements of one's identity do not address the full range of human needs, fears, and concerns as comprehensively or powerfully as the religious elements (1999). Religion provides stability in the form of a knowable world by giving an individual a sense of "locatedness," a connection to the past through origin myths and connection to the future through afterlife beliefs; a sense of predictability through religious norms and expectations, as well as role prescriptions; and an overall stable worldview. As Wellman remarks in chapter 2, religion is not simply about "belief," but it is a total way of *being* in the world, that touches and expresses desires that rational debate cannot invalidate. Since religious worldviews excel at being at the core of one's identity, and threats to that identity are often perceived as threats to the individual's very survival, Seul remarks (563) that it is unsurprising that we see conflicts occurring frequently along religious fault lines. Additionally, competitive pressure may cause the in-group to cohere more tightly around its religiously defined identity.

Existential security theory is supported by these observations. In situations of both societal and individual existential insecurity, be it an intense fear of mortality or perceived threats to identity, religious ideologies are adhered to with greater tenacity. Conversely, in situations of increased existential security, levels of religiosity decrease as the population relies less upon the "worldview defense." Indicators of religiosity such as religious identity, adherence to traditional moral attitudes, and religious participation are increased in hazardous conditions. Importantly, these strong indicators of religiosity can be identified in Northern Ireland. In fact, the region has traditionally had some of the highest levels of religious observance found in the Western world (see Fahey, Hayes, and Sinnot 2006; Hayes and McAllister 1997).

The historic conditions in Northern Ireland leading up to the Troubles created a situation of serious human insecurity for both Catholic and Protestant camps. Institutional divisions, segregated schools, inequalities in housing and employment, as well as the eruption of violence, created not only a pattern of social stratification but also a condition of general, existential threat. Similar to the situation in Zimbabwe that Gladys Ganiel describes in this volume, we can understand that both parties perceived threats to their human security as evidenced by economic insecurity, political oppression, ethnic tensions, educational inequalities, and threats of violence. Fahey et al. remark (2006: 14), "the [T]roubles did not just reinforce the prevailing nationalist-unionist conflict in Northern Ireland. They created it anew, each terrorist act, each security measure and each failed political initiative adding a fresh basis for grievance and polarization." Additionally, Ross remarks that while the distinction between physical and symbolic threat may be conceptually simple to distinguish, in a heated conflict such threats to human security may be more difficult for participants to distinguish: "both fears involve feelings of vulnerability, denigration, and humiliation that link past losses to present dangers" (2007:37). I argue that this threatened situation in Northern Ireland encouraged entrenched religiosity, greater adherence to traditional values, and strong endogamy—that is, marriage only within the accepted religious group. By adhering more closely to these ideologies, the "worldview defense" provided adherents with a greater sense of human security during the Troubles.

Ironically, this intensified religiosity inadvertently caused greater insecurity as well. It amplified the preexisting political polarization between these socially stratified camps. This polarization meant that the population divided into two opposing ethnoreligious groups with fewer individuals remaining neutral or offering cross-confessional political support (Breen and Hayes 1997). The polarization created heightened levels of conflict between the groups, eventually resulting in the outbreaks of violence for which the Troubles are known. The conflict and subsequent violence added to perceived notions of threat, which, in turn, reinforced religiosity. The worldview defense, which was attempting to buffer believers from an existentially insecure environment, was also responsible for the continuation of that same environment of existential threat. Thus, the Catholic and Protestant camps were caught in a self-reinforcing mechanism of existential insecurity, further entrenchment in religious ideologies, heightened polarization between camps, and an increased threat of violence with no interruption in sight (fig. 12.1).

The Importance of Religion in the Conflict

The role of religion in the Troubles has been the subject of much discussion and little agreement. While the conflict has been commonly referred to as a struggle

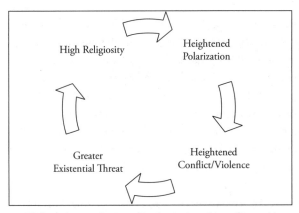

Without the introduction of modernization, the conflict could have been sustained by these patterns of religiosity and affiliation indefinitely.

FIGURE 12.1 Religiosity and Conflict in Northern Ireland. Morrison Griffin 2008.

between the Protestants and the Catholics, the degree to which these terms are considered indicative of religious involvement is not universally established. The term "Protestant" often has been used imprecisely as an alternate term for British, Loyalist, Unionist, Ulsterman, or Orangeman, while "Catholic" is often used to indicate a Republican, Nationalist, Fenian, or Irishman. Norman Richardson and others believe that the terms "Protestant" and "Catholic" are more likely to describe where people went to school or where they live rather than where they go to church on Sundays (Jenkins, Donnan, and McFarlane 1986; Richardson 1998).

Because of the presumed interchangeability of these terms, many scholars like Richardson believe that the religious nature of the dispute has been overemphasized. Richard Jenkins et al. (1986) believe that although religion has a place in the "repertoire of conflict" in Northern Ireland, it is apparent that the situation was primarily concerned with matters of politics and nationalism, not religious issues. Edna Longley has argued that it is better described as a culture war in which both sides have been merely defined by their religious denominations (2001: 13). In an editorial column in the *National Catholic Reporter*, Eoin McKiernan told readers that the "religious conflict in Northern Ireland is a misnomer for political strife" (McKiernan 1997). In 2007, William Cardinal Conway, former archbishop of Armagh, referred to the issues as "basically political, social, and economic" in nature (McCaffrey 1973: 525). Hayes and McAllister suggest that the terms "Protestant" and "Catholic" play no greater role in shaping the conflict beyond providing convenient identifying labels for the protagonists (1995: 65).

However, not recognizing the religious nature of the situation in Northern Ireland would be a serious oversight. The conflict is at many points reinforced by religiously motivated practices and activities, religious perspectives, and religious fears (Richardson 1998: 9). Jenkins et al. and Conway are correct: the conflict *is* about nationalism, economics, welfare, and rights—issues of human security. *And* we must remember that a religious influence underlies each of these issues. These labels are not merely convenient, they are indicative of the identities, and thus worldviews, interests, fears, and desires of the communities. Religious identities and narratives dictate the kinds of actions that populations are willing to execute in their pursuit for greater human security.

In her work "Religion, Identity and Politics in Northern Ireland," Claire Mitchell discusses the consequences of not only ignoring the impact of religion on the conflict, but of reducing the scope of what we define as "religion" (2006: 4). By limiting religious importance in terms of *only* belief, or church structures, or ethnic markers, or participation, we limit our understanding of what religion is and does (Mitchell 2006: 4). Religion is an ethnic marker, but it is *also* made of church structures and is *also* strongly related to political attitudes. The importance of religion as a boundary marker in Northern Ireland cannot be overemphasized (Mitchell 2006: 59). Consequently, religion, and its influence on the pursuit for human security, must be considered seriously. Furthermore, as we examine the development of nationalism and unionism in Ireland, as communities negotiated for greater human security, it will become clear that it is impossible to study the rise of the Irish and Northern Irish nation-state without recognizing the religious foundations. We shall also see how deeply embedded religion has been in the spheres of politics and economics in Northern Ireland, and how that embeddedness has influenced human security.

Competing Histories and Clashing Narratives

"Competing histories," or the conflicting historical memories of the Catholics and the Protestants, complicate their public perspective. Though the Troubles largely began in 1968, the ongoing struggle between the parties has a long history of bloodshed. Furthermore, the Protestant and Catholic accounts of the historical events clash in their content and moral assessments, including the very introduction of the British presence in Ireland. The Catholic narrative describes this initial event as the British invasion of Ireland in 1170, the year at which the oppression of the Irish commenced. However, the Protestant narrative considers the British presence in Ireland to have been established at that time when an Irish warrior king, Diarmait Mac Murchada, recovered his conquered lands with the assistance of a Norman ally, Richard de Clare "Strongbow," who subsequently and *legally* inherited those lands.

We should not assume that this is a common discussion between modern political or religious proponents, but it serves to illustrate the idea of the conflicting shared memories, or competing histories. In *Cultural Contestation in Ethnic Conflicts*, Marc Howard Ross refers to these as "clashing narratives," which "offer emotionally meaningful accounts of the world, defining groups and explaining their motives and actions" (2007: xv). He emphasizes the importance of these narratives in four components: (1) for revealing core worldviews of a group; (2) for revealing fears, threats, and grievances that drive conflict; (3) for privileging certain actions over others; and (4) for (re)constructing and strengthening communities *via* the act of storytelling (30).

Thus, the competing histories are not simply objective events of the past, but rather are indicative of lived experiences. Accordingly, we can (and should) understand the competing histories of the Catholic and Protestant narratives in order to fully comprehend the Northern Ireland conflict. It is especially significant that these conflicting histories are often deeply tied to what the communities perceived as direct threats to their human security. Thus, when the Northern

Irish communities set out to establish their rights and freedoms, the established context of clashing narratives dictated a violent struggle versus a more peaceful approach.

The Republic and Northern Ireland: Background

From 1534 to 1603, English rulers sought to strengthen their control of the island with the least financial burden. To this end, the monarchs introduced the policy of Plantation to Ireland. Since it would be difficult to gain the absolute loyalty of the Catholic elites, the process of granting Irish land to loyal agents of the Crown was both financially and strategically advantageous. At the same time, James I enacted a series of Penal Laws, which significantly reduced the rights of native Irish Catholics. For example, the laws barred Catholics from holding public office. Catholics also had to pay "recusant fines" for not attending Protestant services, nor were they allowed to own a horse worth more than five pounds.

The Plantation of Ulster in 1606 attracted many Protestant settlers from Britain and Scotland by granting generous tracts of land confiscated from the native, Catholic Irish (Darby 1996: 201). As a result, two conflicting Ulster ethnoreligious groups were created: the politically and economically dominant Anglo-Scots settlers (Protestant/Presbyterian) and the dispossessed and politically excluded Irish (Catholic).[2] This is another example of the "clashing narratives" of the groups: while the Protestant community saw the Plantation of Ireland and the Penal Laws as prudent methods for ensuring loyalty to the Crown, the Catholic community saw those same methods as inhumane, as unjust, and as a direct attack on their welfare, rights, and freedoms.

While these two groups recall the following centuries with "clashing narratives," they would often share this sense of injustice, vulnerability, and human insecurity in their histories (Ross 2007: 99). Each "regard themselves as an embattled minority religion in certain contexts, while at the same time asserting their majority status in others" (Fahey et al. 2006). Protestants would see the Gaelic Irish revolt in 1641 as an unprovoked attack against the outnumbered and vulnerable Protestant settlers (Ross 2007: 99). Catholics would forever lament the subsequent retaliation of Cromwell eight years later, killing roughly six hundred thousand Irish.

The year 1916 became a date of special significance for both groups. In 1916, the Easter Rising led by James Connelly and Patrick Pearse was crushed by the British government but gave rise to Irish nationalism. The year marks a significant date for Protestants as well, for it marks the deaths of thousands of soldiers from Northern Ireland in the Battle of the Somme (Norris and Inglehart 2004; Ross 2007: 98). In December 1921, Ireland was declared a "Free State" under the

Anglo-Irish Treaty, and in 1949, it was renamed the Republic of Ireland. Northern Ireland was given the choice to opt out of the agreement, and this was promptly done (McCracken 1995). Of the nine counties in Ulster, only six remained under British rule to become what is now the province of Northern Ireland. These six counties ensured a Protestant political majority, with a third of the population, the Catholic minority, severely opposed to the arrangement.

The newly created Republic of Ireland was not simply Catholic by nature of its population. According to William Crotty, "the Irish Catholic Church became a symbol of Ireland in the minds of the nation's people, the preserver of value, and the one instrument of the society that was not subjugated by the British" (2006: 118). Richard Finnegan asserts, "the Gaelic Ireland movement associated devotion to the Church with Irish cultural identity" (1983: 73). This strong initial connection between the Catholic Church and Irish nationalism would become crucial for both Protestants and Catholics during the Troubles.

After the separation of the six counties, nationalism in Northern Ireland, unsurprisingly, drew the majority of its support from the Catholic population. As a result, Protestant unionists associated Catholicism with a nationalist hostility and disloyalty to the province's government; Catholicism and nationalism were a serious risk for Protestant human security. Thus began the notorious association of Catholics as nationalists and Protestants as unionists. However, it is important to stress that religion was never a mere political marker; the Catholic Church was the symbol and identity for Irish nationalists. Furthermore, the province of Northern Ireland was a symbol for the Protestant community: "a Protestant State for a Protestant people" as James Craig, the first prime minister of Northern Ireland, said (Ross 2007: 14).

It is equally important to stress that perceived existential threats were fundamental to polarization along these religious fault lines. As many have insisted, the grievances between the Catholics and the Protestants have been both economic and social. The Protestant hegemony in Northern Ireland, fearful of the Catholic influence in the province, arranged local government constituencies in order to prevent any significant Catholic authority at Stormont, the Parliament of Northern Ireland (O hEither 1989: 97). As a result, Catholics were increasingly treated as second-class citizens. This pattern of social stratification had the far-reaching consequence of splitting the Protestant and Catholic camps even further into closed groups of identities and interests.

The communities would certainly attend different religious services, but the partitioning extended much further than this. Local electoral boundaries were rigged so that Protestants dominated the local councils where housing and public employment were determined. Following the rebuilding of Belfast after the Second World War, the allocation of housing was sectarian and discriminatory, creating further segregation of the population. As unemployment became a greater issue, Catholics were far less likely to find work than Protestants. The labor market became split to such an extent that Catholics and Protestants rarely found themselves working in the same arenas. Indeed, the camps self-identified with divergent holidays, cultural symbols, and sports activities. The partitioning also extended into the educational system, so that Protestant "controlled" schools had the benefit, and funding, of the government, and Catholic "maintained" schools were significantly disadvantaged, further increasing the employment gap. Unionist supporters justified these social divisions on the grounds of protecting their own human security; if the Catholic nationalists were given any amount of power sharing, they would vote for a united Ireland and, thus, a papal authority.[3]

Troubles and Existential Threat

Encouraged by the civil rights movement in the 1960s, Catholics began to organize and protest the inequalities. However, most Protestants did not accept the claims of the civil rights movement and perceived the Catholic demonstrations for equal rights as a cloaked Catholic nationalist movement. Protestants remained skeptical of the Roman Church's influence in Northern Ireland that would come about if Catholics were permitted to share power. Furthermore, the traditionally large Catholic families were seen as a threat to the Protestant numerical supremacy (O hEither 1989: 89). When Unionist prime minister Terrence O'Neill attempted to recognize the grievances of the Catholic population by implementing some housing and public appointment reforms, many Protestants felt betrayed (Terchek 1977: 54). The Unionist majority and the more extreme Democratic Unionist Party led by Rev. Ian Paisley accused O'Neill of preparing the way for a united Ireland and O'Neill was eventually forced out of office (O hEither 1989: 89). Rev. Paisley began to rally working-class Protestants against the perceived Catholic threat to Protestant human security. Thus, the conflicting perceptions of human insecurity were inextricably tied to the polarization of the communities.

Beginning in 1968, the tensions between the Catholic and Protestant communities erupted into violence. In two civil rights marches held in Derry, many protestors were injured while marching through Protestant neighborhoods. At this time, the Irish Republican Army (IRA), the self-identified defender of the Catholic community, was poorly organized and committed to nonviolent politics.[4] This soon changed. Paramilitary groups, often religiously defined, would begin to play a significant role in the struggles. The Ulster Volunteer Force, heavily armed Protestants dedicated to fighting the IRA, organized the first bombing campaign of the Troubles in an attempt to implicate the IRA. From there, violence fueled both sides. On January 30, 1972, a day now remembered as "Bloody Sunday," thirteen unarmed civilians were killed in Derry when paratroopers opened fire on a crowd of Catholic protestors. The British Embassy in Dublin was bombed in retaliation, killing thirty civilians. The British government abolished Stormont and decided to rule the state directly (O hEither 1989: 97). In 1981, Bobby Sands and ten other IRA members died in a hunger strike in Maze Prison near Belfast while protesting against the British government's refusal to grant them the rights of political prisoners rather than terrorists. The competing histories of the Catholics would see the prisoners as martyrs while the Protestant community would view them as murderers. By 1999, a total of 3,651 people had been killed in the conflict, and the Protestant and Catholic accounts and moral assessments of these deaths continued to create clashing narratives (McKittrick and McVea 2000).

Modernization and Secularization

As discussed earlier, existential security theory suggests that in instances where people feel that their human security is threatened, they will adhere more closely to religious ideologies. An addition to this theory is the assertion that modernization "weakens the influence of religious institutions in affluent societies, bringing lower rates of attendance at religious services, and making religion subjectively less important in people's lives" (Norris and Inglehart 2004: 25). Norris and Inglehart are suggesting that secularization is an evident result of modernization. I pause here to remark that the processes and relationship of modernization and secularization are neither inevitable nor necessarily causal (see Finke and Stark 1992; Hadden 1987; Stark and Iannaconne 1994). A broad-stroke thesis of modernity in the form of scientific progress that characteristically regards religion as an irrelevant player in social and political life is *not* the conception of modernization that is proposed here (Hefner 1998). I define modernization as the process of industrialization, urbanization, rising levels of education and wealth, and the development of economic and political conversations that include greater participation in the international community.[5] Modernity often goes hand in hand with a differentiation of social spheres, which may give rise to a form of secularization, or a "privatized religiosity." I do not propose that every process of modernization is inevitable or that secularization is a predetermined result. Modernization is, rather, the confluence of one or more of these processes, which may or may not create the privatization of religion and the decline of institutional religious practice, which is the mark of secularization that I investigate in this chapter.

I *do* suggest that in this particular context a secularizing trend occurred in Northern Ireland in the era surrounding the Good Friday Agreement. This secularization may be identified by the declining salience of religion measured by a decline in religious participation (church attendance) and traditional beliefs or behaviors, as well as an increase in interconfessional marriages. To illustrate this religious decline, I draw data from the following sources: the World Values Survey (WVS) waves of 1981, 1990, and 1999, and the Northern Ireland Social Attitudes Survey (NISAS) of 1989–1996. Additionally, I supplemented my own findings with those of Tony Fahey, Bernadette C. Hayes, and Richard Sinnott, who use data from the European Values Survey (EVS) waves of 1981, 1990, and 1999–2000, the Northern Ireland Life and Times Survey 1999–2003, and the Irish Social and Political Attitudes Survey 2001–2002.

As measures of modernization, I expected to see a greater degree of perceived economic security and increased levels of education across both ethnoreligious groups, as well as political conversations that address international concerns rather than domestic issues. In the surveys I examined, both Catholics and Protestants should have increasingly answered more optimistically regarding their views toward household income, job stability or opportunity, and general economic increases. I also expected to see indications of increasing education in both groups, represented in the survey data by a rise in the number of students in school past the age of fifteen. Finally, I compared indicators of increased international concerns by the increase of the number of internationally related questions on the Northern Ireland Social Attitudes Survey.

I determined the varying degrees of public religiosity in Northern Ireland by three factors: frequency of church participation/attendance, salience of traditional beliefs and values, and the percentage of interconfessional marriages. In the self-perpetuating model of existential threat, religiosity and polarization during the Troubles, I expected to see high degrees of church participation and adherence to traditional beliefs. Additionally, heightened polarization would result in low levels of intermarriage and interconfessional political support, with few "neutral" individuals. In the surveys of late 1980s–1990s, as Northern Ireland became more modernized, I expected these values to gradually switch, demonstrating lower indications of religiosity and polarization.

Modernization and Secularization in Northern Ireland

Research indicated a strong tendency toward modernization in Northern Ireland in the most recent decades (fig. 12.2). Involvement in education increased as expected. The number of respondents in both camps in the Northern Ireland Social Attitudes Survey who had completed their continuous full-time education before the age of fifteen dropped from 43 percent to 35 percent from 1989 to 1994. The respondents' positive feelings regarding their household income

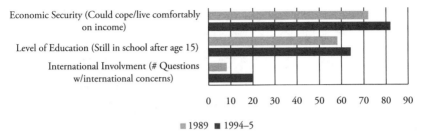

FIGURE 12.2 Modernization Trends.

Morrison Griffin 2009
Devine, P. and Dowds, L.; 1989–1995 Northern Ireland Social Attitudes Survey. Distributed by the Economic and Social Data Service. Crown Copyright material is reproduced with the permission of the Controller of HMSO and the Queen's Printer for Scotland.

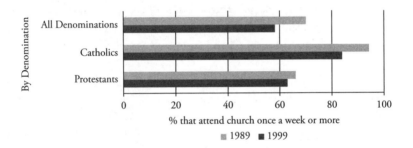

FIGURE 12.3 Church Attendance 1989–1999.

Morrison Griffin 2009
Devine, P. and Dowds, L.; 1989–1999 Northern Ireland Social Attitudes Survey. Distributed by the Economic and Social Data Service. Crown Copyright material is reproduced with the permission of the Controller of HMSO and the Queen's Printer for Scotland.

also increased. Progressively from 1989 to 1994, both Catholic and Protestant respondents were more likely to feel they could cope or even live comfortably on their household income.[6] Additionally, we can see an increase of questions on the NISAS regarding the international community. In 1989, respondents were asked eight questions pertaining to the broader world, and in 1995 the survey contained twenty questions.

Survey data also confirmed the notion of secularization in Northern Ireland. According to the NISAS, the percentage of respondents who claimed to attend church once a month or more declined from 70 percent to 58 percent from 1989 to 1999 (fig. 12.3). This figure is also biconfessional, decreasing from 94 percent of Catholics to 84 percent, and 66 percent of Protestants to 63 percent who attend church at least once monthly.

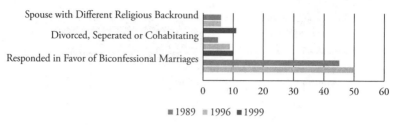

FIGURE 12.4 Religious Marital Values.

Morrison Griffin 2009

Devine, P. and Dowds, L.; 1989–1999 Northern Ireland Social Attitudes Survey. Distributed by the Economic and Social Data Service. Crown Copyright material is reproduced with the permission of the Controller of HMSO and the Queen's Printer for Scotland.

Studies by Queen's University Belfast and the University of Ulster also found that church attendance had declined biconfessionally, dropping in Catholics from 90 percent to 62 percent between 1989 and 2004, in the Presbyterian Church from 50 to 40 percent, and in the Church of Ireland church from 40 to 35 percent (Ganiel 2008).

Finally, according to the NISAS, those in favor of mixed marriages, that is biconfessional marriages, increased from 45 percent in 1989 to 50 percent in 1996. Data also indicated a decrease in traditional values. Respondents who were divorced, separated, or cohabiting without being legally married doubled from 5 percent in 1989 to 10 percent in 1999 (fig. 12.4).

In their work, *Conflict and Consensus: A Study of Values and Attitudes in the Republic of Ireland and Northern Ireland*, Tony Fahey, Bernadette C. Hayes, and Richard Sinnott also confirm a secularization trend in Northern Ireland. They remark, "secularization . . . intensified in the 1990s and the early years of this century, both in the North and the Republic" (2006: 54). Significantly, for the existential security model, this "intensified" shift toward secularization corresponds with the era preceding the Good Friday Agreement. These lowered levels of religiosity would provide a shift within the self-reinforcing mechanism that would allow for decreased levels of polarization and, thus, perceived existential threat.

Fahey et al. continue that it was a "shift from strong and highly institutionalized attachments toward more intermittent and lukewarm adherence and towards various forms of privatized belief and commitment" (56). I am not convinced that religion in Northern Ireland has shifted to a "lukewarm adherence," as the province still evidences some of the highest levels of religiosity in the Western world (Fahey et al. 2006: 30). While the province may have experienced a degree of secularization, it may be an exaggeration to call Northern Ireland a "secularized society." There is by no means a universal project to secularize the province by the majority of opinion, and secularization in Northern Ireland is more accurately described as a decrease in religious salience than as a rise in secularity. In fact, I argue later that the role of the churches will be equally as important for post–Good Friday Agreement reconciliation processes as they may have been for sustaining the conflict.

Critiques and Limitations

There are several critiques that can, and have, been made against the models proposed here and it is worthwhile to examine them. First, existential security theory is based on an assumed, unstated, and contentious cognitive model. As I described earlier, Norris and Inglehart remark, "Both religion and secular ideologies assure people that the universe follows a plan. . . . This belief reduces stress, enabling people to shut out anxiety and focus on coping with their immediate problems" (2004: 19). These remarks are made without any substantiating data. However, as also discussed earlier, the research conducted on the issue of mortality salience and terror management theory speak to this concern. Psychologists have found that when a person's awareness of mortality is increased, a person will, in fact, adhere more closely to his or her previously held ideologies and worldviews.

Moreover, there are limitations to using surveys to determine modernization or secularization. Foremost, while binary polling can be efficient, conducting in-person, open-ended interviews would have resulted in greater depth and accuracy of information. Perhaps more problematic are the subjective interpretations of certain questions and terminologies. For example, in order to determine frequency of prayer, question 199 in the World Values Survey asks the respondent, "How often do you pray to God outside of religious services?" (Norris and Inglehart 2004: 57). Respondents' perceptions of what constitutes "prayer" will be subjective and variable. Additionally, the concept of prayer "outside religious services" does not apply to the Jewish context as every act of prayer is, by definition, a religious service.[7] With this in mind, the World Values Survey and other surveys from which I draw can be considered to have a very Western-Christian bias, presuming a unilateral interpretation of religious terminologies and definitions of "religiosity." However, considering the context of this study, such a bias is a negligible concern. The two religious communities concerned here are both from the Western-Christian tradition, and an assumed vocabulary is not unreasonable in this instance.

Beyond its obvious Western bias, the survey data poses other limitations for this model as well. Because of the lack of earlier surveys, this model is unfortunately unable to demonstrate earlier trends of modernization or secularization.

Especially problematic is any attempt at isolating the modernization variables from one another; rather than taking all the indicators as evidence of modernization, it could be possible that the reduction of religious indicators is solely due to one factor, such as an increase in education or greater immigration.

Finally, it is possible to see religion's role in this model as a purely negative influence. This is not the intention of this study. As Wellman and Lombardi discuss in the introduction, religion may or may not involve violence as it seeks to to establish human security for its participants. Indeed, other case studies in this volume demonstrate how religious nonstate actors are able to achieve greater human security via entirely peaceful means. However, as the Troubles began in the late 1960s, preexisting, clashing narratives associated with religious identities caused these highly polarized communities to respond to perceived existential threats with violence. It is not the purpose of this volume to determine whether religious worldviews are inherently good or evil. Our purpose is to demonstrate the motivating and mobilizing influence of religion and to suggest that we underestimate that power at our own risk.

Policy Implications and Conclusions

Religious identities in Northern Ireland are not merely convenient labels, they are indicative of the identities of the communities: their worldviews, narratives, interests, desires, and fears. Furthermore, it is analytically incoherent to study the rise of the republic and the Northern Irish nation-state without recognizing their religious foundation. Religion has been deeply embedded in the spheres of Northern Irish politics and economics, and thus, human security. During the Troubles, Northern Ireland was caught in a self-perpetuating cycle of continuously strengthened effects of religiosity, polarization, conflict, and threats against human security. However, the increase of secularization that intensified in the 1990s introduced a change into that recursive mechanism that created the space for the Good Friday Agreement.

As Ross notes, "Any given theory of conflict has crucial implications for the theory and practice of conflict management" (2007: xiii). If a conflict is a matter of resource competition, a resolution will be sought via material distributions. However, if a conflict is defined by competing religious identities, then a state must seek a solution that bridges those identities. The conflict in Northern Ireland provides an informative example of religion's power to create individual and group identities and its potential to mobilize those groups toward violence. The decrease in religious salience in Northern Ireland was an important break for the cycle of conflict in the region. The promotion of increased education and improved quality of life are important factors in diminishing ethnoreligious conflicts and increasing human security. However, by recognizing the religious worldviews that inform polarized groups, communities may develop *inclusive* narratives that emphasize a peaceful tolerance of other perspectives. Inclusive narratives that encourage civil practices promoting comfortable, productive relations between Catholics and Protestants will be critical for a peaceful future. Thus, just as these narratives were once responsible for creating a seemingly intractable conflict, churches and states may work together to emphasize narratives that take advantage of biconfessional worldviews.

The Consultative Group on the Past of Northern Ireland has been formed to make recommendations on any steps that might be taken to support Northern Ireland society in building a shared future in light of the past violence. Based on this study, I believe that these recommendations will best succeed when taking into consideration the role of religious worldviews, clashing narratives, and what the communities perceive as "human security." For example, one of the proposals is that of recognition payments. This is a proposal has been met with great hostility, especially by the dominant unionist party, the Democratic Unionist Party. The government would be asked to pay £12,000 to the families of all those killed during the Troubles—including members of paramilitary groups. This would mean families of paramilitary victims, members of the security forces, and civilians who were killed would all be entitled to the same amount. Unionist Jim Nicholson declared, "The proposal endorses the morally flawed notion that a terrorist killed while undertaking a mission of murder has the same status as an innocent civilian murdered in a bomb attack or a member of the security forces murdered in front of their family."[8] One can immediately see the force of clashing narratives in Nicholson's remark regarding the paramilitary "terrorist." A plan that compensates IRA families for their loss will have competing moral assessments. In this case, recognition payments may serve to further segregate the communities over past grievances, rather than reconcile them.

Another proposal is an annual day of reflection and reconciliation. Northern Ireland has a long tradition of expressing communal triumphs and sufferings via parades and holidays, usually as enactments of provocation, mobilization, and division. A biconfessional day of remembrance would be able to tap into this history of expression, while using a traditionally divisive method, to bring the communities together over shared loss. This is an example of a proposal that could begin to construct inclusive narratives and improve conditions of human security.

Indeed, these inclusive narratives seem already to be in motion. In developments of early 2009, Northern Ireland saw a recurrence of violence carried out by dissident republicans, the groups calling themselves the Real IRA and the Continuity IRA.[9] Employees at the Belfast City Council have also received death threats from the group called the North Belfast Republican Brigade. Rather than sparking a new round of retaliation, the violence has actually served to unify the Catholic and Protestant communities. Several thousand Catholics and Protestants have protested the violence in silent rallies in Belfast, Londonderry/Derry, and Newry. It appears that the dissident violence, a violence that draws on the old narratives emphasizing the polarized religious communities and conflicting notions of human security, is becoming outmoded. Instead, Catholics and Protestants are taking ownership of a new worldview, one that envisions human security biconfessionally rather than divisively, one that emphasizes the overwhelming desire for peace.

Notes

Emily Morrison Griffin is an online learning instructor in Comparative Religion for the University of Washington. In June 2009, she received her master of international studies degree from the University of Washington with honors in comparative religion. Her graduating research essays included this chapter, "In Violence and in Peace," as well as an essay entitled "Bhiksunis and Bodhisattvas: The Buddhist View of Women." The author offers her sincere appreciation to University of Washington professors Steven Pfaff, George Behlmer, Cabeiri Robinson, James Wellman, Christine Ingebritsen, and Walter J. Walsh, as well as colleagues Jennifer Callaghan, Megin Freaney, and Cynthia Morrison for their invaluable contributions to this chapter.

1. I am indebted to Professor George Behlmer, University of Washington, for this notion of competing histories.
2. Additionally, Presbyterians would share a degree of discrimination aside the Catholics under the Penal Laws for dissenting against the Church of Ireland. The 1798 Irish Rebellion would see both Presbyterians and Catholics rising together under Theobald Wolfe Tone. Thus, the ethnoreligious groups were not always so dramatically polarized.
3. Article 44 of the 1937 constitution in the republic recognized the "special position of the Holy Catholic Apostolic and Roman Church as the guardian of the Faith possessed by the great majority of the citizens." This article resulted in laws banning contraception, abortion, and divorce. This article was repealed later on, but Protestants point to the article as an example of the incredible influence Catholicism has in the south.
4. In this chapter, for the sake of brevity, I refrain from making explicit the split in philosophies between the Official IRA and the Provisional IRA in Northern Ireland, instead making references to the PIRA or "Provos" as simply the IRA. Please excuse my lack of specificity.
5. This is a modified version of the definition of modernization set forth by Norris and Inglehart (2004: 25).

6. It should be noted, I am not studying the *actual* increase of economic opportunities at this time, but rather the participants' perceptions of their economic welfare, as this is most relevant to the study of perceptions of existential threat or security.

7. My thanks to Professor Martin Jaffee for bringing my attention to this fact.

8. Patrick Sawer, "Families of Dead IRA and Loyalist Killers Could Receive £12,000 for Their Loss," *The Telegraph* (Belfast, Northern Ireland), January 24, 2009.

9. D. McAleese, "Recruitment of New Northern Ireland Police Officers 'Unaffected' by Dissidents," *The Telegraph* (Belfast, Northern Ireland), April 25, 2009.

13

Eastern Christianity and Human Security in Postwar Europe

Lucian N. Leustean

Introduction

At the end of the Second World War, the European continent was deeply divided by political and social fragmentation with large sectors of the population displaced. The continent no longer maintained its earlier geopolitical structure. East and West were two different worlds; they soon engaged in the Cold War rhetoric that would last almost half a century. In this milieu, religious communities sought a means of adapting to the new political settings. They developed ways to resist the new communist regimes even as they ostensibly collaborated with the new rulers. This strategy of survival by collaboration was a function of a long-standing theology of *symphonia* in the Orthodox tradition: a position that marks all governments as the "will of God," even those adamantly opposed to religion. This chapter, however, illustrates that Orthodoxy, by insinuating itself within the very bosom of these political regimes, clinched its survival by ensuring the human security needs of its people. As stated in the introduction to this volume, human security seeks to ensure, enhance, and engage the welfare, rights, and subjective and social desires of populations, particularly those marginalized by political power. This chapter reveals the complex and subtle relationship between the Orthodox religion and the communist regimes that sought either to destroy the church or to use it for their own purposes. The eventual failure of the regimes was due, at least in part, to their underestimation of the contributions made by Orthodoxy to the human security of its peoples. I will argue that religious communities are one of the primary actors in securing the welfare, rights, and social desires of their constituents. I will provide a broad background of the relationship of religion to the communist regimes, the ways in the churches responded to these regimes, and a detailed account of how the Romanian church survived amid communist political powers. Indeed, the church's involvement in both domestic and foreign politics continues to create a primary source of human security in contemporary Eastern Europe more generally (Leustean 2009, 2010).

Religion and Communism

The victor of the eastern front, the Soviet Union, directed political and religious issues in Eastern Europe. Despite widespread religious persecution in the interwar period, the Russian Orthodox Church, the dominant religious confession in the Soviet Union, acquired a new position with regard to state policy during the Second World War. The 1937 census showed that attachment to religious institutions remained high while the anti-German nationalist stance of the Orthodox hierarchy contributed toward war resistance and, ultimately, to military and political mobilization (Ramet 1987: 24).

On September 8, 1943, Joseph Stalin held an audience with the last remaining hierarchs in Moscow, and there was a sudden shift in the relationship between the Soviet regime and the Russian Orthodox Church. Four days later, Metropolitan Sergii was raised to the rank of patriarch, and the church became fully engaged in cooperation with the regime (Conquest 1968). The church was allowed to reopen a large number of buildings, and religious practices started to recover. While the church was domestically controlled because of its being engaged in propaganda, the hierarchy was assigned to an international mission to extend the country's influence in the Orthodox commonwealth (Ramet 1993; Curtiss 1953). The church maintained deep ties to the wider public, representing the public's interests to the new regimes, and all the while, it forged a broader influence on the wider territory of Orthodox nation-states.

By claiming spiritual superiority over other patriarchates, Moscow sent religious delegations in April 1945 to Bulgaria and Yugoslavia, in May 1945 to Romania, and in 1946 to Belgrade. In 1945, Patriarch Alexius visited the ancient Orthodox patriarchates of Antioch, Jerusalem, and Alexandria and extended Russian influence to the Middle East. Furthermore, Orthodox clergy courted the Russian diaspora communities in France, Britain, and the United States. The Soviet Union employed the church in its foreign policy by establishing the Department of External Church Affairs in the Russian Orthodox Church in 1946. This department had the largest number of employees in the patriarchate and acted as the direct liaison with state institutions (Ramet 1987: 4; Spinka 1956; Kolarz 1961; Pospielovsky 1987).

The favored position of the Russian Orthodox Church came at the expense of other religious communities in the Soviet Union. The Latvian, Estonian, and Georgian Orthodox Churches were incorporated into Russian jurisdiction, while the Polish Orthodox Church was offered an autocephalous status that rejected its previous ties to Constantinople. The pattern of offering autocephaly in the Eastern bloc extended to Czechoslovakia, which had a small Orthodox minority; in 1953, it extended further, allowing for the establishment of the Bulgarian Orthodox Patriarchate.

The appointment of Orthodox hierarchs in the region occurred after their mandatory visits to Moscow. Metropolitan Timothy of the Polish Orthodox Church visited Moscow in July 1948 and was made head of his church in November 1948. Metropolitan Justinian of Romania visited in October 1946 and became patriarch in May 1948, and Bishop Paisi from Albania visited in January 1948 and became head of the Albanian Orthodox Church in August 1949 (Ellis 1986).

The political control of churches behind the Iron Curtain was also connected with the oppression of those communities that retained significant networks with the West. The most important church was the Roman Catholic. In the predominantly Orthodox countries in the region, the Greek Catholic Churches were abolished and forcibly integrated into the structures of national Orthodox churches, while the leaders of the Roman Catholic Church suffered severe persecution. An underground religious culture emerged within these churches, and it remained significant throughout the Cold War period. In multiethnic countries in the region, Protestant communities were allowed to exist as long as their leaders were controlled by the regimes, and they suppressed contact with the Western world.

In those countries where religion was perceived as indissolubly tied to national identity, political leaders had to ensure that their authority was drawn from politics and religion. Across the region, communists appeared at mass rallies together with religious hierarchs—mainly because their association with the church's representatives strengthened their own political legitimacy. This had a direct effect: by combining religion with politics the regimes prevented opposition and ensured stronger control of the population (Leustean 2009).

The communists took advantage of the ecclesiastical organization of the church that followed not only the civil law of the state but also its own canon law, which paralleled state structures. Political leaders interfered in church matters and imposed their verdicts while the church presented itself as independent from politics, giving the false notion of religious freedom. Those members of the hierarchy who were seen as undesirable to the regimes were tried by the church and expelled by their hierarchical fellows rather than by communist authorities. Religious trials were followed by civil trials, suggesting that the church was active in supporting the establishment of a new society (Leustean 2009).

The church became engaged in communist discourse, and its prayers were invaded by communist slogans. In turn, by combining religious and communist language, communist regimes increased their authority. The portrayal of Stalin as a "Savior of the people" and the propagandistic construction of "a new man and society" were slogans adopted by both the party and the church. This type of language influenced the ways in which the position of the church and the authority of the communist leadership were regarded in addition to the evolution of their political regimes.

Communists sought control not only through the subservience of church hierarchs but also through a systematic method of controlling opposition. Following the Soviet model of the People's Commissariat for Internal Affairs, communist countries developed their own apparatus of surveillance and state security. By censoring every pastoral visit and sermon of church personnel, the regimes ensured that religion was a method of controlling the people and especially those who preached or showed public dissatisfaction. Even the space of the church confessional was no longer private, and in many cases, words uttered there led directly to political and religious persecution.

The church was effectively transformed into a state department. The employment of religion by the communists had a direct impact on the political evolution of the region and on the place of religion in society. Officially, in all communist countries, people were free to profess their faith, but in practice, the state sought to erase and destroy any form of religious belief (Leustean 2009).

The regimes' stance on religion was especially evident in education from primary to university levels where special courses on atheism were taught (Ramet, 1988, 1990, 1992). Atheism was an academic course even in church seminaries in Bulgaria and Czechoslovakia (Ramet 1987: 5). However, despite antireligious propaganda, in some cases the regimes reserved a special attitude toward religion, and it is still uncertain whether all members of the party were truly antireligious. For example, in Romania, Prime Minister Petru Groza was the son of a priest and a layman within the church's structures; in Bulgaria, Patriarch Kiril was appointed with the help of Prime Minister Valko Chervenkov, one of his former classmates (Kalkandjieva 2009; Leustean 2010). Many communists, in fact, continued to bring up their children in the Orthodox faith, attending religious ceremonies outside their cities where the party could not easily control them. Even during the attempt of the communist regimes to extricate religion from the people's lives, it is clear that Orthodoxy was deeply planted in the subjective desires, rituals, and cultural identity of the people. Communists could not simply obliterate the churches. They could and did use them to legitimize their authority, but even in doing so, the churches prevailed simply by virtue of their surviving; additionally, many were successful in both maintaining and nurturing their traditions by continuing their works and identifying with their congregations and the surrounding populace.

Church-State Relations, Authority, and Human Security

In analyzing the religious factors that influenced the evolution of church-state relations in European communism, Pedro Ramet has set out six main factors:

(1) The size of a religious organization; (2) its amenability to infiltration and control by the secret police; (3) its allegiance to any foreign authority; (4) its behavior during World War II; (5) the ethnic configuration of the country in question; and (6) the dominant political culture of the country

(Ramet 1987: 187, 1998: 10–50).

A large religious organization represented a direct challenge to the spread of communist ideology since it was harder to control than any small group. For this reason, the predominantly Orthodox and Catholic churches in the region continued to exert significant influence in society. The communist authorities found it difficult to control every religious activity of a large organization, and the most efficient means remained the obedience of the hierarchy. In cases where the hierarchy was imprisoned, the authorities established suprachurch structures that became responsible for that particular religious community.

Religious communities that were not dependent on a foreign ecclesiastical authority seemed to benefit from collaboration with the regimes. Orthodox and Protestant churches continued to receive financial support to various degrees. This financial support was critically significant for the control of both the hierarchy and lower clergy that were, therefore, at the whim of their regimes.

In addition to the main factors in church-state relations noted by Ramet, a significant role was played by international religious contacts. These contacts were initiated with the support of the communist regimes that aimed at controlling diaspora opposition and influencing public perception in the West. However, in the long run, the contacts increased the mobility of religious elites and antiregime support. The membership of Orthodox and Protestant communities in the newly established World Council of Churches (1948) and the Conference of European Churches (1959) led to the recognition of these groups. Although meetings in these bodies remained dominated by the Cold War divisions, they represented a significant step in the survival of the institutional communities (Leustean 2009).

Behind the Iron Curtain, religion survived atheist indoctrination, mainly because religious institutions continued to retain a significant authority over the general masses. This authority was different in each particular religious confession; however, it followed a comparable pattern throughout the region. In the case of Orthodox churches, authority was shaped on the concept of *symphonia* that suggests concord with the political realm. The claim that "every regime is the will of God" led church hierarchs to cooperate with the regime despite anti-religious persecution. The power of this principle cannot be underestimated—the assumption was, whether acknowledged by the communists or not, whatever secular influence the communists wanted was only granted by God. Nothing, no matter how secular it might be, could be defined outside the metaphysical boundaries of God's rule. It can be argued that this ecclesiastical doctrine formed a sociological sacred canopy over the regimes, forcing them to formulate themselves in its light. In the case of Protestant churches, these spheres of sacred authority were confined to the actions of their pastors. In the private space of religious meetings and prayers of Protestant congregations, the dissociation from politics increased the authority of these churches and their increasing dissent (Wittenberg 2006: 239; Pfaff 2006). In the case of the Roman Catholic churches, authority remained closely connected with the Vatican's stance against the communist regime and ultimately with the personality of the pope. The pope remained a figure whose authority transcended that of national frameworks of church-state relations and who, fundamentally, would become extremely significant for the fall of the communist regimes.

As Paul Froese argues, religious pluralism after the fall of communism did not automatically lead to a religious revival, which Froese associates with two factors: first, the atheist indoctrination of societies in Eastern Europe and, second, the favored position of some churches within church-state relations (Froese 2008). Froese comments, "Interestingly, years of religious repression have given rise not to new levels of religious freedom but a return to pre-communist relations between church and state" (Froese 2004: 73). The return to previous forms of church-state relations is connected with the public authority of religious communities acquired during the Cold War. Despite various degrees of persecution, religious communities were significant actors for human security, forging social and national identities and ensuring on a deeper, more social-psychological basis the human welfare of populations.

Churches preserved human security by cooperating with new regimes and by continuing their spiritual mission at the local level. From this perspective, the authority of religious institutions was crucial for their survival throughout the Cold War and was amplified after the fall of communism. The abundance of religious symbolism, expressed in hymns, liturgies, and prayer, combined folk elements with national imagery that proved crucial for the authority of Orthodox churches behind the Iron Curtain. The private Orthodox space employed a combination of religious symbolism and national characteristics and led to the church's survival (Alexander 1979; Perica 2002; Chumachenko 2002). Here I note, as authors have throughout this volume, that human security is a critical mechanism of existential identity, nurturing in human communities a sense of trust and hope. Religions are quintessential carriers of trust, identity, and social desires that humans have returned to even as they struggle against violent or oppressive regimes.

In the case of the Roman Catholic Church, the establishment of the Polish Solidarity movement that combined religious with civic organizations had a direct impact on the extension of the church's authority (Kubik 1994). Maryjane Osa writes that "Solidarity became more successful when it was associated with Polish nationalism" (2003: 181). Despite the Catholic Church's being a transnational institution, its authority was closely connected to that of the leading national figure of the church, namely the Polish pope. This sense of trust was critical in galvanizing social and political resistance, and mobilizing people to organize around their social desire to express their interests and fight for their human rights. In a comparable way to the situation of Orthodox churches, human security in predominantly Catholic and Protestant regions was associated with the ways in which churches were nationally organized in contrast to more typical transnational structures.

The relationship between religion and human security behind the Iron Curtain was particularly visible in five areas, namely: political legitimation, infiltration, propaganda, competition, and jurisdictional reorganization.

First, by being politically controlled and engaged in various forms of propaganda, churches offered legitimacy to the communist regimes. However, this legitimation gradually changed when the communists obtained complete power. In those cases where legitimation was no longer necessary, religious communities faced harsh persecution and even annihilation (as in Albania). Conversely, where the regimes wanted to assert a semiautonomous voice in the communist bloc, religious communities had official state support (as in Romania and Serbia).

Second, communists and communist sympathizers infiltrated the hierarchies, and their societal role followed strict party control. A particular form of promoting human security by churches was through the personality of some religious leaders and their close contact with the communist leadership. Patriarch Justinian in Romania, Patriarchs Alexius I and Alexius II in the Soviet Union, Patriarch Kiril in Bulgaria, and Patriarch German in Yugoslavia had close contacts with communist authorities. The influence of these individuals extended even to the here-and-now of everyday religious ceremonies.

Third, the involvement of religious communities in the peace movement from the 1950s until the fall of communism revealed the interest of communist regimes in the human security being promoted by churches. The theme of peace suggested that the political system of the Soviet Union was the most viable human system in history, and thus, peace acquired an eschatological connotation. Churches organized national petitions, which were signed by large numbers of people. In this way, the populace was engaged, particularly at a rural level, in state policy. Protests against the war in Vietnam and the atomic bomb remained prime subjects that brought together the religious and political leaderships of the various communist nations (Leustean 2009).

Fourth, the spiritual conflict over the primacy of patriarchates within the Orthodox commonwealth, and particularly the clash between Moscow and Constantinople, led to the mobilization of a wide range of religious communities from both East and West. In this conflict, churches acted as messengers of national voices behind the Iron Curtain. The communists attempted to change the very foundations of Orthodox Christianity by summoning councils, such as the Pan-Ecumenical Conference in 1948 and the pan-synodal conferences in the 1960s, which could rewrite theological doctrines. These elements indicated that the communist regimes were interested in the human societal contribution of their churches. The communist authorities realized that only a dramatic transformation of the roles of churches could lead to their being controlled.

Finally, the jurisdictional reorganization of religious communities during the Cold War was shaped by the decisions of the communist authorities. In most cases, this was achieved in a process that indicated the interests of the regimes. For example, the Uniate churches were incorporated into the Orthodox structures. The Old Believers were banned, and Orthodox churches were encouraged to assimilate ethnic communities into national frameworks. The recognition of jurisdictional reorganization led to the institutionalization of religion, which the state came to perceive as a partner. This institutionalization cemented the survival of religious communities within the church-state framework. Religious leaders gained authority by collaborating with political authorities; after the fall of communism, this state of affairs became even more amplified.

Case Study: The Romanian Orthodox Church

In theory, Romania is a secular state with a secular politics, but in practice, the Orthodox Church retains considerable influence over social and political life. In the interwar period, the Romanian Orthodox Church and the Greek Catholic Church enjoyed the status of national churches as the country's predominant religious confessions. Though still under military and political influence of the Soviet Union, Romania became a People's Republic on December 30, 1947; it remained a communist state until December 22, 1989. Despite the atheist regime, the Romanian Orthodox Church remained one of the most significant state institutions, having direct influence on the social and political evolution of the state. On the other hand, the communist authorities regarded the Greek Catholic Church as being closely connected to the Vatican. As a result, the state began to integrate it into the structures of the Romanian Orthodox Church in 1948; this practice progressed gradually until the fall of communism (Leustean 2009; Tismaneanu 2003; Deletant 1999).

The regime enjoyed good relations with the Orthodox hierarchy, partly by ensuring that those who were suspected of conducting anticommunist activities were replaced. At the same time, the state pursued strong antireligious propaganda aimed at reducing the influence of the church in society. The regime allowed the church to continue its activity mainly because the hierarchy was politically controlled. This control was effected by placing communists within the religious hierarchy and by fostering internal clashes for ecclesiastical power. Primarily through these means, the communists sought domination of the entire church. Ostensibly, the church was actively engaged in the propagandistic message of the battle for peace, and the Holy Synod was forced to accept regulations and hierarchs favorable to the regime (Vasile 2005).

Despite state control of the church, the hierarchs promoted a nationalist discourse that contrasted with the fierce Sovietization of the country. For example, the decision to canonize the first Romanian saints in 1950 showed that, by preserving references to the national past, the church was interested in promoting a position that would make it stronger. The regime initially opposed the celebration of canonization, but after the rise of Gheorghe Gheorghiu-Dej and the implementation of state policy on constructing a Romanian road to communism, public festivities were permitted. The October 1955 canonization proved that the church continued to have a significant impact on the people, a sign that was clearly indicated by the attendance of approximately 10,000–15,000 people at Cernica monastery, most of whom had walked seventeen kilometers from Bucharest.

Despite the fact that the church restructured its ecclesiastical organization and that important hierarchical figures were deposed or suddenly died, Orthodoxy remained strongly rooted in the lives of ordinary people. Even many of the communist activists who proselytized about benefits of the new regime declared themselves to be religious. Despite political interference in the nomination of the hierarchy, the Orthodox faith remained strong, and throughout the communist period, people remained attached to their church (Leustean 2009).

The Orthodox Church suffered its greatest persecution in 1959 when the regime decreed the modification of the regulations regarding monastic life. The Orthodox monasteries were seen as centers of resistance sheltering former political dissidents and as places through which the church retained its influence in society. State authorities claimed that the new regulations were a rationalization of the religious life. In fact, they were closely linked with the church's role in providing human security that clashed with the party's ideological line.

With the rise of national communism in the early 1960s and the redefinition of Romanian national security, the church promoted more assertive theological and nationalist discourses. The contact between the church and churches abroad in addition to the nationalist message being spread inside the country aided the regime in promoting an independent position within the communist bloc. Romania officially declared an independent path of communism at the Party Plenum in 1964. This position was long anticipated, and the church was one of the institutions that supported the move. The church had previously used Romanian nationalism as a basis for the consolidation of its societal power.

The development of Nicolae Ceauşescu's ultranationalist dictatorship took into account the societal position of the church during Gheorghiu-Dej's leadership. References to the national past, the rise of the cult of personality, and depictions of Ceauşescu as a leader with mythical features were also visible in the church's nationalist discourse. In the 1980s, Ceauşescu was promoted as a semidivine leader whose place in Romanian history would be equal to that of the rulers of the Middle Ages and the founders of the Romanian state (Behr 1991; Deletant 1995; Fischer,1989). The church continued to praise the political leadership, combining national communism with its own theological discourse (Tismaneanu, Dobrincu, and Vasile 2007).

During the Cold War, the church hierarchy was perceived as behaving differently than the ordinary clergy. In relation to political power, it was the religious leadership that stood for the church. For this reason, Patriarch Justinian's strong personality and his contacts with the top communist officials managed to gain the church an important position in society. In his meetings with foreign religious leaders, Justinian claimed to be a socialist and not a communist and that he was doing everything in his position to preserve the church. The results of his policy were clearly indicated by the fact that, despite persecution and antireligious propaganda, at the time of Justinian's death in 1977, the church still had around 8,500 priests, a number similar to that of the first years after the Second World War (Leustean 2009). At the lower clergy level, the church was based on the preservation of folk traditions and religious ceremonies. At a time when churches were being demolished or transformed into museums, local communities turned to religious symbolism and folk traditions to keep the church alive. Human security at a grassroots level was connected with the very societal foundations of the church, which were extremely difficult to influence with political decisions. From this perspective, the church maintained social stability and human security against the Sovietization of the country after the Second World War.

This illustrates in the most powerful form the power of organizations that are committed to human security. No matter the power of the state or the oppressive nature of political authority, associations that ensure human security, in this case the Romanian church, can maintain their power no matter the wider forces. Religion, in particular, acts as a catalyst to human security, guaranteeing the welfare, rights, and subjective identity of peoples over and against wider political forces.

The communists allowed the church to continue its spiritual activity mainly because they saw that using the church was more profitable than persecuting it. In some sense the communists had no choice. The church contributed toward the welfare of the state by engaging the monastic population in lucrative activities. The monasteries' output brought significant financial revenue to the state while at the same time encouraging the reintegration of those clergy who were against the communist authorities. Second, the church continued to preserve the religious sentiments of the people "supporting" the claim that the regime allowed complete religious freedom. Third, the church had important connections abroad and the regime encouraged religious tourism to Romania, thereby promoting the idea of a free and civilized country. Fourth, the church helped the regime to foster a Romanian road to communism and, consequently, the rise of Romanian national communism (Leustean 2009).

By being closely connected with the political realm, the church served its followers. The sanctification of the first Romanian saints, subsidies for rebuilding churches and paying the salaries of the clergy, and personal contacts between the church and top governmental officials contributed to Romanian church-state relations. As a result, public religious opposition was minimal in Romania, and the Communist Party also profited from the positive relationship (Leustean 2009). Because of its combination of national communism and close contacts with the political leadership, the church was one of the most influential actors in the social and political life of the country at the end of Ceauşescu's regime. The combination of religious authority and nationalism acquired during the Cold War ensured that the church had a direct role in providing human security to the Romanian population.

Comparable to the experience of other Orthodox churches behind the Iron Curtain, the relationship between human security and the Romanian Orthodox Church was visible at the levels of political legitimation, infiltration, propaganda, competition, and jurisdictional reorganization. By supporting the regime, the church conferred political legitimacy on the government. Simultaneously, the church was infiltrated by the regime and transformed into a propagandistic agent of the state. Special relationships with the regime motivated the church to obtain a favored position in competition with other churches, particularly the Greek Catholic Church, which as noted earlier was forcibly incorporated into its structures. The jurisdictional position within the communist system of church-state relations had an impact on the reemergence of religion after the end of the

Cold War. The church, which had promoted human security before 1989, had a considerable advantage in the battle for souls in postcommunist Romania, and as a result, it retained a visible, social, and political legitimacy. Despite previous collaboration with the communist regime, the church remained one of the most trusted state institutions—with approximately 88 percent of the population reporting that they trust the church (Flora, Szilagyi, and Roudometof 2005).

Currently, Romania is a secular state that recognizes the status of religious minorities, which is in accord with the international norms of the area. Despite a few attempts in the last years to recognize Romanian Orthodoxy as a "national church," there is no formal agreement (concordat) between the Romanian Orthodox Church and the state. Nevertheless, post-1989 elections revealed that the hierarchs remained in close contact with political leaders (Stan and Turcescu 2007). Politicians turned to the church for gaining votes, while hierarchs turned to the political realm in order to consolidate the church's position in society.

Public Policy Implications

The evolution of churches and human security behind the Iron Curtain reveals that religion was closely connected with the political sphere. This is largely because the Orthodox churches embodied and lived out a long tradition of *symphonia* between church and state. The two were in a relationship in part because, theologically, they cannot be separated. In the Eastern Orthodox faith, political rule only occurs under the wider canopy of a sacred covenant between God and the nation's people. Of course for communists, the church's structures and its hierarchs were ripe for being used as dupes and purveyors of propaganda. Nonetheless, the communist regimes could never fully eradicate the deep relationship between the church and its constituents. I would argue that this relationship was forged by the deep connection between the religion and human security—a security founded on an investment in the human welfare of the people, a sense of trust that never dissipated between the people and the churches, and a social desire and identity wrapped up in the ritual life of the religion that communism could neither compete with nor duplicate. Needless to say, Orthodoxy continues to have a considerable affect on post-1989 political realities for multiple reasons.

Religious communities are prime factors in the transformation of societal and political realms. The adaptation of religious communities to political power during the Cold War has had a direct impact on the current structure of church-state relations. After the fall of communism, religious communities became extremely active in Eastern Europe. During the era of uncertain political systems, churches were perceived as stabile societal actors. In most countries in the region, political leaders engaged in dialogue with religious communities and references to religion fostered political support. In the long term, the ambivalence of religious attitudes toward atheist political leadership benefited both institutions. Religious leaders saw an increase in church membership, while political leaders came closer to religious institutions in search of electoral support.

The comparative analysis of churches behind the Iron Curtain shows that human security is closely linked with religious symbolism, folk traditions, and national identities. The symbolic repertoire of nationalism was extremely important for the adaptation and survival of religious communities. Eastern Europe remained a predominantly rural society in which traditional religiosity was coupled with local identities; this deep link of religion, identity, and nationalism formed a trust that powered the church and its leaders regardless of the propaganda or the violence of the communist regimes. In this sense, social and political trust trumps fear and violence; human security is always more important in garnering political influence and social power. Regimes can only rule by force for so long.

The authority projected by religious communities is fundamental to their survival and adaptation to new regimes. An understanding of the history and influence of religious communities in society is necessary in order to have a better perception of religious presence. Despite widespread antireligious propaganda, religious leaders retained significant societal and political authority. Collaboration with state authorities can be seen as the norm throughout the Orthodox commonwealth because of the concept of symphonia. The symphonic agreement with the state does not necessarily mean the corruption of the religious sphere, but it does imply the search for providing the necessary framework for the existence and enlargement of religious authority. Indeed, the communists were outwitted by a theology that colonized their own political ideology. The Orthodox social ideology was cemented and confirmed by consistent exhibitions of trust in rituals of identity. These rituals offered the church's population a sense of human security with which communists could never compete.

There remains no single rule on the adaptation to political power for politically subservient churches and state-dependent churches. Churches obtain their authority from religious symbolism and national elements rather than from imposing a strict political control or subservience. While religious communities can be grouped in various patterns of adaptability to the political realm, each Eastern European country witnessed various degrees of religious control. The authority of religious communities is closely associated with transformations within theological and national discourses. Throughout the Iron Curtain, churches were engaged in peace propaganda that fostered national interests and led them to adopt new theological programs, as, for instance, the "social apostolate" program was aimed at providing a basis for new church-state relations. The history of church-state relations revealed that, if churches wanted to survive, they had to remain in touch with the political leadership and also concentrate on the spiritual needs of local communities.

An increasing competition for power, resources, and influence still exists among religious groups. This competition is particularly visible in the reorientation of religious communities toward other sources of political power, especially with regard to the increasing number of national interest groups in Brussels and Strasbourg. The fall of communism led religious communities to engage with new political sources of power, particularly in the context of European enlargement. In recent years, Orthodox churches have begun to open representation to European institutions and have promoted a new type of discourse aimed at defining their position toward the supranational European architecture.

Patriarchates in the Orthodox commonwealth remain embroiled in a competition for supremacy. Moscow continues to argue for primacy, clashing with the traditional centers of spiritual power, particularly with the Ecumenical Patriarchate of Constantinople, and relations between the two patriarchates are continually strained. After 1989, the Ecumenical Patriarchate recognized the autonomy of various churches in Eastern Europe and extended its influence outside traditional centers, with new communities in Asia, Australia, and Western Europe. In addition, the migration of Orthodox believers to the West posed challenges to national Orthodox churches that began establishing new communities in diaspora.

Churches that find the means of adapting to new regimes enhance social, political, and economic securities in the long term. This was the case throughout the Cold War and is so today. Churches are searching for innovative theological models to assert a stronger place in society. Even in conditions of extreme persecution, such as in Albania, where the faith officially ceased to exist in the 1960s, the Orthodox Church continued to adapt itself to new conditions and promoted human security at the local level. The Albanian Orthodox Church reemerged in the 1990s with the support of neighboring Orthodox countries, demonstrating that annihilation of religious organizations is extremely difficult as long as they adapt to new political circumstances and retain a significant role in promoting human security.

Relations between the Russian Orthodox Church and the Vatican remain significantly strained. While the pope was allowed for the first time to visit the predominantly Orthodox countries of Romania (1999), Ukraine (2001), and Bulgaria (2002), there remains mutual distrust, accusation of proselytism, and difficulties in the restitution of the properties of the Greek Catholic Churches.

Note

Lucian N. Leustean is lecturer in politics and international relations at Aston University, Birmingham, United Kingdom. He is the author of *Orthodoxy and the Cold War: Religion and Political Power in Romania, 1947–65*, editor of *Eastern Christianity and the Cold War, 1945–91*, and coeditor of *Religion, Politics and Law in the European Union*. The author would like to thank James Wellman for his comments and for his thorough editing, and Daniel Chirot, Steve Pfaff, Scott Radnitz, and James Felak for their constructive feedback.

14

Washed by a Deluge

THE RELIGIOUS STRUGGLE FOR HUMAN SECURITY IN ALGERIA AND POLAND

Sayres S. Rudy

> *The Spirit of History is out walking.*
> *He whistles; he likes these countries washed*
> *By a deluge, deprived of shape and now ready.*
> CZESŁAW MIŁOSZ, "The Spirit of History: Warsaw,
> 1939–1945"

Introduction

Political and economic deprivation under authoritarian socialism inspired religious activists in Poland and Algeria to demand greater welfare and rights. State reforms, intended to divide or distract dissidents, instead unified and concentrated them in Polish labor unions and Algerian political parties. After the respective states responded by declaring martial law, Poland peacefully democratized (1981–1989), but Algeria erupted in war (1992–1997). Why did radical religious struggles for human security under similarly corrupt and coercive secular dictatorships remain peaceful in Poland but turn violent in Algeria?

Vexed by this difference during Algeria's spiraling conflict, one scholar wrote:

> The seizure of power by General Jaruzelski in 1981 may be seen as the first step in the transition to democracy, a decade . . . in which the armed forces and the police were pitted against Solidarity and large segments of Polish society were "mobilized," and civil society began to create political space for itself. Could the aborted elections in Algeria and the seizure of power by the military and technocrats signal the beginning of a similar transition?

I believe that the answer is no, because the FIS, aside from its popularity, in no way resembles Solidarity. (Waterbury 1994: 39)

But why did the Front Islamique du Salut (FIS) contrast so starkly with Solidarność (Solidarity)? Should we really single out Islamists and forgive the state for failing this central European standard? If Muslim voters and Catholic workers diverge in their political strategies, how do religious valuation and social structure produce this discrepancy? How do citizens' cultural values and states' ruling strategies interact to forge such disparate outcomes from similar demands for human security? These questions have grown only more daunting as scholars and practitioners have recognized that abstract concepts like globalization, culture,[1] and tyranny fail to explain such discrepancies.[2] Meanwhile, the discrepancies themselves have only grown more striking; postcommunist Europe has developed wealthy capitalist democracies while the Middle East and North Africa still suffer autocratic rule, contested liberal transitions, fragile social agitations, and potential Islamist appropriations of the "Arab Spring."

In relative obscurity, Algerians are trapped in the violent statism that Poles famously escaped. Even as a lead player in the recent popular Arab uprisings Algeria has received scant attention in public media and minimal scrutiny in scholarly literatures. At best, Algeria conjures dislocated images of its seminal violence: eminent émigrés like Hélène Cixious and Jacques Derrida, Gillo Pontecorvo's "Battle of Algiers," Frantz Fanon's Les Damnés de la Terre, General David Petraeus's musings on counterinsurgency—even the old affront to Americans by their eighteenth-century Muslim captors. Since al-Qaeda gained a foothold there, Algeria has yet again been reduced to its political violence but now as an exemplar of Islam's "democratic dilemma."[3] This caricature conjoins the struggle between ruling secular and Muslim conservative reactionaries, on the one hand, and ruled Islamist revolutionary reactionaries, on the other.[4] Against this morbid and toxic "theocratic impasse," Poland's cosmopolitan civility, legatee of glorious shipyard strikes and charismatic freedom fighters, seems a breath of liberal fresh air. Thus the nagging question returns:

Where is the Muslim *Solidarnosc*? ... The ideal of pro-democracy activism arising spontaneously from the shipyards of Gdansk stands for the hope that in every society, no matter how totalitarian or repressive, there are freedom-loving people who see clearly that democracy is the solution to what ails their country. Yet such popular democracy movements are hard to come by in the contemporary Muslim world. (Feldman 2003: 19)[5]

My puzzle is this: why do religious adherents seeking human security take up violence? Polish Catholics and Algerian Muslims, in and outside religious institutions, initially demanded social provision and political voice—the *welfare* and *rights* components of human security. But martial law, I will argue, had different effects in Algeria and Poland on another index of human security: *subjectivity*, the possession within a political space of social resources effective in improving welfare and rights. Polish political subjectivity was established in labor-intensive work sites whose unions, allied with the church, still had leverage over the industry-dependent state. Polish Catholics did not lose effective citizenship or political subjectivity under martial law; in contrast, Algerian subjects were centralized in voter-intensive electoral sites whose elimination left no resources to coerce rulers. Algerian Muslims lost their effective citizenship and became political objects, internal exiles with no systemic chance to improve their human security. Poles and Algerians equally lacked welfare and rights under martial law but diverged on this third register of human security: political subjectivity. Violence thrives in the absence of subjectivity, or social humanization, where citizens exist in an environment that severs desires and actions by denying citizens reliable means to advocate for *other* aspects of human security. The denial of political subjectivity—of systemic resources to compel state concessions—in Algeria, but not Poland, best explains their divergent paths to a religiously sanctioned human security.

Polish and Algerian religious activism thus informs our conceptual and causal schemas of the politics of human security. We may distinguish, within the concept of human security, social welfare, legal rights, and political subjectivity.[6] From here, we may track the cause of religious violence as a shift in the pursuit of human security from welfare and rights to subjectivity.[7] Religious activists have long sought human security in the forms of welfare and rights; when dehumanized in political systems that deny them any will to improve their welfare or rights, they redesignate subjectivity as the primary category of human security. In vernacular terms, people protest all the time for more goods or freedoms within given social systems, but in radical moments activists adopt antisystemic positions; instead of asking the state to increase social provision, dissidents ask the state to defend its legitimacy. Criticizing the legitimacy rather than efficacy of the state signals the moralization of political protest, where deprivation is no longer an error or disagreement but an injustice, evidence against the state's qualifications to administer welfare and rights. To reclaim political subjectivity from an authoritarian state is thus inherently violent because it requires a direct, zero-sum contest over the very nature of social life. The Algerian Islamists were brutalized into this final form of political resubjectivization.[8] That is, under total state assault, the meaning of human security itself, of securing one's very humanity, changed the frontiers of politics to ensure total war as the final assertion of human will.[9]

My argument requires a comparison of social systems with and without subjectivity or effective citizenship. A robust literature correlating democratic inclusion and decreased political violence in Arab-Muslim countries already confirms my framework,[10] but to complement the democratic pacification thesis, I utilize cross-regional research to reveal dynamics within single regime-types based on alternative resources of political subjectivity—such as politicized labor sites. Alternative or transitional modes of citizen subjectivity could prove crucial in breaking the "democratic-theocratic" impasse in authoritarian Arab-Muslim countries. Contrasting Poland with Algeria shows two such distinct forms of citizen subjectivity operating beneath the regime level: that is, within the shared confines of a despotic secular state with a bankrupt command economy, undergoing social retrenchment. This research design must "control" other differences in the two cases, of course, but no more than any other social explanation.[11]

Indeed, many similarities in Polish and Algerian politics, economics, and ethics allow us to isolate the causal effects of worker and voter subjectivity on religious protests under martial law, while enriching the puzzle. Algeria and Poland had been colonized for over a century, had resisted with religious-nationalist campaigns, and had been decimated in their anti-imperial struggles. Both countries pursued rapid industrialization, urbanization, and command-economic planning, including generous public outlays to incorporate citizens, while growing similarly dependent on foreign commercial banks and Soviet aid. Algeria and Poland developed massive bureaucratic and police states, indenturing citizens in single-party recruitment for political, professional, or social advancement. Specific reversals of socialist planning were made in land-reform, pricing, import-export conditions, and so on in response to government crises and their critics.

In addition to overall developmental similarities, Poland and Algeria had analogous religion-state relations. Polish Catholic and Algerian Muslim institutions predated the modern state and retained a veto power, limiting the effect on secular sovereignty. The Algerian and Polish regimes negotiated and compromised with religious constituents throughout authoritarian rule and popular agitations. They also tried to "co-opt religion" by creating official religious authorities to approve priests or imams and sanction sermons. But Polish and Algerian religious organizations retained their autonomy and popular support to mediate between secular state programs and religious citizen demands.[12] In a sense, churches and mosques buttressed the state by competing with it for popular allegiance and mediating regime-citizen conflicts. By providing social services and refuge for faithful and secular civil society they cushioned the blows of failed government policies. Hence the church and mosques bridged religion and state while insulating adherents from the regime. Finally, Polish and Algerian religionists had equally strong ties, if not divided loyalties, to Catholics and Muslims outside their countries.[13] Polish and Algerian dictators had to contend and bargain with large, powerful, and relatively autonomous religious institutions and movements over terms of human security.

The Muslims and Catholics confronting Algerian and Polish rulers also had comparable conceptions of human security—grounded in community obligation, private property, autonomous faith-based institutions, and distributive justice. With their histories of imperial occupation and coercive centralization, Polish Catholics and Algerian Muslims were nationalistic and jealous of self-determination. Conservative and rural in background, they desired "traditional" education and family planning. Catholic and Muslim anger over political and economic corruption evinced a spiritual contempt for crass material opportunism that fueled a forceful and enduring moral antagonism. In celebrated instances of this ethical compulsion, Catholic and Muslim landowners not only defeated socialist land reforms that threatened religious endowments but also compelled the states to expand church and mosque construction.[14] Churches and mosques offered education, cultural life, social support, and spiritual counsel, constituting a form of parallel state.[15] At the same time, Catholics and Muslims pressured the secular commons, believing that the public sphere must accommodate religious values. Thus, in Algeria and Poland, religion was inseparable from the deliberations of public policy. Churches and mosques had ideological authority in Poland and Algeria, a fact that became evident whenever the states violated it. Political corruption, military violence, and economic suffering prompted institutional and personal resistance from Polish Catholics and Algerian Muslims. With regard to the issue of Polish peace and Algerian violence, it is salient that, before martial law, Polish Catholic demands for change were more radical than Algerian Islamist demands. Polish revolutionaries wanted to dismantle their entire social structure; Algerian Islamists wanted to usurp theirs.

Deepening the puzzle, peaceful Algerian and Polish dissidents suffered similar state coercion. The states had wagered that Polish unions and Algerian parties would stabilize ruling class domination by dividing the oppositions and isolating extremists, but when Solidarity and FIS dissidents further undermined, rather than bolstered, illegitimate governments, Polish and Algerian forces arrested, tortured, killed, and interned political opponents. Activists recalled centuries of colonization and partition, brutal uprisings for religious-national emancipation, horrific assaults by European powers, and atrocities against their populations. Martial law compounded the popular contempt Catholics and Muslims felt for the avarice, inequality, and aggression of military-backed state socialism-cum-capitalism. Moreover, Polish Catholics and Algerian Muslims had struggled peacefully and violently for human security over generations. Roman Catholic or Sunni Islamic scriptural doctrines or cultural mores hardly explain Poland's Catholic nonviolence or Algeria's Islamist violence. Similarly, brutal state retaliation at home or from abroad had not prevented radical or violent protests in the past and do not explain their presence or absence in either case.

Before martial law, Polish Catholics and Algerian Muslims had long militated for similar conceptions of physical, juridical, and subjective human security against comparable attempts to deny them. After martial law, the celebrated Polish peace and unspeakable Algerian violence that I review below remain perplexing. As Poland's pacific revolution still lifts the spirit, Algeria's bloodbath still shocks the conscience: villages slaughtered, women raped, and children bayoneted. Out of relatively similar social, economic, and political conditions and criteria of human security, Poland's Catholic pacifists and Algeria's Muslim militants become binary paradigms of antiauthoritarian agitation. The following case studies exhibit the reasons for which Algerians so violently demanded their political subjectivity while Poles peacefully campaigned for the welfare and rights components of human security. These political histories show how the structure of citizenship or political subjectivity, not the regime type, separated Poland's peace and Algeria's violence.

Polish Catholic citizen subjectivity allied the church to a powerful working class on which the state depended, forging a layered civil society symbiotically tied to the state. Algerian Muslim subjectivity allied mosques to voters running in state elections. When both governments collapsed and forced protest movements into a state of emergency, Algerians, but not Poles, lost all systemic means to advocate for welfare and rights. Poles retained their collective worker resources and economic position, sustaining their political subjectivity. Algerians lost their individual voter resources and, with them, their citizen subjectivity altogether. As a result, Catholic Poles never experienced comprehensive systemic alienation, objectification, or dehumanization; but Algerians were effectively denaturalized with no systemic potential to improve their human security as it eroded from physical and juridical to subjective deprivation.

Algeria

The birth date of Algeria's state or national identity is debated (e.g., Ruedy 1992: 16; Roberts 2003: 53), but Islam was already there. Algerian Muslims lived in social networks of self-ordered saintly lineages or Sufi "brotherhoods." These Islamic ministates fended off Ottoman and French coastal occupiers from 1783 until they were exhausted around 1871. By World War I, Islamists had been pacified, co-opted, or suppressed. French *colons* atomized and capitalized indigenous labor and property, undermining Muslim communal economies and religious autonomy. Growing urbanization, impoverishment, and emigration sustained Islamist activism among natives. Algerian nationalists and Islamists demanded independence, autonomy, or citizenship from France to no avail until colon-Algerian-French atrocities in 1945 presaged the war of liberation (1954–1962). The Front de Libération Nationale (FLN) deployed Islamist rhetoric, internal repression, and protostate organization against France. Since independence, Algeria has declared itself an "Islamic-Socialist" coalition of women, Berbers, Islamists, peasants, workers, state developers, bureaucrats, and the military.

Algerian elites made good on their victory by nationalizing industry and agriculture, "Arabizing" schools, uniting Berber-Arab parties, appointing women legislators, and espousing postcolonial solidarity. The state, courting private groups with discretionary favors and public constituents with social welfare, was a military regime based on patron-client relations, and exchanges between constituents and bureaucrats managed social conflicts for two generations. Import-substitution and capital-intensive industrialization, urban-biased oil-wealth distribution (Chaudhry 1997: 142), and gifts to influential clients tended to balance disparate demands. Algeria financed its insulated socialism with oil rents and commercial borrowing (Frieden 1981: 408). This project began collapsing before the mid-1980s oil glut, global recession, and state fiscal crunch that discredited the political economy (Ammour, Leucate, and Moulin 1974; Bennoune 1988; Entelis 1988). By 1984, nonagricultural employment had reached 2,555,000, but repeating a century-old pattern, "this impressive growth was inadequate to absorb all the new urban job seekers. Unemployment . . . remained very high during the expansionary phase of import-substitution industrialization—22 percent in 1977 and 18 percent in 1984—and rose to 24 percent in 1990 when state-led development was in serious crisis" (Beinin 2001: 148–149; Pfeiffer 1996: 30). Algerians began to mock the state's parasitic nationalism, classless industrialization, and state capitalism as hypocritical ruses that abandoned the people to their crowded apartments, dead-end jobs, and "wall-holding-up"[16] with nothing productive to do in their growing slums.

This policy agenda of rapid economic and political modernization without autonomous civil social forces paralleled efforts to woo powerful Muslims. In an exemplary incident, similar to events in Poland, the state, pursuing agricultural socialism, implemented a land reform and allocation scheme in the early 1970s. The state had tried "limiting the Algerian landlords' property to twenty hectares. The rest would be bought by the state and distributed to peasants who were organized in cooperatives. . . . [The rural Sheikh] Soltani issued a *fatwa* declaring land reform un-Islamic . . . [decreeing] that prayer performed on nationalized land would not be accepted by God. They [allied] with petty intellectuals and landlords who financed them" (Bennoune 2002: 76). The FLN and state bureaucracy withdrew from the countryside, ceding control of peasants to traditional leaders, holy men, and rural power holders (Ottoway and Ottoway 1970: 241). Similarly, ruling elites caved in to Islamists on the state's official commitment to gender equality. In 1962, the National Assembly had 10 (of 196) women, but by 1982 it had none. At the time, the state was growing anxious about the Islamists who were staging mass rallies and fighting with secular students on campuses. Small Islamist challenges to state *and* Muslim elites in the late 1970s had augured a generation of audacious radicals. As Vergés notes, "The first organized Islamist opposition took the form of study groups in the 'free' mosques not subject to the control of the Ministry of Religion" (Vergés 1997: 295; cf. Roberts 2003: 19–24; Willis 1996: ch. 3). As a pacifying gesture, the state passed in 1984 the notorious Family Code, comprehensively domesticating women despite furious feminist protest. Likewise, the Algerian state flattered the Islamists by extending Arabic language teaching to secondary schools. This merely postponed the reckoning of Islamists and secular, Francophone ruling classes as the former reached French-language levels in their training or careers. Finally the Algerian state facilitated construction of a profusion of mosques, hoping to secure conservative Muslim support against any potential Islamist aggression (Willis 1996: 35).

By 1985, Algeria's patron-client balancing act, mixed economy, and exclusive state apparatus were in peril. Islamists, Berbers, women, the poor, workers, capitalists, professionals, bureaucrats, writers, academics, and students sought incompatible changes. Economic reforms, launched in 1979, had diminished state resources by the time oil prices plunged in 1985–1986. Public enterprises were being phased out in favor of services, small industry, market deregulation, and an expanded private sector. Roger Owen observes (1992: 144), "As elsewhere . . . economic liberalization led to greater inequalities of income, increasing unemployment and more obvious corruption, while cuts in subsidies and imports were a stimulus to inflation, currency depreciation and the growth of a black market." These changes, not least the prolific black market controlled by wealthy entrepreneurs, smacked of corruption, but elites were indifferent to popular resentment. Algerians "want[ed] to know, as one student bitterly stated . . . , why more than half of them are jobless 'while we earn billions per year from natural gas and [the former head of the ruling party] lives like a king'" (Vandewalle 1988: 2). Protests culminated in the tumultuous October 1988 riots. Islamists commandeered the uprising as Hamas had in the Palestinian *intifada* to which Algeria's riots were frequently equated. The uprising and state slaughter of hundreds of demonstrators polarized Algeria. As long as ruling elites protected their entrepreneurial-bureaucratic-military prerogative, activists and the state were bound to a contest over the very nature of the public sphere.

The state and Islamists acted quickly. The regime opened the political system to competition in 1989, amending the 1976 constitution to legalize parties and free expression. Islamists organized a party, the Front islamique du salut (FIS)

[Ar. *al-jabha al-islamiyya lil-inqadh*]. In July, the National Assembly established procedures for official party registration, and political parties of all kinds sprang forth, though the Islamist opposition remained dominant. As one commentator notes:

> Algeria was a classic harmonic state. For nearly 30 years, its generals and ruling-party hacks had been absorbing all potential opposition into a quasi-socialist order that celebrated the alleged harmony of "the Algerian people." Islamic leaders and institutions were drafted into this hegemonic project, thereby ironically ensuring, in the wake of liberalization, populist Islam would emerge as the counter-hegemonic force [against] the corrupt rule of a minority that was more French than Arab, or more Berber than Muslim (Brumberg 2002: 57).

Indeed, 1989 is the pivotal date in modern Algerian history but not because of democratic and constitutional reforms. Rather, this was the year the Islamists formed an opposition party and launched their campaign against the military regime, which responded by intensifying the very market and security apparatuses that so many Algerian Muslims, Islamist and otherwise, resented. Indeed, this period inaugurated Algeria's Realpolitik state of exception:

> [T]he moment one accepts that the single most important locus of power in independent Algeria has been the army, the fact that its commanders were no longer members of the Party of the FLN from 1989 onwards can no longer be ignored as a side issue, let alone seen as positive in itself, for it meant that they could no longer be held to account in any political institution whatever. In 1989, they withdrew from the Central Committee of the FLN, and in July 1990 they forced President Chadli to surrender the defense portfolio to the then Chief of Staff, Major General Nezzar; from that point on, they were a law unto themselves to a degree which was without precedent since 1965 (Roberts 2003: 253).

On June 27, 1991, legislative elections were scheduled. Street clashes occurred when the state tried to manipulate voting methods. General Khaled Nezzar postponed elections and arrested Islamist leaders Abassi Madani and Ali Benhadj. This affront prompted a tense meeting of Islamists who narrowly decided to continue in the democratic process. This decision was remarkable; many Islamists already dismissed democracy as "partyism" [Ar. *hizbiyya*], a secular distraction, even before their party leaders had been arrested by the incumbents. Cooler heads of state, too, prevailed. Prime Minister Sid Ahmed Ghozali, who wished to proceed with the vote, called a summit with forty-five political parties to diffuse tensions just as the Gulf Crisis infuriated the Islamist movement (Roberts 2003: 63–81; Willis 1996: 162–165; Stora 2001: 208–209).

It must be emphasized that the Algerian state had decided to experiment with elections deliberately to further state and ruling-class-elite power—not to surrender power or risk losing control. The plan was to distract and divide regime opponents while entrenching the refined police state and trade markets. As elections proceeded without, or instead of, the social reforms that Algerians were campaigning for, the strain benefited the Islamists. "I voted for the FIS out of revenge," said one voter in 1990; another said, "In this country [one has] four choices: you can remain unemployed and celibate because there are no jobs and apartments to live in; you can work in the black market and risk being arrested; you can try to emigrate to France to sweep the streets of Paris or Marseilles; or you can vote for FIS and vote for Islam."[17] The Islamists were poised to win the national legislative elections in early 1992, having won local elections and already ruled in several towns. Islamist government shocked Algerian secularists and even many Muslims with its rigid regulations and puritanical codes. The military, manically anti-Islamist, canceled elections on January 11, 1992, banned the FIS, and declared martial law.

The Islamists then militarized their views and strategies. The annulled elections only intensified the Islamist sense of battling corrupt "foreign" governors for centuries (Laremont 2000). By strategic compromise (1871–1914, 1962–1979, 1989–1992), civil agitation (1920–1954, 1979–1992), or *militancy* –Islamists had fended off domination by centralizing state-builders (1830–1871, 1945–1962, 1992–). Islamists coimplicated democracy, Western hypocrisy, and secular-authoritarian coercion, given the positive or permissive response of putative prodemocracy regimes outside Algeria. As one Islamist leader put it:

> Ethics and human rights are subservient to interests; values are only necessary if they will bring to power "liberals" (as in Eastern Europe), but they are dispensable if the result is power for the genuine and sincere children of the land and an end to minority regimes that are the legacy of the colonial era. To prevent the latter situation, prisons may be packed with political opponents, and the state may resort to torture, economic deprivation, and even rape as has become official policy as evident in Amnesty International's reports on Tunisia and Algeria. Islamists today are the victims, repressed under the pretext—witness Algeria—of saving democracy from themselves (Ghannouchi 2000: 103; cf. Sadiki 2004: 356).[18]

It was a group of generals called the Haut Comité d'État (HCE) that took over Algeria, declaring war on Islamists who deplored the hegemonic secular, military, and crony capitalist order. On February 9, 1992, the HCE declared a state of emergency and

> Five detention centers opened in the Sahara to hold thousands of FIS activists, including 500 mayors and councilors. Special courts, which had been banned under the 1989 constitution, were reestablished to prosecute "terrorists." . . . As time went on, the state closed down all the cultural and charitable organizations of the FIS and ordered the destruction of all unofficial mosques, which were popular with Islamists. In 1992 and 1993, a total of 166 Islamists were sentenced to death (Hafez 2004: 46).

These activists had participated in the state-called elections and had won a plurality, if not a majority, only months earlier. Now "thousands of arrests were made and new judicial councils created to expedite trials began handing down death sentences with chilling regularity" (Waltz 1995: 101). In 1993, Amnesty International "accused the Algerian government of having used torture since the installation of the state of emergency . . . ; torture had 'practically disappeared between 1989 and 1991' [but] was now being used against the 'extremists' and was reported regularly in twenty detention centers" (Stora 2001: 214).

On March 4, 1992, the government banned FIS. On June 29, President Mohammad Boudiaf—recently recalled from exile to parlay his "revolutionary credentials" to repair the country—was assassinated. On July 15, Madani and Benhadj received twelve-year prison terms from the Blida military tribunal. In August, indiscriminate terrorism occurred for the first time at the Algiers airport, and total war ensued between Algerian Islamists and the state. By 1994, the Groupe Armée Islamique and state paramilitaries, equally hated by most Algerians, were massacring people with impunity (Ghemati 1998: 109). Fifty imams were murdered that year for condemning atrocities urged by mujahideen back from Afghanistan (Kiser 2002: 168; Bruce 1995). By 1996, half of the 43,737 prisoners in 116 prisons were accused of terrorism, though Islamist and paramilitary groups imitated and infiltrated each other. As Mohammed Hafez notes, "The gravest development since 1993 . . . was the almost daily killing of Islamists, either through manhunts or clashes during searches. Many human rights organizations condemned the military regime's use of torture, 'disappearances,' and the extrajudicial killing of suspected Islamists" (2004: 46; see also Hafez 2003, 2000). Fatalities, by 1999, reached perhaps 70,000, wrought by the state, its death squads, torture chambers, and concentration camps.[19] Massacres, executions, and disappearances peaked in 1997 when the Armée Islamique du Salut (military wing of FIS) quelled the violence with a unilateral cease-fire and the state called elections.

Militants are still fighting the state and have been only emboldened by the "war on terror" (Rudy 2010). The Algerian conflagration is an entrenched moral conflict between Islamist populists, demanding physical, juridical, and subjective human security and bourgeois-militant ruling elites over the terms of social integration (Labat 1995). Islamists had borne material privation and religious compromise as peacefully as they welcomed the political liberalization of 1989. As fiscal crises had vacated distributive justice by 1988, electoral crises had vacated political subjectivity by 1992. The state, with no more decoys, attacked, further dehumanizing Islamist dissidents and guaranteeing bloodshed.

Poland

The 966 baptism of King Mieszko I consecrated the Catholic nation-state of Poland (Kłoczowski 1979; Davies 1982: 207). By the 1700s, Poland's world-historical *Liberum Veto* gave every noble in parliament (*sejm*) a veto over royal decrees (Davies 1984: 281). Poland's partition by Russia, Prussia, and Austria (1795–1918) seized upon this decentralized governance but deepened Polish-Catholic national identity and resistance (Lukowski and Zawadski 2001: 109). External domination spurred Polish-Catholic nationalism with historical and social variations:

> During the 150 years of national and political subjugation, the church fostered allegiance in the faithful to the collective bodies of nation and Church rather than to religion alone as a road to redemption. Thus, the loyal Catholic Pole did not . . . feel compelled to internalize principles of piety. . . . His Catholicism, as the Church, was perceived in broad social, political, and symbolic terms. . . . As such, it became generally conservative, traditionalist, and highly politicized (Fiszman 1972: 19).

Polish Catholics learned that "rigid conservatism" better secured survival than "supple reformism" and that "it did not need temporal power to support and sustain it . . . that it could even remain aloof from the secular rulers [if] it remained institutionally strong and in touch with the nation's feelings" (Cviic 1983: 93). Partition created a "'culture of dissent' that would be revived under the communist regime," with the church as "guardian and preserver of all that was Polish . . . : the culture, history, language, and traditions" (Ediger 2005: 302). Thus, the great Polish romantics—with "their heroes and heroines larger than life" and "cult of Freedom"—"added a specifically Polish note of Catholic piety" (Davies 1984: 169; cf. Kołakowski 1983: 55). Hardly pacifists, Poles resisted conquest *qua* Catholics:[20]

> During the century of statelessness and beyond, every single Polish generation has produced men careless of their own survival, who have risen with

desperate courage against their tormentors. The Warsaw uprising of August 1944 was but the last performance of a drama which was also enacted in 1733, 1768, 1794, 1830, 1846, 1848, 1863, 1905, and 1920. On each occasion, if asked what they were fighting for, their reply might well have been the same: for "a few ideas . . . which is nothing new" (Davies 1982: 37).

Poles sated their "unquenchable thirst for freedom [and] national independence (Ash 1985: 3) briefly in the interwar period; during Catholic "moral prestige," organizations, education, and unions flourished under Polish self-rule (Lukowski and Zawadzki 2001: 218, ch. 6). Shortly after fighting off the Russians, the Polish state and church agreed to the Concordat of 1925, comprising Vatican recognition, state voice in episcopal designations, and church privileges. Especially under Jozef Piłsudski's creeping dictatorship, church-intellectual relations foreshadowed their tense cooperation decades later. While intellectuals were "put off by the Church's traditionalism, exclusivism, and . . . intense anti-Semitic prejudice," "the Church's concern for easing social tensions helped to weaken the anticlericalism that had been widespread among the left-wing and liberal intelligentsia . . . and promoted the emergence of a new open-minded Catholic intelligentsia" (Cviic 1983: 93; Lukowski and Zawadzki 2001: 218). Polish sovereignty ended with the Nazi invasion that targeted intellectuals, slaughtered a third of the clergy, and destroyed minority communities, leaving Poland almost purely Catholic. From 1944 to 1956, the church and communist party-state, then emerging under Soviet suzerainty, jostled for power. Communists hoped to co-opt Catholics with optional privileges, while Catholics were key to state legitimacy (Davies 1982: 539). The early path to a balance of interests revealed the chasm between communism and Catholicism.[21] In 1949, the church excommunicated party members and the state nationalized church land, confiscated the church's welfare agency, censored Catholic publications, eliminated religious teachings in school, and pulled chaplains from prisons, hospitals, and army units (Cviic 1983: 95). The oscillation between repression and accommodation should not obscure substantive changes in Poland's church-state struggles from polemical discussion (1944–1948), mute coexistence (1949–1956), and spontaneous mass dialogue (1956–1958) to constructive dialogue (1959–) (Will 1984: 155).

The turning point of the 1956 strikes in Poznań forced "changes in party leadership, institutional adjustments, and important concessions to the Catholic Church" (Ekiert 1996: 216). Cardinal Stefan Wyszyński, released from jail, allied with Władysław Gomułka, now head of state. Gomułka, more "socialist" than "communist," was partial to the church's impulses toward "liberation theology" (Dziewanowski 1959: 213). The party sought "acquiescence from the Church hierarchy in return for certain concessions" (Fiszman 1972: 17), notably relinquishing land reforms. Catholics could found "clubs of intelligence," ran for the Sejm, and formed, most tellingly, an independent group called Znak, a collection of Catholic and secular intellectuals and artists that signaled the eventual alignment of Catholics and activist intellectuals (Cviic 1983: 99). Catholic popularity tested the party's patience immediately with the tour of the Black Madonna (1957–1966), "seen by virtually all Polish Catholics," that "strengthened social integration on local and national levels and rejuvenated the religiosity of the Poles . . . [T]his spectacular ceremony . . . defined the cultural frame of the conflict between the Church and the state for decades to come" (Kubik 1994: 108). By most accounts, 1956 marked the "de-Stalinization," "de-totalization," or even "de-Communization" of Poland and the triumph of pragmatism over ideology (Ekiert 1996: part III; Staniszkis 1984: 150.; Wiatr 1994: 252). As important, Poznań set a precedent:

> The Polish crisis in 1980–81 was the culmination . . . of political crises that occurred periodically after 1956 and led to unexpected popular protests and abrupt leadership changes (since 1956 virtually all Polish top leaders had been deposed as a result of unrest) as well as to further erosion of the Stalinist party-state (Ekiert 1996: 217).

And those ratcheting changes "of leadership and policy resulted from labor protests" (Glasman 1996: 86). After student protests of 1968, the church publicly supported the opposition by publishing its articles in the Catholic presses and, "on behalf of the episcopate demanding the release of arrested students, an end to 'drastic' methods of investigation and punishment, and . . . truthful reporting" (Cviic 1983: 97–98). Between 1970 and 1976 the opposition gradually braided Catholics, intellectuals, and labor into a cohesive logic of dissent.

Ferocious worker protests and state coercion after price hikes in 1970 inaugurated a decade of church-state wrangling, labor mobilization, intellectual and professional advocacy, desperate economic development and collapse, and the Solidarity uprising. Replacing Gomułka, Edward Gierek increased investment, foreign borrowing, and price stability; income, infrastructure, and welfare improved. Gierek hoped that economic growth would help "normalize" state ties to the church, workers, and intellectuals whose desires for deeper reforms were converging. Discrete incentives to each group supplemented the material progress. For instance, the state restored to the church properties in the "recovered areas" that the communists had held since 1950 (Monticone 1986: 57), though that act hardly resolved church-state tension (Szajkowski 1983: ch. 2). Later, the state opened "informal" channels to individual workers to appeal for state provisions: "Worker pressure could . . . be . . . leverage to help extract additional resources from hierarchical superiors unresponsive to more orthodox methods" (Pravda 1983: 79; cf. Ekiert, 1996: 229; Staniszkis 1984), but these cheery programs and reconciliations were devised to prevent the profound reforms demanded by dissidents. Just as Algerian elites had abruptly offered elections to social activists to divide and distract them, Polish elites placated opponents with public and private benefits based on doomed policies. As Bauman puts it, "The whole failed political strategy of Gierek's regime was founded in legitimizing the socialist order as one aiding and abetting personal gain and self-interest and pandering to ever growing consumer desires [and] dismantling the vestiges of the welfare state cultivated under Gomulka" (Bauman 1985: 577).

By the mid-1970s, growth and real wages were plunging, prices and debt rising.[22] When protests and strikes, notably in Radom and Ursus, were repressed in 1976, church, workers, and intellectuals formed a diverse opposition. The church and workers were a kind of good cop–bad cop team, with labor threatening production and the church legitimacy. In 1977, Cardinal Wyszyński publicly denounced the "daily humiliations" of those lining up to get "essential needs of the people" by apparatchiks obsessed with "top performance of production" (Szajkowski 1983: 50). At the time, the Committee for the Defense of Workers (KOR), "socialists and liberals, Catholics, Jews, and nonbelievers," organized to defend "a simple and profound belief in human freedom" (Goodwyn 1991: 193, cf. 109–225). Two dynamics were at work in this phase. First, a Polish consensus on dignity and rights united the church, intellectuals, and workers with material and ideological foundations (Cirtautas 1997). Second, the church complemented more than echoed workers and KOR radicals and militants but came under considerable attack.

As Catholics accused the communists of violating church property and education rights in 1976, the state besieged its funding sources and proposed a loyalty oath (Cviic 1983: 101; Monticone 1986: 75). The state's religious affairs director, Kazimierz Kąkol, proclaimed, "While allowing the Church to function, we will never go back on our principles. . . . We will never permit the religious upbringing of children. If we cannot destroy the Church, we shall at least stop it from causing harm" (Kubik 1994: 105). But mutual respect, or interest, prevailed. Mieczysław Rakowski, the "voice of Gierek," vowed: "If the leaders of the Catholic Church in Poland will continue . . . a policy of cooperation as opposed to confrontation and if they will take an active part in building our socialist fatherland, then the Marxists will certainly be ready to help settle problems which still exist today" (Szajkowski 1983: 66). The "established pattern" of "the Church's behavior" held, bridging citizen and state in exchange for concessions to the episcopate (Szajkowski 1983: 47). Note that the church, workers, and intellectuals allied in a dense public realm across distinct institutional and ideological interests and religious identities. Catholic workers and church believers posed a double threat to the state while twice providing human security to the Polish people. Such a dual strategy was impossible in Algeria where public religion lacked any material or social leverage over the state.

Boosted by the 1979 visit of Pope John Paul II, once Cardinal Karol Wojtyła of Krakow, the church had "virtually unlimited socio-cultural power," having 27 dioceses; 7,556 parishes; 15,444 priests; and 42 monastic institutes of 4,207 priests and 1,477 brothers (Walaszek 1986; Will 1984: 153–154). A visitor measuring continuous rule and popular legitimacy might have reckoned that the church was the Polish state and had been taken over by a band of corrupt thugs (Czabański 1993). Discontent reached its height in summer 1980 with the "rebellion of the masses," a "populist . . . egalitarianism . . . that was rational within the confines of an irrational system because it was the only way to deprive the political system of legitimacy" (Michnik 1995 [1983]: 231–232). On August 14, 1980, the Gdańsk shipyard, led by fired electrician Lech Wałęsa and supporters of the sacked Anna Walentynowicz, struck. Ten million workers organized, galvanized by church and KOR support, urban and rural work sites, and past successes in changing state policies and politicians, but "this time, unlike 1970 or 1976, the strikers did not pour out into the streets or attack local Party headquarters; they occupied factories and formed strike committees" (Lukowski and Zawadzki 2001: 272–273). The movement's pacifism is often confused with moderation, but this ignores how extreme their pacifism was. In actuality, it was a total social movement, aiming to change all aspects of public life, but it never sought to seize power; "it concerned itself with institutional reforms, trying to install competent and hard-working managers in industry and wanting to see the freedom of the press respected and censorship abolished . . . a popular movement which behaved like a legislative assembly infinitely anxious to respect legal procedures" (Touraine et al. 1983: 2–3).

For the civil-social radicalism and institutional conservatism of their "self-limiting revolution," the movement, known as "Solidarity," received public religious support (Arato 1993: 629–630). On August 22, the church issued a communiqué saying, "The general council of the Episcopate expresses its esteem both for the workers on strike and their committees and for the authorities for having prevented disturbances of public order" (MacDonald 1981: 72). The Gdańsk Agreement (August 31) legalized independent trade unions, rendering the movement nationally efficient; "when Solidarity called a warning strike, the strike call was followed in the remotest corners of the country: in the tiny station buffet and the village pub as in Ursus or Huta Warszawa" (Ash 1985: 285). Poles taunted the state with "an endless parade of political meetings, mass rallies, and private discussion[s about] anti-Semitism in Poland, the theory and practice of union democracy, or the proper income of steelworkers as a percentage of gross national product" (Ost 1984: x–xi).

On December 13, 1981, the Polish state imposed martial law because, in the words of Vice-Premier Rakowski at Radom (December 3), Solidarity said

> behind closed doors, that they should openly ask for power. . . . Radom simply scared us. . . . They had gone completely crazy. On November 28, when Jaruzelski tried to pass an Emergency Powers act to stop the strikes and asked Solidarity leaders to restrain themselves, the answer was a huge fat laugh. They said, "If the government makes a special law against strikes, there will be a general strike."[23]

As in Algeria, the Polish state arrested, interned, and tortured its opponents in facilities dispersed all over the country (Mur 1984: viii–ix). The state, under General Wojciech Jaruzelski, passed minor reforms with some benefit. While the state returned work councils power to government ministries, workers retained strength at the firm level. The private sector also grew, with employment up from 271,000 in 1980 (5.2 percent) to 717,000 by 1989 (14.7 percent) (Crane 1991: 319–321). In 1982, "as a concession to Poland's growing democratic movement," the state amended the 1952 constitution to form "a quasi-judicial body similar to existing European constitutional courts" to function as long as it did "not challenge [the state's] most fundamental assumptions" (Brzezinski 1993: 159–160).

Meanwhile, church-state reciprocity was changing. On November 8, 1982, Jaruzelski and the Vatican announced a papal visit, a "tactical concession . . . to torpedo the strikes and demonstrations ordered by the Solidarity leaders" (Diskin 1986: 134). The church, which had negotiated a strike in February 1981, described itself as the voice of reason and calm with an adjudicating position between labor and state (Cviic 1993: 106–107). But the church's tactics should not be seen as reactionary, even if conservative relative to Solidarity. In the performances of citizen and state in authoritarian regimes, neutrality is a weapon. Indeed, as Wolicki points out:

> [The Church was central] in the defense of society's subjectivity. . . . It is the mainstay of all forms of public life (even for nonbelievers), both in direct contacts among people and organizationally. What is more, the experience of Solidarity has proved the church's new ability to participate in the formation of a mass labor movement [and activities of] the most creative groups of the intelligentsia. (Wolicki 1995 [1983]: 70–71)

These several government concessions substantiated the pacifism of labor, intellectuals, and religionists that contrasts sharply with Algeria's experience under martial law. This is not to say that dissident Poles were optimistic, assured, or seamless in the 1980s. The Polish opposition was not celebrating in this time; they despaired miserably and even debated violence, but a social logic, embedded and materialized in labor's power to cripple the communist state, had instilled, over several generations, a set of disciplines and interpretations that made violence infinitely less likely than patience to satisfy the desires of the church, Solidarity, KOR, and other anticommunist Poles.[24]

Conclusion

Effective citizenship encourages religious advocates for welfare or rights to secure their human subjectivity within, rather than against, their political system. This inference, drawn from citizenship reform experiments in Polish unionization and Algerian democratization, has political implications. First, if ruling elites wish to avoid violent social opposition, they must afford dissidents effective means for seeking all forms of physical, juridical, and subjective human security.[25] More precisely, if paradoxically, ruling elites must provide their opponents resources to compel the state to improve social welfare and legal rights lest activists cost the state more in the long run in militant agitations for political subjectivity. Second, *multiple* forms of effective citizen-subjectivity endow dissidents with the potential to pursue welfare and rights gains without resorting to violence. This suggests that endangered incumbents may avoid the combustible impasse of all-or-nothing social revolution by extending intermediate forms of effective citizenship.[26] Middle Eastern autocrats, for instance, could prepare for democratization by cultivating political subjectivity at subsidized and negotiated work sites. Third, the "war on terror" between a coalition of militarist, nationalist, and capitalist interests against Islamists demanding physical, juridical, and finally, subjective human security against authoritarian states—as in Algeria in 1989–1992—should end, precisely because it tends to exacerbate the very problems its seeks to resolve, undercutting rather than assuring human security for its relevant populations.

Notes

Sayres Rudy teaches social science and political philosophy at Hampshire College. He thanks James Wellman, Clark Lombardi, James Felak, Daniel Chirot, Christian Novetzke, David Waldner, Amrita Basu, Tim Snyder, David Dornisch, Andrzej Paczkowski, Andrzej Walicki, Lakhdar Brahimi, and anonymous Algerian interviewees for their encouragement and critical discussion.

1. Culture or ideology can *not* explain variable outcomes. As a *constant* it cannot explain change; as a *variable*, its own changes must be explained. Empirical works

confirm this. "Islam" or "Catholicism" cannot explain the variety of Muslim or Catholic political movements over time and space. Religious culture *interacts* with other variables to influence social action.

2. By 2003, the Bush administration and its academic opponents agreed that "poverty and tyranny," rather than "Islam," caused Islamist militancy. Alas, by recoding anti-Muslim racism in a more sophisticated analysis, this apparently enlightened insight merely helped to convert American domestic and foreign policies to the pure Realpolitik of the "global war on terror" (Rudy 2007).

3. As Edward Said argued, ruling "westerners" only deexoticize menacing Arab Muslims and, thus, see them realistically as an extension of military strategy. So the real lives of Arab Muslims supplant fantasies about exotic Orientals only under narrow parameters of martial priorities and policy mandates. In this way, Arab Muslim experiences are ignored or instrumentalized

4. Reactionary states and movements are often said to cause each other; a quintessential case is Saudi Arabia (Vitalis 2007).

5. Feldman poses the puzzle poorly. Muslims did form a "popular democratic movement" in Algeria precisely because they saw "democracy as the solution to what ail[ed] their country" *if it brought them to power*. One presumes Feldman means Islamists are not "freedom-loving" since they are not liberals. But this tendentiously confuses democracy, liberalism, and freedom.

6. These three components of human security are (1) physical (welfare); (2) juridical (rights); (3) subjective (power). Physical safety and juridical rights do not secure resources to compel the state to respect civilian demands. Political subjectivity is then one primal right that conditions effective demands for other rights, e.g., food, shelter, free speech. Which component of human security is the primary condition of the others is, however, indeterminate. Citizens need minimal caloric intake, legal space, and coercive capacity to advance their human security. Of course, they lack, and see themselves as lacking, these aspects of human security in varying ways across time and place. So it helps to be specific about how physical, juridical, or subjective capacities are weighted objectively and subjectively in particular contexts (cf. Geuss 2001).

7. It should be plain that human security is defined by particular social desires in specific contexts; there is no universal notion of human security. Welfare, rights, and subjectivity are placeholders to be "filled" by localized social demands. Human security is whatever people demand. It is an error to speak of being "for" or "against" human security, of human security "rising" or "falling," and so forth. Rather, politics should be seen as a competition over different conceptions of human security, of the rise or fall of certain beliefs about human security held by discrete persons or movements. This clarification reveals a widely ignored fissure in the concept of human security between data/statistics and theory/ethics. For instance, if we equate a statistical rise in disposable income with "more" human security, we are advocating that specific equation against critics who disagree over how to weigh income gains relative to

overall human security. In general, any conception or implementation of human security places a set of commitments (or theories about goods and "the Good") over opposing sets of commitments or theories of human security. People who define human security differently still value it equally. Physical, juridical, or subjective reforms mark decisions among contentious demands for human security, not between those for and against human security. Finally, physical, juridical, and subjective capacities are locally evaluated and objectively conditioned. A drop in caloric intake is a politically interpreted fact that effects social action. Likewise, the empirical presence of citizen- subjectivity is an objective fact that is desired and evaluated differently across contexts (Rudy 2004).

8. This revisits Fanon's (2004 [1963]) claim that imperial dehumanization causes rehumanizing violence; but against Fanon, I hold that oppressive regimes— imperial, authoritarian—differ in systemic subjectivity and so in recourse to violence for human security. It should go without saying that I do not apologize for Islamist violence or take any normative position toward my findings. If one needs to do so, I am opposed to the conditions under which Islamists turn to sustained collective violence as I am to inaccurate, hasty, or detached nostalgia for Gandhi, Mandela, and other nonviolent radicals. What Islamists in Grozny, Algiers, and Gaza have experienced is closer to the Jewish experience of Nazi-occupied Warsaw than to the Great Salt March. As Orwell rightly sneered, it is the common dream of those in power that their exploitation and brutality be met with only peaceful resistance.

9. Mine is a causal account of how social desires in discrete political settings pursue and conceive subjectivity as a part of human security. Violent rehumanization, and its dehumanization of the Other, can mark a caused pursuit of human freedom, dignity, or subjectivity as social actors define it against their lived experience. This process is nonagential; I oppose the liberal dogma that assigns everyone "agency" as if "agency" were either a philosophically strong concept or an empirically universal social reality.

10. Democratic inclusion has incorporated Islamists peacefully in Turkey, Jordan, Yemen, and Lebanon; political exclusion and aggression have militarized Islamists in Afghanistan, Palestine, Chechnya, Xianian, Algeria, Iraq, Uzbekistan, Pakistan, FATA, and the Ferghana Valley. In exceptional cases, the state has simply massacred Islamist opponents (preinvasion Iraq, Syria).

11. It reflects a potent confusion about social explanation that I face less "methodological" resistance to the same argument when I present it for Algeria or Poland in isolation than for Algeria and Poland in combination. It would appear that theory is agreeable but the comparison needed to justify it is not! Note that all explanations, including counterfactual narrative historiographies, require comparison and therefore bear the same burdens of variable analysis.

12. Algerian rulers claimed to derive legitimacy from their Islamic faith and participation in the liberation war against France. The Algerian state thus "sacralized" itself

in religious and revolutionary terms as directly representing Algerians' fundamental beliefs. Poland's leaders, in contrast, sanctified communism in secular and modern terms as negotiating with or transforming Poles' basic beliefs. But neither Algeria's religious nor Poland's secular "sacralization" project succeeded. Both regimes had to bargain and pay for "legitimacy" and were anyway discredited, or "desacralized," long before they imposed martial law.

13. This does not imply that Algerian Muslims or Polish Catholics gave their primary allegiances elsewhere or could not legitimize national-secular states. It is simply one, and a minor one, of their shared traits that their religious movements had global support.

14. This wrangling over assets should not be construed as either a religiously coded material contest or a materially coded secular-religious contest. Material wealth is required to defend beliefs and to build institutions, whatever faith they express. Note, too, that the presence of religious agitation against secular states implies neither a basic conflict between religious and secular beliefs nor any inherent polarity in the social logics of secular and religious faith, symbols, rituals, desires, or sacrifice.

15. States typically have mundane and coalitional commitments that do not map over those of leading religious groups.

16. Young unemployed men, known as *hittistes* or "wall-leaners," joined the Islamist movement en masse.

17. Youssef Ibrahim, "Militant Muslims Grow Stronger as Algeria's Economy Grows Weaker," *New York Times*, June 25, 1990, qtd. in Tessler and Grobschmidt (1995: 155).

18. The secular state explicitly claimed, in contrast, to be defending citizens from the theocratic "Iranization" of Algeria. Indeed, this exemplifies the point that both parties to the conflict are invoking at this moment opposed conceptions of human security.

19. The official death toll for 1992–1997 was 26,536; the US State Department and most estimates were 70,000 ("Algeria" 1999).

20. This does *not* imply continual or seamless Polish-Catholic national identity, unity, or uniformity.

21. Joseph Stalin himself had famously demurred that imposing communism on Catholic Poland was like saddling a cow.

22. Poland's largely commercial foreign debt ballooned from $1.2 billion in 1971 to $23.5 billion in 1980 (Ekiert 1996: 224).

23. Oriana Fallaci, "Interview with Mieczyslaw Rakowski," *Washington Post*, February 21, 1982, qtd. in Tymowski (1982: 2).

24. I cannot answer here all counterclaims but two require comment. First, religious principles cannot account for variations in religious practice, so I set aside cultural generalities about Islam and violence. Second, the literature equivocates on the Soviet Union's affect on Polish social protest (Singer 1982; Mastny 1999; Moreton

1982; Summerscale 1981; Sar 1985; Dallin 1958). Factors such as the Helsinki accords and US-USSR tension in Afghanistan made it implausible in 1980 that the Soviets would invade Poland to suppress the uprising; opposition figures argued this at the time. If this were false, mass protests should have drawn the Soviets in; they did not. Finally, potential counterviolence is, historically, a poor predictor for initial violence.

25. In the current era, authoritarian capitalism has, manifestly, every interest in provoking militarism between state and citizens.

26. If this seems somehow reactionary, mind that "effective citizenship" is tied to measurable gains in human security and so is, itself, a claim for radical inclusion. It is precisely the violent history of the zero-sum total war that urges me to find gradual transitions.

15

The Soka Gakkai and Human Security

Daniel A. Métraux

Introduction

Japan's Soka Gakkai provides an illuminating example of how a modern Asian Buddhist movement seeks to provide for the human security of not only its millions of members but also for the people of Japan and, by extension, all humankind. What makes the Soka Gakkai unique among engaged Buddhist organizations across Asia is its high degree of political activity and power. Together with its closely affiliated political party, the Komeito, a member of Japan's governing coalition between 1999 and 2009, the Gakkai has a consequential agenda that seeks to alter the social and political framework of the Japanese state. Soka Gakkai leaders criticize the current state of Japanese society, which they liken to a rudderless boat without any ethical foundation, sense of purpose, or clear direction. They offer an alternative view of Japanese society in which their form of Buddhism would reshape the religious foundation of a peaceful and psychologically and materially enriched society. They argue that Japanese society, shaped in their own image, would better provide for the human security of the people and the national security of the state. The transformation of Soka Gakkai as a nonstate religious actor to a potent state actor is precisely what makes it so unusual in this volume. Its members have merged their deep interest in the welfare, rights, and subjective desires of their religion with the broader hopes and dreams of a nation. Contesting, as this chapter shows, for the very heart of Japan's national security apparatus, they seek to maintain Japan's solely defensive military posture toward the world as not only the best strategy for its human security but for its national security as well.

The Soka Gakkai has not only institutionalized its influence within the formal machinery of the Japanese state[1] but has also chosen to be a significant political actor using its considerable social capital and potent political party to work through legitimate institutional means for change. This has not always been the case. Throughout the 1950s, the Soka Gakkai was a relatively radical movement that remained outside mainstream Japanese society, but since the foundation of the Komeito in the 1960s, it has considerably moderated its activities and has become a very mainstream movement, especially after the Komeito joined the coalition government in 1999.

This chapter examines the Soka Gakkai's depiction of the problems facing not only Japan but humankind as a whole as well as its proposals for their resolution. The Soka Gakkai's goal is the creation of a harmonious and prosperous Japan that will lead the way to a more peaceful world and a resolution of such challenges as global warming. The latter part of this study provides an analysis of how the Soka Gakkai and the Komeito used the party's position as a vital coalition partner with the ruling conservative Liberal Democratic Party (LDP) to forestall attempts by the government to revise Japan's 1947 "peace" constitution.

The Soka Gakkai's Worldview

The Soka Gakkai is a thirteen-million-member, broadly based new religious movement[2] with a religious ideology based on its own interpretation of the teachings of the medieval scholar and monk Nichiren (1222–1282), the founder of Japan's only native school of Buddhism. Nichiren taught that the stability of the state and the quality of life of its inhabitants depend on the successful propagation of Buddhist teachings found in the Lotus Sutra.[3] Nichiren lived during the Kamakura period (1185–1333), when Japan was beset by constant domestic strife, foreign invasion, and devastating natural disasters.

Like many other Buddhist scholars of his day, he held the view that Japan and its people were suffering because they were living during the age of Mappô (understood as the period of the degeneration of the Dharma, Buddhist law of nature) when people were forgetting the saving truths of Buddhist scripture. Nichiren proclaimed that peace, harmony, and human security could only be achieved if the doctrines of the Lotus Sutra became the spiritual foundation of Japanese society.

Central to today's Soka Gakkai worldview is that humankind is still embedded in the age of Mappô. Despite the impressive achievements in science, health, and technology, the twentieth century was the bloodiest period in human history, and the start of the twenty-first century has not been much better. Serious problems such as hunger, tribal and ethnic warfare, deadly terrorism, and many other forms of suffering plague people everywhere. According to the Soka Gakkai, the cause for these problems lies in the lack of a religious foundation for modern society.

The human life-condition of Japanese and people everywhere is dominated by such attitudes as greed, animosity, and indifference to the suffering of others. The demon of human misery in all of us must be expunged before the world can find true peace.

Like Nichiren, the Soka Gakkai argues that religion must serve as the basis of any morally just society. The primary social and political role of any religion is to remove the basic causes of human discontent and to lead humankind to true happiness, harmony, and prosperity in life. Religion is essential to the philosophical, social, and political betterment of society as a whole, and religion must enter into every sphere of society, including politics, in order for change to occur for the better. Thus, a society with a firm religious (read Buddhist) foundation would enjoy a higher degree of human security than one devoid of such a base.

The foundation of the Soka Gakkai movement is expressed through the term "human revolution" (*ningen kakumei*), which involves the transformation of individual character through the adoption of the "true Buddhism of Nichiren." The widespread propagation of Nichiren Buddhism, says the Soka Gakkai, would lead people everywhere to become more humane, compassionate, and peaceful than in the past. All people possess the potential for both evil and good (Buddha nature), but those who espouse Nichiren Buddhism will experience a profound transformation of their character from bad to good.[4] These "transformed" people would then devote their lives, earnestly working to better society through efforts to clean the environment, to improve the lives of the disadvantaged, to restore peaceful relations between states, and so on.

Thus, the goal of the Soka Gakkai is to provide greater human security by having more and more people experience its "human revolution" and then work to improve the human condition in whatever field they choose to enter. The Gakkai also seeks to improve human security through its activist involvement in such fields as education and politics so that even those who are not followers of the movement may benefit from its reforms and programs. For example, because it believes that all Japanese would benefit if the country remains a peaceful and demilitarized society, Soka Gakkai has used its political muscle to preserve Article 9 of the current Japanese constitution, which prohibits Japan from maintaining its own military.

Before moving on, I need to clarify the Soka Gakkai's relationship with Nichiren Buddhism and its former parent sect, Nichiren Shoshu, and its attitude toward the tendencies of intense Japanese nationalists such as Tanaka Chigaku (1861–1939),[5] the infamous proponent of Nichirenism, the fiercely nationalistic blend of Nichiren Buddhism and state Shinto. During World War II, the Gakkai so strongly denounced Tanaka and Nichirenism, as well as Japan's war effort as a whole, that its leaders were imprisoned for the duration of the war. Furthermore, the Soka Gakkai has moved sharply away from the exclusivism it exhibited in the 1950s and has become much more inclusive in its approach to society. This shift occurred as the Soka Gakkai endeavored to become a more accommodating part of mainstream Japanese society.

The Soka Gakkai and Human Security

The Soka Gakkai offers an illuminating case study of the role that one religious organization can play in the realm of human security. It strongly advocates such universal values as pacifism and greatly enhanced social welfare programs for all, but the very fact that it is a distinct denominational group raises questions about its ability to realize its human security goals in a society where nearly 90 percent of the population does not belong to the organization.

The great difference between the Soka Gakkai and other large religious movements in Japan and elsewhere is that it has the political muscle and wherewithal to actually realize some elements of its sociopolitical agenda. Before the 2009 landslide victory by Japan's Democratic Party, the LDP-Komeito coalition ruled Japan for nearly ten years. Moreover, during this period, Komeito controlled enough seats in both chambers of the Japanese Diet[6] to hold the balance of power between the two major conservative parties. The price for Komeito's support in a coalition government with the ruling Liberal Democratic Party was the adoption of several of its policies, including the preservation of Article 9.

The Soka Gakkai stresses that human security starts with the basic needs of all the people: "We need shelter, air to breathe, water to drink, food to eat." People need to be safe: "We need to work, to earn, to care for our health, to be protected from violence." People cannot live in isolation: "We need community, friends, family." People need to be respected—"to have self-respect and to respect others. We need access to love, culture, faith." Man must have a sense of contribution and purpose: "We need the chance to reach our highest potential."[7]

The Soka Gakkai stresses that human security can only be achieved through the transformation of the world—from a culture of violence and greed into a culture of peace, compassion, and respect. The essence of Buddhist faith is the interconnectedness of all things and all matter. Thus, even the activities of just one person, community, or nation can have a direct effect on everything else. The only real way to root out violence, greed, and intolerance is decidedly *not* through the destruction or subjugation of any one person or community of persons but rather through the transformation of the human spirit.[8] After all, "one cannot achieve peace through violence, but rather through understanding."

The Soka Gakkai asserts that it advances human security through its programs that promote peace education and culture and through individual "human revolutions" of its members. Personal change comes through Buddhist faith and practice, but the Soka Gakkai combines this individual practice with a variety of broader educational and practical activities, including peace education, intercultural exchange, an enhanced educational system, and the creation of a strong political party, the Komeito. The Komeito sees itself as responsible for enhancing the public welfare of the Japanese people, promoting peaceful relations abroad, especially with China, and protecting Japan's current "peace constitution."[9]

The Soka Gakkai believes that it is advancing the human security of the Japanese people with its highly publicized peace education campaigns. Komeito Diet representative Endo Otohiko asserts that "over 60 years have passed since World War II ended with Japan's total defeat. Young Japanese who have no memories of the horrors of war must be reminded of what happened then and what could happen again if they allow our country to adopt a warlike stance against its neighbors."[10] Komeito Deputy Chairperson and House of Councillors member Hamayotsu Toshiko suggests that her party and the Soka Gakkai are preserving the security and promoting the welfare of the Japanese through peace education.[11]

The peace education campaign began in 1957 when the Soka Gakkai's second leader, Toda Josei, made a very public speech in front of a large crowd of Soka Gakkai members, calling for the abolition of nuclear weapons. Since then, the Soka Gakkai has inundated its followers with endless speeches and publications on the danger of war and has staged many public exhibitions across Japan and throughout the world, including several at the United Nations in New York. These exhibitions through pictures, testimonies of survivors, and graphic videos show the horror and suffering that accompanies war. There are also exhibits about what can happen if we continue to destroy our environment. The message here is that if the Japanese can understand the horrible experiences of the 1930s and 1940s, they will be less likely to seek military solutions to problems in the future.

The Soka Gakkai maintains its campaign for the abolition of nuclear weapons to this day. Writing on the topic of "Human Security and Nuclear Abolition" in 2009, the Soka Gakkai's spiritual leader, Ikeda Daisaku, noted:

When we address the issue of nuclear abolition, I think that it would be useful to make an approach from the perspective of Human Security. Such an approach will enable us to explain to people how nuclear abolition has multifaceted effects on various issues directly linked to human survival and human life. In this way, I believe that this approach has a great potentiality of bringing the nuclear abolition issue to a great many people and thus expanding the circles of people who address the issue of nuclear abolition. Moreover, I trust that it would enable us to have people's moral common sense of abhorrence toward nuclear weapons be clearly reflected in international discussions.[12]

The Soka Gakkai notes that a culture of peace "consists of values, attitudes, behaviors, and ways of life that reject violence and prevent conflicts by tackling their root causes" and that such a culture solves problems "through dialogue and negotiation among individuals, groups, and nations."[13] Thus, one must firmly establish the awareness that no society can base its security and well-being on inflicting terror and misery on another; we must create a new set of global ethics. "The theory of nuclear deterrence," the organization argues, "in seeking to ensure the security of one state by threatening others with overwhelming destructive power, is diametrically opposed to the global ethics the new era demands."[14]

The Soka Gakkai promotes "humanistic education" through its own school system in Japan that extends from kindergarten to graduate school.[15] The Gakkai asserts that its schools differ from other entities in Japan in that "Soka education" places far less emphasis on rote learning and testing and more on developing the character, values, and potential of each individual child. The principal of the Soka High School in Tokyo told me in 2008 that "unlike other schools in Japan, we put the welfare of the individual child first."[16]

The Soka Gakkai also endeavors to advance international understanding through its Min-On culture programs, its strong support for the United Nations, and frequent published dialogues between Soka Gakkai International (SGI) leaders and other major world figures. Environmental awareness is a constant theme in numerous Gakkai exhibitions, talks, and publications as well as in several small environmental stations set up by the Gakkai in Japan and Brazil. One leader of the Soka Gakkai asserted that "there is no greater danger facing human security today than global warming and the on-going destruction of our environment."[17]

Despite these many active campaigns to promote peace education and the like, the Soka Gakkai argues that its main goal is not to bring actual change itself but rather to foster high-quality people who, through their own actions, will bring about positive social change. It sees itself as "the catalyst which can help people transform their character and develop a deep concern for human security, but it is up to these people themselves to become socially active in society to bring about positive change."[18] Meaningful social transformation can only occur when "reformed citizens" obtain enough influential positions in society to be able to persuade other citizens to adopt their proposals.

The Soka Gakkai, however, does employ direct action to promote its social agenda through the Komeito. The organization realizes that its growth potential is limited and that the way to bring meaningful reform is to elect enough candidates to national, prefectural, and local offices. Ideally, these elected officials will work with other sympathetic politicians to bring about positive change. Gakkai leaders stress that while their movement's main goals are the religious and spiritual needs of its members, politics is a critical arena in shaping the future human security of the country.

The Komeito's success in local and national elections, since the 1950s, and its role as the coalition partner of the ruling Liberal Democratic Party, after 1999, gave the Soka Gakkai the ability to exert its influence on the national scene. Even with the defeat of the coalition government in 2009, the Komeito has a secure voting base of several million Soka Gakkai voters who are concentrated in enough areas to elect Gakkai candidates. Nonetheless, various surveys indicate that a quarter to a third of Komeito voters are nonmembers who either support the party's basic policies, who do not wish to vote for the other major parties, or who see their vote as a way of showing disdain for the two mainstream parties, the Liberal Democratic Party and the Democratic Party.

Soka Gakkai International

Since the 1960s, the Soka Gakkai has become a significant international movement, claiming more than 2 million members outside Japan along with 10 million domestic members. The largest concentrations of foreign members are in South Korea, North America, South America, and Southeast Asia, with smaller concentrations in Europe, Africa, and Oceania. My research on SGI chapters across Southeast Asia, Australia, and Canada indicates that SGI has attracted a small native membership in every country that has an SGI organization. For example, SGI members in Singapore are almost entirely Chinese and SGI-Korea is made up almost entirely of Koreans.

Members abroad join for most of the same reasons that they do in Japan; they believe that this form of Buddhism offers them happiness here and now, a sense of empowerment, companionship with weekly or monthly small group meetings and social gatherings, and, for young educated Asians who have cut their ancestral Buddhist ties, a renewed link to Buddhism. Foreign members, especially in Korea and Southeast Asia, tend to be young, highly educated, and ambitious—they believe that this type of Buddhism empowers them to succeed at whatever they do best, while generating a feeling that they are making a positive contribution to world peace while building a network of friends through SGI.[19]

Effectiveness of SGI's Security Goals

When researching the Soka Gakkai's approach to human security, one must also determine the effectiveness of its peace education programs, who and how many people are in some way affected by them, and what the limitations of these programs are. Over the past few years, I conducted several focus group discussions with rank-and-file Soka Gakkai members in Japan, met with various Soka Gakkai leaders, including Ikeda Daisaku and Komeito Diet members, and discussed the Soka Gakkai with numerous Japanese scholars and journalists not affiliated with the movement.

It is clear that the Soka Gakkai's peace and environmental education campaigns have had a strong, even powerful, effect on its members. Discussions with ordinary members reveal a deep, even passionate, concern for peace and support for environmental conservation programs. There was a great outcry in 2003 and 2004 when the Komeito supported measures by its coalition partner, the LDP, to send Japanese Self-Defense troops to Iraq, where they were to work behind the lines in reconstruction programs. Soka Gakkai exhibitions, talks, and publications receive considerable attention from members. There is also support and devotion for Ikeda.

I doubt very much, however, that many ordinary nonmember Japanese know or care very much about the Soka Gakkai or its activities. When I conducted a survey of 235 Doshisha University students a few years ago asking their opinions about the Gakkai and how much they knew about its peace education programs, over 80 percent responded that they had a negative image of the movement and about 60 percent thought that its "peace movement" is little more than promotional propaganda. The few respondents with a positive image were either Soka Gakkai members, were related members, or were friends of members.

There was absolutely no coverage of the Soka Gakkai in the Japanese press during my past few visits to Japan. Several members have argued that the Japanese media has a negative bias against their organization and that it only pays attention when there is some scandal involving the movement or one of its leaders.[20] I interviewed a prominent television journalist who confirmed that there was indeed a deliberate policy at his station not to offer any coverage of the Soka Gakkai unless its activities directly affected Japanese politics in some manner or there was a verifiable new scandal involving the Gakkai or its leaders.[21]

One may logically conclude, then, that much of the Soka Gakkai's campaign for human security has only reached an audience of its own membership, but even if its impact is largely limited to its members, their friends, and their families, this number still includes many millions of Japanese who support the Gakkai's peace, environmental, and educational programs. But as we will see in the next section, the Soka Gakkai, using its considerable political clout, has played a key role in preserving Article 9 of the constitution and in promoting better relations between Japan and China.

The Soka Gakkai, Komeito, and the Preservation of Article 9

Article 9 of the Japanese constitution has become one of the most contentious issues in Japanese politics. It reads as follows:

> ARTICLE 9. Aspiring sincerely to an international peace based on justice and order, the Japanese people forever renounce war as a sovereign right of the nation and the threat or use of force as means of settling international disputes. (2) In order to accomplish the aim of the preceding paragraph, land, sea, and air forces, as well as other war potential, will never be maintained. The right of belligerency of the state will not be recognized.

The constitution, written by a team of Americans and ratified by the Japanese in 1947 at the height of the Allied occupation of Japan (1945–1952), remains in force today, never once having been amended. Article 9 prohibits the use of military force as a means of settling international disputes. It was specifically included under the instructions of the Supreme Commander for the Allied Powers General Douglas MacArthur, but after the occupation ended in 1952, it was up to the Japanese government to interpret what actually was and was not allowed. By 1954, the government had established that while it was inherently illegal for Japan to have a military force that would be involved in military operations outside Japan, sufficient forces to defend the country in case of attack by an external force was permissible.

Many conservatives in Japan, including conservative members of Japan's Parliament, propose amending the article to allow Japan to play a more active role in its own defense and to have a "normal" military that could develop collective security arrangements with other powers, including the United States. Many individuals and groups in Japan, including the Soka Gakkai, oppose any revision; they argue that a constitutional change could rattle Asian neighbors with bitter memories of past Japanese imperialism and that the principles of Article 9 can be applied to such issues as human rights, disarmament, the environment, and development.

The Komeito's position on Article 9 is dictated by the strong pacifist stance of its patron, the Soka Gakkai, and its spiritual leader, Ikeda Daisaku, regards the preservation of the "Peace Constitution" as a sacred article of faith. I interviewed several Komeito leaders, all of them Soka Gakkai members, who share Ikeda's support for the current version of Article 9. They and many other Soka Gakkai members believe that the welfare and quality of life of the Japanese people depends on their country remaining at peace and having peaceful relations with its neighbors.

Makiguchi Tsunesaburo and Toda Josei, the founders of the early Soka Gakkai, fervently believed that Nichiren Buddhism holds the key to world peace. Toda saw Japan's great destruction in World War II as a fulfillment of Nichiren's prophecy that ruin would come to the country and that the people of Japan had abandoned the "True Buddhism" of Nichiren in favor of some other faith, in this case, State Shinto. But Toda was also convinced that a new peaceful and prosperous Japan would emerge, like a phoenix from the ashes of defeat, if Nichiren Buddhism was propagated across the country and was allowed to become the dominant faith of the land.

Scholars who have studied the Soka Gakkai and other religious groups in Japan have frequently asked whether they, in fact, support "absolute pacifism" or "conditional pacifism." It is evident that although many followers of Soka Gakkai support the ideals of "absolute pacifism," their politically involved leaders have shifted to a more pragmatic or "realistic" conditional stance. Robert Kisala, a leading scholar on Japan's new religions who has studied six new religious organizations, finds that there are varying views as to what constitutes absolute pacifism. This position can mean a stance that rejects violence absolutely, but it can also mean a more long-term view that sees peace as the ultimate goal, but does not rule out the use of force for just means along the way (Kisala 1999). Kisala suggests that there is a distinct correlation between these two, quite different interpretations of pacifism and the social position of people who espouse them. Only those people willing to remain on the periphery of society can maintain the absolutist stance. When the movement shifts to the center in an effort to join mainstream society, it is forced to come to terms with questions about issues such as national defense and social order.

Kisala found in the cases of Soka Gakkai and Rissho Koseikai that the absolute option has been withdrawn because the two have become mass movements, involving millions of followers. Yet the achievement of peace remains a strong demand, and both groups participate in the international peace movement. Kisala stresses that the Japanese are very dedicated to the preservation of their cherished "peace constitution" and have strongly resisted any attempts to revise it, but when it comes to the active carrying out of a program for peace, the notion remains a romantic ideal that clashes with feelings of national superiority, with the result that there has been little opposition to conservative "reinterpretations" of the constitution to permit extensive de facto rearmament. Kisala makes note of Ikeda's and the Soka Gakkai's many peace-related activities but comments that a "further look at Ikeda's stated positions, however, leads to the conclusion that his fundamental position should be more accurately described as one of multi-nationalism rather than pacifism, for he does not absolutely rule out the use of force" (Kisala 1999).

Japanese Politics and the Question of Article 9

Article 9 of the 1947 constitution imposed on Japan by American occupation authorities gives Japan a national identity closely identified with peace and non-proliferation. When the 1954 Japan Self-Defense Establishment Law came into effect, the Japanese government interpreted the article to mean that, as a sovereign nation, Japan has the right of self-defense and that it is allowed an infrastructure for homeland security. This interpretation specified that Japan could develop a minimal military force for defensive purposes only[22] and that it could respond with "minimum necessary force" if invaded, but that it could not send forces abroad and could not participate in any collective defense arrangements (Samuels 2004). This interpretation limited the size of Japan's postwar military, and it limited the use of force to self-defense. This proscription meant that Japan could not maintain the capacity to conduct full-scale "modern warfare" and that it could not assist allied nations, like the United States, who came under attack. It even implied that Japan could not assist an American warship that came under attack while defending Japan (Samuels 2004).

The fact that Article 9 has never been changed is structurally linked to the requirement that to amend the constitution requires a two-thirds vote in each house of the national Diet and a majority of voters in a national referendum. For the first five decades of the postwar era, progressive political parties led by the Japan Socialist Party controlled over a third of the seats in both houses of the Diet, thus forestalling any constitutional reform that they might oppose. Another inhibiting factor was the existence of three political blocs, two of which had enough power to block reform of Article 9. Professor Richard J. Samuels, in his 2007 book *Securing Japan: Tokyo's Grand Strategy and the Future of East Asia*, identifies these three blocs, each with its own distinct view on Article 9: the antimainstream, the mainstream, and the pacifists.

The antimainstream group consists of a conservative grouping of politicians within the LDP who built a strong alliance with various industrialists and other conservative groups in Japanese society. According to Samuels (2007), "They favored a combination of rearmament and conventional alliances. To achieve these ends, they called for revision of the constitution's antiwar Article 9, argued that Japan should rebuild its military capabilities, and sought a reciprocal security commitment with the United States as a step toward their holy grail of 'autonomous defense.'"

In his book, Samuels describes the mainstream faction and its allies, led by the postwar prime minister Yoshida Shigeru, as a group of pragmatic conservative LDP politicians. These "liberal internationalists" held the view that "economic success and technological autonomy were the prerequisites of national security and that an alliance with the world's ascendant power was the best means to buy time until the former could be achieved. They rejected military spending in favor of a broader plan for state-led development of the private sector" (29). These pragmatists dominated Japanese government during the period when the three pillars of Japan's postwar security apparatus were established: Article 9, the Self-Defense Forces, and the U.S. Japan Security Treaty. Their power during the first half century of the postwar era beat back attempts by the revisionists to change the direction of Article 9.[23] This "Yoshida School," as noted, stressed that the foundations of national security rested with economic success and technological autonomy.

During the 1960s, 1970s, and 1980s, most Japanese favored the views of this faction. Peter Katzenstein, looking back at this era, argues that public attitudes favored a passive stance over an active stance along with a policy of alignment with the United States over a policy of equidistance between the United States and the Soviet Union. Furthermore, he argued that the Japanese preferred political dependence over a policy of autonomy and minimal rather than extensive military spending. The public favored economic strength, peaceful diplomacy, and a low-key consensus approach. Katzenstein argues that many of these same feelings persist, even today, although a higher number favor some revision for Article 9 (Katzenstein 2008).

The third group consisted of intellectuals, labor activists, and leftist politicians who viewed Japan as a "peace nation" and strongly opposed the use of organized violence. As strong supporters of Article 9 and opponents of major rearmament and the US-Japan Security Treaty, they sought a doctrine of "unarmed neutrality." As Samuels observes (2004: 6), "These groups did not trust Japan with a full military capability, preferring instead to rely on international public opinion, diplomacy, and passive resistance to counter security threats." They greatly expanded their grassroots networks during the 1950s and became a substantial political and economic force by 1960 (6). Leftist parties led by the Socialists had considerable success from the 1950s to the 1990s. However, because the Socialist Party has virtually disappeared as a viable political force since the 1990s, the political clout of this third group has been severely diminished.

The Soka Gakkai and Komeito fit very much into this third group throughout the 1990s, but the collapse of both leftist socialist parties and their replacement by a more moderate and nationalist Minshuto (Democratic) Party left Soka Gakkai–Komeito very much adrift. It was only at this time that the Soka Gakkai–Komeito developed a more cooperative attitude toward the LDP.

The significant strength of each of these factions kept any change to Article 9 from occurring. The mainstream faction working in an informal alliance with the leftists effectively preserved the integrity of Yoshida's goals, long after he himself was dead. But in the 1990s, the dynamic began to change. Japan was stung by swift international criticism of its failure to provide anything more than money to support the United States and its allies in the Gulf War of 1991, and public support to deploy minesweepers to the Persian Gulf soared. Revisionists, eyeing this change in public sentiment, criticized Article 9 as a major obstacle to "international cooperation" and as a cause of significant embarrassment. They scored well in 1992, when the Diet passed the Peace Keeping Operations (PKO) bill allowing SDF participation in United Nations peacekeeping operations.

Step-by-step, throughout the 1990s and into the new century, Japan began to face new security challenges that enhanced public support for stronger military capabilities to defend the nation. The balance of power within the LDP also began to shift markedly as the pragmatists slowly but surely began to noticeably decline. Today, revisionist leaders who strongly champion a stronger role for Japan in international affairs dominate the party and are pushing strongly for revision of Article 9 so that Japan might become a "normal" power once more.

The LDP issued a plan, discussing how it would like to alter Article 9:

> The LDP insists on language establishing "armed forces for national self-defense" and proposes that Japan explicitly provide itself the right of collective self-defense as well as the use of armed force when engaged in UN peacekeeping. The LDP proposes to delete Paragraph Two and Replace it with a renunciation of war and a declaration of the so-called "three non-nuclear principles" (no production, possession, or introduction of nuclear weapons). So, on the whole, by retaining the renunciation of war, referring to a new pacifism as a basic concept, and by stating its respect for human rights, the LDP draft does respect the original intent of Article Nine. (Samuels 2007: 8)

During the long term of Prime Minister Koizumi Junichiro (2001–2006), a strong proponent of constitutional revision, his government took decisive steps to broaden Japan's military reach. He used the 9/11 terrorist incident to win Diet approval for the first dispatch of Japanese warships out of the areas surrounding Japan since 1945. With Japanese naval tankers and destroyers in the Indian Ocean, Koizumi enacted the Emergency Powers Bill, which authorizes military mobilization in case of an attack on Japan. His government's 2003 Iraq Reconstruction Bill authorized the temporary dispatch of Japanese troops to that war-torn country. Koizumi and the LDP apparently gained broad public support for these actions.

But what has kept the LDP from bringing this issue to a vote in the Diet? The obvious answer is that it simply does not have the votes. The then major opposition party, the Democratic Party of Japan (Minshuto), has also issued position papers advocating collective defense, but it may have held back its support because it did not wish the LDP to receive credit for what might be a popular issue. Another important roadblock is the Soka Gakkai and Komeito. The LDP could not afford to lose the Komeito as its coalition partner as it needed Komeito votes to remain in power from 1999–2009.

Ultimately, in reality if not in theory, the LDP was getting its way. Rather than actually revising Article 9, the government steadily engaged in constitutional interpretation. This expansion of constitutional interpretation, since the 1980s, has seen a great expansion of the term "self-defense" to include collective defense activities such as convoying with American ships, patrolling sea-lanes up to a thousand miles away from the Japanese mainland, and refueling American ships in the Indian Ocean. Thus, while few in Japan actually want Japan to become a major military power on its own, there is a growing consensus that Japan, working closely with the United States, should play a greater role as an equal partner with the United States in the defense of Japan and the advancement of its interests in Asia (Katzenstein 2008).

No Compromise on Changing Article 9

Although the Soka Gakkai and Komeito were willing to compromise with the LDP on the issue of Iraq, they are not so obliging when it comes to the issue of Article 9. There are clear limits to the extent to which the Soka Gakkai will compromise its pacifist stance. Maintaining Article 9 and the essence of Japan's peace constitution is very important. Terasaki Hirotsugu, the Soka Gakkai's chief public relations officer, noted in a 2007 interview that

> Article 9 upholds Japan's commitment to world peace and its role as an active participant in constructive programs to foster a more peaceful and humane world. Any change in Article 9 that would encourage Japan to advance as a major military power would run counter to the goals of the Soka Gakkai movement. As a Buddhist organization we are deeply committed to the principles of pacifism and we cannot support any measures that would dilute this stand.[24]

Komeito Diet members Hamayotsu Toshiko and Endo Otohiko, when interviewed separately in March 2006, stressed their strong support for Article 9 and absolute opposition to change its format to meet the demands of the LDP revisionists. Instead, they both urged the adoption of a third clause that would make it possible to send troops abroad only on United Nations—sponsored peace and humanitarian missions, saying that such a clause "would further commit Japan to a path of nonviolence and nonbelligerence."[25]

The strong stance of both the Komeito and Soka Gakkai has gone a long way in preserving Article 9 in theory if not entirely in fact. At the very least, it has slowed the train of political reform. Helen Hardacre reflected on the Komeito's role in this process, saying:

> The leading political party was unable to proceed with its highest priority revision because of Komeito opposition, which itself originates with Ikeda Daisaku. Had the LDP succeeded in committing the country to collective self-defense, Japan would undoubtedly have been drawn even further into the "US Imperium," and thus Komeito's opposition on this point is highly consequential. (Hardacre 2005)

The 2009 election ended the Komeito's role as a coalition partner in Japan's government. The LDP did very badly, losing 177 seats and having its share of the popular vote drop to 27 percent from 48 percent in the 2005 election. The Komeito held its Soka Gakkai base and a fair share of its independent vote, winning 21 seats compared to 31 in 2005, but holding most of its popular vote—12 percent in 2009, compared to 13 percent in 2005.[26] The 2009 election has left the fate of Article 9 hanging in abeyance. While the Liberal Democratic Party renewed its desire to revise Article 9 during the 2009 election campaign and the Komeito adhered to its more pacifistic stance, the Democratic Party focused on domestic economic and social welfare issues and made no real mention of its feelings about constitutional reform. Immediately after their victory the Democrats announced that their focus would be on reviving Japan's economy and bettering relations with China and other Asian neighbors. Article 9 and constitutional reform is definitely not on the new government's immediate agenda (*Asahi Shimbun* 2009). Therefore, it seems that the Soka Gakkai–Komeito efforts to preserve Article 9 between 1999 and 2009 have borne fruit.

The Soka Gakkai is a hybrid in Japanese society. It is, on the one hand, an intensely religious organization that proselytizes over its version of the teachings of Nichiren and cares for the spiritual needs of its millions of followers; on the other hand, it is a very active political organization that has a significant number of members in both houses of Japan's Diet and was a member of Japan's governing coalition from 1999 until 2009.

The Soka Gakkai seeks to advance the human security of Japan through an intensive campaign of both transforming the individual personalities of its individual followers and offering them and the general public broad peace and environmental educational programs. There is ample evidence to show that while these programs have had a profound effect on Soka Gakkai members (who make up about 8 percent of the Japanese population), they have had very little effect on the public as a whole. It is in the area of politics, however, where the Soka Gakkai has had a broader effect on the course of the Japanese nation.

As a political party, the Komeito has had to make numerous compromises in the more idealistic stands of the Soka Gakkai membership. This includes agreeing to support the sending of Japanese troops to Iraq as peace keepers in 2003–2004 and sending some Japanese ships off the Horn of Africa in March 2009 to protect Japanese and allied shipping from Somali pirates. On the other hand, the Komeito's support for Article 9 has been adamant and uncompromising—a situation that led to the LDP's inability to enact constitutional reform, although its policies are slowly eroding the true effectiveness of the article.

The Soka Gakkai, despite being a religious organization, is convinced that political action is necessary to advance the human security of the Japanese people. It is very necessary to be socially active through broad educational programs and the like, but if right-wing politicians control the government, they will enact legislation that might restore Japan as a "normal" military power—an act that the Gakkai thinks is directly threatening to the human security of Japan. Thus through the Komeito, the Gakkai joined the ruling coalition and is very proud of the fact that although it has been forced, at times, to compromise some of its views, it effectively checked many of the schemes and aims of the LDP in the name of human security.

The Soka Gakkai demonstrates that there are limitations to what one religious organization can do in its promotion of human security. Particular religious denominations existing in a free and democratic society like Japan, even ones with huge memberships like Soka Gakkai, are generally restricted in their effectiveness to their core membership. The fact that Soka Gakkai has effectively extended its key values to its membership, here 8–10 million Japanese and more than 2 million members abroad, is significant, but its inability to reach the other 115 million Japanese is also significant.

The Soka Gakkai's successful entry into electoral politics and its effectively joining the ruling government coalition in 1999 is an indication that large religious organizations can affect society as a whole through their political involvement. The Gakkai's strong support for Article 9 would have meant little had it not had the Komeito to exercise its political muscle as a member of the coalition cabinet. The fact that Komeito gets a lot of non–Soka Gakkai votes indicates that politics allows religious organizations to extend their reach beyond their own denominational following. However, the fact that the LDP has been chipping away at Article 9 shows that there are limits to a religious group's political sway.

Finally, what about the Soka Gakkai's ability to facilitate better relations between Japan and its Asian neighbors? While there are very real limitations to its power due to its minority status in Japan, it does have a record of accomplishment. Because the Gakkai maintained close private ties with China, even during the Cultural Revolution of the 1960s, it could and did act as a go-between of the Chinese and Japanese governments, which finally recognized each other in 1972 (Métraux 1984).[27] Further, through its strong support for Article 9 and its publication of stories concerning atrocities committed by Japanese troops in World War II, Soka Gakkai has earned the trust of neighboring states and can play an important role in improving relations between them and Japan. All in all, religious organizations, particularly those that have large memberships and can exercise significant political muscle, can play a part in advancing their human security goals, but the fact that their effectiveness can be circumscribed by their denominational membership shows that there are limitations to their abilities in this regard.

Nonetheless, against the backdrop of this volume, the power of religion to advocate and express the need for human security underscores the necessity for governments to take seriously the power of religious groups to express the social and subjective desires of their populations. It further underlines the need for governments to take seriously the ability of religious groups to motivate and mobilize populations, in this case Japan, but in other cases as well, showing again that when governments focus only on national security and overlook the power of human security they tend to undermine both.

Notes

Daniel A. Métraux is professor of Asian studies at Mary Baldwin College and adjunct professor of history in the graduate program at Union Institute and University. He has taught at Doshisha Women's College in Kyoto, Japan, visited China twice as a Fulbright Scholar, and has been a visiting fellow at the Australian National University. He has written extensively on Japanese and East Asian religion and politics including *The Soka Gakkai Revolution* (1994) and *Aum Shinrikyo and Japanese Youth* (2000). He has served as president of the Southeastern Chapter of the Association for Asian Studies and editor of the *Southeast Review of Asian Studies*.

1. While the Soka Gakkai has been very much involved in Japanese politics since the mid-1950s, none of its international chapters are involved in any political activities.

2. The current wave of new religious movements in Japan began in the late nineteenth century, but those movements have experienced considerable growth in the postwar era. The Soka Gakkai, literally, the "Value Creation Society," founded by school teacher and principal Makiguchi Tsunesaburo (1871–1944) in 1930, began as an educational reform movement but became primarily a religious movement under its second president, Toda Josei (1900–1958), immediately after World War II.

The Soka Gakkai had only about a million members at the time of Toda's death but exploded in size under its third president and current spiritual leader, Ikeda Daisaku (1928–), claiming 13 million members (10 million in Japan—8 percent of the population) in 2009. The Soka Gakkai served as a lay religious group for the Nichiren Shoshu sect of Japanese Buddhism under Presidents Toda and Ikeda until the early 1990s, when the two organizations split, and the Soka Gakkai became an independent Buddhist movement. (Soka Gakkai International response to author's query, August 2009.)

3. The Lotus Sutra or Sutra on the White Lotus of the Sublime Dharma purports to be a discourse delivered by the Buddha near the end of his life. The ultimate "teaching" of the sutra is that the Buddha will save all beings that embrace its doctrines. Devotees of the Lotus Sutra attest that it is the highest of all sutras in that it fully crystallizes the Mahayana notion of the salvation of all sentient beings. Nichiren declared that one only needs to chant the Japanese title of the Sutra (*nam-myoho-renge-kyo*) repeatedly to achieve Buddhahood.

4. The transformation of the individual lies at the very heart of the Soka Gakkai movement. The Soka Gakkai follows the traditional Tendai-Nichiren Buddhist concept of the "Ten Worlds" (*jukai*). These "worlds' are psychological states that range from pure evil to pure good or Buddhahood. All people simultaneously possess the potential for great good or evil, but generally, the human spirit exists with a mixture of both good and bad. The transformation of the human spirit occurs when the individual, through Buddhist faith and practice, moves his or her personality from a lesser to a greater state of good. The Soka Gakkai asserts that this personal change and transformation can be greatly enhanced through education. The result has been an intense and very public campaign to promote peace education and greater concern for the protection of the environment.

5. Tanaka was a Japanese Buddhist scholar and a preacher of Nichiren Buddhism. Noted also for his work as an orator, writer, and ultranationalist in the Meiji (1868–1912), Taisho (1912–1926), and early Showa (1926–1989) periods, he is considered the founder of Nichirenism, which was espoused by other right-wing Japanese nationalists of the 1930s as well.

6. In the 2005 House of Representatives election in Japan, the Komeito won 13.3 percent of the vote and 31 of 480 seats. The Komeito holds 20 of 242 seats in the House of Councilors, as of 2009. See "Results of the 2005 Election for the House of Representatives," *Japan Times*, September 12, 2005, and "Seats Won in the House of Councillors Election," *Japan Times*, July 30, 2007.

7. Soka Gakkai 2003 leaflet, "Transforming the Human Spirit from a Culture of Violence to a Culture of Peace."

8. Interview with Terasaki Hirotsugu, executive director of the Soka Gakkai Office of Public Information, Tokyo, March 10, 2009.

9. Interview with Terasaki, 2009.

10. Interview with Endo Otohiko, then senior vice-minister of finance at the Finance Ministry, Tokyo, May 2, 2008.

11. Interview with Hamayotsu Toshiko at her Diet office, Tokyo, March 22, 2006.

12. Unpublished 2009 Soka Gakkai document, "The Rationale Behind the 'People's Decade of Action for Nuclear Abolition.'"

13. Soka Gakkai, "Transforming the Human Spirit."

14. Soka Gakkai, "Transforming the Human Spirit."

15. The Soka Gakkai runs primary and secondary schools in Tokyo and Osaka, Soka University in Hachioji near Tokyo, Soka University of America near Los Angeles, and kindergartens in Sapporo, Singapore, Malaysia, and Hong Kong.

16. Interview with Shirokawa Masatoshi, school principal, Soka High School, Tokyo, April 30, 2008.

17. Interview with Terasaki Hirotsugu, Tokyo, March 20, 2007.

18. Interview with Terasaki, 2009.

19. For a detailed discussion of SGI chapters in Southeast Asia, see Métraux (2001). Further, Professor Shimazono Susumu of Tokyo University has suggested several reasons for the success of Japanese new religious movements like Soka Gakkai abroad:

    One of the common characteristics of the New Religions is their response to strongly felt needs of individuals in their daily lives, their solutions to discord in interpersonal relations, their practical teachings that offer concrete solutions for carrying on a stable social life, and their provision, to individuals who have been cut off from traditional communities, of a place where congenial company and a spirit of mutual support may be found. As capitalistic industrialization and urbanization advance, large numbers of individuals are thrown into new living environments, thus providing conditions that require spiritual support for the individual. . . . Japanese religions are abundantly equipped with cultural resources that answer the needs of just these people in treading the path towards the urban middle class. (Susumu 1991: 1163)

20. Japan's sensationalist magazines and newspapers often accuse the Soka Gakkai, Ikeda Daisaku, and other leaders of sensational scandals including personal use of organizational funds, bizarre sex escapades, and much more. While several of the accusations of illicit use of funds have proven to be true—one leader was caught stealing large sums of money—the Soka Gakkai has successfully brought libel suits against some of these publications.

21. Interview with political television journalist Tsukamoto Akira, Tokyo, March 10, 2004.

22. The Japan Self-Defense Forces, generally referred to as Self-Defense Forces, are the united military forces of Japan established after the postwar Allied occupation of Japan ended in 1952.

23. This move begs the question whether Japan can actually afford a vast military expansion. The Japanese government is already deeply in debt.

24. Interview with Terasaki, 2007. Pacifism is a major element in some strands of Buddhism, but there are also traditions such as warrior Buddhist monks in Japanese history.

25. Interview with Hamayotsu, 2006.

26. "Democratic Party Wins Japanese Election," *Asahi Shimbun*, September 1, 2009.

27. Daniel A. Métraux, "How Soka Gakkai Helped Cement Sino-Japanese Relations in 1972," *Asahi Evening News*, July 17, 1984, p. 4.

16

Postscript: Lessons for Policymakers about Religion and Human Security

James K. Wellman, Jr., and Clark B. Lombardi

THIS BOOK GREW out of a multiyear project designed to determine whether human security is being affected by religious behavior and, if so, to explore the nature of its impact. Participants in the project were asked to discuss and help formulate workable definitions of human security and of "religion" and then to produce case studies in which human security in a particular country was (or was not) affected by religion.

Our working definition of human security included a broad concern for human welfare, human rights, and subjective and cultural interest in autonomy and a sense of freedom. In this way, we have argued that people are "insecure" when they are in danger of physical harm or material want; if they are suffering violations of human rights and are unable to improve their conditions; or if they feel alienated, psychologically distressed, or sociologically oppressed—for example, during a period of dislocation as refugees. We found this a helpful guide for our research and a fruitful avenue for ongoing research on the topic of human security. In like fashion, we identified religion as *a socially enacted desire for the ultimate, embodied in practices that have ultimate significance.* We are aware that all definitions are limited and in part shaped by the research interests and the data that a scholar or public policymaker has before them. But we have found these definitions helpful as a guide for research.

Participants were not asked to identify lessons that academics or policymakers should draw from their studies. Looking at the case studies, however, we think that together they suggest a number of important lessons for policymakers who wish to promote human security.

1. *The goals of the human security movement resonate with the goals of some, but not all religious actors around the world.* The human security movement is a historically recent event. It has used the logic of the "realist" movement in foreign

affairs and has pressured states to study and promote the welfare, rights, and desires of citizens, in ways that most states have generally not done in the past. The message of the human security movement is, in addition, one that resonates with a particular strain of religiosity that has long flourished in many of the world's global religions. Within many of the world's religions are strains that insist that all humans, no matter their station or condition, deserve care. Within these same religions are often also traditions that take a more exclusivist and parochial view of religion's strictures and the relative worth of human groups.

2. *Religion's motivating abilities and its powerful organizational structures make the religious friends of human security effective and potent allies, but also make the religious enemies of human security, similarly, complex and menacing foes.* Religions have a remarkable capacity both to provide human security and to harm it. Ignorance of or indifference to religion on the part of states and policymakers overlooks the potential religious actors have in the delivery of human security, as well as underestimating the power of religious actors to affect states for the worse.

- *Some religious actors promote conflict with alarming efficiency, while others are powerful advocates of peace.* Religions often create moral dichotomies between good and evil; enemy construction is good for group formation but often very bad at accommodating modern pluralistic populations. Religions can also trump universal moral discourse by claiming a "suspension of the ethical" in light of a transcendental demand. In the latter case, examples are prolific, not only in the past, but also in the present. They range from the Japanese sect Aum Shinrikyo, which in 1995 carried out the sarin gas attack in a Tokyo subway, to the violence of various forms of al-Qaeda over the last twenty years, to the US Christian groups that have supported the assassinations of doctors involved in providing abortions. On the other hand, the case study of Northern Ireland shows how religion can help resolve seemingly intractable problems. In Northern Ireland, religion certainly had a part in fostering the violence between the Protestant unionists and the mainly Catholic nationalist communities, but it has now become a part of the solution by creating more inclusive forms of discourse. As the chapter on Northern Ireland notes, the increasing salience of secularized values and commerce has moved the debate toward forms of reconciliation. The parties in the religious conflict accommodated the call for peace, partially to join a growing interest in civility and partially to take advantage of modernizing economic and social effects.

- *Some religious actors promote worldviews that are inconsistent with international human rights, while others are uniquely powerful advocates of worldviews that align with such rights.* Some religious actors promote worldviews that are inconsistent with international human rights norms. The case studies in this volume present provocative evidence, however, not only that other religious groups champion rights-friendly ethical paradigms but also that these religious figures can serve as crucial counterweights to illiberal religious figures. One of the case studies from India is particularly suggestive in this vein—demonstrating that liberal voices within a particular religion can play a uniquely important role in disempowering illiberal voices within that same religion. This can promote not just intercommunal peace but also women's rights and other fundamental human rights.

• *Religious groups often play an important role in providing food, welfare, and shelter for citizens in a particular nation.* Religious groups have an extraordinary ability to motivate adherents to act, including an ability to motivate followers to act against their own self-interest. They often also build up, through the process of proselytization and management of religious behavior, strong organizations. As a result, they have an ability to help ensure that followers help to provide the components of physical well-being to all citizens in a troubled society. The case studies in this book are replete with examples of religious groups inspiring action that provides food and shelter for the needy within their own communities as well as providing for the needy who are not members of their own community.

• *Religious groups, even powerful ones, sometimes have only a minimal impact on human security.* Some powerful religions promote, in troubled regions, quietist philosophies that lead their adherents to be passive and have no effect on the human security situation at all. The Latin American studies exemplify two sides of the coin. In the case study of Guatemala, Pentecostal congregations, though extremely well organized and potentially powerful, have been ineffectual in their impact on corrupt social and political structures. However, in Brazil, in a close study of a religious group in the municipality of Araçuaí, in the Jequitinhonha Valley of northeastern Minas Gerais, religious actors have successfully resisted their political oppression and continue to advocate for their basic rights.

3. *Religions promote human security most significantly when they complement a robust state concern for human security and not when they provide a substitute for it.* The ability of religious groups to provide food, shelter, and sometimes physical security often makes them allies of weak or failing states. They compensate for state failures and provide security and thus help to prevent desta-

bilizing unrest. In some cases this very act of care paradoxically harms human security in the long run.

- One problem is that some religions, whether by their own doing or by the decision of the state, act alone in the promotion of human security. As it turns out, they are far less effective than they would be if they demanded as a condition of their work that the state work with them. This is particularly true when religious actors are outsiders or nonstate actors who may do great good for vulnerable human populations but simultaneously allow states to hoard their resources and to ignore their own responsibilities.

- A second problem comes when religious groups are so effective that they are willing and able to displace current state elites (or, alternatively, powerful religious actors might have no intention of displacing elites, but elites fear it nevertheless). Scholars isn this volume discuss this situation in Egypt and in Turkey. States may initially feel that they benefit from "using" religions to take care of the poor, but they begin to fear that they are "losing" in the long run, since these religious groups tend to become independent powers invested with authority, trust, and respect that would otherwise be attributed to the state. Religions that come to play an indispensable role in meeting needs that are normally met by the state may also feel empowered to cease supporting the state and, instead, try to replace it. When religions move from empowering the state to threatening the state, violence, either instigated by the threatened state or by newly emboldened religious actors, can create new human security problems. In short, it appears that in the long run, religions are most helpful to human security when they complement a robust state concern for human security and not when they provide a substitute for it.

4. *Policymakers can and should draw on the expertise of scholars of religion to help them harness the power of religion to promote the positive contributions of religions to human security and to minimize the negative.* Scholars of religion can help states and policymakers differentiate between religious groups (or subgroups within a particular religious tradition) whose interests and activities work against the goal of promoting human security and those groups (or subgroups of a particular religious organization) whose interests and activities are synergistic with the goal of promoting human security. Scholars of religion can help also in another way. One of the most important findings in our case studies is that civilian populations are often quite ignorant about what religions are doing in their own populations. In Pakistan, for instance, there is widespread ignorance of extremist Islamic groups and the violence that they do to others. Many do not understand what these groups are doing, but the data shows that

if they did, they would not support it. Thus, again, more knowledge of religion can help promote human security.

To sum up, this initial examination makes it clear that religion often has an important impact on human security. Those who wish to promote human security must ask whether religion, the state, and international actors are working synergistically to promote the physical, sociological, and psychological welfare of people as well as their fundamental human rights. If this is not the case, they would be well advised to try to effect changes in the behavior of both religious actors and states so that productive partnerships take place. To do this, they will need both to encourage scholars of human security to consider the impact of religion, and to urge scholars of religion to think about how they can help to illuminate this important, but understudied phenomenon.

Bibliography

Abbas, Hassan. 2007a. "Increasing Talibanization in Pakistan's Seven Tribal Agencies." *Terrorism Monitor* 5(18): 1–5.

Abbas, Hassan. 2007b. "Is the NWFP Slipping out of Pakistan's Control?" *Terrorism Monitor* 5(22): 9–12.

Abbas, Hassan. 2008. "A Profile of Tehrik-i-Taliban Pakistan." *CTC Sentinel* 1(2): 1–4.

Abdo, Geneive. 2000. *No God but God: Egypt and the Triumph of Islam*. New York: Oxford University Press.

Abed-Kotob, Sana. 1995. "The Accommodationists Speak: Goals and Strategies of the Muslim Brotherhood of Egypt." *International Journal of Middle East Studies* 27(3): 321–339.

Agnes, Flavia, ed. 2002. *Of Lofty Claims and Muffled Voices*. Mumbai: Majlis.

Aktar, Ayhan. 2000. *Varlık Vergisi ve Türkleştirme Politikaları* [Wealth Tax and Turkification Policies]. Istanbul: İletişim.

Alexander, Stella. 1979. *Church and State in Yugoslavia since 1945*. Cambridge: Cambridge University Press.

Alkire, Sabina. 2003. "A Conceptual Framework for Human Security." Working Paper No. 2, Centre for Research on Inequality, Human Security and Ethnicity (CRISE), Oxford University.

Al-Tilmisani, Umar. 1987. "Do the Missionaries for God Have a Program?" *Liwa al-Islam*, June.

America's Development Foundation. 2007. "The Angolan Citizens Participation Initiative Final Report." Cooperative Agreement 690–04–00025. Alexandria, VA: America's Development Foundation. Available at http://www.adfusa.org/files/751_file_ADF_Angola_Citizen_Participation_Initiative_Final_Report.pdf.

Ammour, Kader, Christian Leucate, and Jean-Jacques Moulin. 1974. *La Voie Algérienne: Les Contradictions d'un Développement National*. Paris: F. Maspéro.

Amnesty International. 2009. "Amnesty International Chief Challenges Zimbabwe Prime Minister to Implement Human Rights Reforms." Available at http://www.amnesty.org/en/news-and-updates/news/amnesty-international-chief-challenges-zimbabwe-prime-minister-implement-human-rights-reforms-20090623.

Anan, Kofi. 2000. *Millenium Report of the Secretary-General of the U.N.: We the Peoples—The Role of the United Nations in the 21st Century.* New York: United Nations Department of Public Information.

Anderson, Allan. 2005. "New African Initiated Pentecostalism and Charismatics in South Africa." *Journal of Religion in Africa* 35 (1): 66–92.

Appleby, R. Scott. 2000. *The Ambivalence of the Sacred: Religion, Violence, and Reconciliation.* Lanham, Md.: Rowman & Littlefield.

Arato, Andrew. 1993. "Interpreting 1989." *Social Research* 60 (3): 609–646.

Arruti, José Maurício A. 2006. *Mocambo: Antropologia e História do Processo de Formação Quilombola.* Bauru, Brazil: EDUSC.

Asad, Talal. 1993. *Genealogies of Religion: Discipline and Reasons of Power in Christianity and Islam.* Baltimore, Md.: Johns Hopkins University Press.

Asad, Talal. 2003. *Formations of the Secular: Christianity, Islam, Modernity.* Stanford, Calif.: Stanford University Press.

Asad, Talal. 2007. *On Suicide Bombing.* New York: Columbia University Press.

Ash, Timothy. 1985. *The Polish Revolution: Solidarity.* New York: Vintage.

AU (African Union). 2005. Non-Aggression and Common Defense Pact. *Adopted by the Fourth Ordinary Session of the Assembly Held at Abuja Nigeria on Monday, 31 January 2005.* Available at http://www.africa-union.org/root/au/documents/treaties/text/Non%20Aggression%20Common%20Defence%20Pact.pdf.

Avalos, Hector. 2005. *Fighting Words: The Origins of Religious Violence.* Amherst, N.Y.: Prometheus Books.

Awadi, Hisham. 2004. *In Pursuit of Legitimacy: The Muslim Brothers and Mubarak, 1982–2000.* London: Tauris.

Aydın, Davut, Ali Çarkoğlu, Murat Çızakça, and Fatoş Gökşen. 2006. *Türkiye'de Hayırseverlik: Vatandaşlık, Vakıflar ve Sosyal Adalet* [Humanitarianism in Turkey]. İstanbul: TÜSEV.

Barve, Sushobha. 2003. *Healing Streams: Bringing Back Hope in the Aftermath of Violence.* New Delhi: Penguin Books.

Bastos, Santiago, and Aura Cumes. 2007. *Mayanización y Vida Cotidiana: La Ideología Multicultural en la Sociedad Guatemalteca.* Guatemala City: FLACSO.

Basu, Kaushik, and Sanjay Subrahmanyam. 1996. *Unravelling the Nation: Sectarian Conflict and India's Secular Identity.* New Delhi: Penguin Books.

Bauman, Zygmunt. 1985. Review of *Ideology in a Socialist State: Poland 1956–1983*, by Ray Taras. *Soviet Studies* 37(4): 577–578.

Bayat, Asef. 2007. *Making Islam Democratic: Social Movements and the Post-Islamist Turn.* Stanford, Calif.: Stanford University Press.

BBC Online. 2007a. "Zimbabwe Inflation Reaches 2,200 per cent." April 26. Available at http://news.bbc.co.uk/1/hi/business/6597993.stm, accessed June 23, 2009.

BBC Online. 2008. "Zimbabwe's Turbulent Priests." May 13. Available at http://news.bbc.co.uk/1/hi/world/africa/7396539.stm, accessed 7 July 2009.

BBC Online. 2009a. "Zimbabwe Rival to Enter Coalition." January 20. Available at http://news.bbc.co.uk/1/hi/world/africa/7860161.stm, accessed July 18, 2009.

BBC Online. 2009b. "Zimbabwe Abandons its Currency." January 29. Available at http://news.bbc.co.uk/1/hi/world/africa/7859033.stm, accessed June 23, 2009.

BBC Online. 2009c. "Can Tsvangirai Fix Zimbabwe's Basket-Case?" February 12. Available at http://news.bbc.co.uk/1/hi/business/7885343.stm, accessed July 20, 2009.

Beard, Virginia Parish. 2008. "Demanding Democracy and Rejecting in Africa: The Role of Religion and Regime Experience." Paper presented at the 2008 Meeting of the Midwest Political Science Association, April 3–6, 2008, Chicago.

Behr, Edward. 1991. *Kiss the Hand You Cannot Bite: The Rise and Fall of the Ceauşescus.* New York: Villard Books.

Beinin, Joel. 2001. *Workers and Peasants in the Modern Middle East.* Cambridge: Cambridge University Press.

Bellah, Richard N. 1975. *The Broken Covenant: American Civil Religion in the Time of Trial.* 2nd ed. Chicago: University of Chicago Press.

Bennoune, Karima. 2002. "A Disease Masquerading as a Cure: Women and Fundamentalism in Algeria." In Betsy Reed, ed., *Nothing Sacred: Women Respond to Religious Fundamentalism and Terror.* New York: Nation Books. Pp. 351–369.

Bennoune, Mahfoud. 1988. *The Making of Contemporary Algeria, 1830–1987: Colonial Upheavals and Post-Independence Development.* Cambridge: Cambridge University Press.

Benson, Rodney, and Daniel C. Hallin. 2007. "How States, Markets and Globalization Shape the News: The French and US National Press, 1965–97." *European Journal of Communication* 22 (1): 27–48.

Bergen, Peter, and Michael Lind. 2007. "A Matter of Pride: Why We Can't Buy Off the Next Osama bin Laden." *Democracy Journal* (Winter): 8–16.

Berger, Peter L. 1967. *The Sacred Canopy: Elements of a Sociological Theory of Religion.* Garden City, N.Y.: Doubleday.

Berger, Peter L. 1999. *The Desecularization of the World: Resurgent Religion and World Politics.* Washington, D.C.: Ethics and Public Policy Center.

Berkes Niyazi, Ahmad Feroz. 1998. *The Development of Secularism in Turkey.* London: McGill University Press.

Bhargava, Rajeev. 1998. *Secularism and Its Critics.* Delhi: Oxford University Press.

Bhebe, Ngwabi, and Terence O. Ranger, eds. 2001. *The Historical Dimensions of Democracy and Human Rights in Zimbabwe.* Harare: Zimbabwe University Publications.

Bigelow, Anna. 2004. "Sharing Saints, Shrines, and Stories: Practicing Pluralism in India." Ph.D. diss., University of California Santa Barbara.

Bigelow, Anna. 2010. *Sharing the Sacred: Practicing Pluralism in Muslim North India.* New York: Oxford University Press.

Bird, Litany. 2006. "Chortling Churchmen." *The Zimbabwean.* June 8. Available at http://www.thezimbabwean.co.uk/200606087223/opinion-analysis/chortling-churchmen.html.

Birmingham, David. 2002. "Angola." In Patrick Chabal, David Birmingham, Joshua Forrest, Malyn Newitt, Gerhard Seibert, and Elisa Silva Andrade, eds., *A History of Postcolonial Lusophone Africa*. Bloomington: Indiana University Press. Pp. 137–185.

Birmingham, David. 2006. *Empire in Africa: Angola and Its Neighbors*. Athens: Ohio University Press.

Bond, Patrick, and Masimba Manyanya. 2002. *Zimbabwe's Plunge: Exhausted Nationalism, Neoliberalism and the Search for Social Justice*. Pietermaritzburg: University of Natal Press.

Bourdieu, Pierre. 1977. *Outline of a Theory of Practice*. Cambridge: Cambridge University Press.

Bozan, İrfan. 2007. *Devlet ile Toplum Arasında* (Between State and Society). İstanbul: TESEV Yayınları.

Bratton, Michael, Annie Chikwana, and Tulani Sithole. 2005. "Propaganda and Public Opinion in Zimbabwe." *Journal of Contemporary African Studies* 23 (1): 77–108.

Bratton, Michael, and Nicolas van de Walle. 1997. *Democratic Experiments in Africa: Regime Transitions in Comparative Perspective*. Cambridge: Cambridge University Press.

Breen, Richard, and Bernadette C. Hayes. 1997. "Religious Mobility and Party Support in Northern Ireland." *European Sociological Review* 13 (3): 225–239.

Briscoe, Ivan, and Martín Rodríguez Pellecer. 2010. "A State under Siege: Elites, Criminal Networks, and Institutional Reform in Guatemala." The Hague: Instituut Clingendael. Available at http://www.clingendael.nl/publications/2010/20100913_cru_publication_ibriscoe.pdf.

Browers, Michaelle L. 2009. *Political Ideology in the Arab World: Accommodation and Transformation*. Cambridge: Cambridge University Press.

Bruce, James. 1995. "The Azzam Brigades: Arab Veterans of the Afghan War." *Jane's Intelligence Review*, April 1, p. 175.

Brumberg, Daniel. 1997. "Rhetoric and Strategy: Islamic Movements in the Middle East." In Martin Kramer, ed., *The Islamism Debate*. Tel Aviv: Moshe Dayan Center for Middle Eastern and African Studies. Pp. 11–34.

Brumberg, Daniel. 2002. "The Trap of Liberalized Autocracy." *Journal of Democracy* 13 (4): 56–68.

Brusco, Elizabeth E. 1995. *The Reformation of Machismo: Evangelical Conversion and Gender in Colombia*. Austin: University of Texas Press.

Brzezinski, Mark F. 1993. "The Emergence of Judicial Review in Eastern Europe: The Case of Poland." *American Journal of Comparative Law* 41 (2): 153.

Buğra, Ayşe. 2002. "Political Islam in Turkey in Historical Context: Strengths and Weaknesses." In Neşecan Balkan and Sungur Savran, eds., *The Politics of Permanent Crisis: Class, Ideology and State in Turkey*. New York: Nova Science Publishers. Pp. 107–144.

Buğra, Ayşe. 2008. *Kapitalizm, Yoksulluk ve Türkiye'de Sosyal Politika* (Capitalism, Poverty and Social Policy in Turkey). İstanbul: İletişim Yayınları.

Bulaç, Ali. 2001. *Avrupa Birliği ve Türkiye* (The European Union and Turkey). İstanbul: Eylül Yayınları.

Burdick, John. 1998. *Blessed Anastácia: Women, Race, and Popular Christianity in Brazil.* New York: Routledge.

Burdick, John. 2010. "Religion and Society in Contemporary Latin America." *Latin American Politics and Society* 52 (2): 167–176.

Burleigh, Michael. 2005. *Earthly Powers: The Clash of Religion and Politics in Europe from the French Revolution to the Great War.* New York: HarperCollins.

Burleigh, Michael. 2007. *Sacred Causes: The Clash of Religion and Politics, from the Great War to the War on Terror.* New York: HarperCollins.

Buruma, Ian. 2010. *Taming the Gods: Religion and Democracy on Three Continents.* Princeton, N.J.: Princeton University Press.

Buzan, Barry, and Lene Hansen. 2009. *The Evolution of International Security Studies.* Cambridge: Cambridge University Press.

Cahen, Michel, and Christiane Messiant. 1998. "La Chronique documentaire et des médias: L'Interlusonet." In Michel Cahen, ed., *Des Protestantismes en "Lusophonie Catholique."* Paris: Karthala. Pp. 513–520.

Calder, Bruce J. 2001. "The Role of the Catholic Church and Other Religious Institutions in the Guatemalan Peace Process, 1980–1996." *Journal of Church and State* 43 (4): 773–797.

Campagna, Joel. 1996. "From Accommodation to Confrontation: The Muslim Brotherhood in the Mubarak Years." *Journal of International Affairs* 50 (1): 278–304.

Campos, Bernardo L. 1996. "In the Power of the Spirit: Pentecostalism, Theology and Social Ethics." In Benjamin F. Gutiérrez and Dennis A. Smith, eds., *In the Power of the Spirit: The Pentecostal Challenge to Historic Churches in Latin America.* Louisville, Ky.: Presbyterian Church (USA), Worldwide Ministries Division; Mexico City: AIPRAL; and Guatemala City: CELEP. Pp. 41–50.

Cantón Delgado, Manuela. 1998. *Bautizados en Fuego: Protestantes, Discursos de Conversión y Política en Guatemala (1989–1993).* La Antigua, Guatemala: Centro de Investigaciones Regionales de Mesoamérica.

Çarkoğlu, Ali, and Ersin Kalaycıoğlu. 2007. *Turkish Democracy Today: Elections, Protest and Stability in an Islamic Society.* London: I. B. Tauris.

Çarkoğlu, Ali, and Binnaz Toprak. 2006. *Değişen Türkiye'de Din, Toplum ve Siyaset* [Religion, Society, and Politics in a Changing Turkey]. İstanbul: Tesev Yayınları.

Çarkoğlu, Ali, and Barry M. Rubin, eds. 2006. *Religion and Politics in Turkey.* London: Routledge.

Casanova, José. 1994. *Public Religions in the Modern World.* Chicago: University of Chicago Press.

Chatterjee, Partha. 1993. *The Nation and Its Fragments: Colonial and Postcolonial Histories.* Princeton, N.J.: Princeton University Press.

Chaudhry, Kiren Aziz. 1997. *The Price of Wealth: Economies and Institutions in the Middle East.* Ithaca, N.Y.: Cornell University Press.

Chesnut, R. Andrew. 1997. *Born Again in Brazil: The Pentecostal Boom and the Pathogens of Poverty*. New Brunswick, N.J.: Rutgers University Press.

Chesnut, R. Andrew. 2003. *Competitive Spirits: Latin America's New Religious Economy*. Oxford: Oxford University Press.

Chitando, Ezra. 2005. "'In the Beginning Was the Land': The Appropriation of Religious Themes in Political Discourses in Zimbabwe." *Africa* 75 (2): 220–239.

Chumachenko, Tatiana A. 2002. *Church and State in Soviet Russia: Russian Orthodoxy from World War II to the Khrushchev Years*. Trans. Edward E. Roslof. Armonk, N.Y.: M. E. Sharpe.

Cirtautas, Arista Maria. 1997. *The Polish Solidarity Movement: Revolution, Democracy and Natural Rights*. New York: Routledge.

Clarence-Smith, Gervase. 2003. "Le Problème ethnique en Angola." In J. P. Chrétien and G. Prunier, eds., *Les Ethnies ont une histoire*. Paris: Edition Karthala L'UMR MALD (CNRS-Paris I). Pp. 405–416.

Clark, Janine. 2004a. "Social Movement Theory and Patron-Clientelism: Islamic Social Institutions and the Middle Class in Egypt, Jordan, and Yemen." *Comparative Political Studies* 37 (8): 941–968.

Clark, Janine A. 2004b. *Islam, Charity, and Activism: Middle-Class Networks and Social Welfare in Egypt, Jordan, and Yemen*. Bloomington: Indiana University Press.

Cleary, Edward L. 1999. "Latin American Pentecostalism." In Murray W. Dempster, Byron D. Klaus, Douglas Petersen, eds., *The Globalization of Pentecostalism: A Religion Made to Travel*. Oxford: Regnum Books International. Pp. 131–150.

Cohen, Yehuda. 2003. *Why Religion? About One of the Strongest and Most Productive Motifs in Human Life*. Jerusalem: Priests' Publications.

Cole, Juan. 2010. *Engaging the Muslim World*. 2nd ed. New York: Palgrave Macmillan.

Collins, Randall. 2004. *Interaction Ritual Chains*. Princeton, N.J.: Princeton University Press.

Collins, Randall. 2010. *The Micro-sociology of Religion: Religious Practices, Collective and Individual*. ARDA Guiding Paper Series. State College, Pa.: Association of Religion Data Archives at Pennsylvania State University. Available at http://www.thearda.com/rrh/papers/guidingpapers.asp.

Comerford, Michael. 2004. "Alternative Voices: The Angolan Peace Movement." *Accord* 15: 32–36.

Commission on Human Security. 2003. *Human Security Now: Protecting and Empowering People*. New York: Commission on Human Security, 2003.

Concerned Citizens' Tribunal—Gujarat. 2002. *Crime against Humanity: An Inquiry into the Carnage in Gujarat, Findings and Recommendations*. 2 vols. Mumbai: Citizens for Peace and Justice.

Conferência Episcopal de Angola e São Tomé—CEAST 1988. "On Peace." CEAST, Luanda.

Conferência Episcopal de Angola e São Tomé—CEAST 1984. "On Reconciliation." CEAST, Luanda.

Conferência Episcopal de Angola e São Tomé—CEAST 1976. "On War and Religious Freedom." CEAST, Luanda.

Connor, Catherine, Yogesh Rajkotia, Ya-Shin Lin, and Paula Figueiredo. 2005. *Angola Health System Assessment*. Bethesda, Md.: Partners for Health Reformplus Project, Abt Associates.

Conquest, Robert. 1968. *Religion in the USSR*. London: Bodley Head.

Conselho Nacional Eleitoral—CNE. 2008. "Primeiros resultados parciais divulgados pela CNE." Available at http://www.cne.ao/noticias.cfm?id=281.

Crane, Keith. 1991. "Institutional Legacies and the Economic, Social, and Political Environment for Transition in Hungary and Poland." *American Economic Review* 81 (2): 318–322.

Crotty, William. 2006. "The Catholic Church in Ireland and Northern Ireland: Nationalism, Identity, and Opposition." In P. C. Manuel, L. C. Reardon, and C. Wilcox, eds., *The Catholic Church and the Nation-State: Comparative Perspectives*. Washington, D.C.: Georgetown University Press. Pp. 117–130.

Curtiss, John Shelton. 1953. *The Russian Church and the Soviet State, 1917–1950*. Boston: Little Brown.

Cviic, Christopher. 1983. "The Church." In Abraham Brumberg, ed., *Poland: Genesis of a Revolution*. New York: Vintage. Pp. 92–108.

Czabański, Krzystof. 1993. "Privileges." In Abraham Brumberg, ed., *Poland: Genesis of a Revolution*. New York: Vintage. Pp. 156–163.

Dahl, Robert A. 1998. *On Democracy*. New Haven, Conn.: Yale University Press.

Dallin, Alexander. 1958. "The Soviet Stake in Eastern Europe." *Annals of the American Academy of Political and Social Science* 317: 138–145.

Danielson, Robert Eugene. 2007. *Nasser and Pan-Arabism: Explaining Egypt's Rise in Power*. Monterey, Calif.: Naval Postgraduate School.

Darby, John. 1996. "An Intractable Conflict? Northern Ireland: A Need for Pragmatism." In K. Rupesinghe and V. A. Tishkov, eds., *Ethnicity and Power in the Contemporary World*. Tokyo: United Nations University Press. Pp. 199–209.

Davies, Norman. 1982. *God's Playground, a History of Poland in Two Volumes*. Vol. 2, *1795 to the Present*. Oxford: Clarendon/Oxford University Press.

Davies, Norman. 1984. *Heart of Europe: A Short History of Poland*. Oxford: Oxford University Press.

Dayal, John. 2002. *Gujarat 2002: Untold and Retold Stories of the Hindutva Lab*. Delhi: Justice and Peace Commission and All India Christian Council.

Dedring, Juergen. 2004. "Human Security and the UN Security Council." In Hideaki Shinoda and How-Won Jeong, eds., *Conflict and Human Security: A Search for New Approaches of Peace-Building*. IPSHU English Research Report Series No.19. Hiroshima, Japan: Institute for Peace Science, Hiroshima University. Pp. 45–94.

Deletant, Dennis. 1995. *Ceauşescu and the Securitate: Coercion and Dissent in Romania, 1965–1989*. Armonk, N.Y.: M. E. Sharpe.

Deletant, Dennis. 1999. *Communist Terror in Romania: Gheorghiu-Dej and the Police State, 1948–1965*. New York: St. Martin's Press.

Demerath, N. J. 2003. "Civil Society and Civil Religion as Mutually Dependent." In Michele Dillon, ed., *Handbook of the Sociology of Religion*. New York: Cambridge University Press. Pp. 348–359.

Diskin, Hannah. 1986. "The Pope's Pilgrimage to Jaruzelski's Poland: A Test of Power Revisited." In J. L. Black and J. W. Strong, eds., *Sisyphus and Poland: Reflections on Martial Law*. Kanata, Ont.: Frye. Pp. 133–144.

Dow, James, and Alan R. Sandstrom. 2001. *Holy Saints and Fiery Preachers: The Anthropology of Protestantism in Mexico and Central America*. Westport, Conn.: Praeger.

Dube, Jimmy G. 2006. *A Socio-Political Agenda for the Twenty-First Century Zimbabwean Church: Empowering the Excluded*. Lewiston, N.Y.: Edwin Mellen Press.

Durkheim, Emile. 1995 [1915]. *The Elementary Forms of the Religious Life*. London: MacMillan.

Dziewanowski, M. K. 1959. *The Communist Party of Poland: An Outline of History*. Cambridge, Mass.: Harvard University Press.

Eagleton, Terry. 2010. *Reason, Faith, and Revolution: Reflections on the God Debate*. New Haven, Conn.: Yale University Press.

Ediger, Ruth M. 2005. "History of an Institution as a Factor for Predicting Church Institutional Behavior: The Cases of the Catholic Church in Poland, the Orthodox Church in Romania, and the Protestant Churches in East Germany." *East European Quarterly* 39 (3): 299.

Ekiert, Grzegorz. 1996. *The State against Society: Political Crises and Their Aftermath in East Central Europe*. Princeton, N.J.: Princeton University Press.

Ekiert, Grzegorz, and Andrew A. Michta. 1997. "The State against Society: Political Crises and Their Aftermath in East Central Europe." *Slavic Review* 56 (2): 337.

Eliade, Mircea. 1996. *Patterns in Comparative Religion*. Rosemary Sheed, translator. Lincoln, NE: University of Nebraska Press.

Ellis, Jane. 1986. *The Russian Orthodox Church: A Contemporary History*. Bloomington: Indiana University Press.

Ellis, Stephen, and Gerrie ter Haar. 2004. *Worlds of Power: Religious Thought and Political Practice in Africa*. Johannesburg: Wits University Press.

Elshtain, Jean Bethke. 2003. *Just War against Terror: The Burden of American Power in a Violent World*. New York: Basic Books.

Engineer, Asgharali. 1984. *Communal Riots in Post-Independence India*. Hyderabad, India: Sangam Books.

Engineer, Asgharali. 1985. *On Developing a Theory of Communal Riots*. Bombay: Institute of Islamic Studies.

Engineer, Asgharali. 1989. *The Muslim Community of Gujarat: An Exploratory Study of Bohras, Khojas and Memons*. Delhi: Ajanta Publications.

Entelis, John. 1988. "Algeria under Chadli: Liberalization without Democratization, or: Perestroika, Yes, Glasnost, No!" *Middle East Insight* 6 (3): 47–64.

European Stability Initiative. 2005. *Islamic Calvinists Change and Conservatism in Central Anatolia.* Berlin: European Stability Initiative.

European Union Election Observation Mission. 2008. "Final Report on the Parliamentary Elections." EU Election Observation Mission, Angola, September 5.

Eyerman, Ron, and Andrew Jamison. 1991. *Social Movements: A Cognitive Approach.* Cambridge: Polity Press.

Fahey, Tony, Bernadette C. Hayes, and R. Sinnott. 2006. *Conflict and Consensus: A Study of Values and Attitudes in the Republic of Ireland and Northern Ireland.* Leiden: Brill.

Fahmy, Ninette S. 1998. "The Performance of the Muslim Brotherhood in the Egyptian Syndicates: An Alternative Formula for Reform?" *Middle East Journal* 52 (4): 551–562.

Fair, C. Christine. 2004. "Militant Recruitment in Pakistan: Implications for Al Qaeda and Other Organizations." *Studies in Conflict and Terrorism* 27 (6): 489–504.

Fair, C. Christine. 2007. "Pakistan Loses Swat to Local Taliban." *Terrorism Focus* 4 (37): 3–4.

Fair, C. Christine. 2008. "Who Are Pakistan's Militants and Their Families?" *Terrorism and Political Violence* 20 (1): 49–65.

Fair, C. Christine. 2009a. "Antecedents and Implications of the November 2008 Lashkar-e-Taiba Attack Upon Mumbai." Testimony presented before the House Homeland Security Committee, Subcommittee on Transportation Security and Infrastructure Protection, March 11.

Fair, C. Christine. 2009b. "Pakistani Attitudes towards Militancy in and Beyond Pakistan." In V. Krishnappa, Shanthie Mariet D'Souza and Priyanka Singh, eds., *Saving Afghanistan.* New Delhi: Academic Foundation. Pp. 93–112.

Fair, C. Christine, Clay Ramsay, and Steven Kull. 2008. *Pakistani Public Opinion on Democracy, Islamist Militancy, and Relations with the US: A Joint Study of WorldPublicOpinion.org and the United States Institute of Peace.* Washington, D.C.: WorldPublicOpinion.org.

Fanon, Frantz. 2004 [1963]. *The Wretched of the Earth.* Trans. Richard PhilcoxNew York: Grove Press.

Fanon, Frantz. 2008 [1952]. *Black Skin, White Masks.* New York: Grove Press.

Feldman, Noah. 2003. *After Jihad: America and the Struggle for Islamic Democracy.* New York: Farrar, Straus and Giroux.

Ferris, Elizabeth. 2005. "Faith-Based and Secular Humanitarian Organizations." *International Review of the Red Cross* 87 (858): 311–325.

Fetzer, Joel S., and J. Christopher Soper. 2005. *Muslims and the State in Britain, France, and Germany.* Cambridge: Cambridge University Press.

Finke, Roger, and Rodney Stark. 1992. *The Churching of America: 1776–1992: Winners and Losers in Our Religious Economy.* New Brunswick, N.J.: Rutgers University Press.

Finnegan, Richard B. 1983. *Ireland: The Challenge of Conflict and Change.* Boulder, CO: Westview Press.

Fischer, Mary Ellen. 1989. *Nicolae Ceauşescu: A Study in Political Leadership.* Boulder, CO: L. Rienner.

Fish, Steven M. 2002. "Islam and Authoritarianism." *World Politics* 55 (1): 4–37.

Fiszman, Joseph R. 1972. *Revolution and Tradition in People's Poland: Education and Socialization.* Princeton, N.J.: Princeton University Press.

Fletcher, Lehman B. 1996. *Egypt's Agriculture in a Reform Era.* Ames: Iowa State University Press.

Flora, Gavril, Georgina Szilagyi, and Victor Roudometof. 2005. "Religion and National Identity in Post-Communist Romania." *Journal of Southern Europe and the Balkans* 7 (1): 35–55.

Fox, Jonathan. 2008. *A World Survey of Religion and the State.* Cambridge: Cambridge University Press.

Freedom House. 2008. *Freedom in the World Report.* Washington, D.C.: Freedom House.

Freedom House. 2009. *Freedom in the World 2009.* Washington, D.C.: Freedom House.

Freire, Paulo. 2000. *Pedagogy of the Oppressed.* New York: Continuum.

Freston, Paul. 1993. "Brother Votes for Brother: The New Politics of Protestantism in Brazil." In Virginia Garrard-Burnett and David Stoll, eds., *Rethinking Protestantism in Latin America.* Philadelphia: Temple University Press. Pp. 66–110.

Freston, Paul. 2004. *Evangelicals and Politics in Asia, Africa, and Latin America.* Cambridge: Cambridge University Press.

Freston, Paul. 2008. *Evangelical Christianity and Democracy in Latin America.* New York: Oxford University Press.

Frieden, Jeff. 1981. "Third World Indebted Industrialization: International Finance and State Capitalism in Mexico, Brazil, Algeria, and South Korea." *International Organization* 35 (3): 407–431.

Froese, Paul. 2004. "After Atheism: An Analysis of Religious Monopolies in the Post-Communist World." *Sociology of Religion* 65 (1): 57–75.

Froese, Paul. 2008. *The Plot to Kill God: Findings from the Soviet Experiment in Secularization.* Berkeley: University of California Press.

Gandhi, Rajmohan. 1999. *Revenge and Reconciliation.* New Delhi: Penguin Books.

Ganiel, Gladys. 2007. "Religion and Transformation in South Africa? Institutional and Discursive Change in a Charismatic Congregation." *Transformation: Critical Perspectives on Southern Africa* 63: 1–22.

Ganiel, Gladys. 2008. "Beyond Pietism and Prosperity: Religious Resources for Reconstruction and Reconciliation in Zimbabwe," African Peace and Conflict Network working paper. Available at http://www.africaworkinggroup.org/files/Ganiel.pdf.

Ganiel, Gladys. 2009. "Spiritual Capital and Democratization in Zimbabwe: A Case Study of a Progressive Charismatic Congregation." *Democratization* 16 (6): 1172–1193.

Ganiel, Gladys. 2010a. "Pentecostal and Charismatic Christianity in South Africa and Zimbabwe: A Review." *Religion Compass* 5: 130–143.

Ganiel, Gladys. 2010b. "Ethnoreligious Change in Northern Ireland and Zimbabwe: A Comparative Study of How Religious Havens Can Have Ethnic Significance." *Ethnopolitics* 9 (1): 103–120.

Garrard-Burnett, Virginia. 1998. *Protestantism in Guatemala: Living in the New Jerusalem*. Austin: University of Texas Press.

Garrard-Burnett, Virginia. 2001. "Tongues People and Convolutionists: Early Pentecostalism in Guatemala, 1915–1940." Paper presented at the thirteenth Congress of the Latin American Studies Association, Washington, D.C. September.

Garrard-Burnett, Virginia. 2004. "'God Was Already Here When Columbus Arrived': Inculturation Theology and the Maya Movement in Guatemala." In Edward L. Cleary and Timothy J. Steigenga, eds., *Resurgent Voices in Latin America: Indigenous Peoples, Political Mobilization, and Religious Change*. New Brunswick, N.J.: Rutgers University Press. Pp. 125–154.

Garrard-Burnett, Virginia. 2010. *Terror in the Land of the Holy Spirit: Guatemala under General Efraín Ríos Montt, 1982–1983*. Oxford: Oxford University Press.

Garrard-Burnett, Virginia, and David Stoll. 1993. *Rethinking Protestantism in Latin America*. Philadelphia: Temple University Press.

Gaskill, Newton J. 1997. "Rethinking Protestantism and Democratic Consolidation in Latin America." *Sociology of Religion* 58 (1): 69–91.

Geertz, Clifford. 1973. *The Interpretation of Cultures*. New York: Basic Books, Inc., Publishers.

Geertz, Clifford. 1973. "Thick Description: Toward an Interpretive Theory of Culture." In *The Interpretation of Cultures: Selected Essays*, by Clifford Geertz. New York: Basic Books. Pp. 3–30.

Geuss, Raymond. 2001. *History and Illusion in Politics*. Cambridge: Cambridge University Press.

Ghannouchi, Rashid. 2000. "Secularism in the Arab Maghreb." In Azzam Tamimi and John L. Esposito, eds., *Islam and Secularism in the Middle East*. New York: New York University Press. Pp. 97–123.

Ghemati, Abdelkrim. 1998. "A qui profite l'escalade dans l'horreur?" *Confluences Méditerranée*, special issue: "La parole aux Algéries: Violence et politique en Algérie," no. 25, J. Chagnollaud, ed. Paris: Edition L'Harmattan.

Gifford, Paul, ed. 1995. *The Christian Churches and the Democratisation of Africa Conference Entitled "The Christian Churches and Africa's Democratisation": Revised Papers*. New York: Brill.

Gifford, Paul. 1998. *African Christianity: Its Public Role*. Bloomington: Indiana University Press.

Glasman, Maurice. 1996. *Unnecessary Suffering: Managing Market Utopia*. Brooklyn: Verso.

Global Witness. 2002. *All the President's Men: the Devastating Story of Oil and Corruption in Angola's Privatised War*. London: Global Witness.

Goldbard, Arlene. 2006. *New Creative Community: The Art of Cultural Development*. Oakland, CA: New Village Press.

Goldbard, Arlene, and Don Adams. 2001. *Creative Community: The Art of Cultural Development*. Oakland, CA: New Village Press.

Goodwyn, Lawrence. 1991. *Breaking the Barrier: The Rise of Solidarity in Poland*. New York: Oxford University Press.

Gooren, Henri. 2001. "Reconsidering Protestant Growth in Guatemala, 1900–1995." In James W. Dow and Alan R. Sandstrom, eds., *Holy Saints and Fiery Preachers: The Anthropology of Protestantism in Mexico and Central America*. Westport, Conn.: Praeger. Pp. 169–203.

Govender, Shun, and Beatrice Mutale Skagestad. 2009. *Civil Society and Oil for Development in Angola: Ways to Enhance Strategic Cooperation among Non-State Actors*. Pretoria: Institute for democracy in South Africa.

Government of India. 2006. *Social, Economic and Educational Status of the Muslim Community of India: A Report* [Sachar Committee Report]. New Delhi: Government of India.

Grann, David. 2011. "A Murder Foretold." *New Yorker* 87 (7): 42–61.

Green, John Clifford, Mark J. Rozell, and Clyde Wilcox. 2003. *The Christian Right in American Politics: Marching to the Millenium*. Washington, D.C.: Georgetown University Press.

Grobbelaar, Neuma. 2003. "Angola in Search of Peace: Spoilers, Saints and Strategic Regional Interests." Working Paper 14, Netherlands Institute of International Relations "Clingendael," Conflict Research Unit, The Hague.

Guelke, Adrian. 2003. "Religion, National Identity and the Conflict in Northern Ireland." In W. Safran, ed., *The Secular and the Sacred: Nation, Religion, and Politics*. Portland, Ore.: Frank Cass. Pp. 101–121.

Güney, Aylin, and Filiz Başkan. 2008. "Party Dissolutions and Democratic Consolidation: The Turkish Case." *South European Society and Politics*, 13(3): 263–281.

Gupta, Dipankar. 1997. "Civil Society in the Indian Context: Letting the State off the Hook." *Contemporary Sociology* 26 (3): 305–307.

Gupta, N. L. 2000. *Communal Riots in India*. New Delhi: Gyan Publication House.

Hadden, Jeffrey K. 1987. "Toward Desacralizing Secularization Theory." *Social Forces* 65 (3): 587–611.

Hafez, Mohammed M. 2000. "Armed Islamist Movements and Political Violence in Algeria." *Middle East Journal* 54 (4): 572–591.

Hafez, Mohammed M. 2003. *Why Muslims Rebel: Repression and Resistance in the Islamic World*. Boulder, CO: Lynne Rienner.

Hafez, Mohammed. 2004. "From Marginalization to Massacres: A Political Process Explanation of GIA Violence in Algeria." In Quintan Wiktorowicz, ed., *Islamic*

Activism: A Social Movement Theory Approach. Bloomington: Indiana University Press. Pp. 37–60.

Hammar, Amanda, Brian Raftopoulos, and Stig Jensen, eds. 2003. *Zimbabwe's Unfinished Business: Rethinking Land, State and Nation in the Context of Crisis*. Harare: Weaver Press.

Hampson, Fen Osler. 2008. "Human Security." In Paul D. Williams, ed., *Security Studies: An Introduction*. London: Routledge. Pp. 229–243.

Hardacre, Helen. 2005. "Constitutional Revision and Japanese Religions." *Japanese Studies* 25 (3): 235–247.

Harrigan, Jane, and Hamed El-Said. 2009. *Economic Liberalisation, Social Capital and Islamic Welfare Provision*. Basingstoke, U.K.: Palgrave Macmillan.

Harris, Sam, 2005. *Religion, Terror, and the Future of Human Reason*. New York: W.W. Norton.

Hart, David Bentley, 2009. *The Atheist Delusions: The Christian Revolution and its Fashionable Enemies*. New Haven, Conn.: Yale University Press.

Hasan, Mushirul, 2001. *Legacy of a Divided Nation: India's Muslims since Independence*. Delhi: Oxford University Press.

Hasan, Zoya. 2004. "Social Inequalities, Secularism and Minorities in India's Democracy." In Mushirul Hasan, ed., *Will Secular India Survive?* Gurgaon, Haryana: ImprintOne. Pp. 239–262.

Hasan, Zoya, and Ritu Menon. 2004. *Unequal Citizens: A Study of Muslim Women in India*. New Delhi: Oxford University Press.

Hasdorff, Terri. 2006. "Faith-Based Organizations and U.S. Programming in Africa." Testimony before the Subcommittee on Africa, Global Human Rights and International Operations, International Relations Committee, U.S. House of Representatives, September 28. Washington, D.C. Available at http://www.usaid.gov/press/speeches/2006/ty060928.html.

Hayden, Robert M. 2002. "Antagonistic Tolerance: Competitive Sharing of Religious Sites in South Asia and the Balkans." *Current Anthropology* 43 (2): 205–231.

Hayes, Bernadette C., and Ian McAllister. 1995. "Religious Independents in Northern Ireland: Origins, Attitudes, and Significance." *Review of Religious Research* 37 (1): 65–83.

Haynes, Jeff. 2004. "Religion and Democratization in Africa." *Democratization* 11 (4): 66–89.

Hayes-McCoy, Gerard Anthony. 1995. "The Tudor Conquest: 1534–1603." In Theodore William Moody and Francis Xavier Martin, eds., *The Course of Irish History*. Niwot, Colo.: Roberts Rinehart. Pp. 174–188.

Hedström, Peter, and Richard Swedberg. 1998. *Social Mechanisms: An Analytical Approach to Social Theory*. Cambridge: Cambridge University Press.

Hefner, Robert W. 1998. "Multiple Modernities: Christianity, Islam, and Hinduism in a Globalizing Age." *Annual Review of Anthropology* 27 (1): 83–104.

Hefner, Robert W. 2003. *Civil Society and Civil Religion as Mutually Dependent*. In Michele Dillon, ed., *Handbook of the Sociology of Religion*. New York: Cambridge University Press, 2003. Pp. 348–359.

Heper, Metin, and Tanel Demirel. 1996. "The Press and the Consolidation of Democracy in Turkey." *Middle Eastern Studies* 32 (2): 109–123.

Herbert, David. 2003. *Religion and Civil Society: Rethinking Public Religion in the Contemporary World*. Aldershot, U.K.: Ashgate.

Heywood, Linda. 2006. "The Angolan Church: The Prophetic Tradition, Politics, and the State." In Paul C. Manuel, Lawrence C. Reardon, and Clyde Wilcox, eds., *The Catholic Church and the Nation-State: Comparative Perspectives*. Washington, D.C.: Georgetown University Press. Pp. 191–206.

Hickey, John. 1984. *Religion and the Northern Ireland Problem*. Dublin: Gill and Macmillan.

Hill, Geoff. 2005. *What Happens After Mugabe? Can Zimbabwe Rise from the Ashes?* Cape Town: Zebra Press.

Hinton, Alexander Laban. 2010. *Transitional Justice: Global Mechanisms and Local Realities after Genocide and Mass Violence*. New Brunswick, N.J.: Rutgers University Press.

Hitchens, Christopher. 2009. *God Is Not Great: How Religion Poisons Everything*. New York: Hachette Book Group.

Hodges, Tony. 2004. *Angola: Anatomy of an Oil State*. Oxford: Fridtjof Nansen Institute and James Currey.

Holland, Heidi. 2008. *Dinner with Mugabe*. Johannesburg: Penguin Books.

Hopwood, Derek. 1982. *Egypt, Politics and Society, 1945–1981*. London: Allen & Unwin.

Huggins, Martha Knisely. 1998. *Political Policing: The United States and Latin America*. Durham, N.C.: Duke University Press.

Human Rights Watch. 1999. *Human Rights Watch World Report 1999—Algeria*. 1 January 1999, available at: http://www.unhcr.org/refworld/docid/3ae6a8aa18.html.

Human Rights Watch. 2002. *India: "We Have No Orders to Save You": State Participation and Complicity in Communal Violence in Gujarat*. New York: Human Rights Watch.

Human Rights Watch. 2003. *Compounding Injustice: The Government's Failure to Redress Massacres in Gujarat*. New York: Human Rights Watch.

Human Rights Watch. 2004. *Media and Political Freedoms in Angola*. London: Human Rights Watch.

Human Security Network. 1999. *A Perspective on Human Security: Chairman's Summary, 1st Ministerial Meeting of the Human Security Network, May 20, 1999*. Lysøen: Human Security Network.

Hume, David. 1981 [1779]. *Dialouges Concerning Natural Religion*. Indianapolis, Ind.: Bobbs-Merrill.

Huntington, Samuel P. 1993. "The Clash of Civilizations?" *Foreign Affairs* 72 (3): 22–49.

Huntington, Samuel P. 1996. *The Clash of Civilizations and the Remaking of World Order*. New York: Simon & Schuster.

Inglehart, Ronald, and Christian Welzel. 2005. *Modernization, Cultural Change, and Democracy: The Human Development Sequence*. Cambridge: Cambridge University Press.

Instituto Nacional de Estatística. 2002. "Household Income and Expenditure Survey 2001." In United Nations System in Angola, United Nations Development Group, *Angola—the Post War Challenges: Common Country Assessment 2002*. New York: United Nations.

Iwanow, Boris, ed. 1960. *Religion in the USSR*. Munich: Institut zur Erforschung der USSR.

James, William. 1982. *The Varieties of Religious Experience: A Study in Human Nature*. New York: Penguin Classics.

Jayasinghe, Saroj. 2007. "Faith-based NGOs and Healthcare in Poor Countries: A Preliminary Exploration of Ethical Issues." *Journal of Medical Ethics* 33: 623–626.

Jeffery, Patricia, and Amrita Basu. 1998. *Appropriating Gender: Women's Activism and Politicized Religion in South Asia*. New York: Routledge.

Jeffrey, Paul. 1998. *Recovering Memory: Guatemalan Churches and the Challenge of Peacemaking*. Uppsala, Sweden: Life and Peace Commission.

Jenkins, Philip. 2006. *The New Faces of Christianity: Believing the Bible in the Global South*. New York: Oxford University Press.

Jenkins, Philip. 2007. *God's Continent: Christianity, Islam, and Europe's Religious Crisis*. New York: Oxford University Press.

Jenkins, Richard, Hastings Donnan, and Graham McFarlane. 1986. *The Sectarian Divide in Northern Ireland Today*. London: Royal Anthropological Institute of Great Britain and Ireland.

Jonas, Susanne. 2000. *Of Centaurs and Doves: Guatemala's Peace Process*. Boulder, CO: Westview Press.

Juergensmeyer, Mark. 2000. *Terror in the Mind of God: The Global Rise of Religious Violence*. Berkeley: University of California Press.

Kadıoğlu, Ayşe, 2007. "Başörtüsü ... Nereye kadar?" [The Veil ... until Where?]. *Radikal* 2, December 9, 2007.

Kalaycıoğlu, Ersin. 2005. "The Mystery of the Türban: Participation or Revolt?" *Turkish Studies*. 6 (2): 233–251.

Kalaycıoğlu, Ersin, and Binnaz Toprak. 2004. *İş Yaşamı, üst Yönetim ve Siyasette Kadın* [Women in Business Life, Upper Management and Politics]. İstanbul: TESEV Yayınları.

Kalkandjieva, Daniela. 2009. "The Bulgarian Orthodox Church." In Lucian N. Leustean, ed., *Eastern Christianity and the Cold War, 1945–91*. London: Routledge. Pp. 79–98.

Kalyvas, Stathis N. 1996. *The Rise of Christian Democracy in Europe*. Ithaca, N.Y.: Cornell University Press.

Kalyvas, Stathis N. 2003. "Unsecular Politics and Religious Mobilization." In Thomas Kselman and Joseph A. Buttigieg, eds., *European Christian Democracy*. Notre Dame: University of Notre Dame Press. Pp. 293–320.

Kamsteeg, Frans H. 1998. *Prophetic Pentecostalism in Chile: A Case Study on Religion and Development Policy*. Lanham, Md: Scarecrow Press.

Karaman, Hayreddin, 2009. Türkiye ve İslam Dünyası'nda Gündem [The Public Agenda in Turkey and the Islamic World]. Istanbul: Nesil.

Katzenstein, Peter J. 2008. *Rethinking Japanese Security: Internal and External Dimensions*. Abingdon: Routledge.

Kepel, Gilles. 1995. "Islamists versus the State in Egypt and Algeria." *Daedalus* 124 (3): 109–127.

Kepel, Gilles. 1985. *Muslim Extremism in Egypt: The Prophet and Pharaoh*. Berkeley: University of California Press.

Khan, Iftikhar Ali, and R. K. Ghai. 2000. *History of the Ruling Family of Sheikh Sadruddin, Sadar-i-Jahan of Malerkotla, 1449 A.D. to 1948 A.D.* Patiala: Publications Bureau, Punjabi University.

Kisala, Robert. 1999. *Prophets of Peace: Pacifism and Cultural Identity in Japan's New Religions*. Honolulu: University of Hawaii Press.

Kiser, John W. 2002. *The Monks of Tibhirine: Faith, Love, and Terror in Algeria*. New York: St. Martin's Press.

Klaiber, Jeffrey L. 1998. *The Church, Dictatorships, and Democracy in Latin America*. Maryknoll, N.Y.: Orbis Books.

Klaus, Byron D. 1999. "Pentecostalism as a Global Culture: An Introductory Overview." In Murray W. Dempster, Byron D. Klaus, Douglas Petersen, eds., *The Globalization of Pentecostalism: A Religion Made to Travel*. Irvine, CA: Regnum Books International. Pp. 127–130.

Kłoczowski, Jerzy. 1979. "The Polish Church." In William James Callahan and David Higgs, eds., *Church and Society in Catholic Europe of the Eighteenth Century*. Cambridge: Cambridge University Press. Pp. 122–137.

Kołakowski, Leszek. 1983. "The Intelligentsia." In Abraham Brumberg, ed., *Poland: Genesis of a Revolution*. New York: Random House. Pp. 54–67.

Kolarz, Walter. 1961. *Religion in the Soviet Union*. New York: Macmillan.

Konda, 2007. *Biz Kimiz: Toplumsal Yapı Araştırması 2006* [Who Are We? A Study of Societal Structure]. Istanbul: Konda Araştırma ve Danışmanlık.

Krishna, Anirudh. 2002. *Active Social Capital: Tracing the Roots of Development and Democracy*. New York: Columbia University Press.

Krishna, Chaitanya, and Abdul Gafoor Abdul Majeed Noorani. 2003. *Fascism in India: Faces, Fangs, and Facts*. New Delhi: Manak Publications.

Kronstadt, K. Alan. 2008. *U.S.-Pakistan Relations*. Washington D.C.: Congressional Research Service, http://fpc.state.gov/documents/organization/115888.pdf.

Kubik, Jan. 1994. *The Power of Symbols against the Symbols of Power: The Rise of Solidarity and the Fall of State Socialism in Poland*. University Park: Pennsylvania State University Press.

Kukkuk, Leon. 2007. "Comments." *Open Democracy*. Available at http://www.opendemocracy.net/article/democracy_power/africa_democracy/angola_choice.

Kuran, Timur. 1998. "Moral Overload and Its Alleviation." In Avner Ben-Ner and Louis Putterman, eds., *Economics, Values, and Organization.* New York: Cambridge University Press. Pp. 231–266.

Kurtz, Stanley, 2007. "Doc Jihad, Part II." *National Review Online.* Available at http://article.nationalreview.com/?q=NzNhZDAzMjU1YjE1NTc5OWM0ZGE1MGJl MzVjNjgoNWU=.

Kurzman, Charles, and Ijlal Naqvi. 2010. "Do Muslims Vote Islamic?" *Journal of Democracy* 21(2): 50–63.

Kuru, Ahmet T. 2008. "Passive and Assertive Secularism: Historical Conditions, Ideological Struggles, and State Policies toward Religion." *World Politics* 59 (4): 568–594.

Labat, Séverine. 1995. *Les Islamistes Algériens: Entre les Urnes et le Maquis.* Paris: Seuil.

Langfur, Hal. 2006. *The Forbidden Lands: Colonial Identity, Frontier Violence, and the Persistence of Brazil's Eastern Indians, 1750–1830.* Stanford, Calif.: Stanford University Press.

Langohr, Vickie. 2004. "Too Much Civil Society, Too Little Politics: Egypt and Liberalizing Arab Regimes." *Comparative Politics* 36 (2): 181–204.

Laremont, Ricardo René. 2000. *Islam and the Politics of Resistance in Algeria, 1783–1992.* Trenton, N.J.: Africa World Press.

Leaning, Jennifer, and Sam Arie. 2000. "Human Security: A Framework for Assessment in Conflict and Transition." Working Paper Series 11/8, Harvard Center for Population and Development Studies, Cambridge, Mass. Available at http://www.certi.org/publications/policy/human%20security-4.PDF.

Leiken, Robert S., and Steven Brooke. 2007. "Essays—The Moderate Muslim Brotherhood." *Foreign Affairs* 86 (2): 107–121.

Leustean, Lucian N. 2008. "Orthodoxy and Political Myths in Balkan National Identities." *National Identities* 10 (4): 421–432.

Leustean, Lucian N. 2009. *Orthodoxy and the Cold War: Religion and Political Power in Romania, 1947–65.* Basingstoke, U.K.: Palgrave Macmillan.

Leustean, Lucian. 2010. *Eastern Christianity and the Cold War, 1945–91.* London: Routledge.

Levine, Daniel H. 2008. "Conclusion: Evangelicals and Democracy: The Experience of Latin America in Context." In Paul Freston, ed., *Evangelical Christianity and Democracy in Latin America.* New York: Oxford University Press. Pp. 207–223.

Levine, Daniel H. 2009. "The Future of Christianity in Latin America." *Journal of Latin American Studies.* 41 (1): 121–145.

Levine, Daniel H., and David Stoll. 1997. "Bridging the Gap between Empowerment and Power in Latin America." In Suzanne H. Rudolph and James Piscatori, eds., *Transnational Religion and Fading States.* Boulder, CO: Westview Press. Pp. 63–103.

Lewis, Bernard. 2003. *What Went Wrong? The Clash between Islam and Modernity in the Middle East.* New York: Oxford University Press.

Lincoln, Bruce. 2003. *Holy Terrors: Thinking about Religion after September 11*. Chicago: University of Chicago Press.

Lipset, Seymour Martin, and Jason M. Lakin. 2004. *The Democratic Century*. Norman: University of Oklahoma Press.

Lobe, Jim, and Katie Mattern. 2009. "Tsvangirai Gets Obama's Seal of Approval." *The Zimbabwean*, July 13. Available at http://www.thezimbabwean.co.uk/2009071322714/weekday-top-stories/tsvangirai-gets-obamas-seal-of-approval.html.

Lombardi, Clark Benner. 2006. *State Law as Islamic Law in Modern Egypt: The Incorporation of the Sharia into Egyptian Constitutional Law*. New York: Brill.

Long, Charles. 1986. *Significations: Sings, Symbols, and Images in the Interpretation of Religion*. Philadelphia: Fortress Press.

Longley, Edna. 2001. "Multi-Culturalism and Northern Ireland: Making Difference Fruitful." In *Multi-Culturalism: The View from the Two Irelands*, by Edna Longley and Declan Kiberd. Cork, Ireland: Cork University Press. Pp. 1–44.

López R., Darío. 1998. *Los Evangélicos y los Derechos Humanos: La Experiencia Social del Concilio Nacional Evangélico del Perú 1980–1992*. Lima: CENIP.

Löwy, Michael. 1996. *The War of Gods: Religion and Politics in Latin America*. London: Verso.

Luckmann, Thomas, 1967. *The Invisible Religion: The Problem of Religion in Modern Society*. New York: MacMillan.

Lukes, Steven, 2004 [1974]. *Power: A Radical View*. 2nd ed. Basingstoke: Palgrave Macmillan.

Lukowski, Jerzy, and W. H. Zawadzki. 2001. *A Concise History of Poland*. Cambridge: Cambridge University Press.

MacDonald, O., ed. 1981. "Communiqué from the Conference of the General Council of the Polish Episcopate." *The Polish August: Documents from the Beginnings of the Polish Workers' Rebellion, Gdansk, August 1980*. Seattle: Left Bank Books.

MacFarlane, Neil, and Yuen Foong Khong. 2006. *Human Security and the U.N.* Bloomington: Indiana University Press.

Madsen, Stig Toft, 1991. "Class, Kinship and Panchayat among Jats of Western Uttar Pradesh." *Anthropos* 86 (6): 351–365.

Madsen, Stig Toft, 1996. "Clan, Kinship and Panchayat Justice among the Jats of Western Uttar Pradesh." In N. Jayaram and Satish Saberwal, eds., *Social Conflict*. Oxford in India Readings in Sociology and Social Anthropology. Delhi: Oxford University Press. Pp. 402–412.

Marcum, James. 1978. *The Angolan Revolution*. Vol. 2, *Exile Politics and Guerrilla Warfare (1962–1976)*. Cambridge, Mass.: MIT Press.

Mardin, Şerif. 1991. *Türk modernleşmesi: Makaleler IV.* İstanbul: İletişim.

Mardin, Şerif. 2005. "Turkish Islamic Exceptionalism Yesterday and Today: Continuity, Rupture and Reconstruction in Operational Codes." *Turkish Studies* 6 (2): 145–165.

Mardin, Şerif. 2006. *Religion, Society, and Modernity in Turkey*. Syracuse: Syracuse University Press.

Martin, David. 1990. *Tongues of Fire: The Explosion of Pentecostalism in Latin America*. Oxford: Blackwell.

Martin, David. 2001. *Pentecostalism: The World Their Parish*. Oxford: Blackwell.

Martin, David. 2005. *On Secularization: Towards a Revised General Theory*. Aldershot, U.K.: Ashgate.

Martin, Francis Xavier. 1995. "The Normans: Arrival and Settlement: 1169-c.1300." In Theodore William Moody and Francis Xavier Martin, eds., *The Course of Irish History*. Niwot, Colo.: Roberts Rinehart. Pp. 123–144.

Mastny, Vojtech. 1999. "The Soviet Non-Invasion of Poland in 1980–1981 and the End of the Cold War." *Europe Asia Studies* 51 (2): 189–211.

Maxwell, David. 2000. "'Catch the Cockerel before Dawn': Pentecostalism and Politics in Post-Colonial Zimbabwe." *Africa: Journal of the International African Institute* 70 (2): 249–277.

Maxwell, David. 2005. "The Durawall of Faith: Pentecostal Spirituality in Neo-Liberal Zimbabwe." *Journal of Religion in Africa* 35 (1): 4–32.

Maxwell, David. 2007. *African Gifts of the Spirit: Pentecostalism and the Rise of a Zimbabwean Transnational Religious Movement*. Oxford: James Currey.

McAdam, Doug, John D. McCarthy, and Mayer N. Zald. 1996. *Comparative Perspectives on Social Movements: Political Opportunities, Mobilizing Structures, and Cultural Framings*. Cambridge: Cambridge University Press.

McCaffrey, Lawrence J. 1973. "Irish Nationalism and Irish Catholicism: A Study in Cultural Identity." *Church History* 42 (4): 524–534.

McCracken, J. L. 1995. "Northern Ireland: 1921–66." In Theodore William Moody and Francis Xavier Martin, eds., *The Course of Irish History*. Niwot, Colo.: Roberts Rinehart. Pp. 313–323.

McKiernan, Eoin, 1997. "When Northern Irish Stone Catholics, It's Not about Religion." *National Catholic Reporter* 33 (23): 19.

McKittrick, David, and David McVea. 2000. *Making Sense of the Troubles*. Belfast: Blackstaff.

Messiant, Christine, Brigitte Lachartre, and Michel Cahen. 2008. *L'Angola Postcolonial*. Vol. 1, *Guerre et Paix sans Démocratisation*. L'Angola Postcolonial. Paris: Karthala.

Métraux, Daniel Alfred. 1994. *The Soka Gakkai Revolution*. Lanham, Md.: University Press of America.

Métraux, Daniel Alfred. 2001. *The International Expansion of a Modern Buddhist Movement: The Soka Gakkai in Southeast Asia and Australia*. Lanham, Md.: University Press of America.

Michnik, Adam. 1995 [1983]. "Three Fundamentalisms." In M. Bernhard and H. Szlajfer, eds., M. Chmielewska- Szlajfer, tr., *From the Polish Underground: Selections from Krytyka, 1978–1993*. University Park: Pennsylvania State University Press. Pp. 231–238.

Mill, John Stuart. 1985 [1859]. *On Liberty*. London: Penguin Classics.

Miller, Donald E. 2007. "2006 SSSR Presidential Address—Progressive Pentecostals: The New Face of Christian Social Engagement." *Journal for the Scientific Study of Religion* 46 (4): 435–445.

Miller, David, and Tetsunao Yamamori. 2007. *Global Pentecostalism: The New Face of Christian Social Engagement.* Berkeley: University of California Press.

Mitchell, Claire. 2006. *Religion, Identity and Politics in Northern Ireland: Boundaries of Belonging and Belief.* Aldershot, U.K.: Ashgate.

Mitchell, Richard P. 1969. *The Society of the Muslim Brothers.* London: Oxford University Press.

Mitchell, Timothy. 1999. "No Factories, No Problems: The Logic of Neo-Liberalism in Egypt." *Review of African Political Economy* 26 (82): 455–468.

Molesky-Poz, Jean. 2006. *Contemporary Maya Spirituality: The Ancient Ways Are Not Lost.* Austin: University of Texas Press.

Monticone, Ronald C. 1986. *The Catholic Church in Communist Poland, 1945–1985: Forty Years of Church-State Relations.* Boulder, CO: East European Monographs.

Moore, Clement Henry. 1994. *Images of Development: Egyptian Engineers in Search of Industry.* Cairo: American University in Cairo Press.

Morales Sic, José Roberto. 2007. *Religión y Política: El Proceso de Institucionalización de la Espiritualidad en el Movimiento Maya Muatemalteco.* Guatemala City: FLACSO.

Moreton, Edwina. 1982. "The Soviet Union and Poland's Struggle for Self-Control." *International Security* 7 (1): 86–104.

Morris, Brian. 2006. *Religion and Anthropology: A Critical Introduction.* New York: Cambridge University Press.

Moustafa, Tamir. 2000. "Conflict and Cooperation between the State and Religious Institutions in Contemporary Egypt." *International Journal of Middle East Studies* 32 (1): 3–22.

Muchena, Deprose T. 2004. "The Church and Reconciliation: A Mission Impossible?" In Brian Raftopoulos and Tyrone Savage, eds., *Zimbabwe: Injustice and Political Reconciliation.* Cape Town: Institute for Justice and Reconciliation. Pp. 257–270.

Mukonyora, Isabel. 2008. "Foundations for Democracy in Zimbabwean Evangelical Christianity." In Terence O. Ranger, ed., *Evangelical Christianity and Democracy in Africa.* Oxford: Oxford University Press. Pp. 131–160.

Munson, Ziad. 2001. "Islamic Mobilization: Social Movement Theory and the Egyptian Muslim Brotherhood." *Sociological Quarterly* 42 (4): 487–510.

Mur, Jan. 1984. *A Prisoner of Martial Law: Poland, 1981–1982.* San Diego: Harcourt Brace Jovanovich.

Müsiad. 1994. *İş hayatında Islam Insanı (Homo Islamicus)* [The Islamic Human in Business Life]. No. 9. Istanbul: Müsiad Araştırma Raporları.

Muzaffar, Chandra. 2005. "Religious Conflict in Asia: Probing the Causes, Seeking Solutions." In Gerrie Ter Haar, ed., *Bridge or Barrier: Religion, Violence and Visions for Peace.* Leiden: Brill. Pp. 57–79.

Nasr, Seyyed Vali Reza. 1999. *International Relations of an Islamist Movement: The Case of the Jama'at-i Islami of Pakistan*. New York: Council on Foreign Relations.

Nasr, Seyyed Vali Reza. 2005. "The Rise of Muslim Democracy." *Journal of Democracy* 16 (2): 13–27.

Nasr, Seyyed Vali Reza. 2007. *The Shia Revival: How Conflicts Within Islam Will Shape the Future*. New York: Norton.

Neves, Tony. 2007. "Angola, A Paz e os Direitos Humanos nas Mensagens da Igreja Católica (1989–1994)." *Res-Publica Revista Lusófona de Ciência Política e Relações Internacionais* 5–6: 179–194.

Norris, Pippa, and Ronald Inglehart. 2005. *Sacred and Secular: Religion and Politics Worldwide*. Cambridge: Cambridge University Press.

Norton, Augustus R. 2009. *Hezbollah: A Short History*. Princeton, N.J.: Princeton University Press.

Nye, Joseph, 2005. *Soft Power: The Means to Success in World Politics*. New York: Public Affairs.

OAS (Organization of American States). 2003. *Declaration on Security in the Americas*. Adopted at the third plenary session of October 28. Available at http://www.oas.org/documents/eng/DeclaracionSecurity_102803.asp.

Ó hEithir, Breandán. 1989. *A Pocket History of Ireland*. Dublin: O'Brien Press.

Ogata, Sadako, and Johan Cels. 2003. "Human Security: Protecting and Empowering the People." *Global Governance* 9 (3): 273–282.

O'Neill, Kevin Lewis. 2010. *City of God: Christian Citizenship in Postwar Guatemala*. Berkeley: University of California Press.

Öniş, Ziya. 2001. "Political Islam at the Crossroads: From Hegemony to Coexistence." *Contemporary Politics* 7 (4): 281–298.

Öniş, Ziya. 2009. "Conservative Globalism at the Crossroads: The Justice and Development Party and the Thorny Path to Democratic Consolidation in Turkey." *Mediterranean Politics* 14 (1): 21–40.

Öniş, Ziya, and Emin Fuat Keyman. 2003. "A New Path Emerges." *Journal of Democracy* 14 (2): 95–107.

Orlet, Christopher, 2005. "From Breadbasket to Dustbowl." *American Spectator Online*, April 13. Available at http://spectator.org/archives/2005/04/13/from-breadbasket-to-dustbowl.

Osa, Maryjane. 2003. *Solidarity and Contention: Networks of Polish Opposition*. Minneapolis: University of Minnesota Press.

Ost, David. 1984. Introduction to Jan Mur, ed., *A Prisoner of Martial Law, Poland: 1981–1982*, trans. L. Vallee. San Diego: Harcourt Brace Jovanovich. Pp. x–xix.

Ostheimer, Andrea. 2000. "Aid Agencies: Providers of Essential Resources?" In Jakkie Cilliers and Christian Dietrich, eds., *Angola's War Economy: The Role of Oil and Diamonds*. Pretoria: Institute of Security Studies. Pp. 115–140.

Ottaway, David, and Marina Ottaway. 1970. *Algeria: The Politics of a Socialist Revolution*. Berkeley: University of California Press.

Owen, Roger. 1992. *State, Power, and Politics in the Making of the Modern Middle East.* London: Routledge.

Oyebade, Adebayo. 2007. *Culture and Customs of Angola.* Westport, Conn.: Greenwood Press.

Özel, Soli. 2003. "After the Tsunami." *Journal of Democracy* 14 (2): 80–94.

Panner, Morris, and Adriana Beltrán. 2010. "Battling Organized Crime in Guatemala." *Americas Quarterly* (Fall): 38–42.

Péclard, Didier. 1998. "Religion and Politics in Angola: The Church, the Colonial State and the Emergence of Angolan Nationalism, 1940–1961." *Journal of Religion in Africa* 28 (2): 160–186.

Perica, Vjekoslav. 2002. *Balkan Idols: Religion and Nationalism in Yugoslav States.* New York: Oxford University Press.

Petersen, Douglas. 1996. *Not by Might, Nor by Power: A Pentecostal Theology of Social Concern in Latin America.* Oxford: Regnum Books International.

Petersen, Douglas. 2004. "Latin American Pentecostalism: Social Capital, Networks, and Politics." *Pneuma: The Journal of the Society for Pentecostal Studies* 26 (2): 293–306.

Pew Forum on Religion and Public Life. 2006. *Spirit and Power: A 10 Country Survey of Pentecostals.* Washington, D.C.: Pew Research Center.

Pfaff, Steven. 2006. *Exit-Voice Dynamics and the Collapse of East Germany: The Crisis of Leninism and the Revolution of 1989.* Durham, N.C.: Duke University Press.

Pfeiffer, Karen. 1996. "Between Rocks and Hard Choices: International Finance and Economic Adjustment in North Africa." In Dirk Vandewalle, ed., *North Africa: Development and Reform in a Changing Global Economy.* New York: Palgrave Macmillan. Pp. 25–63.

Pospielovsky, Dimitry. 1987. *A History of Marxist-Leninist Atheism and Soviet Antireligious Policies.* New York: St. Martin's Press.

Pravda, Alex. 1983. "The Workers." In Abraham Brumberg, ed., *Poland: Genesis of a Revolution.* New York: Vintage. Pp. 68–91.

Proyecto Interdiocesano Recuperación de la Memoria Histórica (Guatemala), Catholic Institute for International Relations, and Latin America Bureau. 1999. *Guatemala, Never Again!* Maryknoll, N.Y.: Orbis Books.

Putnam, Robert D., Robert Leonardi, and Raffaella Nanetti. 1993. *Making Democracy Work: Civic Traditions in Modern Italy.* Princeton, N.J.: Princeton University Press.

Qutb, Sayyid. 1996. *Sayyid Qutb and Islamic Activism: A Translation and Critical Analysis of "Social Justice in Islam,"* trans. William E. Shepard. New York: Brill.

Raftopoulos, Brian. 2003. "The State in Crisis: Authoritarian Nationalism, Selective Citizenship and Distortions of Democracy in Zimbabwe." In Amanda Hammar, Brian Raftopoulos, and Stig Jensen, eds., *Zimbabwe's Unfinished Business: Rethinking Land, State and Nation in the Context of Crisis.* Harare: Weaver Press. Pp. 217–241.

Raftopoulos, Brian. 2004a. "Unreconciled Differences: The Limits of Reconciliation Politics in Zimbabwe." In Brian Raftopoulos and Tyrone Savage, eds., *Zimbabwe:*

Injustice and Political Reconciliation. Cape Town: Institute for Justice and Reconciliation. Pp. viii–xxii.

Raftopoulos, Brian. 2004b. "Current Politics in Zimbabwe: Confronting the Crisis." In Brian Raftopoulos and Tyrone Savage, eds., *Zimbabwe: The Past is the Future.* Zimbabwe: Weaver Press. Pp. 1–18.

Raftopoulos, Brian, and Karin Alexander. 2006. *Reflections on Democratic Politics in Zimbabwe.* Cape Town: Institute for Justice and Reconciliation.

Ramet, Pedro. 1987. *Cross and Commissar: The Politics of Religion in Eastern Europe and the USSR.* Bloomington: Indiana University Press.

Ramet, Sabrina P. 1988. *Eastern Christianity and Politics in the Twentieth Century.* Durham, N.C.: Duke University Press.

Ramet, Sabrina P. 1990. *Catholicism and Politics in Communist Societies.* Durham, N.C.: Duke University Press.

Ramet, Sabrina P. 1992. *Protestantism and Politics in Eastern Europe and Russia: The Communist and Postcommunist Eras.* Durham, N.C.: Duke University Press.

Ramet, Sabrina P. 1993. *Religious Policy in the Soviet Union.* Cambridge: Cambridge University Press.

Ramet, Sabrina P. 1998. *Nihil Obstat: Religion, Politics, and Social Change in East-Central Europe and Russia.* Durham, N.C.: Duke University Press.

Ranger, Terence O. 2008. *Evangelical Christianity and Democracy in Africa.* Oxford: Oxford University Press.

Rappaport, Roy. 1999. *Ritual and Religion in the Making of Humanity.* Cambridge: Cambridge University Press.

Razzack, Azra, and Anil Gumber. 2002. *Differentials in Human Development: A Case for Empowerment of Muslims in India.* New Delhi: NCAER.

Reilly, Charles A. 2009. *Peace Building and Development in Guatemala and Northern Ireland.* New York: Palgrave Macmillan.

Richardson, Anna. 2000. "Negotiating Humanitarian Access in Angola: 1990–2000." New Issues in Refugee Research Working Paper No. 18, June, United Nations High Commission on Refugees, Geneva.

Richardson, Norman. 1998. *A Tapestry of Beliefs: Christian Traditions in Northern Ireland.* Belfast: Blackstaff Press.

Riesebrodt, Martin. 2010. *The Promise of Salvation: A Theory of Religion.* Chicago: University of Chicago Press.

Robbins, Joel. 2004. "The Globalization of Pentecostal and Charismatic Christianity." *Annual Review of Anthropology* 33: 117–143.

Robbins, Joel. 2010. "Anthropology of Religion." In Allan Anderson, Michael Bergunder, André Droogers, and Cornelis van der Laan, eds., *Studying Global Pentecostalism: Theories and Methods.* Berkeley: University of California Press. Pp. 156–178.

Roberts, Hugh. 2003. *The Battlefield: Algeria, 1988–2002: Studies in a Broken Polity.* London: Verso.

Rocha, Glauber, director. 1964. *Black God, White Devil.* Koch-Lorber Films.

Roosevelt, Franklin Delano. 1941. Franklin D. Roosevelt Annual Message to Congress, January 6, 1941; Records of the United States Senate; SEN 77A-H1; Record Group 46; National Archives. Available at http://www.ourdocuments.gov/doc.php?flash =true&doc=70&page=transcript and also at http://www.americanrhetoric.com/ speeches/fdrthefourfreedoms.htm.

Ross, Marc Howard. 2007. *Cultural Contestation in Ethnic Conflict.* Cambridge: Cambridge University Press.

Rudy, Sayres. 2004. "Subjectivity, Political Evaluation, and Islamist Trajectories." In Birgit Schäbler and Leif Stenberg, eds., *Globalization and the Muslim World.* Syracuse: Syracuse University Press. Pp. 39–79.

Rudy, Sayres. 2007. "Pros and Cons: Americanism versus Islamism in the 'War on Terror.'" *Muslim World* 97 (1): 33–78.

Rudy, Sayres. 2010. "Barring the Algerian Subject: Carcerality and Resistance under Market-Statism." In Laleh Khalili and Jillian Schwedler, eds., *Policing and Prisons in the Middle East: Formations of Coercion.* New York: Columbia University Press. Pp. 97–118.

Ruedy, John. 1992. *Modern Algeria: The Origins and Development of a Nation.* Bloomington: Indiana University Press.

Saberwal, Satish, and N. Jayaram. 2003. "Social conflict." In V. Das, ed., *The Oxford India Companion to Sociology and Social Anthropology.* Delhi: Oxford University Press. Pp. 532–562.

Sachikonye, Lloyd M. 2004. "The Promised Land: From Expropriation to Reconciliation and Jambanja." In Brian Raftopoulos and Tyrone Savage, eds., *Zimbabwe: Injustice and Political Reconciliation.* Cape Town: Institute for Justice and Reconciliation. Pp. 1–18.

Sadiki, Larbi. 2004. *The Search for Arab Democracy: Discourses and Counter-Discourses.* New York: Columbia University Press.

Said, Edward W. 1979. *Orientalism.* New York: Vintage Books.

Samson, C. Mathews. 2003. "The Martyrdom of Manuel Saquic: Constructing Maya Protestantism in the Face of War in Contemporary Guatemala." *Le Fait Missionnarie/Social Sciences and Missions* 13: 41–74.

Samson, C. Matthews. 2008. "From War to Reconciliation: Guatemalan Evangelicals and the Transition to Democracy, 1982–2001." In Paul Freston, ed., *Evangelical Christianity and Democracy in Latin America.* New York: Oxford University Press. Pp. 63–96.

Samuels, Richard J. 2004. "Constitutional Revision in Japan: The Future of Article 9." Brookings Institution for North East Asia Policy Studies, December.

Samuels, Richard J. 2007. *Securing Japan: Tokyo's Grand Strategy and the Future of East Asia.* Ithaca, N.Y.: Cornell University Press.

Sanchíz Ochoa, Pilar. 1998. *Evangelismo y Poder: Guatemala ante el Nuevo Milenio.* Sevilla: Universidad de Sevilla, Secretariado de Publicaciones.

Sanford, Victoria, and Martha Lincoln. 2010. "Body of Evidence: Feminicide, Local Justice, and Rule of Law in 'Peacetime' Guatemala." In Alexander Laban Hinton, ed., *Transitional Justice: Global Mechanisms and Local Realities after Genocide and Mass Violence*. New Brunswick, N.J.: Rutgers University Press. Pp. 67–94.

Sanneh, Lamin O. 2008. *Disciples of All Nations: Pillars of World Christianity*. Oxford: Oxford University Press.

Sar, Marcin. 1985. "The Evolution of Centripetal Fraternalism: The Soviet Union and Eastern Europe." *Annals of the American Academy of Political and Social Science* 481: 92–103.

Schmitter, Philippe C., and Terry Lynn Karl. 1991. "What Democracy Is ... and Is Not?" *Journal of Democracy* 2(3): 75–88.

Schubert, Benedict. 1999 [1997]. "Os Protestantes na Guerra Angolana Depois da Independência." *Lusotopie* 405–413.

Schubert, Benedict. 2000. *A Guerra e as Igrejas: Angola 1961–1991*. Basel: P. Schlettwein.

Schwedler, Jillian, 2006. *Faith in Moderation: Islamist Parties in Jordan and Yemen*. Cambridge: Cambridge University Press.

Seiple, Robert A., and Dennis Hoover. 2004. *Religion and Security: The New Nexus in International Relations*. Lanham, Md.: Rowman & Littlefield.

Selka, Stephen. 2007. *Religion and the Politics of Ethnic Identity in Bahia, Brazil*. Gainesville: University Press of Florida.

Sen, Amartya. 1999. *Development as Freedom*. New York: Anchor Books.

Seul, Jeffrey R. 2001. "'Ours Is the Way of God': Religion, Identity, and Intergroup Conflict." *Journal of Peace Research* 36 (5): 553–569.

Shani, Giorgio. 2007. *Sikh Nationalism and Identity in a Global Age*. Abingdon, U.K.: Routledge.

Shaxson, Nicholas, João Neves, and Fernando Pacheco. 2008. *Drivers of Change, Angola*: *Summary of Findings*. London: Chatham House.

Shehata, Samer, and Joshua Stacher. 2006. "Special Report: The Brotherhood Goes to Parliament." *Middle East Report* 240: 32–39.

Shifter, Michael. 2011. "Central America's Security Predicament." *Current History* 110 (733): 49–55.

Shimazono Susumu. 1991. "Expansion of Japan's New Religions." *Japanese Journal of Religious Studies* 18 (2–3): 105–132.

Sigmund, Paul E. 1999. *Religious Freedom and Evangelization in Latin America: The Challenge of Religious Pluralism*. Maryknoll, N.Y.: Orbis Books.

Singer, Daniel. 1981. *The Road to Gdansk: Poland and the USSR*. New York: Monthly Review Press.

Skovgaard-Petersen, Jakob. 1997. *Defining Islam for the Egyptian State: Muftis and Fatwas of the Dār al-Iftā*. Social, Economic and Political Studies of the Middle East and Asia series. Vol. 59. Ed. Reinhard Schulze. Leiden: Brill.

Smart, Ninian. 1999. *Dimensions of the Sacred: Anatomy of the World's Beliefs*. Berkeley: University of California Press.

Smilde, David. 2007. *Reason to Believe: Cultural Agency in Latin American Evangelicalism*. Berkeley: University of California Press.

Smith, Christian. 1991. *The Emergence of Liberation Theology: Radical Religion and Social Movement Theory*. Chicago: University of Chicago Press.

Smith, Christian. 2003. *Moral, Believing Animals: Human Personhood and Culture*. New York: Oxford University Press.

Smith, Christian. 2006. Review of *Sacred and Secular: Religion and Politics Worldwide*, by Pippa Norris and Ronald Inglehart. *Journal for the Scientific Study of Religion* 45 (4):623–624.

Smith, Dennis. 2006. Los teleapóstoles guatemaltecos: Apuntes históricos y propuestas para la investigación. Paper presented at the 26th Congress of the Latin American Studies Association, March 15–19, San Juan, Puerto Rico.

Soares, Geralda Chaves. 2010. *Na Trilha Gerreira dos Borun*. Belo Horizonte: Instituto Metodista.

Somer, Murat. 2007. "Moderate Islam and Secularist Opposition in Turkey: Implications for the World, Muslims and Democracy." *Third World Quarterly* 28 (7): 1271–1289.

Somer, Murat. 2010. "Media Values and Democratization: What Unites and What Divides Religious-Conservative and Pro-Secular Elites?" *Turkish Studies* 11 (4): 555–577.

Somer, Murat. 2011. "Does It Take Democrats to Democratize? Lessons from Islamic and Secular Elite Values in Turkey." *Comparative Political Studies* 44 (5): 511–545.

Somer, Murat, and Gönül Tol. 2009. "New Muslim Pluralism and Secular Democracy in Turkey and the EU." In Elizabeth Prugl and Markus Thiel, eds., *Diversity in the European Union*. New York: Palgrave Macmillan. Pp. 95–111.

Spinka, Matthew. 1956. *The Church in Soviet Russia*. New York: Oxford University Press.

Stahn, Carsten. 2007. "Responsibility to Protect: Political Rhetoric or Emerging Legal Norm?" *American Journal of International Law* 101 (1): 99–120.

Stan, Lavinia, and Lucian Turcescu. 2007. *Religion and Politics in Post-Communist Romania*. Oxford: Oxford University Press.

Staniszkis, Jadwiga. 1984. *Poland's Self-Limiting Revolution*. Princeton, N.J.: Princeton University Press.

Stark, Rodney, and Roger Finke. 2000. *Acts of Faith: Explaining the Human Side of Religion*. Berkeley: University of California Press.

Stark, Rodney, and Laurence R. Iannaccone. 1994. "A Supply-Side Reinterpretation of the 'Secularization' of Europe." *Journal for the Scientific Study of Religion* 33 (3): 230–52.

Stauffer, Robert E. 1975. "Bellah's Civil Religion." *Journal for the Scientific Study of Religion* 14 (4): 390–395.

Steigenga, Timothy J. 1999. "Guatemala." In Paul E. Sigmund, ed., *Religious Freedom and Evangelization in Latin America: The Challenge of Religious Pluralism.* Maryknoll, N.Y.: Orbis Books. Pp. 150–174.

Steigenga, Timothy J. 2001. *The Politics of the Spirit: The Political Implications of Pentecostalized Religion in Costa Rica and Guatamala.* Lanham, Md.: Lexington Books.

Steigenga, Timothy J. 2007. "The Politics of Pentecostalized Religion: Conversion as Pentecostalization in Guatemala." In Edward L. Cleary and Timothy J. Steigenga, eds., *Resurgent Voices in Latin America: Indigenous Peoples, Political Mobilization, and Religious Change.* New Brunswick, N.J.: Rutgers University Press. Pp. 256–279.

Steigenga, Timothy J. 2010. Review of Virginia Garrard-Burnett, *Terror in the Land of the Holy Spirit: Guatemala under General Efraín Ríos Montt, 1982–1983,* and Kevin Lewis O'Neill, *City of God: Christian Citizenship in Postwar Guatemala.* H-Net *Reviews in the Humanities and Social Sciences,* June. Available at http://www.h-net.org/reviews/showrev.php?id=29678.

Steigenga, Timothy J., and Edward L. Cleary. 2007. *Conversion of a Continent: Contemporary Religious Change in Latin America.* New Brunswick, N.J.: Rutgers University Press.

Stoll, David. 1990. *Is Latin America Turning Protestant? The Politics of Evangelical Growth.* Berkeley: University of California Press.

Stora, Benjamin. 2001. *Algeria, 1830–2000: A Short History.* Ithaca, N.Y.: Cornell University Press.

Sultana, Anila. 1996. "Muslim Institutions and Organizations in Malerkotla and Their Impact on the Muslim Community." *Punjab History Conference Proceedings,* Twenty Eighth Session: 263–70.

Summerscale, Peter. 1981. "Is Eastern Europe a Liability to the Soviet Union?" *International Affairs* 57 (4): 585–598.

Swatos, William H., and Peter Kivisto. 1998. *Encyclopedia of Religion and Society.* Walnut Creek, Calif.: AltaMira Press.

Szajkowski, Bogdan. 1983. *Next to God—Poland: Politics and Religion in Contemporary Poland.* London: Pinter.

Tal, Nachman. 2005. *Radical Islam in Egypt and Jordan.* Brighton: Sussex Academic Press and Jaffee Center for Strategic Studies.

Tamimi, Azzam, and John L. Esposito. 2000. *Islam and Secularism in the Middle East.* London: C. Hurst.

Taves, Ann. 2009. *Religious Experience Reconsidered: A Building Block Approach to the Study of Religion and Other Special Things.* Princeton, N.J.: Princeton University Press.

Terchek, Ronald J. 1977. "Conflict and Cleavage in Northern Ireland." *Annals of the American Academy of Political and Social Science* 433: 47–59.

Tessler, Mark. 2002. "Do Islamic Orientations Influence Attitudes toward Democracy in the Arab World? Evidence from Egypt, Jordan, Morocco, and Algeria." *International Journal of Comparative Sociology* 43 (3): 229.

Tessler, Mark, and Marilyn Grobschmidt, 1995. "Democracy in the Arab World and the Arab-Israeli Conflict," In D. Garnham and Mark Tessler, eds., *Democracy, War, and Peace in the Middle East*. Bloomington: Indiana University Press. Pp. 135–169.

Tezcür, Güneş M. 2010. *Muslim Reformers in Iran and Turkey: The Paradox of Moderation*. Austin: University of Texas Press.

Thale, Geoff, and Elsa Falkenburger. 2006. *Youth Gangs in Central America: Issues in Human Rights, Effective Policing and Prevention*. Washington, D.C.: Washington Office on Latin America.

Thompson, Randy, and James K. Wellman, Jr. 2011. "From the Social Gospel to Neo-conservativism: Religion and U.S. Foreign Policy." *Interdisciplinary Journal of Research on Religion* 7: 1–41.

Tibbi, Bassam. 2008. "Why They Can't Be Democratic." *Journal of Democracy* 19 (3): 43–48.

Tiburcio, James. 2010. "Human Security in Angola: The Role of Religious Non-state Actors." *Journal of Human Security* 6 (2): 47–57.

Tismaneanu, Vladimir. 2003. *Stalinism for All Seasons: A Political History of Romanian Communism*. Berkeley: University of California Press.

Tismaneanu, Vladimir, Dorin Dobrincu, and Cristian Vasile. 2007. *Comisia prezidenţială pentru analiza dictaturii comuniste din România: Raport final* [Presidential Commission for the Analysis of the Communist Dictatorship in Romania: Final Report]. Bucharest: Humanitas.

Toft, Monica Duffy, Daniel Philpott, and Timothy Samuel Shah, eds. 2011. *God's Century: Resurgent Religion and Global Politics*. New York, New York: W.W. Norton.

Toprak, Binnaz, İrfan Bozan, Tan Morgül, and Nedim Şener. 2008. *Türkiye'de Farklı Olmak* [Being Different in Turkey]. İstanbul: Boğaziçi University.

Touraine, Alain. 1978. *The Voice and the Eye: An Analysis of Social Movements*. Cambridge: Cambridge University Press.

Touraine, Alain, François Dubet, Michel Wieviorka, and Jan Strzelecki. 1983. *Solidarity: The Analysis of a Social Movement: Poland, 1980–1981*, trans. David Denby. Cambridge: Cambridge University Press.

Tunaya, Tarık Zafer. 2007. *İslamcılık Akımı* [The Islamism Movement]. İstanbul: İstanbul Bilgi Üniversitesi.

Tymowski, Andrzej. 1982. *Solidarity under Siege*. New Haven, Conn.: Advocate.

"UK Policy on Zimbabwe." N.d. Available at http://ukinsouthafrica.fco.gov.uk/en/working-with-south-africa/uk-policy-zimbabwe/.

UNDP (United Nations Development Programme). 1994. *Human Development Report: New Dimensions of Human Security*. New York: Oxford University Press.

UNDP. 1999. *Human Development Report 1999*. New York: Oxford University Press.

UNDP. 2009. *Arab Human Development Report: Challenges to Human Security in the Arab Countries.* New York: UNDP.

UN (United Nations) General Assembly. 2005. "World Summit Outcome." General Assembly Resolution 60/1: para.1, October 24.

UN (United Nations) Secretary General. 2005. "In Larger Freedom: Towards Development, Security and Human Rights for All: Report of the Secretary General." UN Doc. A/59/2005. Available at http://www.un.org/largerfreedom/contents.htm.

UN Secretary General. 2010. "Human Security (Follow-up to the Outcome of the Millennium Summit): Report of the Secretary-General." U.N. Doc. A/64/701. Available at http://responsibilitytoprotect.org/Human%20Security%20Report%20 2010.pdf.

United States Department of State. 2006. *Report on International Religious Freedom.* Washington, D.C.: United States Department of State.Available at http://www.state.gov/g/drl/rls/irf/2006/71332.htm.

United States Department of State. 2007. *Report on International Religious Freedom.* Washington, D.C.: United States Department of State. Available at http://www.state.gov/g/drl/rls/irf/2007/.

United States Department of State. 2008. *Report on International Religious Freedom.* Washington, D.C.: United States Department of State.

Van Butselaar, Jan. 2005. "The Promise of the Kingdom and the Reality of Sin: Christian Religion, Conflict, and Visions for Peace." In Gerrie Ter Haar and James Busuttil, eds., *Bridge or Barrier: Religion, Violence and Visions for Peace.* Leiden: Brill. Pp. 121–152.

Van den Bof, K, 2008. "Radical Worldview Defense in Reaction to Personal Uncertainty." Paper presented at the Extremism and the Psychology of Uncertainty Conference, Claremont Graduate University, April 6.

Vandewalle, Dirk J. 1988. *Autopsy of a Revolt: The October Riots in Algeria.* Washington, D.C.: Institute of Current World Affairs.

Van Dijk, Rijk. 2003. "Pentecostalism and the Politics of Prophetic Power: Religious Modernity in Ghana." In Niels Kastfelt, ed., *Scriptural Politics: The Bible and the Koran as Political Models in the Middle East and Africa.* London: Hurst. Pp. 155–184.

Varadarajan, Siddharth. 2002. *Gujarat: The Making of a Tragedy.* New Delhi: Penguin Books.

Varshney, Ashutosh. 2002. *Ethnic Conflict and Civic Life: Hindus and Muslims in India.* New Haven, Conn.: Yale University Press.

Vasile, Cristian. 2005. *Biserica Ortodoxă Română în primul deceniu communist* [The Romanian Orthodox Church in the First Communist Decade]. Bucharest: Curtea Veche.

Vásquez, Manuel A., and Marie F. Marquardt. 2003. *Globalizing the Sacred: Religion across the Americas.* New Brunswick, N.J.: Rutgers University Press.

Vergés, Meriem. 1997. "Genesis of a Mobilization: The Young Activists of Algeria's Islamic Salvation Front." Joe Stork and Joel Beinin, eds., *Political Islam: Essays from Middle East Report.* Berkeley: University of California Press. Pp. 292–308.

Vines, Alex, Nicholas Shaxson, Lisa Rimli, and Chris Heymans. 2005. *Angola*. Drivers of Change Position Paper 3. London: Chatham House.

Vitalis, Robert. 2007. *America's Kingdom: Mythmaking on the Saudi Oil Frontier*. Stanford, Calif.: Stanford University Press.

Walaszek, Zdzislawa. 1986. "An Open Issue of Legitimacy: The State and the Church in Poland." *Annals of the American Academy of Political and Social Science* 483: 118–134.

Wallace, Chuma, Brian Raftopoulos, and Karin Alexander. 2006. *Reflections on Democratic Politics in Zimbabwe*. Cape Town, South Africa: Institute for Justice and Reconciliation.

Walsh, John. 2003. "World in Review: Egypt's Muslim Brotherhood—Understanding Centrist Islam." *Harvard International Review* 24 (4): 32–36.

Waltz, Susan Eileen. 1995. *Human Rights and Reform: Changing the Face of North African Politics*. Berkeley: University of California Press.

Walzer, Michael. 2004. *Arguing about War*. New Haven, Conn.: Yale University Press.

Warren, Jonathan. 2000. "Masters in the Field." In France Widdance Twine and Jonathan Warren, eds., *Racing Research, Researching Race: Methodological Dilemmas in Critical Race Studies*. New York: New York University Press. Pp. 135–164.

Waterbury, John. 1994. "Democracy without Democrats? The Potential for Political Liberalization in the Middle East." In Ghassan Salamé, ed., *Democracy without Democrats? The Renewal of Politics in the Muslim World*. London: I. B. Taurus. Pp. 23–47.

Wellman, James K., Jr., ed. 2007. *Belief and Bloodshed: Religion and Violence across Time and Tradition*. Lanham, MD: Rowman & Littlefield.

Wellman, James K., Jr. 2008. *Evangelical vs. Liberal: The Clash of Christian Cultures in the Pacific Northwest*. New York: Oxford University Press.

White, Jenny B. 2002. *Islamist Mobilization in Turkey: A Study in Vernacular Politics*. Seattle: University of Washington Press.

Whyte, J. H. 1995. "Ireland: 1996–82." In Theodore William Moody and Francis Xavier Martin, eds., *The Course of Irish History*. Niwot, Colo.: Roberts Rinehart. Pp. 342–361.

Wiatr, Jerzy. 1994. "From Communist Party to 'The Socialist-Democracy of the Polish Republic." In Kay Lawson, ed., *How Political Parties Work: Perspectives from Within*. New York: Praeger. Pp. 229–248.

Wickham, Carrie Rosefsky. 2002. *Mobilizing Islam: Religion, Activism, and Political Change in Egypt*. New York: Columbia University Press.

Wickham, Carrie Rosefsky. 2004. "The Path to Moderation: Strategy and Learning in the Formation of Egypt's Wasat Party." *Comparative Politics* 36 (2): 205–228.

Wightman, Jill M. 2007. Healing the Nation: Pentecostal Identity and Social Change in Bolivia." In Edward L. Cleary and Timothy J. Steigenga, eds., *Resurgent Voices in Latin America: Indigenous Peoples, Political Mobilization, and Religious Change*. New Brunswick, N.J.: Rutgers University Press. Pp. 239–255.

Wilkinson, Steven. 2005. *Religious Politics and Communal Violence.* New Delhi: Oxford University Press.

Will, James E. 1984. "Church and State in the Struggle for Human Rights in Poland." *Journal of Law and Religion* 2 (1): 153–176.

Williams, Paul. 2008. *Security Studies: An Introduction.* London: Routledge.

Williams, Rina Verma. 2006. *Postcolonial Politics and Personal Laws: Colonial Legal Legacies and the Indian State.* New Delhi: Oxford University Press.

Willis, Michael. 1996. *The Islamist Challenge in Algeria: A Political History.* New York: New York University Press.

Wilson, Everett. 1997. "Guatemalan Pentecostals: Something of Their Own." In Edward L. Cleary and Hannah W. Stewart-Gambino, eds., *Power, Politics, and Pentecostals in Latin America.* Boulder, Colo.: Westview Press. Pp. 139–162.

Wittenberg, Jason. 2006. *Crucibles of Political Loyalty: Church Institutions and Electoral Continuity in Hungary.* New York: Cambridge University Press.

Wolicki, Krzysztof. 1995 [1983]. "About the Future." In Michel Bernhard and Henryk Szlajfer, eds., *From the Polish Underground: Selections from Krytyka, 1978–1993,* trans. Maria Chmielewska-Szlajfer. University Park: Pennsylvania State University Press. Pp. 69–92.

Woodberry, Robert D., and Timothy Shah. 2005. "The Pioneering Protestants." In Larry J. Diamond, Marc F. Plattner, and Philip J. Costopoulos, eds., *World Religions and Democracy.* Baltimore: John Hopkins University Press. Pp. 117–131.

World Bank. 2007. *Angola: Oil, Broad-Based Growth, and Equity.* Washington, D.C.: World Bank.

Wright, Elliott. 2008. "Church Promoted Voting as Sacred 'Must' Prior to Angola's Election." GBGM News Archive of the General Board of Global Ministries— United Methodist Church.

Xavier, Ismail. 1982. "*Black God, White Devil*: The Representation of History." In Randal Johnson and Robert Stam, eds., *Brazilian Cinema.* New York: Columbia University Press. Pp. 134–148.

Yang, Fenggang. 2011. *Religion in China: Survival and Revival under Communist Rule.* New York: Oxford University Press.

Yavuz, M. Hakan. 2003. *Islamic Political Identity in Turkey.* Oxford: Oxford University Press.

Yavuz, M. Hakan, ed. 2006. *The Emergence of a New Turkey: Democracy and the AK Parti.* Salt Lake City: University of Utah Press.

Yusufzai, Rahimullah. 2007. "The Emergence of the Pakistani Taliban." *Jane's Information Group,* December 11, www8.janes.com.

Zahab, Mariam Abou, and Olivier Roy. 2004. *Islamist Networks: The Afghan-Pakistan Connection.* London: C. Hurst.

Zubairy, Mohammed Khalid. 2000. *Malerkotla: Itihas Ke Darpan Mein.* Malerkotla: Tarkash Publications.

Index

Bold font indicates reference to illustrative matter.

abortion, 32, 226n3, 286n2
    See also women's rights
Ahmedabad, 114, 119
Alexius, Patriarch of Moscow and all
    Russia, 229, 234
Algeria, 19, 29, 28, 241, 248–54,
    260–62
al-Qaeda, 65n14, 71, **78**, **79**, 84, 87,
    89n3, 89n11, 244, 286n2
Anan, Kofi, 4–5
Angola (Republic of Angola), 175,
    188–206 Arab Human
    Development Report (2009), 7, 16
Arab Spring, 244
Araçuaí (municipality), 139–40, 142–48,
    287
Arie, Sam, 8, 17n2
Article 9 (Constitution of Japan),
    267–68, 272–81
Asad, Talal, 24–25, 29
Atatürk, Kemal, 34–35
al-Azhar, 51–52

Banna, Hassan al-, 50, 55, 62
    See also Muslim Brotherhood
Bedi, Sahib Singh, 97

Bharatiya Janata Party (BJP), 96, 116
Bigelow, Anna, 99, 100, 107
Boudiaf, Mohammad, 253
Bloody Sunday (1972), 218–19
    See also Ireland; the Troubles
Brazil, 12, 14, 130–48
Buddhism, 265–69, 271, 274
    and human security, 43, 265, 266–67,
        268, 279–80
    and pacifism, 278, 284n24

Caballeros, Harold, 153, 165, 166,
    171n24
Casanova, José, 26
Catholic Church,
    in Angola, 190–93, 195–99, 206
    and Article 44 (Irish Constitution),
        226n3
    in Brazil, 133–34, 136, 146
    and communism, 230, 232, 233–34,
        255, 257
    in France, 21 in Guatemala, 151, 152–55
    Greek Catholic Church, 230, 235,
        238, 241
    in Ireland, 214, 215–19, **221**, 222
    and human security, 154–55, 234

Catholic Church (*Cont.*)
  and liberation theology, 146, 191, 255
    (*see also* liberation theology)
  and Maya Catholics, 157–59
  in Poland, 234, 255
  and Protestants, 193, 210–17
  and popular religion, 133, 153–54
  in Zimbabwe, 175–76
Ceauşescu, Nicolae, 237, 238
CEG
  See Guatemalan Episcopal Conference
    (CEG)
Center for Popular Culture and
  Development (CPCD), 143–147
  and Children of Araçuaí Choir, 143
China, 23–24, 28, 269, 272, 279, 281
Christianity
  *See under specific locales and
    denominations*—Angola; Araçuaí;
    Brazil; Catholic Church; China;
    Congregationalist Church; Egypt;
    EPC Churches; Evangelical
    Christianity; Guatemala;
    Ireland; Jequitinhonha Valley;
    Maya religion; Mount Pleasant
    Community Church (MPCC);
    neo-Pentecostalism; Orthodox
    Church; Pentecostalism; Poland;
    Romania; Romanian Orthodox
    Church; Zimbabwe
CICIG
  See International Commission Against
    Impunity in Guatemala (CICIG)
civil religion, 23–24
civil society, 37, 88, 94–95, 102, 104–6,
  110–11, 142, 144
Clash of Civilizations, 10
COIEPA (Inter-Ecclesiastical Committee
  for Peace in Angola), 199
Cold War, 3–4
  and emergence of human security, 3–4
  religion during, 230, 233, 235,
    237–39, 241

Commission on Human Security, 5, 7
Committee for the Defense of Workers
  (KOR), 257–58, 260
communism, 15, 23, 229–35, 234,
  236–38, 239, 241
*Conferencia Evangélica de Iglesias de
  Guatemala* (CIEDEG), 156
  See also Evangelical Conference of
    Churches of Guatemala (CIEDEG)
Congregationalist Church, 192–94,
  196–97
conscientização, 146, 148n4
Constitution of Japan, 266–67, 269,
  273–75, 277–80
Council of Christian Churches of
  Angola, 199
Copts, 48, 60
CPCD
  See Center for Popular Culture and
    Development

Dargah(s), 97, 101, 121n9
da Silva, Luiz Inácio Lula (Lula), 139–40
Declaration on Security in the
  Americas, 7
Democratic Party of Japan (Minshuto),
  276–77
Democratic Unionist Party of Ireland,
  218, 225
Deobandis, 70–71, 89n8, 101, 105, 129
Deprivatization, 26
Directorate of Religious Affairs
  (Turkey), 35
Diwali, 108, 112n18

Eastern Europe, 229, 233, 239–41, 252
Easter Rising (1916), 216
Egypt, 21, 48–66
El Shaddai Congregation (Guatemala),
  152, 153, 165
Endo Otohiko, 269, 278
EPC churches (evangelical/Pentecostal/
  charismatic), 173–78

European Court of Human Rights, 36
European Union, 37, 199, 201
Evangelical Alliance, 151, 153, 156, 199
    See also under Angola; Guatemala
Evangelical Christianity, 10, 153, 164
    in Angola, 190–91, 193
    in Brazil, 192
    and "biblical principles," 153, 166
    and democratization, 164, 191
    discourse of, 10, 161
    and Evangelical Alliance, 151, 153,
        156, 199 (*see also under* Angola;
        Guatemala)
    and Evangelical Conference of Churches
        of Guatemala (CIEDEG), 156
    and Evangelical Congregationalist
        Church of Angola, 193–94,
        196–97, 207n6
    Full Gospel Church of God (IDEC),
        156–57, 161, 163, 169n13
    in Guatemala, 148, 151–54, 155–56,
        164
    and human security, 153–54, 164
    and Maya religion, 159, 170n14
    and politics, 10, 152–53
    See also Angola; EPC (evangelical/
        Pentecostal/charismatic) churches;
        Guatemala; Maya religion;
        neo-Pentecostalism; Pentecostalism
Evangelical Conference of Churches of
    Guatemala (CIEDEG), 156
Evangelical Congregationalist Church
    (Angola), 193–94, 196–97, 207n6
evangelical/Pentecostal/charismatic
    (EPC) Christians
    See EPC churches
Existential Security Theory, 209–212,
    222–223

Fanon, Frantz, 244, 262n8
FATA
    See Pakistan: Federally Administered
        Tribal Areas (FATA)

FIS
    See Front Islamique du Salut (FIS)
FNLA
    See Angola, Republic of: National
        Liberation Front of Angola (FNLA)
Four Freedoms Speech (1941), 3–4
Freire, Paulo, 134–35, 148n4
Front Islamique du Salut (FIS) (Algeria),
    243–44, 250–53
Full Gospel Church of God (IDEC),
    156–57, 161, 163, 169n13

gay rights, 32–33, 42
gender equality, 12, 33, 42, 46n21,
    120–23, 126, 250
Gheorgiu-Dej, Gheorge, 236–37
Gomulka, Wladyslaw, 255–56
Good Friday Agreement (1998), 208,
    210, 219, 222–23, 224
Guatemala, 14, 150–168, 171n24,
    187n2
Guatemalan Episcopal Conference
    (CEG), 151, 154–55
Gujarat, 113, 114–16, 118–27
Gülen movement, 40–41
Gurdwaras, 97, 103, 109
Guru Arjan Dev Ji, 97

haa da naara, 98–99, **99**, 106
Haider Shaikh
    See Shaikh, Haider
Hamayotsu Toshiko, 269, 278
Hardacre, Helen, 179
Hinduism, 13, 99–108
    and communal violence, 13, 99–101,
        103, 107, 111n5
    and Muslims, 13, 100–102, 117,
        119–20, 124, 129n1
    as privileged group in India, 117
    and Sikhs, 100–102
Holden, Roberto, 193
homosexuality, 32–33, 42 *See also* gay
    rights; gender equality

Hudaybi, Ma'mun al-, 60
human autonomy, 30, 43, 112, 152, 168
Human Development Reports of 1999, 4
    Arab Human Development Report
        (2009), 7, 16
    New Dimensions of Human Security
        (1994), 4, 6
human rights, 5, 7–8, 10, 67–68, 151
    in Angola, 199–200, 202, 204–206
    and Egyptian Organization for
        Human Rights, 60
    and European Court of Human
        Rights, 36
    and European Union standards of
        human rights, 42
    fundamental human rights, 1–2, 11,
        287n2, 289
    and Guatemala's Human Rights office,
        155
    and human security, 19, 30, 113, 117,
        189, 211, 234, 285
    international human rights norms,
        88n2, 187, 286n2
    and popular religion, 131
    and Religion, 20, 153, 286n2
    and secular groups, 44, 60
    and subjectivity, 191
    in Zimbabwe, 172
human security, 1–5, 19–20, 30–34,
        42–50, 63–64, 114–18, 125–28,
        156–63, 173–75, 180–87, 268–71,
        285–89
    in Algeria, 243, 244–45, 248, 254
    in Angola, 189–92, 198–99, 200, 202,
        204–206
    in Brazil, 130–31, 132–33, 134, 135,
        146–47
    and civil society, 105–6
    and Cold War, 3–4 defining, 1, 5–9,
        19, 25–29, 30, 43, 160, 268
    in Guatemala, 150–63, 167–68

    in Gujurat, 113, 118–20
    and human rights, 19, 30, 113, 117,
        189, 211, 234, 285
    in India, 116–18 in Ireland, 209–214,
        224–26
    in Japan, 265, 266–71, 279–81
    in Malerkotla, 94, 105, 110
    in Mumbai, 113, 114–116, 125
    vs national security, 1, 4, 19, 63, 113,
        189
    objective components of, 8, 43
    in Pakistan, 86–88
    in Poland, 243, 244–45, 248, 258
    and political participation, 198–99
    short-term, 173, 181, 185, 186
    subjective components of, 8, 11, 27,
        43, 113, 117
    and subjectivity, 244–45, 261nn6–8
        (*see also* subjectivity)
    in Zimbabwe, 172–73, 173–75,
        180–87
Human Security Network, 7
Huntington, Samuel, 10

Id Milan, 106, 108
IDEC, 156–57, 161, 163, 169n13
Iglesia de Dios del Evangelio Completo
        (IDEC), 156–57, 161, 163,
        169n13
    See also Full Gospel Church of God
        (IDEC); Guatemala
Ikeda Daisaku, 269, 272, 273, 274, 279,
        281n2, 283n20
India, 94–96, 98–100, 105, 113–128
industrialization, 21–22, 129, 246,
        149, 175
Inglehart, Ronald, 210, 211, 219, 223
Inter-Ecclesiastical Committee for Peace
        in Angola (COIEPA), 199
International Committee of the Red
        Cross (ICRC), 197

Ireland, 14, 209–226, 286n2
Irish Republican Army (IRA), 218–19,
  225, 226n4
Islam, 10, 13, 30–34, 36–41
  and Dargah(s), 97, 101, 121n9
  and democracy, 32, 33, 36–38
  in India, 113, 115–18, 120–22,
    123–125
  and Islamic revival, 10, 17n4
  and militancy, 115, 127–28
  and Personal Laws, 123, 129n2
  vs secularism, 33–36, 40–43, 45n4
  Sharia, 50, 55, 70, 90n12
  Shia, 70–72, **81**, 95, 121–22
  Sufi, 35–36, 96, 125n1, 248
  Sunni, 35–36, 51–52, 70, 95, 147
  in Turkey, 31–32, 34–41
  and women, 32, 33, 122–27 (*see also*
    Muslims; women's rights)
Islamism, 10, 31, 36–37, 41, 48, 67–70
  in Algeria, 244, 245, 247, 249–54,
    262n8
  in Egypt, 48, 51–52, 54, 55–61, 64n4,
    64n14
  in Pakistan, 68, 70–72, 77–78, 80, 82
  in Turkey, 31–32, 34, 36–37, 41

Jamaat-e-Islami, 70, 101, 105–106,
  120–22, 126, 129n1
Jamaat-e-Ulema-e-Hind, 120–22, 126,
  129n1
Jama'at-I-Islami
  See *Jamaat-e-Islami*
Jama'at ul Dawa, 72–73
Japan, 5, 15, 265–281
Japan-United States Security Treaty, 276
Jequitinhonha Valley, 130–31, 133–37,
  146, 186n2
Jindal, Kewal Kishan, 107
Justice and Development Part (AKP), 34,
  38, 41, 42, 45n9

Justinian, Patriarch of Romania, 230,
  234, 237

Kashmir, 70–73, 80–83, 86–87, 89n8,
  89n21, 115–116
Katzenstein, Peter, 276
Khan, Iftikhar Ali, 106
Khan, Sher Muhammad, 98, 106
  See also under Malerkotla (Punjab,
    India)
Kisala, Robert, 274
Koizumi Junichiro, 277
Komeito1, 265–66, 268, 272, 273–74,
  276–80
Kukas 97, 108, 112n14

labor unions, 31
Laden, Osama bin, 78–79 (*see also under*
  Pakistan)
Lancaster House Agreement, 174
  See also Zimbabwe
Landless Workers Movement (MST), 137
Leaning, Jennifer, 8, 17n2
Levine, Daniel, 164
Liberal Democratic Party (LDP) of
  Japan, 266, 275–80
liberation theology, 133–34, 160, 191
  in Angola, 191
  in Brazil, 133
  in Guatemala, 160
  and Marxism, 133
  in Poland, 255
Lula
  See da Silva, Luiz Inácio Lula

Makiguchi Tsunesaburo, 274, 282
Malerkotla (Punjab, India), 94–96,
  97–111
Mam (people), 157–58
Marques, Maria Lira, 135–44
Marx, Karl, 21

Mayareligion, 155–56, 158–59

Maya Movement (in Guatemala), 155–56

Mbundu (people), 193, 196

Médecins sans Frontières, 197

Metropolitan Justinian
  See Justinian *under* Romanian
    Orthodox Church

Mexico, 150, 151, 158

modernity/modernization, 11, 18, 21,
    26, 34, 38–40, 219–20, 223–24
  definitions of, 219

Molina, Otto Pérez, 166

moral dissonance, 31

Mount Pleasant Community Church
    (MPCC), 177–86

Movement for Democratic Change
    (MDC) (Zimbabwe), 172–73, 185

MPCC *See* Mount Pleasant Community
    Church (MPCC)

MPLA *See* Popular Movement for the
    Liberation of Angola (MPLA)

Mugabe, Robert, 172–175

multilateral organizations, 1, 5–7

Mumbai (Maharashatra, India), 113,
    114–16, 118–19, 121–23, 125

Muslims, 35–36, 45n10, 94–96, 100–2,
    116–18

Muslim Brotherhood, 48–64

Nakshibendi (Sufi Islam), 36
  See also Islam; Islam: Sufi; *tariqats*

Namdharis (Namdaris), 97, 108, 112n14

Nanak Dev Ji (Guru), 97, 108

National Liberation Front of Angola
    (FNLA), 193, 194, **201**

neo-Pentecostalism, 151–53, 165, 167,
    169n6

Neto, Augustino, 193, 194, 196
  See also Angola; Popular movement
    for the Liberation of Angola
    (MPLA)

New Dimensions of Human Security
  See United Nations: *United Nations*

Development Report (1994)

"new social movements," 182

Nichiren Buddhism, 266–68, 274, 279,
    281–82nn2–5
  and human security, 266, 279
  and Lotus Sutra, 266, 282n3
  and Nichirenism, 267–68, 282n5
  and Tanaka Chigaku, 267, 282n5
  and Nichiren Shoshu, 267,
    281–82nn2–3
  and Soka Gakkai, 266–67, 274, 279

Nichiren Shoshu, 267, 281–82nn2–3

Non-Aggression and Common Defence
    Pact (2005), 7

nongovernmental organizations
    (NGOs), 6, 20, 40–42, 51, 58,
    189–90, 197, 205

nonstate actors
  See *under* religious actors

Norris, Pippa, 210, 211, 219, 223

NWFP, 70, 84, 90n11

Obama, Barack, 44, 187

Ogata Sadako, 5, 7

Operation Blue Star (1984), 99

Organization of American States (OAS), 7

Orthodox Church, 23, 228–31, 235–39,
    241
  and Catholic Church, 232, 241
  during Cold War, 233, 235, 238
  and communism, 229–31
  Eastern, 239
  and human security, 228–29, 232–35,
    236, 237–41
  Russian, 229, 241
  and Soviet Union, 229, 231, 234, 235,
    236, 237
  and *symphonia*, 228, 232–33, 239, 240

Paisley, Rev. Ian, 218

Pakistan, 13, 68–88, 90n11, 90n13,
    91n14, 91n17, 92n21

Panchayat, 104n12

Partido dos Trabalhadores, 139

Peace Keeping Operations (PKO) bill, 277

Pedagogy of the Oppressed, 134

Pentecostalism, 151–53, 156–57, 159–68
  as contributors to democracy, 161
  and education, 164
  and human security, 152–53, 156–57, 160, 163–65
  and liberation theology, 177
  and popular religion, 157, 166–67 (*See also* Full Gospel Church of God (IDEC))
  and "progressive" Pentecostalism, 170n16, 177
  and prosperity gospel, 165, 177
  and religious revival, 164
  as response to modernization, 153
  spiritual practices, 161
  theology of, 160–61
  and women, 153
  worship services, description of, 161–63

Personal Laws, 123–24, 127–28, 129n2
  Hindu, 129n2
  Muslim, 123–24, 127–28

pluralism, 25, 31–34, 37, 40–41
  ethnic, 166
  political, 32–33, 40–41
  religious, 153–56, 166, 233
  social, 41–42, 44

pluralistic democracy, 32, 34, 37

Poel, Franciscus Henricus van der *See* Xico, Frei

Poland, 243–48, 254–60, 263n21
  compared to Algeria, 244–45, 246–47, 248

Polish Solidarity Movement, 234

political subjectivity *See* subjectivity

Popular Movement for the Liberation of Angola (MPLA), 191, 194–204, 207n9

prosperity gospel, 152, 162, 165, 177, 186

Public Order and Security Act (Zimbabwe), 175

Punjab (India) *See* Malerkotla

Ramet, Pedro, 232

Ranger, Terence, 175–77

Rashid Brothers, 96, 107

Recovery of Historical Memory Project (Guatemala), 155

Red Cross, 197
  See also International Committee of the Red Cross (ICRC)

religion (overview), 9–11
  adopted definition of this volume, 9, 285
  definitions of, 9, 21, 24, 25–29
  and (de)privatization, 18, 23, 26 (*see also* Casanova, José)
  and human security (*see* Religion and human security)
  and modernity/modernization, 25, 153 (*see also* modernity/ modernization)
  and politics (overview), 10, 23, 24
  private, 24
  public, 24–26
  vs secularism, 20–25, 164 (*see also* Islam: vs secularism)
  See also religious actors *and specific case studies: i.e. locales and traditions*

religion and human security, 1–3, 8–11, 18–29, 173–76, 185, 189–90, 210, 234–40
  and *Arab Human Development Report* (2009), 26
  in Buddhism, 43, 265, 266–67, 268, 279–80
  and Catholic Church, 154–55, 234
  and EPC churches (evangelical/ Pentecostal/charismatic), 177, 185

religion and human security (*Cont.*)

  and Evangelical Christianity, 153–54, 164

  and *Jamaat-e-Islami*, 120–22, 126

  and Mount Pleasant Community Church (MPCC), 180–82, 184, 186

  and Muslim Brotherhood, 54, 56–59, 62

  and Nichiren Buddhism, 266, 279

  and Orthodox Church, 228–29, 232–35, 236, 237–41

  and Pentecostalism, 152–53, 156–57, 160, 163–65

  and popular religion (folk traditions), 240

  and practical theology, 156–63

  relationship behind the Iron Curtain, 234–35

  and religion as detrimental to human security, 22, 286–87

  and religion as promoting human security, 20–21, 24, 28–29 285–87

  and religious pluralism, 153–56

  and religious revival, 67, 69

  and religious symbolism, 240

  and ritual, 20, 24, 239–40

  and Romanian Orthodox Church, 237–38

religious actors (overview), 9–10, 36–41, 42–43, 110, 112–128, 186

  as competing with states to provide human security, 173–75, 181, 185, 189–90, 236

  and effect on human security, 30–32, 41–44

  as nonstate actors, 10, 31–38, 40–43, 110, 114–116, 210–211

  and secular actors, 31–32, 124–26, 192

  and violence, 244–45

  See also specific case locales and traditions

religious revival, 2, 8, 10, 11, 18, 22, 26, 86–87, 164

  and Asad, Talal, 24–25

  after fall of Communism, 233

  in Hinduism, 13

  and impact on human security, 10, 67, 69

  in Islam, 10, 17n4

  in Pentecostalism, 164

  and religious pluralism, 233

Religious Studies, 18, 29

Responsibility to Protect (R2P), 5

ritual as facilitator of human security, 20, 24, 239–40

Rocha, Sebastião, 143

Romania, 15, 228–29, 235–39

Romanian Orthodox Church, 228–29, 235–39

Savimbi, Jonas, 193, 196, 198

Sen, Amartya, 5, 7

Shaikh, Haider, 100, 101–2

Sharia, 50, 55, 70, 90n12

Sikhs

  and Diwali, 108, 112n18

  Kukas, 97, 108, 111n2, 112n14 (*see also* Kukas; Namdharis (Namdaris); *see also under* Malerkotla (Punjab, India))

  in Malerkotla (*see under* Malerkotla (Punjab, India))

  and *matataak*, 100

  and Operation Blue Star (1984), 99

  and *Vaada Ghallughara* (Great Massacre), 97

socialism, 134, 143, 243

Soka Gakkai, 15, 265–74, 277–81, 282n4, 283n15, 283n19

  goals of, 266, 267, 270–71, 274

  and "human revolution" (*ningen kakumei*), 267, 279–80, 282n4

and human security, 267, 268–71,
   280
as international organization, 270
and media, 272, 283n20
Nichiren, influence of, 266, 282n4
and Nichiren Buddhism, 266–67, 274,
   279
as nonstate religious actor, 265–66
and pacifism, 268, 270, 273–74,
   278–79, 284n24
and peace education campaigns,
   268–69, 270, 271–72, 282n4
and political activity, 265, 268,
   270–71, 279–81, 281n1 (*see also*
   Komeito)
and Soka Gakkai International (SGI)
   270–72
as state actor, 265–66 success of, 280,
   283n19
and Toda Josei, 269, 274, 281n2 (*see
   also* Toda Josei)
and United Nations, 267, 269, 270,
   277, 278
worldview of, 266–69
and World War II, 267, 269, 273,
   274–75, 281, 281n2 (*see also*
   Article 9)
Soviet Union, 23, 231
Stahn, Carsten, 5
Stalin, Joseph, 229, 231, 256, 263n11
subjectivity, 244–48, 260, 261nn6–9
Sustainable Araçuaí, 143, 145
suvidha, 104

tariqat, 35, 37
Taliban
   Afghan Taliban, 71, 88n2, 91n17,
      92n21
   Pakistan Taliban, 70–71, 88n2, 90n13,
      91n14, 92n21, 92n24
Tanaka Chigaku, 267, 282n5
   See also Japan; Nichiren Buddhism

Terasaki Hirotsugu, 278
Terror Management Theory (TMT),
   211, 223
Tilmisani, Umar al-, 51, 53
Toda Josei, 269, 274, 281n2
Tokyo, Japan, 270, 275, 286
the Troubles (Ireland), 209, 213–20,
   224–25
Tsvangirai, Morgan, 185, 187
Turkey, 20, 23, 31–44, 45n9, 46n16,
   46n21

ulama, 34
Ulster Volunteer Defense Force (UVF),
   218
Union for the Total Independence of
   Angola (UNITA), 191–97, 200,
   201, 204, 207n9
United Nations, 1, 3–5, 197 and Angola,
   197–98, 204
   and *Arab Human Development Report*
      (2009), 7, 26
   and Children and Youth Code
      (Guatemala), 155
   and emergence of human security,
      3–5
   and *Human Development Report*
      (1994), 4, 6–7
   and *Human Development Report*
      (1999), 4
   and United Nations Development
      Programme (UNDP), 4, 7
   and United Nations High
      Commission for Refugees, 197
   and United NationsSecretary General
      Report: "In Larger Freedom:
      Towards Development, Security
      and Human Rights for All," 5
United States Agency for International
   Development (USAID), 203
United States and Japan Security Treaty,
   276

van der Poel, Franciscus Henricus
      See Xico, Frei
Vision conValores (VIVA), 153
Vision with Values
      See *Vision con Valores* (VIVA)
voter subjectivity
      See subjectivity
Voz da Revolução (Voice of the
      Revolution), 204

"War on Terror," 17n4, 70, 154, 160,
      161n2, 254
women's rights, 13, 19,115, 122–23
      and employment, 46n16, 46n21
      in governance, 60
      Muslim headscarf, 32, 33, 39 (*see also*
      under Muslims)

worker subjectivity
      See under subjectivity
Workers Party (PT) (Brazil), 139–145
worldview defense, 211–13, 223, 224, 225

Xico, Frei (Franciscus Henricus
      van der Poel), 132–38,
      143–44, 146–47

Yoshida Shigeru, 275–76

Zeta Drug Cartel (Mexico), 151
Zimbabwe, 172–87
Zimbabwe African National
      Union—Patriotic Front
      (ZANU-PF), 172, 174, 175,
      181, 184–85, 188n3